340.11
Paint. R

AMERICAN NERO

The History of the Destruction of the Rule of Law, and Why Trump Is the Worst Offender

RICHARD W. PAINTER

AND PETER GOLENBOCK

BenBella Books, Inc.
Dallas, TX

BenBella Books, Inc.
10440 N. Central Expressway, Suite 800
Dallas, TX 75231
www.benbellabooks.com
Send feedback to feedback@benbellabooks.com
BenBella is a federally registered trademark.

Printed in the United States of America
10 9 8 7 6 5 4 3 2 1

Library of Congress Cataloging-in-Publication Control Number: 201904662
ISBN 9781948836012 (trade cloth)
ISBN 9781950665273 (electronic)

Editing by Lee Oglesby and Alexa Stevenson
Copyediting by Scott Calamar
Proofreading by Michael Fedison
Indexing by WordCo Indexing Services
Text design by Aaron Edmiston
Text composition by Katie Hollister
Cover design by Sarah Avinger
Printed by Lake Book Manufacturing

Distributed to the trade by Two Rivers Distribution, an Ingram brand
www.tworiversdistribution.com

To William H. Painter (1927–2018)
And to Wendy Grassi, Wendy Golenbock, and Robert Golenbock,
love you all.

CONTENTS

INTRODUCTION

Three Narcissists: One Ancient, One Colonial, and One Modern

THE FIRST QUESTION A READER MIGHT ASK IS WHY THIS book is entitled *American Nero*. What does Nero have to do with Donald Trump? There was a Roman emperor famous for building a wall, but it was not Nero. The reason the book is called *American Nero* is because the emperor, like Donald Trump, was a notorious narcissist who put himself above everyone else, causing chaos and confusion with every irrational decision.

Nero Claudius Caesar Augustus Germanicus (December 15, 37–June 9, 68 AD) was the last Roman emperor of the Julio-Claudian dynasty. Nero was a man with low self-esteem who would cheat the system and declare himself a winner whenever he could. He rigged the Olympic Games in 67 AD to win the chariot race, even though he'd been thrown out of the chariot while making a turn. During public performances, he would "wow" his audience with his singing ability, though in fact he had a weak voice. The audience dared not reveal to him the truth about his meager talent lest he feed them to the lions.

Nero was *obsessed* with popularity and loyalty—the loyalty of others to him, of course. He paid informants to spy on the senators to see who was loyal to him and who wasn't. He wanted to know who applauded his stage performances, who flattered him and fawned on him. He especially wanted to know who mocked him.

Publius Clodius Thrasea Paetus was one senator who didn't make the cut. He refused to take an oath of loyalty, kept his hands in his lap during Nero's performances, and stormed out of the senate when Nero defended himself for murdering his own mother. Nero had him tried for treason, found guilty, and forced to commit suicide.

Nero felt his mother, Agrippina, favored her other son, Britannicus. Agrippina had criticized Nero for shacking up with a slave. Nero, like all narcissists, wouldn't abide criticism, so he banished his mother from the castle. She died mysteriously. Britannicus died suddenly and mysteriously while attending a banquet.

Nero killed his wife, Octavia. Though he had her death ruled a suicide, Nero sent Octavia's head to his mistress, Poppaea, as a gift.

It didn't stop at murder. In ten years, Nero stripped the senate of all its power, and in a display of arrogance and poor judgment, he decided he no longer needed to heed the wishes of the senators.

Nero was a nativist. He sought to rid his country of Christians, whom he relentlessly persecuted.

"Mockery of every sort was added to their deaths," the historian Tacitus wrote. "Covered with the skins of beasts, they were torn by dogs and perished, or were nailed to crosses, or were doomed to the flames and burnt, to serve as a nightly illumination when daylight had expired."

Nero was said to have ordered the execution of the Apostle Paul, and in one of the worst fake news events of world history, when Rome burned down, he blamed the Christians for its destruction.

Nero bankrolled a lavish, expensive lifestyle with funds from the Roman government. To build an extravagant villa, an edifice to himself, he raised taxes and stole money from the local temples. In one of his last moves, he reinstated a policy that allowed him to confiscate property from anyone suspected of treason. Of course, he alone decided who was suspected of treason.

In 65 AD, Nero discovered a plot to assassinate him, so he killed many of those involved, including former advisors and close friends.

Now he was universally hated. Nero had no friends left. He had killed them all. When his own army deserted him, he knew it was time to flee.

Nero was assailed by his enemies for being greedy, frivolous, and self-indulgent, and the senate ordered him to be beaten to death. In his own defense, he claimed to be an artist who was misunderstood. As he heard the hoofbeats of the horses bearing the men ordered to carry out his execution, Nero refused to give them the satisfaction and ended his life by suicide.

Nero was the fifth Roman emperor, succeeding Augustus, Tiberius, Caligula, and Claudius in that order. These emperors succeeded a series of authoritarian leaders who had gradually transformed Rome from a republic to a dictatorship. Much of the political foundation for the rise of dictators and emperors including Nero had been laid ninety years earlier during the populist dictatorship of Julius Caesar, who ruled from 49 to 44 BC.

Most dictatorships emerge out of other authoritarian governments, as happened after the French Revolution, which began in 1789, and the Russian Revolution in 1917. Rome was one of two examples in history of a major economic and military power being transformed from a republic into a dictatorship. The second example was the transformation of the Weimar Republic into Nazi Germany in 1933.

Our objective in writing this book is to help make sure there is not a third.

KING GEORGE III

Great Britain's King George was not as horrific a leader as Nero, but like Nero he was very much focused on his authority as king, and he reacted to political unrest in petty and destructive ways. George's reaction to instability in the American colonies in large part precipitated the American Revolution.

George was twelve when his father died and left him heir to the throne. When he became king, he had no previous government experience. Born wealthy, he'd never worked for anyone else. Though he was commander in chief, he had never served in the military.

Though George was frugal, cheap even—he advocated importing cheap labor to drive down wages and increase profits—he spent lavishly on his new royal palace, Buckingham House.

George's family had immigrated to Great Britain from Hannover, Germany, to become its rulers after the death of Queen Anne, the last of the Stuart monarchs. Many British citizens, including nobility, saw the Hanoverian dynasty as foreigners. Indeed both King George I and II spoke imperfect

English. George III was obsessed with proving himself to be British, proclaiming, "I glory in the name of Britain" when he ascended to the throne.

Many witnesses described George's pathological mania.

They spoke of his "incessant loquacity" and his habit of talking until the foam ran from his mouth. Sometimes he suffered from convulsions, and his pages had to sit on him to keep him safe on the floor.

The press accused George of preferring war to peace and of restricting the liberties of English citizens. His advisor was George Grenville, an ultra-conservative Whig politician.

King George saw America as a parent saw a child. If America was disobedient, George felt, it must be punished. During a period of financial difficulty for England, Grenville advised George to make the colonies pay their own administrative costs. The colonists were going to *pay* for their protection and well-being. First came the Stamp Act in 1765, and then indirect taxes on the colonies from the Townshend Acts. When in 1773 Britain passed the Tea Act (called the Intolerable Acts in America), imposing yet another tax, the colonies united in protest and tossed the tea into the harbor.

Faced with such disobedience, George declared, "The colonies must either submit or triumph. We must not retreat."

Two years later, the Continental Congress declared independence.

George was the main character in the 1991 play by Alan Bennett, *The Madness of George III*. Because of porphyria, a rare metabolic disorder, George suffered from severe insomnia. He would stay up all night ranting, writing letters to cabinet members, generals, and even to citizens airing his complaints. Nothing was too petty for him to complain about, from the stipends of parish clergy to the pension of the royal laundress. One can only imagine what King George III would have been like on Twitter.

Though he sought to emphasize his loyalty to Britain, George is remembered as the monarch whose refusal to compromise cost Britain one of its most valuable possessions.

DONALD J. TRUMP

So, why does this book about the forty-fifth president of the United States discuss King George III, and why is it named after a narcissistic emperor of ancient Rome?

Many psychologists and psychiatrists are convinced that we are faced with an extreme narcissist whose psychological disorders are a threat to our national well-being and our government. In an age of nuclear weapons, which neither Nero nor King George III had at their disposal, our president's psychological disposition could threaten the survival of the human race.

At best, Trump is a real threat to our democracy and the rule of law.

An article written by one of this book's authors, Richard Painter, and clinical psychologist Dr. Leanne Watt, observed:

> Anti-social symptoms include a disregard for the rights of others, a tendency to break the law, lack of remorse, frequent lying, failure to honor financial obligations, interpersonal exploitation, risk-taking and revenge-seeking in response to perceived slights.
>
> Hallmark narcissistic symptoms include an exaggerated self-importance, sensitivity to criticism, lack of empathy, a need for admiration and attention, entitlement and exploitation with a need for personal gain.
>
> Together, these symptoms could severely undermine a president's ability to lead.

At the time, almost eight hundred mental health professionals had come forward to warn the public about Trump's alarming behavior.

"Though remote," concluded the article, "we cannot rule out the possibility that a president in a downward mental health spiral could destroy important global partnerships, alter century-old alliances, and leave the United States vulnerable to terror attacks or war."

From his speeches, negotiations with Congress, and tweets, we can see clearly that we have a raging narcissist in the White House.

It is also clear that his narcissism has already had a severe impact on our government. For a narcissist, laws are meant for *other people*. Laws that do not reinforce their own sense of superiority are to be ignored.

Examples from Trump's tenure so far are many, including:

- Taking foreign government payments in violation of the Constitution
- Refusing to disclose where his business empire gets its money even though there is good reason to believe that he is financially and politically dependent upon foreigners, including perhaps the Russians
- Repeatedly attempting to obstruct the FBI investigation and special counsel's investigation of Russian interference
- Attacking the special counsel, Robert Mueller
- Threatening to put Hillary Clinton in jail
- Threatening the free press, a direct challenge to the liberties afforded under the First Amendment
- Attacking Muslims because of their religion, a direct challenge to freedom of religion

And the list goes on and on.

Historians and the general public often wonder whether we have ever had a president display such extreme narcissism and refusal to abide by the rules that apply to everyone else. Has any president so blatantly and consistently violated the Constitution and the rule of law?

As we explain in this book, the answer is clearly "NO." We have had presidents—and other government officials—who at times have violated laws set forth in our Constitution, statutory laws, and laws based on principles of common human decency. Our history is a very imperfect one, and we recount several of those imperfections in the first part of this book.

We demonstrate, however, that Donald Trump's narcissism has put him in the unique position of exploiting the historical imperfections of the United States to elevate himself by rubbing salt in the wounds of his fellow Americans.

He thus raises himself up while putting the rest of us down.

First, some generalizations about pre-Trump history, which is the subject of the first part of this book. There has never before been a combination of representative democracy and a society as large and diverse as ours in the

United States. Unlike many countries that are far more ethnically homogenous, we are a nation in which people of many different races, ethnicities, and religions must work together to build and defend a representative democracy.

The United States is a great experiment of whether a very diverse mixture of people can live together in a democracy. We believe the answer is yes, but that remains to be seen.

We started off with a substantial portion of our population, African Americans, enslaved. Women could not vote. Native Americans were either exterminated or forced to live in poverty on reservations. Immigrants were sometimes allowed to come to the United States and sometimes not, but they often faced discrimination from those who were already here. Sometimes there were laws in place to protect citizens' rights, sometimes not. Sometimes, perhaps often, our laws were ignored.

That being said, the trajectory of the United States until 2016 was generally headed in a positive direction. The rule of law—set forth in our Constitution—has helped bring us together to form a union approaching if not achieving perfection.

Then came the election of Donald Trump. In the second half of this book, we explain why his presidency has been the greatest challenge to the rule of law that this country has faced since the Civil War.

This book is about the rule of law: the internal and external threats to the rule of law, the role that narcissism and other psychological disorders can play in undermining the rule of law, and the ways in which ordinary citizens who care about their country can respond. Since the founding of this country, violations of the rule of law have made for some colorful yet troubling moments.

We will begin this story with the Salem witch trials, and we'll end the book with the Mueller investigation, which President Trump snidely calls "the worst witch hunt in our history." We will also briefly relate how Trump, after declaring himself "exonerated" of involvement in Russia's interference in the 2016 election, immediately turned to pressuring another former Soviet Republic, Ukraine, to dig up dirt on former vice president Joe Biden, a likely opponent of Trump in the 2020 election.

Our goal is that, by the time you are finished reading, you'll have the perspective to determine just how great a threat our forty-fifth president is to our nation.

The makers of fake news in **1690** who brought the witch trials in Salem, Massachusetts, for a brief moment unleashed real monsters onto our land.

This president has done the same.

CHAPTER 1

The Rule of Law in America

Freedom of thought is the only guarantee against an infection of mankind by mass myths, which, in the hands of treacherous hypocrites and demagogues, can be transformed into bloody dictatorships.
—ANDREI SAKHAROV

THE RULE OF LAW IS A POLITICAL PHRASE THAT GOES back to sixteenth-century England, when citizens were burdened by English kings' "divine right" to rule. Nobody would think of prosecuting a sitting king. The king could not violate the law because he *was* the law. He could hire and fire crown prosecutors at his will.

This was essentially a "unitary executive" style of government: one king and one government under the king. The king was chosen by God and was accountable only to God. Everyone else obeyed the king.

We will return to the unitary executive theory of executive power later in this book, explaining how the modern iteration envisions a ruler—even an elected ruler like a president—with the powers of a medieval king.

John Locke, the English philosopher who influenced American revolutionaries, opposed this vision of authoritarian rule:

"The natural liberty of man is to be free from any superior power on earth, and not to be under the will or legislative authority of man, but to have only the law of nature for his rule," Locke wrote. "The liberty of man, in society, is to be under no other legislative power, but that established, by consent, in the commonwealth, nor under the dominion of any will, or restraint of any law, but what that legislative shall enact, according to the trust put in it."

When the founders wrote the Declaration of Independence, they started with the principle of the consent of the governed—the only legitimate government would be one with a "social compact" between citizens and government. The founders also sought to guard against the tendency of those in power to abuse their authority. The government they set up had limits. It was divided into branches to limit its power.

The founders wrote the Declaration of Independence to explain why they no longer would tolerate and submit to King George's tyranny.

The founders believed in the protection of individual rights, and they were willing to go to war to get them.

The first attempt at central governance was way too weak. Under the Articles of Confederation, the federal government couldn't tax, regulate commerce, make treaties, or protect the rights of states or individuals. After the Revolutionary War, the founders made a second attempt with the Constitution, which divided the government into three branches: executive, legislative, and judicial. Each branch was expected to act as a check on unlimited power of any other branch.

From our beginnings to now, citizens of the United States have lived under a rule of law. What that means is that our laws are (relatively) stable, limited in scope, and apply to *every* citizen—including those who make them.

The rule of law means the law reigns supreme. "The law is king," wrote Thomas Paine in his pamphlet "Common Sense." When John Adams helped write the Massachusetts constitution, he sought to set up "a government of laws and not of men."

As James Madison wrote in *The Federalist Papers*, "If the American people shall ever be so debased as to tolerate a law not obligatory on the legislature as well as the people, the people will be prepared to tolerate any thing but liberty." He wrote, "No one is above the law in respect to enforcement;

no one is privileged to ignore the law, just as no one is outside the law in terms of its protection."

The founders hoped to elect virtuous leaders with wisdom, courage, honesty, humility, responsibility, and a sense of justice. But, just in case, they gave Congress and the federal courts the tools to keep a less-than-virtuous president in check. The House and Senate could impeach a president who committed "high crimes and misdemeanors" in office.

The framers created this impeachment remedy with the expectation that Congress would take action if ever faced with a president who acted like Nero or King George.

Those elected to the legislature were depended upon to have the wisdom, courage, and sense of justice necessary to take action whenever they saw the president overstepping his bounds. They were expected to put their country and its Constitution first, and their partisanship and personal loyalties second.

In US history, only two presidents before Trump have been impeached by the House. Neither was convicted by the Senate. Andrew Johnson was impeached for his refusal to implement post–Civil War Reconstruction. He was acquitted. Bill Clinton was impeached for lying under oath about having sex with an intern. He was acquitted. Richard Nixon resigned before being impeached, and for good reason.

But no president in our history more closely matches the founder's fears than Donald Trump. It has become obvious that the country is being run by a narcissistic oligarch with enormous financial conflicts of interest and extraordinarily bad judgment, who obstructs justice and repeatedly lies, and who likely owes his presidency to the influence of a foreign power.

It would be hard even for a talented novelist to come up with a president such as Trump. He has attacked political institutions—Congress, the Justice Department, the FBI, the cabinet, and the federal courts—without concrete proposals to improve them. He has loudly proclaimed to be "draining the swamp," but the financial conflicts that he brought to Washington have done the exact opposite. By "draining the swamp," he's actually attempted to destroy the rule of law. By "draining the swamp," he disrupted investigations of his conflicts of interest, payoffs to women to keep quiet about affairs, Russian involvement in the election, and anything else that might embarrass him.

The authors of this book are confident this country can come out of this national nightmare, but it's worth exploring the history that brought us to this point and asking how America could return to its best self.

Meanwhile, Donald Trump fiddles while the rule of law burns.

CHAPTER 2

Assaults on the Rule of Law in Early America

If our nation is ever taken over, it will be taken over from within.
—*JAMES MADISON*

THERE WAS A RULE OF LAW ON AMERICAN SHORES FOR millennia before the first European immigrants arrived. The tribal law of Native Americans embodied a deep yet varied understanding of the relationship of human beings to each other, to the earth, and to their creator.

The Iroquois League of nations is often noted as the most powerful of the northeastern tribes. In the Iroquois society, land was owned and worked in common. Hunting was done in groups. Villagers shared the catch. Families shared homes. There was no private ownership of land or property.

The women with seniority in an Iroquois village named the men to represent them at village and tribal councils. It was the women who chose the tribal chiefs for the ruling council for the Five Nations of the Iroquois. Women attended meetings and voted. Laws and history were passed down through an oral tradition, song, dance, and traditional ceremonies. However, warfare was a persistent problem. Like Europeans, the Iroquois tried to avoid war with treaties.

One of the most important stories handed down through generations was the coming of Dekanawida, the man who became known as the Great Peacemaker. His spokesperson was Hiyonwantha, later named Hiawatha by Henry Wadsworth Longfellow. Hiyonwantha (her name has sometimes been spelled "Ayenwathaaa" or "Aiionwatha") was an Onondaga woman living among the Mohawks.

The Peacemaker arrived when there was fierce fighting among the Mohawk, Oneida, Onondaga, Cayuga, and Seneca tribes. He arrived on Lake Onondaga in a canoe made of white stone, proclaiming that peace had come.

The Peacemaker would preach peace as the desire of the Creator. It took forty years for the five tribes to agree to end hostilities.

Sometime between 1450 and 1600, the Five Nations, joined together as the Iroquois Confederacy, agreed to the Great Law of Peace. (In 1722, a sixth tribe, the Tuscarora, joined the confederacy.)

The Great Law of Peace, 177 articles written on wampum belts and passed down through oral tradition, promoted unity, harmony, and respect for others.

The three principles of the Great Law of Peace were:

1. **Righteousness**—to treat each other fairly
2. **Health**—incorporating well-being of mind, body, spirit, and peace between nations
3. **Power**—to maintain peace and well-being of the members of the confederacy

The government of the Great Law of Peace ("of the people, by the people, and for the people") included two houses and a grand counsel; a women's council, similar to a supreme court; checks and balances between branches; separation of powers; freedom of religion; and freedom of speech.

The grand counsel consisted of fifty sachem chiefs, each from a clan of the tribe. Decisions often were decided by consensus, though each sachem chief had veto power. As a result, most decisions were made at the tribal level.

The Iroquois were visited often by the Founding Fathers, including George Washington, Benjamin Franklin, and Thomas Jefferson. These men were familiar with the Great Law of Peace, and several Iroquois delegates were in attendance when the Declaration of Independence was written. In 1987, the United States Senate acknowledged that the Great Law of Peace had been a model for our Constitution.

Before the American Revolution, the Iroquois kept their treaty promises to the British and prevented the French from gaining a stronghold in the area. They were dependent on British goods. During the American Revolution, the Oneida and the Tuscarora sided with the Americans, while the other tribes sided with the British. When the Americans won, they forced six pro-British tribes to the northern lands still owned by Britain.

We now jump back to the time when Europeans first came to America. We note the great irony of contemporary American politicians attacking immigrants, when the history of our country has benefited greatly from immigrants, beginning with the Pilgrims.

The American immigration story is now four hundred years old, and much of it involves those who arrived without permission: immigrants who wanted a new life or believed that God called them here.

The first European immigrants to permanently settle in North America came in the 1620s. And yes, the *Mayflower* passengers actually left their country illegally. They snuck out. The Pilgrims, who were opposed to the Church of England, first fled to Holland, set up a community, and then in 1620 sailed to America *without permission* and *without speaking the native language*. Native Americans welcomed them, at least at first. They didn't turn the *Mayflower* back because they didn't have proper papers. Millions of Americans are descended from those who arrived without permission. Until the late nineteenth century, many immigrants came here without first asking anyone for permission to come.

These immigrants brought new concepts of the rule of law, drawn almost entirely from experiences in their countries of origin. They also borrowed from the Native American rule of law, but they gradually built a government based on European political philosophy and legal concepts.

Still, there were several obstacles to the establishment of the rule of law in the New World. These have been salient features of American history since colonial times.

We will refer to these throughout this book.

The most significant obstacles to a democratic rule of law are the problems surrounding:

1. Religious intolerance
2. Violations of due process
3. Myths and alternative facts
4. Attacks on the free press
5. Corruption

RELIGIOUS INTOLERANCE

Religion has been centrally important to most civilizations since the dawn of time. Sadly, it's also often been a source of strife, oppression, and warfare.

Most early European settlers came to America for religious freedom, to get away from state religion and rulers in countries throughout Europe. If you lived in a Protestant country like England, you were expected to worship only the type of Protestantism approved by the king. In a Catholic country like France, you were expected to be Catholic. Going back to the Crusades in Spain, Greece, and even Austria, Christians were often at odds with Islam. Jews were sometimes tolerated but at one time or another were expelled from most European countries.

Those brave souls who sailed to America, it turned out, were not so tolerant themselves. Even as late as the American Revolution, eight of the thirteen colonies were ruled by powerful Christian religious groups. Not only did state government leaders sometimes force strict religious observance on the residents, but they also levied taxes to pay the salaries of the ministers. Those who practiced a different version of Christianity faced persecution.

In Boston in the early years, for instance, everyone was obliged to go to church on Sunday. There was a Congregationalist meetinghouse in *every* New England town. Massachusetts and Connecticut were run by the Puritans, who enforced their religious beliefs by law. Religious dissenters were treated as harshly as they had been in England.

In many colonies there was a battle between the Anglicans and the Puritans, offshoots of the Congregationalists. Other groups in the colonies included Catholics, Quakers, Dutch Calvinists, Scottish Presbyterians, German Reformed, French Huguenots, Baptists Methodists, Unitarians, and Jews. The sect with the most power varied from colony to colony.

Rhode Island, founded by Roger Williams, was an exception, embracing tolerance of all religions. Williams had been a minister in Salem, Massachusetts, and he became fluent in the languages of the Narragansett and Wampanoag tribes. He preached that the settlers should not take land from the Native Americans without a valid treaty, and he promoted the separation of church and state.

"Forced religion stinks in God's nostrils," said Williams, and many felt he went too far when he declared that the magistrates of the city should have no say in spiritual matters. Outrage ensued.

Furious Puritan leaders decided to ship Williams back to England. John Winthrop, the strict Puritan founder of the Massachusetts Bay Colony, tipped Williams off, and with the aid of some Native American friends, Williams escaped to what would later become Rhode Island.

Rhode Island became a haven for dissenters because of Williams. Jews, for example, settled in Newport, where the Touro Synagogue (built 1759–63) is the oldest synagogue in the United States.

The period now known as the Great Awakening arose in the 1730s and '40s. A minister named Jonathan Edwards traveled the colonies leading a movement that focused on salvation through personal conversion. The Evangelical sect—which still exists today—was embraced by the poor.

The movement that followed the Great Awakening encouraged believers to question the right of the state and local governments to adjudicate religious issues, leading to the adoption of the separation of church and state in the Constitution. Early American Evangelicals thus were strongly opposed to government entanglement with religion.

After the Revolution, America was essentially a Protestant nation, but newcomers joined forces to oppose state religions. The resistance culminated in a philosophical battle that pitted Thomas Jefferson and James Madison against Patrick Henry's 1784 bill proposing a tax-supported religion in Virginia.

Madison, the leader of the separation of church and state faction, in 1785 wrote, "The Religion then of every man must be left to the conviction and conscience of every man; and it is the right of every man to exercise it as these may dictate. This right is in its nature an unalienable right [. . .] We maintain therefore that in matters of Religion, no man's right is abridged by the institution of Civil Society, and that Religion is wholly exempt from its cognizance."

Madison also wrote, "We are teaching the world the great truth that Governments do better without Kings & Nobles than with them. The merit will be doubled by the other lesson that Religion Flourishes in greater purity, without than with the aid of Government."

In 1786 Madison reintroduced a bill that had been set aside by the legislature nine years earlier. Against a state tax-supported religion, Thomas Jefferson's bill proclaimed religious freedom, banned compulsory attendance or support of any religious institution, and forbade religious tests for public office. It passed with an overwhelming margin.

Jefferson's statute was a model for the First Amendment and Article VI, Clause 3 of the Constitution, which states that there shall be "no religious test for public office."

The United States has a long history of religious discrimination by individuals against each other, but our Founding Fathers recognized early on that the *government* should not restrict or penalize people for their religion. The First Amendment thus reads:

"Congress shall make no law respecting an establishment of religion, or prohibiting the free exercise thereof." After the Civil War, the Fourteenth Amendment applies this and other parts of the Bill of Rights to the states.

The framers could not have been clearer about the relationship between religion and government. Political figures who flouted the rule of law throughout history often ignored this.

VIOLATIONS OF DUE PROCESS

Religious persecution is closely linked to another antagonist to the rule of law: denial of life, liberty, or property without due process. In Europe for centuries, people were often imprisoned, had their assets confiscated, and were executed based on *accusations* that they did not follow the predominant religion, were disloyal to rulers, or both. At times in Puritan New England, it was no better.

Recall Hester Prynne in Nathaniel Hawthorne's *The Scarlet Letter.* Accused of adultery, Prynne had to walk around town wearing a scarlet letter *A* on her chest. Never mind that her fellow adulterer was the town minister. Other common punishments included being tied to a post in the middle of town and public stoning, which could result in death.

Before 1692, there had been rumors of witchcraft in villages neighboring Salem, Massachusetts. Cotton Mather, an important outspoken Boston minister, strongly believed in witches. He wrote about the strange behavior he had witnessed in six children and called their strangeness "witchcraft." His fear and imagination-based observations fueled the hysteria that came afterward.

Between February 1692 and May 1693 fear rose up among the parishioners. That fear turned into hysteria and a particularly nasty undermining of the rule of law. Two girls, aged nine and eleven, began having fits, screaming, crawling under furniture, and contorting themselves. A doctor said he didn't know why they were acting that way.

The two girls were the first to be accused and arrested for being witches. A vicious rivalry between two families fueled the insanity. One woman was accused of witchcraft because she married a servant. Another woman was accused because she was a South American Indian slave, and she was accused of having magical powers over children. Those accused were interviewed for several days and sent to jail.

As the fear of witches spread, accusations flooded in. A special court was empaneled. Cotton Mather expressed support for the prosecutions.

A series of trials ensued. In all, twenty people were convicted, fourteen of them women. Twelve were hanged. Five (including two infants) died in prison.

The Salem witch trials became a cautionary tale about the dangers of religious extremism, false accusations, and lack of due process.

It was the fear of the unknown that was grossly exaggerated and became the basis for undermining the rule of law.

Enter the politics of accusation. In this case, the mere accusation became guilt—*there was no due process*—and that pattern made it very easy to destroy people you didn't like just by accusing them. People were accused of witchcraft just because others held grudges against them.

When the mere accusation is enough for conviction, that's perhaps the most frightening violation of the rule of law imaginable, one that would rear its ugly head too often in American history.

The framers thus sought to embed in the rule of law a protection against accusation without due process that had been badly lacking in early Puritan New England and Europe. The Fifth Amendment was this protection.

It reads:

> No person shall be held to answer for a capital, or otherwise infamous crime, unless on a presentment or indictment of a Grand Jury, except in cases arising in the land or naval forces, or in the Militia, when in actual service in time of War or public danger; nor shall any person be subject for the same offence to be twice put in jeopardy of life or limb; nor shall be compelled in any criminal case to be a witness against himself, nor be deprived of life, liberty, or property, without due process of law; nor shall private property be taken for public use, without just compensation.

The framers did not want to see a Spanish Inquisition or another Salem witch trial.

MYTHS AND ALTERNATIVE FACTS

The Salem witch trials were among the New World's earliest exposures to the damage that can be done by an essential human character flaw: the tendency to form opinions and make judgments based on myths instead of demonstrable evidence. Collective adherence to falsehood—reinforced by lying—would threaten the rule of law again and again for centuries.

Galileo had been persecuted by the Catholic Church for refusing to believe the world was flat—even though scientific evidence showed otherwise. In Salem, the settlers not only believed in witches, despite a lack of scientific or even biblical evidence, but they became convinced they could use judicial processes to determine who was a witch. The myth so dominated Salem that mob rule took hold.

More recently, Americans have confronted myths about human origins. There was the famous Scopes Monkey Trial in 1925 in which public school science teacher John Scopes was indicted for violating a Tennessee law that prohibited teaching evolution. Myths and "alternative facts" are often politicized: by Jeffersonian Democrats who idealized the French Revolution, by early twentieth-century American communists and socialists who idealized the Russian Revolution, by deniers of clear scientific evidence of climate change in the 2000s, and most recently by people, including President Trump, who trust Fox News more than information gathered by professionals in multiple intelligence agencies.

There is yet another category of even more pernicious myths—when one group of human beings believes another group of human beings is morally or intellectually inferior. These myths exist globally but have been particularly tragic for our country. These myths were used to justify slavery and then Jim Crow; to destroy Native American civilizations; and to demean, abuse, and imprison countless immigrant groups.

A demagogue may invoke negative characteristics of a religious group such as Jews or Muslims by building on existing myths. Anti-Semitism has never been about anything the Jews actually did. Its deliberate fabrications are systematically spread to engender hatred. For centuries, Christians repeated the "blood libel"—that as part of the Passover ritual, Jews sacrificed Christian babies. The myth of Jewish world domination was spread by the book *The Protocols of the Learned Elders of Zion*, which was probably forged in the early 1900s by the Tsarist secret police in response to political unrest in Russia. But in the twentieth century, it was spread in the United States by many anti-Semites, including Henry Ford.

Irrational fear can be a terrible thing, putting due process to the test time and time again. When our country was gripped by fear of rebels during the Civil War, President Lincoln suspended habeas corpus. Fear of communists in the early 1920s led to the Red Scare and midnight raids; a fear of Japanese nationals led to internment of Americans of Japanese ancestry during World War II; fear again of communists in the 1940s and 1950s led to McCarthyism; and after the 9/11 attacks came the fear of Muslims.

The ability, and failure, of due process to stand up to myth and fear has been a critically important part of the story of the rule of law in America.

ATTACKS ON THE FREE PRESS

England passed the Bill of Rights in 1689, but the bill ignored freedom of the press. The English government decided who could own a printing press, and if one dared to speak out against the king or Parliament, he could face the common-law crime of seditious libel. Only members of Parliament could speak their minds without fear of arrest.

Let's be clear: The freedom of the press in our Constitution did *not* come from England. It came rather from colonists' resentment of the strict control over ideas and information.

In the years leading to the American Revolution, colonists published more than three dozen newspapers, hundreds of political pamphlets, and a flood of one-page broadsides, often written under pseudonyms, that held the disparate colonies together. Thomas Paine's "Common Sense" made the first forceful argument for independence and became the most popular of the four hundred pamphlets distributed in the American colonies. Paine mocked the divine right of kings.

He wrote, "Every thing that is right or reasonable pleads for separation. The blood of the slain, the weeping voice of nature cries, 'TIS TIME TO PART."

In Boston, the *Gazette* printed diatribes against the crown. The *Boston Chronicle* was owned by a loyalist who supported the crown and did what he could to out the *Gazette* writers.

The authors championed freedom from British rule and used pseudonyms to stay anonymous so as not to incur the wrath of royal governors and councils that could charge them with sedition and throw them in jail.

In 1732, the king appointed William Cosby to be New York colony's royal governor. Cosby was an unpopular autocrat who broached no opposition. He tried to extort the former governor, Rip Van Dam, then sued him.

Cosby got permission to hold the trial before a three-judge special court. The chief justice, Lewis Morris, objected, saying that what Cosby was trying to do was illegal. The other two justices, James De Lancey and Frederick Philipse, sided with Cosby.

Cosby in retaliation fired Morris and made De Lancey the chief justice.

Morris and Van Dam tried to get King George II to recall Cosby, and they published attacks in the *New York Weekly Journal*. Morris hired a printer, Peter Zenger, to publish diatribes against the governor, who Morris rightly characterized as a tyrant. Morris's articles were printed under a pseudonym.

This went on for several months, until Cosby had had enough.

Uncertain of the author, Cosby sued Zenger—for seditious libel.

When Cosby asked the New York Colonial Assembly to prosecute, it refused. The regular courts also refused. When Cosby demanded that the Assembly order the public hangman to ceremonially burn issues of the *New York Weekly Journal*, the Assembly refused.

Cosby, unable to try Zenger legally, was left to try him before the special jerry-rigged three-man court he himself had set up. The makeshift court set a high bail of four hundred pounds, and Zenger was jailed.

Avoiding the grand jury, Cosby had his attorney general, Richard Bradley, issue an "information" against Zenger, charging him with printing items that were "false, scandalous, malicious, and seditious."

Zenger languished in jail for an entire year.

The trial began on August 4, 1735. With James De Lancey, a close friend of Cosby, as the chief judge, Zenger didn't stand a chance. Defense attorneys James Alexander and William Smith argued that the appointments of Judges De Lancey and Philipse were illegal because they were "at the Governor's pleasure."

In retaliation, Judge De Lancey ordered the disbarment of Alexander and Smith.

Cosby was one steel-nosed autocrat.

John Chambers, a young lawyer favorable to Cosby, was named Zenger's attorney, but Alexander and Smith were able to convince top-rated lawyer Andrew Hamilton to take the case. Hamilton, no relation to Alexander, was the most famous defense attorney in the American colonies. He had been the attorney general of Pennsylvania.

During his argument, Hamilton said to the jury, "The question before the Court and you, Gentlemen of the jury, is not of small or private concern. It is not the cause of one poor printer, nor of New York alone, which you are now trying. No! It may in its consequence affect every free man that lives under a British government on the main of America. It is the best cause. It is the cause of liberty."

Chief Justice De Lancey instructed the jurors that their job was to decide but one question: Had Zenger published the issues of the *New York Weekly Journal*?

Hamilton then surprised everyone by admitting to the jury that Zenger had done just that.

He then argued that Zenger had every right to print them so long as he was telling the truth.

"If Attorney General Bradley can prove the words were not true," said Hamilton, "I will agree they were libelous."

Chief Justice De Lancey, caught by surprise by Hamilton's defense, ruled that truth did not matter in libel cases. He said it was up to the court to judge whether the words were libelous.

Hamilton turned and spoke directly to the jurors.

"Are we to believe that truth is a greater sin than falsehood?" he asked. "If we leave the matter of libelous words up to judges, this would render juries useless."

He continued, "It is you that we must now appeal for witness to the truth."

Telling the truth, he said, does not cause governments to fall. Rather, "abuse of power" causes governments to fall.

Zenger printed the truth. No libel had taken place, and the jury should find him not guilty.

"Truth ought to govern the whole affairs of libels."

Governor Cosby tried to fix the jury, another violation of the rule of law. Some men on the list were not freeholders, as required, and some held commissions and offices at the Governor's pleasure, including his baker, tailor, shoemaker, and candlemaker. Hamilton got them all tossed from the jury.

The jury deliberated for ten minutes and found Peter Zenger not guilty. The crowded courtroom cheered as Judge De Lancey was defeated.

After the Zenger trial, few seditious libel cases were brought for fear that juries would refuse to convict.

When the Bill of Rights was adopted, the first amendment was:

Congress shall make no law . . . abridging the freedom of the press.

In 1798, the United States Congress passed the Sedition Act, bringing back the possibility of jail for talking or writing against the government. The United States was fighting France on the high seas, and the Federalists, led by Alexander Hamilton, took advantage of wartime fears and argued for bills that they said would strengthen national security. The Federalist-controlled Congress passed three laws curtailing immigrants' rights and passed a fourth law permitting prosecution of those accused of voicing or printing remarks against the United States government. The laws were designed to silence outspoken Republicans critical of the war with France.

The law led to the prosecution of fourteen men, mostly journalists, and mostly Republicans. Some were imprisoned.

Republicans Thomas Jefferson and James Madison declared the Sedition Act to be in violation of the First and Tenth Amendments. Because of backlash from the passage of the Alien and Sedition Acts, Jefferson defeated John Adams for the presidency in 1800.

The Sedition Act was repealed in 1802, and the three anti-immigrant acts were allowed to expire.

Freedom of the press remained a cornerstone of our democracy.

CORRUPTION

Since the earliest days of our country, we have had problems with corruption—the comingling of a politician's financial interests with government interests.

The founders were well aware of the risk of corruption of American officials by foreign governments, particularly the great powers of Europe: Great Britain, France, Austria-Hungary, and Russia, whose monarchs were enormously wealthy. The founders were so worried about foreign influence that they insisted that the president must be a natural-born citizen (we heard about that clause endlessly from Donald Trump spewing alternative facts about President Obama's birth certificate). More importantly, the emoluments clause of the Constitution provides:

> No Title of Nobility shall be granted by the United States: And no Person holding any Office of Profit or Trust under them, shall, without the Consent of the Congress, accept of any present, Emolument, Office, or Title, of any kind whatever, from any King, Prince, or foreign State.

Officials in the United States government may accept *no title of nobility, no gift, no profits or advantages* (the definition of "emoluments" in Samuel Johnson's 1755 *Dictionary of the English Language*), no offices, no titles *of any kind* without consent from Congress. That includes the most lowly federal employee as well as the president of the United States.

Controversies under this clause have generally been modest (for instance, a gold snuffbox given to Benjamin Franklin by the French king) until Trump assumed office in 2017. The first federal court decision interpreting the emoluments clause, *Maryland v. Trump*, was not until 2018.

Related to the foreign emoluments clause is the domestic emoluments clause, designed to avoid favoritism between states. It is directed solely at the president and reads:

> The President shall, at stated Times, receive for his Services, a Compensation, which shall neither be increased nor diminished during the Period for which he

shall have been elected, and he shall not receive within that Period any other Emolument from the United States, or any of them.

That clause also has not been controversial until recently. It also is part of the pending litigation against President Trump.

The founders, however, overlooked a serious domestic conflict of interest. They wrote their own corruption into the Constitution when they declared that African American slaves were to be counted as three-fifths of a person. They condoned slavery because it made agricultural plantation owners rich. Economic self-interest of public officials as well as racism is thus an important part of the slavery story and its tragic aftermath.

Another area of corruption came when we tried to establish a financial system under Alexander Hamilton, Washington's treasury secretary. Hamilton set up the first central bank of the United States. Great Britain had had a central bank since 1696. The Federalists believed that the United States needed a central bank to be a financial power. The other thing we needed was to pay back in full both the federal and state debts incurred during the Revolutionary War.

So far, so good. Hamilton was doing the right thing to establish the credit worthiness and sound financial footing of the United States.

Opposing Hamilton were the Democrat-Republicans, sometimes called the "Jeffersonians," who didn't like the idea of a central bank. The populist Jeffersonians feared the concentrated economic power of a central bank. Furthermore, some Jeffersonians didn't like having to pay off the states' debts, because most had been incurred in states such as Massachusetts and New York, states not represented by the Jeffersonians.

The Southerners struck a deal to allow the central bank and to pay off $25 million of the states' debt. In exchange, Congress moved the capitol from New York City to a site on the Potomac River that became Washington, DC.

Once it was agreed that all the state debts would be paid off, some members of Congress and their allies began buying at a fraction of their value the debt certificates from Revolutionary War veterans and farmers who had funded the revolution.

The speculators were close to Treasury Department officials who were close with Congress; they made themselves rich by buying this paper at twenty-five cents on the dollar. These speculators had inside information and made millions off the backs of ordinary Americans.

William Maclay, a Jeffersonian senator from Pennsylvania, wrote extensively about this in his published diary. Maclay was hostile to Alexander Hamilton, President Washington, other Federalists, and the big-city financiers who dominated the political scene. He and other Jeffersonians were very critical of what was going on in the Treasury Department under Hamilton.

In his *Journal*, Maclay wrote on January 15, 1790:

> I call not at a single house or go into any company but traces of speculation in certificates appear. Mr. Langdon [Sen. John Langdon of New Hampshire], the old and intimate friend of Mr. Morris [Sen. Robert Morris of Pennsylvania], lodges with Mr. Hazard [Jonathan Hazard, Rhode Island's delegate to the Continental Congress]. Mr. Hazard has followed buying certificates for some time past. He told me he had made a business of it; it is easy to guess for whom. I told him, "You are, then, among the happy few who have been let into the secret." He seemed abashed, and I checked by my forwardness much more information, which he seemed disposed to give.
>
> The Speaker gives me this day his opinion, that Mr. Fitzsimmons [congressman from Pennsylvania] was concerned in this business as well as Mr. Morris, and that they stayed away [from Congress] for the double purpose of pursuing their speculation and remaining unsuspected.

Later, Maclay wrote, "I really fear the members of Congress are deeper in this business than any others. Nobody doubts but all commotion originated from the Treasury."

Whether Hamilton and his associates leaked inside information to inquiring speculators is subject to debate.

James Madison, a Democrat-Republican, proposed paying the speculators the highest market price to date for the certificates, with the balance going to the original note holders, but he was voted down. The speculators who bought the notes were paid in full.

It was the first insider trading scandal in America. The only thing Congress did about it was to pass an obscure law prohibiting the treasurer and secretary of the treasury from trading in state and federal bonds while they were in office. The bill said nothing about members of Congress speculating in the public funds. The bill had been uniquely targeted to the treasury secretary, because some in Congress did not trust Alexander Hamilton.

Jeffersonians feared corruption in the First Bank of the United States. When Jefferson became president in 1801, he abolished many of Hamilton's taxes but allowed the bank to remain intact.

When the bank's charter came up for renewal in 1811, the Democrat-Republicans controlled Congress. The bill to continue the bank was defeated by one vote.

This fear of corruption made it very hard for the central bank to gain popular support, even though having a central bank was a sound economic policy.

We celebrate Alexander Hamilton today in the musical, but the truth is that Hamilton never dealt with the corruption problem in the central bank. A Second Bank of the United States, established in the 1820s and presided over by Nicholas Biddle, also had serious corruption problems, with payoffs made to Senator Daniel Webster, among others. The Second Bank of the United States was then defeated by the notoriously anti-bank president Andrew Jackson. Hamilton's dream of a national bank for the United States would not be realized until the Woodrow Wilson administration established the Federal Reserve in 1914.

We see this same problem in the financial sector today. When there is corruption in the banking industry, the public loses faith in the financial system. Populist politicians take advantage of unrest to attack the financial system, along with the independence of our central bank, jettisoning good economic policies along with the bad.

If there was one flaw in the early Federalist administrations, it was that rural Americans felt that the rich and powerful controlled government—an opinion that many rural Americans hold today. The little guy—farmers and local business owners—felt that Wall Street bankers and their friends were getting very rich and powerful while their own incomes and futures were stagnant. In the 1790s, those who lived outside the big cities saw bankers and speculators making fortunes while country folk fought just to keep their heads above water. Resentment and anger arose over the unfair economic system.

The result was the Whiskey Rebellion.

In 1791, President Washington imposed the first tax on a domestic product: whiskey. The tax revenue would be used to pay off the war debt. Farmers who distilled extra grain into whiskey were outraged because they felt they had *no say* in Congress. Their reaction was similar to the Boston colonists after Britain passed the Tea Act. In both cases, protestors used violence and intimidation to keep officials from collecting the tax.

In July 1794, a US marshal arrived in western Pennsylvania to serve writs on distillers who hadn't paid the whiskey tax. More than five hundred armed men attacked the home of the local tax inspector.

George Washington himself rode with a band of thirteen thousand militiamen from Pennsylvania, Maryland, New Jersey, and Virginia. The insurgents dispersed before the militia arrived, but Washington had twenty protest leaders arrested. Later, all were acquitted or pardoned.

When elected leaders are chosen by the rich and powerful, ordinary people get angry. That's what led to the demise of the Federalist Party when Thomas Jefferson was elected in 1800. In the 1820s, that populist anger led to Andrew Jackson's election. Jackson was a rough guy who loved to put his boots up on the couch. He was not a gentleman like his predecessors. He attacked our banking system instead of regulating it and rooting out corruption. He liked to engage in violence. He made a career of killing Native Americans, yet he was viewed as the champion of the common man.

It is critical for the survival of democracy that ordinary people feel the government is not corrupt and represents them. We have struggled with the corruption problem since the beginning of our country's history. Today, President Trump, who ran against Wall Street and promised to "drain the swamp," hangs a portrait of Andrew Jackson in the Oval Office, appeals to white populists, and attacks the central bank. In August of 2019, he tweeted that the chairman of the Federal Reserve was as much an enemy of the United States as the leader of China. And yet, as we will see, the corruption problem in America has recently grown worse, not better.

CHAPTER 3

The Civil War and Its Legacy

*Let every American, every lover of liberty, every well-wisher to his posterity,
swear by the blood of the Revolution, never to violate in the least particular,
the laws of the country; and never to tolerate their violation by others.*
—ABRAHAM LINCOLN

T HE CIVIL WAR WAS A COMPLETE BREAKDOWN OF THE
rule of law. It might have been avoided if the founders had put aside
their own financial interests and freed slaves on their plantations. Instead,
they retained their slaves and embedded slavery into the Constitution, allowing Southern states to count slaves for congressional representation while still
denying slaves voting rights.

When we talk about slavery and the Civil War, we usually talk about
racism. It's important we continue to address racism, but what gets overlooked are the enormous financial conflicts of interest by the founders, some
of whom were extremely wealthy and owned many slaves.

Financial conflicts of interest have consequences—tragic consequences—that have not been emphasized enough by scholars who write
about slavery. Our founders failed to acknowledge the inherent and fundamental immorality of slavery. Slavery had been banned in Great Britain.

We knew it was wrong, and yet the founders used their financial interests to distort the meaning of morality in the Bible and the Constitution. Slavery was about racism and also about *money*.

Valuing slave labor over morality is the greatest instance of the tragic consequences of financial conflicts of interest in a representative democracy. Although trade disputes and other disagreements also played a role in the Civil War, corruption and racism set up our republic to descend into chaos and warfare less than a century following its founding.

Shortly after the start of the Civil War, the right to due process came under attack. President Lincoln suspended habeas corpus. Habeas corpus gives people who have been imprisoned or detained the right to appear before a court to determine if that imprisonment is lawful. Article 1, Section 9 of the Constitution provides:

> The privilege of the writ of habeas corpus shall not be suspended, unless when in cases of rebellion or invasion the public safety may require it.

This is the only common-law tradition in the Constitution, and the Constitution also explicitly says when it can be overridden. President Lincoln took that opportunity.

When the Sixth Massachusetts Union Regiment marched in the streets of Baltimore a week after the firing on Fort Sumter and Virginia's secession, the Union soldiers were attacked by a mob supporting Southern secession. Four soldiers were killed, thirty-six soldiers wounded, and twelve civilians killed. Following the bloodshed, the governor of Maryland and the mayor of Baltimore asked Lincoln not to send any more troops to the city. Lincoln replied that if the troops had to go through Baltimore, they would go through Baltimore. In response, locals cut telegraph wires and damaged railroads to try to stop the advance of Union troops.

Fearing that Maryland would secede, Lincoln suspended habeas corpus and had four civilians thrown in jail without a hearing in order to ensure the safety of the military supply lines between Philadelphia and Washington, DC. He also suspended the writ of habeas corpus between Philadelphia and New York and along the Florida coast.

Lincoln would imprison pro-secessionist Maryland legislators so they could not vote to secede from the Union. John Merryman, a farmer, was arrested on suspicion of treason and imprisoned at Fort McHenry without a hearing. His lawyers petitioned the Supreme Court.

Roger Taney, the chief justice of the Supreme Court and federal court judge of Maryland, ordered Merryman to be brought before him. The commander of Fort McHenry refused, citing President Lincoln's suspension of the writ.

Taney called Lincoln's action unconstitutional and said that only Congress could suspend habeas corpus.

Lincoln ignored Taney, a Maryland slaveholder who earlier had written the notorious *Dred Scott* decision denying liberty to slaves, even in free states. Taney—who rightly stood up to Lincoln's infringement of due process but perpetuated the problem of slavery—would die on October 13, 1864, the same day Maryland outlawed slavery.

The charges against Merryman were eventually dismissed.

Following the Battle of Antietam on September 24, 1862, Lincoln broadened his suspension of the writ of habeas corpus. He wrote, "All Rebels and Insurgents, their aiders and abettors within the United States, and all persons discouraging volunteer enlistments, resisting military drafts, or guilty of any disloyal practice, affording aid and comfort to Rebels against the authority of the United States, shall be subject to martial law and liable to trial and punishment by Courts Martial or Military Commission."

The policy was first implemented by Secretary of State William Seward and then by Secretary of War Edwin Stanton. As many as 38,000 were imprisoned and held without a hearing during the war.

The Habeas Corpus Act, passed by Congress in March 1863, required the government to provide names of those imprisoned to civilian judges and to have them charged by a grand jury. They were to be released if the requirement wasn't met.

Once again, Lincoln, acting outside the rule of law, ignored Congress's mandate.

In 1870, five years after the end of the Civil War, Congress passed the Enforcement Act of 1870, empowering the president to enforce the first section of the Fifteenth Amendment, which gave African American men the right to vote. Passed during the Reconstruction Era, the law prohibited discrimination by state officials in voter registration on the basis of race, color, or previous condition of servitude. It created penalties for those who broke the law and empowered federal courts to enforce the act. It allowed the president to call upon the army to quell disturbances and to send federal marshals to polling places if violations of the act were detected.

After the amendment was passed, Confederate general Nathan Bedford Forrest, in an attempt to stop African Americans from bettering their lot, organized a paramilitary terrorist group of former Confederate soldiers to push back against Reconstruction and keep African Americans submissive. This group, the Ku Klux Klan, dressed in white outfits including hoods that covered their faces, allowing the wearers to remain anonymous. Riding in large groups, the Klan terrorized former slaves and those who supported them with intimidation, assaults, destruction of property, and murder. For this reason, the Enforcement Act of 1870 was also often referred to as the First Ku Klux Klan act.

During and after the Civil War, the United States thus faced a challenge to the rule of law that was in some ways similar to the challenge we faced after September 11, 2001. How far should our federal government go in suppressing civil liberties and curtailing due process in order to combat the threat of terrorism?

In an attempt to stop these terrorist acts, President Ulysses S. Grant declared martial law. Passed by Congress and signed by Grant on October 17, 1871, the Second Enforcement Act, better known as the Ku Klux Klan Act, suspended habeas corpus for KKK members arrested by federal troops. Explained Grant in his proclamation, "Whereas such unlawful combinations and conspiracies for the purposes aforesaid are declared by the act of Congress aforesaid to be rebellion against the Government of the United States; and Whereas by said act of Congress it is provided that before the President shall suspend the privileges of the writ of habeas corpus he shall first have made proclamation commanding such insurgents to disperse."

Grant thus engaged in his own "war on terror" against the Ku Klux Klan, the oldest and the most deadly domestic terrorist organization in American history. The act was passed to make sure that sympathetic Southern legislators did not release arrested Klansmen. Grant's suspension of habeas corpus was brief and mostly affected South Carolina.

THE PROBLEM OF RECONSTRUCTION

The handling of Reconstruction had an aftereffect on our politics. Abraham Lincoln's Republican Party started with noble objectives. Their effort to rectify the legacy of slavery and its racist foundations was tragically undermined by the age-old problem of corruption. Reparations for freed slaves were part of the Republican platform, and many freed slaves expected to gain ownership of the land they had worked. Union general William Sherman seemed to bolster that claim when he promised freed slaves forty acres and a mule. Some land redistribution took place, but not much and not for very long.

What happened instead was a river of corruption as white Northerners came to take control of Southern governments for the purpose of personal gain. These people became known as carpetbaggers, named after the carpetbags they carried. They were outsiders who ran for public office in communities they didn't know or care about.

The carpetbaggers said they had come to help the freed slaves, but their primary goal was to stuff their own pockets and rip off the people of the South. For a period after the war, Southerners were not allowed to vote, and the carpetbaggers got themselves elected into Southern state legislatures.

Once again, America experienced the ugliness of corruption. The effort to reconstruct the South after the Civil War and to give voting rights and economic opportunity to African Americans was very much undermined by the corruption that took over both political parties. After Lincoln's assassination in 1865, the Republican Party became embroiled in corruption, as did the Democrats and the entire country.

But first came the impeachment of Lincoln's successor, Andrew Johnson.

THE IMPEACHMENT OF ANDREW JOHNSON

The North-South divide led not only to the first assassination of a president—Abraham Lincoln was assassinated on April 15, 1865, by Southern sympathizer John Wilkes Booth—but also to the first impeachment of a president: Lincoln's successor, Andrew Johnson.

Lincoln, a Republican, after the Civil War had tried to unify the country by choosing as his running mate Johnson, a Democrat with Southern sympathies. But six weeks after his second term began, Lincoln was assassinated. Lincoln's death allowed Johnson as president to go easy on the Southern states while Lincoln's progressive Republicans who controlled Congress fumed.

Johnson, a protégé of President Andrew Jackson, was authoritarian, narcissistic, and defiant of Congress. He had represented Tennessee in the Senate and had been the only Southern senator not to resign and side with the Confederacy. Despite his loyalty to the United States, Johnson's sympathies were with the Southern states, which he wanted quickly to bring back into the Union, even if it meant doing little to hold accountable the men who had led the rebellion or to make the lives of African Americans less odious.

The congressional Republicans, who controlled both houses, passed laws trying to restore representative government in the South, hold the guilty accountable, and rescue the former slaves from demeaning and inferior conditions that would persist without federal intervention.

The provisions of the (first) Reconstruction Act of 1867, for example, called for the following:

1. The former Confederate States of America (CSA) will be divided into five military districts under the direction of Union military officers, who are supported by federal troops.
2. Military courts can be used to try cases involving civil and property rights violations as well as criminal trials.
3. States need to enact new constitutions that grant voting rights to black men ("Freedmen").
4. High-ranking Confederate officials are temporarily barred from political participation.

5. States must ratify the Fourteenth Amendment in order to be
    represented in Congress.

Johnson vetoed each of these laws, and Congress then overrode his vetoes.
But only Tennessee among the former Confederate states agreed to carry out
the laws. With Johnson urging the Southern state lawmakers to push for more
autonomy (which would virtually guarantee continued white supremacy),
Congress was unable to stop state laws and practices severely limiting the
rights of blacks.

Blacks were kept from voting in North Carolina. South Carolina passed a
law that "no Negro could pursue the trade of an artisan, mechanic, or shop-
keeper," or any other trade or employment besides that of husbandry, without a special license. An Alabama law said that "any stubborn or refractory
servants" or "servants who loiter away their time" should be fined fifty dollars, and if they could not pay, they'd be hired out for six months' labor.

A Mississippi law was even more Draconian. It said that every Negro
under eighteen who was an orphan or not supported by his parents must
be apprenticed to a white person, preferably the former owner of the slave.
It was clear that the basic rights of four million African Americans were
not going to be protected in the Southern states as long as Andrew Johnson
was president. Racial animus led to bloody race riots in Memphis and New
Orleans.

For Republicans, Johnson stood for everything that Abraham Lincoln
abhorred. Despite the fact that Johnson had remained steadfastly loyal to the
Union in the Civil War, congressional Republicans considered Johnson to be
a traitor. They referred to him as "the great criminal." Because he was stubborn and authoritarian, others called him "King Andrew."

Those who mourned the death of Abraham Lincoln felt that Johnson
was an illegitimate president. General Benjamin Butler, in his opening statement of the impeachment trial, said of Johnson, "By murder most foul he
succeeded to the Presidency, and is the elect of an assassin to that high office."

It fell to Congress to figure out a way to dethrone Johnson. Congress
passed the Tenure of Office Act, a law that made it illegal for Johnson without Senate approval to fire officials who had been previously appointed with
the advice and consent of the Senate.

Johnson had been threatening to fire his secretary of war, Edwin Stanton, a firm proponent of Reconstruction, and the Republicans were betting that Johnson would risk a confrontation and fire him anyway. If he did so, they promised, he would be impeached.

Headstrong and bullheaded, Johnson went ahead and fired Stanton.

In March of 1868, the Republican House hit Johnson with eleven accusations of high crimes and misdemeanors, most related to his firing of Stanton, even though Johnson's real offense was his obstruction of congressional efforts to advance Reconstruction. The tension between parties was so great that a second Civil War was predicted.

The Senate trial began on March 5, 1868, and it appeared that Johnson would actually be convicted, but in this blatantly political drama there was one important factor that saved him. Because Johnson had become president after Lincoln's assassination, and a new vice president had not been nominated and confirmed by Congress as the Constitution requires, the next person in line to be president according to the law at the time was the president pro tempore of the Senate, Benjamin Wade, one of the most liberal and outspoken Radical Republicans in Congress.

Originally a Whig, Wade joined the Republican Party and established a reputation as one of the most radical politicians of the era, favoring a woman's right to vote, trade union rights, and full equality for African Americans. Wade opposed the spread of slavery before the war, was a foe of the Fugitive Slave Act of 1850, and was strongly opposed to passage of the Kansas-Nebraska Act of 1854, which spread slavery westward. During the war, Wade didn't think Lincoln was freeing the slaves fast enough and criticized him often. After the war, Wade took his stand with the Radical Republicans, a group of congressmen that advocated for severe punishment of the South and its white citizens.

Andrew Johnson was certainly unpopular, but Wade was equally unpopular among other more conservative Senate factions, including some Republicans, and it was the dislike of Wade that in part led to the impeachment attempt falling one vote short. Wade, sure of victory, was selecting his cabinet in May 1868 when the vote was taken.

After the impeachment trial and his acquittal, Andrew Johnson issued a blanket amnesty to all Confederate soldiers, including Jefferson Davis, the president of the Confederacy. After Union general Ulysses S. Grant was elected president in 1868, Andrew Johnson refused to attend his inaugural the following year. If he had attended, Grant had said that he would not have allowed Johnson to ride with him to the ceremony, as was the custom.

Andrew Johnson had been impeached by politicians who hated him for political reasons (the second impeachment of a president, Bill Clinton in 1998, would have some of the same characteristics). But the attempt to remove Johnson failed, proving just how difficult it is to remove a sitting president.

GRANT AND HIS LEGACY

The Ulysses Grant administration was one of the most corrupt in American history. Though Grant was a great general, perhaps the officer most responsible for winning the Civil War, he was ill equipped to be president. He hired military leaders, men whom he knew and trusted, men who were as new to politics as he was.

What Grant couldn't comprehend was that many of his military friends were crooks. As with Trump today, Grant was a sucker for flattery. His personal secretary, Orville Babcock, controlled whole sections of the federal government. Babcock was indicted twice: first for the Whiskey Ring, the most famous scandal of the Grant administration.

Whiskey distillers in Missouri, Illinois, and Wisconsin had evaded taxes for years by bribing Treasury Department agents, who would overlook the taxes of seventy cents per gallon and split the illegal gains with the distillers.

Treasury Secretary Benjamin Bristow eventually broke up the ring, seized the distilleries, and made hundreds of arrests. Among those indicted was Babcock and Grant's other private secretary, Horace Porter.

Grant then appointed a special prosecutor to go after the ring. Babcock, it turned out, had been one of the ringleaders. The supervisor of internal revenue accused Babcock of taking $25,000 in bribes. Even when Grant was presented with evidence of Babcock's guilt, he refused to believe it.

When Grant was accused of protecting Babcock, he fired the first special prosecutor in American history, John Henderson, a former senator, just a month before Babcock's trial, replacing Henderson with another attorney.

With the president siding with Babcock, the prosecution never stood a chance. Despite this flagrant interference with an investigation of his own administration, Grant paid no meaningful political price.

There were other scandals. Two Grant appointees set up an extortion ring at the New York Custom House and were accused of charging exorbitant fees from private merchants. There was a postal ring—lucrative postal contracts were given to profiteers who were paid a lot of money for fictitious routes or for low-quality service. Interior Secretary Columbus Delano, accused of taking bribes for fraudulent land grants, was forced to resign on October 15, 1875. Grant's attorney general, George H. Williams, was rumored to have taken bribes to dismiss some cases of fraud. When informed that Williams's wife, Kate Hughes, had received a $30,000 payoff, Grant forced Williams to resign.

The corruption didn't stop there. Just as the Whiskey Ring graft trials were coming to an end, a House investigation committee accused War Secretary William W. Belknap of taking extortion money in exchange for appointing Caleb Marsh, a friend of Carita Belknap, the secretary's second wife, to run the lucrative Indian trading post at Fort Sill. Native Americans would buy food and clothing at the fort at exorbitant prices. Marsh, a resident of New York City, became quite wealthy.

One of those who testified against Belknap was Lieutenant Colonel George Custer.

Belknap, who was impeached, resigned.

Grant, who again said he knew nothing about this, never asked Belknap why he was resigning.

Then there was the secretary of the navy, George Robeson. Congress had approved a $56 million budget for navy construction projects. but discovered in 1876 that $15 million of that money was unaccounted for. The committee believed Robeson had embezzled it.

Robeson was accused of taking bribes from a grain dealer to give the company profitable contracts. The committee found that Robeson had received a $320,000 vacation cottage and a valuable team of horses. The contractor also paid off $10,000 of Robeson's debts. His annual salary was $8,000, but he had tucked away $300,000 in cash. The committee, however, wasn't able to prove the grain company had provided him with the money. All they could do was admonish him.

The second time Orville Babcock was indicted came in September 1876, when corrupt building contractors in Washington, DC, were tried for graft by prosecutor Columbus Alexander, a reformer and critic of the Grant administration. On the night of April 23, 1874, burglars broke into the safe in the district attorney's office and took the evidence. They substituted fake evidence that suggested that prosecutor Alexander was involved in the theft.

The conspiracy was revealed when two of the burglars confessed. Prosecutor Alexander was exonerated in court. Babcock was named as one of the conspirators who wanted to punish Alexander for his efforts to clean up Washington. Babcock was acquitted. Later it was revealed that the jury had been tampered with.

Enter Wall Street.

The Gold Ring scandal saw the Grant administration become embroiled in an attempt to corner the gold market.

In 1869, immensely wealthy speculators Jay Gould and Jim Fisk attempted to convince Grant not to sell treasury gold. This would increase the sales of agricultural products overseas (thus increasing business for Gould's Erie Railroad). Gould and Fisk got Grant's brother-in-law, Abel Corbin, to help persuade Grant. In exchange for the inside information they needed to carry out this plan, Gould gave Assistant Secretary of the Treasury Daniel Butterfield a $10,000 bribe.

On June 5, 1869, Gould and Fisk met with Grant while he rode on one of Gould's steamships from New York to Boston. Grant wasn't persuaded, and the treasury continued to sell gold.

In late August, Grant met with A. T. Stewart, his first cabinet nominee for treasury secretary, to talk about whether to sell the treasury gold. Stewart, fearing an upset in the sales of agriculture products, advised him not to. On that recommendation, Grant ordered Treasury Secretary George Boutwell to stop selling the gold. Boutwell had been selling $1 million worth of gold a week.

On September 6, 1869, Gould and Fisk bought the Tenth National Bank and began purchasing gold in large quantities. As the price of gold rose precipitously, Grant became suspicious. Still, two weeks passed before he figured out what Gould and Fisk were up to. Grant cautioned his brother-in-law to get out of the gold market. Gould then started selling off his gold, while Fisk kept buying.

By September 21, the price of gold had risen from $37 to $141 an ounce. At that point, Gould and Fisk owned between $50 million and $60 million in gold.

Grant ordered the treasury to release $5 million in gold, and on Friday, September 23, 1869—the first Black Friday—Boutwell released $4 million in gold and ordered the Tenth National Bank closed. This stopped Gould and Fisk from cornering the market and also ruined many other investors.

Stock sales on Wall Street dropped by 20 percent. The price of agricultural products fell sharply, devastating many farmers across the country.

Gould and Fisk, who refused to pay off their obligations, had expert legal representation and were never indicted for their profiteering.

Assistant Treasury Secretary Butterfield resigned.

Grant's reputation took another beating.

The gold panic wrecked the economy for months.

This was an early example of a theme that would arise again in the years leading up to the stock market crash of 1929 and the Great Depression and again in the financial crisis of 2008 and its aftermath. Corruption and recklessness in the financial sector repeatedly intersected with corruption in the public sector to create economic and political crises.

Despite the corruption surrounding the Grant administration, the president never argued that he was above the law. He demonstrated his fealty to the Constitution in 1872 after he was arrested for driving his horse and carriage at breakneck speed down M Street NW in Washington, DC.

William West, an African American who had fought for the North in the Civil War, was patrolling the streets, and he flagged down Grant and gave him a warning for traveling too fast. A mother and child recently had been run over by a horse and carriage, and patrolman West so informed the president and asked him to obey the speed limits.

The next day Grant again came barreling through at top speed, and West again made him stop. Grant apologized, saying what many modern-day motorists say, that he hadn't realized he was going so fast.

"I'm very sorry, Mr. President, but I have to do it," said the patrolman. "Duty is duty, and I will have to place you under arrest."

After Grant accompanied West to the police station, he was ordered to put up twenty dollars as collateral. A trial was held the next day. He didn't appear, and he was not fined.

But Grant didn't contest the arrest or fine, and he didn't issue a statement saying the president was above the law.

It was the only time in American history that a president was arrested.

As the Grant administration became known for its terrible corruption, Southerners became very resentful, and instead of directing this anger at the corrupt politicians in DC, they indulged in a deep racial hatred of African Americans. Racism—a threat to the rule of law in America from the very beginning—once against reared its ugly head.

When the Union Army left the South in 1877, the carpetbaggers soon left too. Blacks were associated with the carpetbaggers. Some freed slaves, used by carpetbagger politicians and others, were left to fend for themselves against the angry Southern whites. Southern whites retaliated by installing Jim Crow laws, a system intended to perpetuate legal slavery. Blacks in the South, kept from voting well into the twentieth century, were powerless in the face of such flagrant discrimination. When the Supreme Court decided in *Plessy v. Ferguson* in 1896 that public accommodations could be separate but equal, segregation of schools, public transportation, restaurants, and even bathrooms became the official law of the land.

The racism was bad in itself, but what we wish to stress again is that the corruption at the founding of our country and the failure to address the moral issue of slavery in the Constitution allowed slavery to exist in America. Further corruption with carpetbaggers, the Grant administration, and beyond fed white resentment and made the treatment of blacks much worse from the Civil War into the present.

It's also worth noting that after the carpetbaggers left, there were movements across the country to accommodate the South and bring the nation together. Autonomous once again, the South celebrated itself with statues of Confederate heroes and romantic notions of the Civil War. Robert E. Lee, Stonewall Jackson, and other generals were depicted not as traitors, but as beloved heroes. Yale University even named one of its colleges after John C. Calhoun, a Southern senator and vice president who defended slavery and claimed that owning slaves was the key to success.

The ugliness of slavery, the massive slaughter during the Civil War, and the corruption that followed were thus downplayed so Northern industrialists and their bought politicians could celebrate the post–Civil War economic expansion, while Southerners found an uneasy and reluctant place in the Union by oppressing former slaves and romanticizing the past.

For decades, political power eluded the South. It only returned when the South aligned itself with one of the two political parties. In return for that support, and the balance of power that came with it, the party embraced by Southern politicians was expected to loyally support the South—the *white* South—and its political agenda.

Up until the mid-1960s, the white South was steadfastly loyal to the Democratic Party, an alliance used to carry out populist attacks on Northern industrial elites and Republican politicians beholden to them. The Democratic flag bearers were an uneasy alliance of Southerners (some more progressive than others, but most imbued with deep prejudices against African Americans); agrarian champions such as William Jennings Bryan, who lost four presidential races; and Northern politicians who claimed to represent the rising working class (including corrupt urban machines such as New York City's Tammany Hall; New York governor Al Smith, in 1928 the first Catholic to run for president; and the patrician FDR, who won the White House in 1932).

For decades, even the most progressive Democrats had to accommodate Southern racists. President Woodrow Wilson of New Jersey grew up in the South and shared that racism. Others looked the other way. (It was Eleanor Roosevelt, not her husband, who spoke out most forcefully when African American opera star Marian Anderson was barred from singing at the Daughters of the American Revolution's Constitution Hall in 1939.)

This alignment lasted until the 1960s and 1970s when the white South shifted away from the Democrats and toward the Republican Party. This was due in part to the Civil Rights Acts of 1964 and 1965 under Democratic president Lyndon Johnson, Bobby Kennedy's support of civil rights, Republican Richard Nixon's pursuit of a "Southern strategy," and Republican Ronald Reagan's reinforcement of a GOP Southern strategy in 1980.

This shift—which we will discuss later—empowered the GOP, but also threatened the rule of law, with a combination of immense industrial wealth, which had always been strong in the Republican Party, and the socially conservative—some argue still racist—white South. These two factions of the GOP have warred for decades, with the social conservatives gaining power and eventual dominance. By 2016, Donald Trump was poised to ride to power on the alliance of concentrated wealth, Southern social conservatism, and lingering racism throughout the country.

But we're getting ahead of ourselves on modern-day Republican politics. That the Democrats attempted to combine progressive politics with social conservatism and, often, racism from the nation's founding until the 1960s is itself worthy of note. This brought many contradictions for America's oldest political party, ranging from Thomas Jefferson's famous words in the Declaration of Independence that "all [white] men are created equal," to Andrew Jackson's vision of a populist democracy that excluded Native Americans and blacks, to former presidential candidate William Jennings Bryan's testimony against public schools teaching Darwin's theory of evolution in the Scopes Monkey Trial in the 1920s, and finally to the infamous Richard J. Daley machine that ruled Chicago with an iron fist and as late as 1972 refused to bring African American delegates to the Democratic National Convention.

It wasn't until the election of Democrat Woodrow Wilson in 1912 that the country had a Southern president after the Civil War. Wilson had been president of Princeton University and governor of New Jersey, but he was a Virginian. His reforms at Princeton included curbing the social influence of eating clubs populated by the scions of wealthy industrial families (mostly from the North), but he also prohibited the admission of African Americans, fearing their presence would offend Southern students.

President Wilson's administration (1913–1921) is remembered not only for its many accomplishments, such as enacting and enforcing antitrust laws and other restrictions on big businesses, mostly from the North, and appointing the first Jewish Supreme Court justice, Louis Brandeis, in 1916, but also for a resurgence of racism. Blacks were excluded from federal employment, much more so than during the preceding Teddy Roosevelt and William Taft administrations, and Wilson was allied with powerful Southern governors.

On March 21, 1915, the White House held a private screening of *Birth of a Nation,* a silent film celebrating the rise of the Ku Klux Klan. The film, a justification of white supremacy, was a box office smash. President Wilson said, "The white men were roused by a mere instinct of self-preservation . . . until at least there had sprung into existence a great Ku Klux Klan, a veritable empire of the South, to protect the Southern country."

NORTHERN INDUSTRIALISTS TAKE OVER THE GOP

Around the turn of the twentieth century, Republicans quickly fell under the control of Northern industrialists, including Andrew Carnegie and John D. Rockefeller, who saw donating to and supporting the Republican Party as a way to control government. They could keep labor costs low while fighting labor unions. They also supported high tariffs on imports to protect their own manufacturing industries, making high tariffs (as well as opposing the income tax) an important part of the GOP platform up through President Herbert Hoover's disastrous implementation of tariffs in 1930, and the ensuing trade war that prolonged the Great Depression. (The GOP should have learned its lesson about protectionism from the 1930s, but it has flirted yet again with protectionism under Donald Trump.)

These industrialists used their money to make sure that the Republican Party would do their bidding.

During William McKinley's presidency, beginning in March 1897, we started to see *big* money come into politics. After McKinley's assassination in 1901, his vice president, Teddy Roosevelt, became president. Roosevelt was a progressive who disapproved of the corrupt practices of big business. This caused a wide split in the Republican Party. Those backing the wealthy and powerful industrialists supported William Howard Taft instead of Roosevelt for the Republican nomination in 1908. This pro-business Taft wing of the Republican Party existed through the 1950s.

Teddy Roosevelt, in retaliation, formed the Bull Moose Party. But again, it was *corruption* that caused this split in the party. Roosevelt wanted public funding for elections. He wanted to break up monopolies and trusts.

On October 14, 1912, Roosevelt was in Milwaukee, Wisconsin, to make a speech about the sins of private citizens having too much economic and political power when a disturbed man named John Schrank shot him. Schrank, a saloonkeeper, had been stalking Roosevelt around the country before getting a clear shot. When arrested, Schrank proclaimed that "any man looking for a third term ought to be shot."

The .32-caliber bullet, aimed at Roosevelt's heart, first struck his eyeglass case and then the pages of the speech he was to give. By the time it broke his skin, it had slowed considerably, so Roosevelt insisted on making his speech.

After telling the audience he had been shot, he pulled the torn, blood-stained manuscript from his breast pocket and said, "It takes more than that to kill a Bull Moose . . . The bullet is in me now, so that I cannot make a very long speech, but I will do my best."

The assassination attempt, Roosevelt said, "emphasizes to a particular degree the need of the Progressive movement. Friends, every good citizen ought to do everything in his or her power to prevent the coming of the day when we shall see in this country two recognized creeds fighting one another, when we shall see the creed of the 'have nots' arraigned against the creed of the 'haves.'"

Roosevelt spoke of the importance of labor unions. He boasted of his work to bolster the antitrust laws and the interstate commerce law, which gave government control over the railroads. He talked of taking government control of Standard Oil, "Big Sugar," and "the Tobacco Trust."

He chided Woodrow Wilson, who was then governor of New Jersey and running against him for president, for saying that the states were the proper authorities to deal with the trusts.

"Well," Roosevelt said, "about eighty percent of the trusts are organized in New Jersey. The Standard Oil, the Tobacco, the Sugar, the Beef, all those trusts are organized in the state of New Jersey and the laws of New Jersey say that their charters can at any time be amended or repealed, and Mr. Wilson has been governor for a year and nine months and he has not opened his lips. The chapter describing what Mr. Wilson has done about trusts in New Jersey would read precisely like a chapter describing snakes in Ireland, which ran: 'There are no snakes in Ireland.' Mr. Wilson has done precisely and exactly nothing about the trusts."

He asked the men and women of Wisconsin to stand with him. He went on, "I will say that, friends, because the Republican Party is beaten. Nobody needs to have any idea that anything can be done with the Republican Party."

He spoke of how Taft had wrecked the party for good by stealing the presidential nomination in 1912.

"They stole that nomination from me," he said, "but it was really from you . . . But you are the people they dread. They dread the people themselves, and those bosses and the big special interests behind them made up their mind that they would rather see the Republican Party wrecked than see it come under the control of the people themselves."

Roosevelt then spoke of Wilson's commitment to states' rights, instead of power for the federal government. He said that Wilson opposed the bill to abolish child labor, a bill that would prohibit women from working more than eight hours a day, and a law to provide a minimum wage for women.

His message was clear: Wilson, although a progressive like Roosevelt, relied too heavily upon the mantra of states' rights that had permeated the Democratic Party since the days of Jefferson. True Progressive reform, Roosevelt argued, required a powerful federal government on the side of the people rather than special interests.

In November, Roosevelt was defeated by Woodrow Wilson in a three-way race that included President William Taft, a Republican. Schrank, his would-be assassin, was committed to a mental hospital, where he died in 1943.

William Howard Taft's head of the Department of the Interior, Richard Ballinger, had contributed to the Republican Party split. Ballinger rekindled that ancient problem of corruption that had plagued the Grant administration, had been driven back by Teddy Roosevelt, and saw a resurgence once Roosevelt was gone. Ballinger also began what is now a century-long practice of politicians using the Interior Department to open up public lands on sweetheart terms to mining, timber, oil, and other industries owned by political supporters, with little respect for environmental consequences or the reasons why the Teddy Roosevelt administration and Congress had set aside lands for conservation in the first place.

Despite Taft's purported policy of land conservation, 15,868 acres in Montana were sold to large corporations (General Electric, Guggenheim, and Amalgamated Copper). Ballinger at first ignored the story, then accused reporters of opposing development in the West. Ballinger was dogged by accusations of favoritism.

An even more serious charge involved coal development in the Chugach National Forest by Clarence Cunningham, a Seattle developer and an associate of Ballinger. The deal was financed by a corporation associated with J. P. Morgan and the Guggenheim family of New York City. The group had staked thirty-three claims, even though Alaska land laws were designed to benefit small farmers and prevent monopolies.

Cunningham was one of Ballinger's former clients. For several months in 1908, between the time Ballinger was employed as land commissioner and interior secretary, he had acted as an agent for the Cunningham/Morgan/Guggenheim development group with the federal government, lobbying then interior secretary James Garfield. Now that Ballinger was interior secretary, Cunningham expected continued loyalty and was not disappointed.

Upon becoming interior secretary, Ballinger also reassigned General Land Office investigator Louis R. Glavis, and fired him when Glavis complained about Ballinger's dealings. President Taft, who had approved of the Glavis firing, exonerated Ballinger. A scandal in the press followed. *Collier's* magazine published Glavis's account of the incident and, when Congress started an investigation and Ballinger threated to sue *Collier's*, the magazine hired Boston lawyer, and future Supreme Court justice, Louis D. Brandeis to represent it and Glavis.

Woodrow Wilson's successor, Warren Harding, had perhaps the biggest scandal since the Grant administration. In a sensational investigation, Senator Thomas Walsh revealed that a group known as the Ohio Gang, members of Harding's administration, had taken bribes to lease oil reserves at Teapot Dome in Wyoming to private companies.

Not three months after taking office, President Harding signed an executive order transferring custody of federal oil reserves from Secretary of the Navy Edwin Denby to the secretary of the interior. Three sites—the naval reserves at Elk Hills, California; Buena Vista, California; and Teapot Dome, Wyoming—were being held out as an insurance policy in case there was a shortage of oil.

On April 3, 1922, in secret and without competitive bidding, Albert Fall, the secretary of the interior, leased the Teapot Dome reserve to Harry Sinclair's Mammoth Oil Company. On December 11, 1922, he leased the Elk Hills reserve to Edward Doheny's Pan American Petroleum Company.

Later it was discovered that Fall had received $260,000 from Sinclair, and that Doheny had "lent" him $100,000.

The scandal was publicized in 1924, a year after Harding died of a heart attack and was succeeded by Calvin Coolidge. Secretary of the Interior Fall was convicted of conspiracy and bribery and became the first member of a president's administration to go to prison while in office. After the public outcry, Secretary of the Navy Denby resigned. Harry Sinclair was also jailed for contempt of court and attempting to bribe jurors.

Charles Forbes, head of the Veterans' Bureau, was another member of Harding's Ohio Gang. Forbes sold government property for less than it was worth in exchange for large payments. He resigned and fled to Europe after he was caught. In 1924, a Senate investigation found that Forbes had taken in more than $200 million. He was convicted of conspiracy to defraud the United States by rigging federal contracts and served two years in Leavenworth federal penitentiary.

Yet another Harding administration scandal arose in the Justice Department. Attorney General Harry Daugherty was suspected of profiting from the sale of government supplies of alcohol. He was also charged with selling pardons and failing to enforce prohibition laws. He was never convicted.

Some historians have sought to redeem the reputation of President Harding. He was unfaithful in marriage, but the corruption he tolerated was probably no worse than what was encouraged later under Richard Nixon and certainly less than Donald Trump's corruption.

The most recent sympathetic biography of Harding is from John Dean, a famous former lawyer who grew up in Marion, Ohio, where Harding lived. Dean, the White House counsel for President Nixon, testified against Nixon and others in the Watergate scandal. Dean was convicted of obstructing justice and lost his law license, but his frequent television commentary against the Trump administration reminds us that corruption in politics has gotten worse. The trajectory from Teddy Roosevelt to Taft to Harding to Nixon to Trump has *not* moved in the right direction.

CHAPTER 4

Immigration, the Red Scare, and Japanese American Internment

We are a nation of many nationalities, many races, many religions—bound together by a single unity, the unity of freedom and equality. Whoever seeks to set one nationality against another, seeks to degrade all nationalities.
—*FRANKLIN D. ROOSEVELT*

AMERICA HAS BEEN A COUNTRY OF IMMIGRANTS SINCE the Pilgrims established the first successful European settlement in Plymouth, Massachusetts, in 1620. (An earlier attempt at Jamestown, Virginia, was an abysmal failure, in part because of hostile relations between English settlers and Native Americans.) Conflict between immigrants and Americans who were already here has also been a part of our history. The first conflict was with the Native American tribes, many of whom were decimated by the late nineteenth century.

Then, as the United States filled with wave after wave of immigrants from Europe and from other parts of the world, conflict intensified between immigrant groups that had arrived earlier (from England, Scotland, Ireland,

and Germany) and had consolidated political power, and those that came later (Italians, Eastern Europeans, Chinese, Japanese, and others).

This conflict was often political and cultural, and it sometimes had religious overtones (particularly if immigrants were Jewish, Catholic, or from predominantly Buddhist or Hindu countries in Asia). Many immigrants faced prejudice, including the family of Donald Trump, whose grandfather Friedrich Trump emigrated from Germany in 1885. After two world wars, his son Fred Trump hid that heritage from other New Yorkers. (The Trumps pretended they were of Swedish origin.)

The United States is unique among powerful nations because the vast majority of its citizens (excluding Native Americans) have family roots elsewhere. Such is not true of Russia, China, Japan, or the powers of Europe. We are alone among superpowers in having a predominant language—English— that was not spoken here four hundred years ago. In the twenty-first century, we will need to combine representative democracy with a society in which no single ethnic group is the majority.

In this chapter we pick up America's immigration story and its impact on the rule of law midstream—in the early twentieth century. Many European immigrants and descendants of African slaves, and a relatively small number of other immigrants, had arrived much earlier, but many other immigrants were just arriving.

These later waves of immigrants became a source of fear, rooted in ethnic prejudice, religious prejudice, and the concern that tumultuous political and social upheavals in Europe would spread to the United States.

In the early twentieth century, US government officials feared that many immigrants were loyal to their countries of origin or to political movements therein. This fear intensified with the massive immigration between 1880 and the 1920s, as well as the growth of anarchism and Marxism in Europe. During the First World War, Americans of recent European origin were suspected of being loyal to different sides. Then, with the Russian Revolution of 1917 and its violent aftermath came a renewed fear of communism.

There was also a cultural component of the fear of immigrants. Status quo–loving Americans feared the change the newcomers were bringing. On top of all of this, there were economic concerns—many immigrants were poor, and their arrival coincided with the growth of union-organizing movements in the United States. Employers feared unions (union-organizing and union-busting tactics were sometimes violent) and feared the immigrants who sometimes joined and occasionally organized unions.

In 1915, before the United States entered World War I, President Woodrow Wilson warned against "hyphenated Americans"—specifically German-Americans, Italian-Americans, Irish-Americans, and Russian émigrés, saying that they "poured the poison of disloyalty into the very arteries of our national life." He called them "creatures of passion, disloyalty, and anarchy," and declared that they "must be crushed out." Wilson was not an aberration. He was elected twice, and many Americans shared his views.

Right after World War I, German, Russian, Italian, and Jewish immigrants were singled out for investigation, arrest, and contempt. Fear of Bolshevism was often the excuse.

When the Bolshevik Revolution began in Russia in 1917, it took everyone by surprise. When the Bolsheviks took control of Russia two years later, it became apparent that the agenda of the new country—the Union of Soviet Socialist Republics—was the Marxist ideology of global communism. The Bolsheviks seized power violently, and the violence would only get worse in coming decades.

It became evident that the Soviet Union would do all it could to undermine capitalist countries, including democracies. This meant destabilizing the new representative democracies set up in Europe after World War I, including Czechoslovakia and Hungary, formed out of the Austro-Hungarian Empire. These countries had communist parties that ran candidates in elections, but many communists didn't want to play by democratic rules. Undermining other countries' governments through fomenting armed revolution was *central* to communist ideology.

Since the days of Czarist Russia, but especially after the Russian Revolution, the Russians have been interfering with and undermining liberal democracy. After World War I the Russians sowed mistrust in representative democracies throughout Europe through both covert and violent means as well as assisting, and sometimes controlling, foreign communist parties during elections. We address Russian and Soviet subversion of Western democracies in chapters 5 and 20 and note that, even if the communist mantra is gone, foreign interference in elections remains a serious, very real threat to our democracy.

After World War I the Soviets attempted to undermine the rule of law in the United States by sending its spies into our country and encouraging Americans to sign up for cells of the Communist Party USA (CPUSA), some of which were colluding with the Soviets. The United States also had a Socialist Party—a labor union movement—which the Russians unsuccessfully tried to turn into a communist movement. Communists fought to take over labor unions, claiming that their primary goal was to improve workers' pay and living conditions. Most American labor unions reacted by embracing a staunchly anti-communist philosophy—making it clear that Soviet intervention in American politics was most unwelcome.

These Soviet-inspired communist activities brought fear to the United States in the decade after World War I and beyond.

This Soviet interference into our democratic process was a *real* threat to the rule of law. But how we respond to a threat can also subvert the rule of law. As in the other instances of external or internal threat, including the suspension of habeas corpus during the Civil War and our reaction to the terrorist attacks of 9/11, the Soviet threat generated a resurgence of the problems that have always stood between our society and a genuine rule of law. Whenever such threats arise, the problem of due process immediately comes into play, often reinforced by the problems of alternative facts as well as ethnic and religious bigotry.

The rule of law again and again comes under threat not only from external sources (such as Soviets or Russians fomenting violence or interfering in elections) but from our poor reactions to that external threat. We had *two* periods in our history when we overreacted to the Russian threat. The first was the Red Scare after World War I. The second was McCarthyism after World War II, which we will discuss in Chapter 7.

Although this fear of violent communism could have been directed toward Americans of any ethnic group, the groups most often attacked for actual or perceived "communist" connections were from countries most closely associated with the threat—Jews of Russian or Eastern European background and, because of the enormous political upheaval and active anarchist movement in Italy, Italians.

In June 1919, a series of bombings by Italian anarchists set our country on edge. Letter bombs were mailed to government officials, businessmen, and law enforcement officials. Most never reached their target, but a few people were injured, including a US senator's housekeeper whose hands were blown off. Another bomb damaged the homes of New York judge Charles C. Nott and Attorney General A. Mitchell Palmer. Three radicals were arrested.

In those days, immigration policy was run by the Labor Department (immigration policy is in large part an issue of labor economics, although from time to time real or perceived national security issues come into play as well). Only the secretary of labor could issue arrest warrants and deportation orders for foreign violators of the immigration acts.

Palmer, the attorney general, decided he needed more power to intervene in the immigration issue, and in August 1919 he named J. Edgar Hoover, who was only twenty-four years old, to head a new division of the Justice Department: the General Intelligence Division (GID). Hoover's job was to identify and investigate members of radical groups.

On November 7, 1919, the second anniversary of the Russian Revolution, federal agents and local Boston police made a series of violent raids against the Union of Russian Workers in a dozen American cities and beat some workers badly. Some who were arrested were American citizens and not members of the targeted group. Some were teachers conducting night classes in a shared space. There were more arrests than warrants. In New York City alone, 650 people were swept up and arrested.

When Congress questioned Palmer, he said his task force had amassed more than sixty thousand names of suspected anarchists, socialists, and communists. Forty-three were deported.

Palmer, wanting more power, pushed for a new sedition act that gave him authority to raid on a broader scale.

The Justice Department conducted raids in thirty cities in twenty-three states on January 2, 1920, and continued for the next six weeks. More than three thousand were arrested, and many others were jailed for long periods before being released. There were searches without warrants, and miserable conditions in jail, as some of those arrested were beaten. Raids were often conducted in meeting halls. Sometimes every person there was arrested, whether they belonged to the group or not. Some were American citizens.

Wrote Francis Kane, the US attorney for the Eastern District of Pennsylvania, "People not really guilty are likely to be arrested and railroaded through their hearings. We appear to be attempting to repress a political party. By such methods we drive underground and make dangerous what was not dangerous before."

Kane resigned in protest.

Palmer replied by saying such raids protected America and were urgently needed.

"There is no time to waste on hairsplitting over infringement of liberties," he said.

A few weeks later, Assistant Secretary of Labor Louis Post canceled more than 2,000 of Palmer's warrants, saying they were illegal. Of the 10,000 arrested, 3,500 were imprisoned and 556 resident aliens were deported.

Palmer wanted Post fired. President Wilson defended Post but urged Palmer to "not let the country see red."

In May 1920, the newly formed American Civil Liberties Union reported on Palmer's unlawful activities. They cited illegal entrapment by agent provocateurs and unlawful incommunicado detention. Noted legal scholars including the future Supreme Court justice Felix Frankfurter denounced the Palmer raids and deportations and the lack of due process.

In June 1920, Massachusetts federal judge George Weston Anderson effectively ended the raids when he ordered seventeen of those arrested discharged and wrote, "A mob is a mob, whether made up of Government officials acting under instructions from the Department of Justice, or of criminals and loafers and the vicious classes."

Yet fear of immigrants—especially Jews and Italians—continued. On September 16, 1920, a terrorist attack on Wall Street, blocks from the site of the 9/11 attacks eighty-one years later, provided yet another excuse to associate immigrants with terrorism. A bomb exploded outside the JP Morgan and Company headquarters, killing thirty-eight people. The attackers were never found, but widespread public opinion was that they were anarchists, and likely immigrants. Xenophobia reached new heights. (In 1944 the FBI reopened the investigation and concluded, without any specific evidence, that the attackers were probably Italian anarchists.)

Meanwhile, two Italian immigrants, Nicola Sacco and Bartolomeo Vanzetti, were accused of shooting two men in an armed robbery in Braintree, Massachusetts, on April 15, 1920. The trial was rife with prejudice toward Italians. Even though there was testimony that they were innocent, the jury found them guilty on July 14, 1920, and sentenced them to death, partly because they were anarchists. The judge expressed his antipathy toward the defendants and later boasted about his role in the case to prominent members of the Boston bar. For the next seven years there were protests against their execution. Still, a three-man commission upheld the verdict, and they were executed at midnight on August 23, 1927. There were protests in every major city in the United States and around the world. There was rioting in Paris, London, and other European cities.

On the fiftieth anniversary of their execution, Massachusetts governor Michael Dukakis in 1977 declared a Nicola Sacco and Bartolomeo Vanzetti Memorial Day, saying they were unfairly convicted and that "any disgrace should be forever removed from their names."

The Sacco and Vanzetti case undermined the rule of law, because it was not a fair trial. Sacco and Vanzetti were presumed to be terrorists simply because they were socialists and were Italian. Other than that, the state did not have much of a case.

Congress also responded to this "threat" by passing the Immigration Act of 1924, which greatly restricted immigration from Southern and Eastern Europe, especially by Italians, Slavs, and Jews. The act also set quotas on immigrants from other countries, preventing immigration by many Arabs, Asians, and others.

This act was passed at a time of relative economic prosperity, but by late 1929, Wall Street had collapsed. The country was soon in the midst of the Great Depression and massive unemployment. This brought about a new threat from immigration—a very real threat to the jobs and public assistance for Americans who were already here. The Franklin Roosevelt administration thus had little choice but to continue harsh immigration restrictions throughout the 1930s and early 1940s. The political fear of immigrants of the 1920s was now compounded by economic fear and, later, by fear of renewed turmoil and war in Europe. Many Americans wanted nothing to do with foreigners, even if this meant turning away immigrants who, when they returned home, would very likely become victims of Nazi genocide.

JAPANESE INTERNMENT

Ethnic profiling took another tragic turn after the Japanese attacked Pearl Harbor on December 7, 1941. Hours after the destructive air strike, the FBI rounded up more than 1,200 Japanese community and religious leaders in Hawaii. They were detained solely for their ethnicity. Their assets were frozen. More than 1,500 Japanese Americans were sent to camps on the mainland.

On the West Coast, the FBI searched thousands of Japanese American homes for weapons and other contraband such as shortwave radios, cameras, and flashlights. In Hawaii, fishing boats belonging to Japanese Americans were seized.

Three men—Lt. Gen. John DeWitt, Secretary of War Henry Stimson, and Attorney General Francis Biddle—planned to round up Japanese, Italian, and German Americans. During hearings, Culbert Olson, the governor of California, and Earl Warren, the state attorney general, called for all Japanese to be removed from the state.

On February 19, 1942, President Franklin Roosevelt signed Executive Order 9066, which created military zones in California, Washington, and Oregon that were to be cleared of Japanese Americans. About 127,000 people, mostly US citizens who had never been to Japan, were relocated to ten internment camps in Colorado, Arizona, Wyoming, Arkansas, Idaho, California, and Utah. Given six days to dispose of their belongings, many, not knowing if they would ever return, sold their homes for a fraction of the value. Some were taken to relocation centers, where they lived for months before being sent to permanent camps. In Portland, Oregon, 3,000 Japanese Americans lived in a livestock pavilion. Another de facto camp was the Santa Anita Assembly Center, where 18,000 people were kept. About 8,500 people lived in the stables.

Each camp held around 10,000 imprisoned Japanese Americans.

In defiance of the order, Fred Korematsu, an American-born citizen, refused to leave his home and was arrested. After his conviction, he appealed, and the case went to the US Supreme Court in 1944. His conviction was upheld by a 6–3 vote.

"Pressing public necessity may sometimes justify the existence of such restrictions," wrote Justice Hugo Black. "Racial antagonisms never can."

The court, however, held that because it was impossible to "separate the disloyal from the loyal," the order applied to all Japanese Americans.

In 1944, Mitsuye Endo, the daughter of Japanese immigrants living in Sacramento, California, brought a case before the Supreme Court from an internment camp. She filed a habeas corpus petition. When the government offered to free her, she refused. She wanted to free all those in the camps.

The US Supreme Court held there was no legitimate, legally sanctioned reason for holding loyal, law-abiding Japanese American citizens once the government determined they weren't threats to the nation's security.

The last internment camp closed in March 1946.

More than forty years later, the US government gave reparations to those who lost property during imprisonment. In 1988, surviving prisoners were awarded $20,000 each.

President Bill Clinton awarded Fred Korematsu the Presidential Medal of Freedom.

The *Korematsu* decision has never been overturned although the Supreme Court in 2018, in a 5–4 decision upholding President Trump's travel ban from Muslim countries (which the court distinguished from the Japanese internment), noted that the *Korematsu* decision was no longer considered good case law.

During the Second World War, Japanese Americans weren't the only ethnicity discriminated against. The US government also restricted freedoms for 600,000 Italian Americans. Shortly after the Pearl Harbor attack, the FBI arrested hundreds of Italian Americans.

General DeWitt, who had recommended rounding up Japanese Americans, called for all "enemy aliens" over the age of fourteen to be removed from the coasts to the interior. J. Edgar Hoover supported him.

Many Italian Americans, though not imprisoned, were forced to register and carry photo IDs at all times. They were subject to travel restrictions, and required to hand over all cameras, weapons, flashlights, and shortwave radios.

Italian-language schools were closed, and Italian American organizations were monitored by the FBI.

Several thousand Italians were forced to move from San Francisco Bay. According to New York Yankees star Joe DiMaggio, Italians were not allowed within a mile of the harbor. His father, DiMaggio said, was forbidden to run his restaurant on the pier because he was a "foreign national."

"He was not even allowed to stop by his restaurant for a glass of wine and a few pieces of bread," said DiMaggio, who served in the military during the war. "I had nothing to say in the matter. I just shut up and did my tour.

"A million Italian-Americans served in the war, and more than half that number had to worry about owning a flashlight and carrying an Enemy Alien card. It makes me angry to this day."

CHAPTER 5

Russian Assault on the Rule of Law

The Soviet Union, as everybody who has the courage to face the fact knows,
is run by a dictatorship as absolute as any other dictatorship in the world.
—FRANKLIN D. ROOSEVELT

INTERFERING IN THE POLITICS OF OTHER NATIONS IS AN
ancient and pervasive strategy for gaining diplomatic and military advantage. Almost every European nation hatched plots in neighboring countries during the Middle Ages, and then around the globe in the colonial era. Popes interfered frequently in national politics during the Middle Ages and after the Reformation.

The United States owes its independence in part to French interference against the British during the American Revolution. Knowing the potential dangers, the United States in the 1820s adopted the Monroe Doctrine, deeming European interference anywhere in the Western Hemisphere to be a hostile act.

By the beginning of the twentieth century, the United States turned to the same game of interference, first in the Philippines under President William McKinley, then in Latin America. The United States seized the Panama Canal after orchestrating a Panamanian "revolution" against Colombia. By the 1950s, the United States responded to communist expansionism by inter-fering in Latin America, Southeast Asia, and the Middle East, with covert operations and military engagements in Chile, Iran, Vietnam, and other countries.

Russia isn't the only country to interfere with the affairs of other nations, but it relies upon this strategy perhaps more than any other nation. The Rus-sians, moreover, are very good at it.

Russia's centuries-long history of overcoming geographic and linguistic disadvantages by playing European powers against each other is part of this story. The ideological commitment of post-1917 Bolshevik communism to spread proletariat revolution around the world is another part of the Russian story.

When it comes to undermining the rule of law in democracies, Russia is the world champion.

Under autocratic rule, Russia gained expertise in the art of espionage. Going back to Peter the Great, Russia had a very ambivalent relationship with the West. Russia had been humiliated after Napoleon's invasion, and though Napoleon was defeated in 1812, the Russians never stopped feeling threatened by the West. Russia responded by sending spies to countries all over Europe and beyond.

One of the first incidents of Russian interference in American affairs occurred in 1871 during the presidency of Ulysses S. Grant, who was negoti-ating with Great Britain to settle claims stemming from the Civil War. Great Britain had built the *Alabama,* a Confederate warship, and Grant wanted reparations.

The Russians and Americans had been allies. During the Crimean War between 1853 and 1856, the Americans had supplied the Russians with arms to fight the British, French, and Turks. Under the rule of Czar Alexander II, Russia had been the only European nation to support the North, but in 1871 as the Americans and the British negotiated a financial settlement, the Rus-sians feared that a deal between the US and Britain would improve relations between the two countries, so they came up with a plan to stir up trouble.

As these negotiations over reparations played out, there was a fight over money owed to Benjamin Perkins, an American who had arranged the sale of munitions to Russia, but claimed that Russian agents never paid him for the arms and powder. Perkins's widow wanted the million dollars her husband was owed. She hired lobbyists and went to newspapers for support.

Russian Ambassador Konstantin Catacazy, whom American officials described as odious and dishonest, had been saying nasty things about President Grant and Secretary of State Hamilton Fish. Catacazy, trying to scuttle America's negotiations with Britain, planted fake stories in the media of illegal financial skullduggery and produced fake documents to pit the two sides against each other.

Catacazy launched a campaign in the press and lobbied members of Congress. One fake story he told the *New York Sun* was that Assistant Secretary of State Bancroft Davis was taking bribes in exchange for supporting Perkins's widow. The paper called Davis a "cunning and coldblooded scamp."

The *New York World* published "fake news"—a letter Catacazy wrote to derail the talks with Britain. *New York Times* investigative reporters revealed that Catacazy's statements were "false and malicious," and called his work "mischievous intermeddling."

Grant ordered Catacazy banished from the country.

In his State of the Union address, Grant said, "It was impossible, with self-respect or with just regard to the dignity of the country, to permit Mr. Catacazy to continue to hold intercourse with this Government after his personal abuse of Government officials, and during his persistent interferences, through various means, with the relations between the United States and other powers."

In a letter to his superiors, Catacazy insulted Secretary of State Fish. The letter appeared in the *Chicago Tribune*, and when President Grant read it, he was furious.

When Catacazy went to the White House, the president refused to see him.

Ambassador Catacazy's bad behavior almost caused the cancellation of the three-and-a-half-month grand tour of the United States planned for Czar Alexander's fourth son, twenty-one-year-old Grand Duke Alexei Alexandrovich Romanov. But the Grand Duke's tour proceeded, and his charm apparently glossed over Russian intentions perhaps more accurately portrayed by the actions of Catacazy.

New York was one of thirty-four cities the grand duke was visiting on his goodwill tour, followed by Niagara Falls and Chicago, which had burned to the ground in the Great Fire only weeks before. He was an honored guest in every city at dinners, balls, and theater performances. Germans and Poles protested his visit. There was talk in New York that Polish nationals were going to kill him.

Arriving in North Platte, Nebraska, by special train, the grand duke was the guest of General Philip Sheridan. Colonel George Armstrong Custer was part of their contingent, and their guide was Buffalo Bill Cody.

They drank a lot, and on his twenty-second birthday on January 14, 1872, Romanov hunted buffalo. The Russian was a lousy shot, but Cody made sure he got to kill an old and slow buffalo, much to the joy of his royal highness.

One of America's first visiting celebrities, Romanov returned to Russia in December.

The Americans and British completed their negotiations. This time, Russian interference had failed.

Meanwhile, the Russian monarchy was plagued by a growing revolutionary movement. In 1881, the grand duke's father, Czar Alexander, was killed by a terrorist's bomb.

After Russia, under Czar Nicholas II, suffered an ignominious defeat in the Russo-Japanese War in 1904–1905, Russia lost a great deal of influence in China and what was then Manchuria.

Things did not improve over the next ten years, and they got worse with the start of World War I.

By early 1917, Russia was on the verge of collapse.

Some Russian revolutionaries, along with intellectuals who supported them, turned to German philosopher Karl Marx for inspiration about a different, and presumably better, social order.

Marx believed that laws existed to oppress the working class. Under communism, he suggested, *everyone* would be treated equally. In sum—as soon as a society moved away from conventional, bourgeois legal norms, violently or otherwise—a new rule of law for the working class would somehow come into being.

This ideology was a very suitable tool for anyone eager to destroy the existing rule of law in their own country or another, and it turned out to be lethal. What type of regime might replace the bourgeois rule of law was an afterthought for some. For others with political power in mind, the aftermath of communist revolution was part of a concealed plan.

The revolt knocked Russia out of the war against Germany and Austria.

Czar Nicholas was ordered to abdicate. Having no choice, he agreed. The Romanov family and their loyal servants were kept prisoners in the Alexander Palace, and after being moved twice, on the night of July 16, 1918, they were murdered at the instructions of Vladimir Lenin.

The brutal, unjust rule of law that existed for centuries under czars was destroyed. What would replace it was far worse.

The communist revolution, it turned out, was no panacea for Russian workers. Emma Goldman, an anarchist who had been deported from America, lived in Russia in 1920 and 1921. She wrote a piece on the conditions there titled "There Is No Communism in Russia" that described an authoritarian, centralized government. As for the factories and the tractors, she said, they weren't nationalized, as Marx had theorized. They were taken by the government.

She concluded, "I think there is nothing more pernicious than to degrade a human being into a cog of a soulless machine, turn him into a serf, into a spy or the victim of a spy. There is nothing more corrupting than slavery and despotism."

Soon thereafter, Lenin died, and a ruthless Joseph Stalin took over. Freedom died as the Russian Revolution sank into a totalitarian state. All criticism, all opposition, was eliminated. Stalin killed anyone he thought to be a traitor, and he saw traitors everywhere. To maintain control, Stalin killed an estimated twenty million people over twenty-five years.

In the end, those in power convinced themselves and others that their position was synonymous with the national interest. Inevitably those in power always saw the need to eliminate all threats to that power. Russians built concentration camps before Nazis did. Lenin and Trotsky created 315 concentration camps in the Soviet Union by 1923. Stalin would later refine these camps into holding cells and chambers of horror for millions. Stalin began his purges. Meanwhile, the NKVD, the secret police that terrorized the populace, stepped up surveillance. Party purges in non-Russian republics were particularly violent. By the time the purges ended in 1938, millions of Soviet leaders, officials, and citizens had been imprisoned, exiled, or executed.

When Stalin took over in Russia in 1924 after the death of Vladimir Lenin, he displaced millions of Ukrainian farmers. When they refused to go into communes, he shipped them to Siberia. There was a famine, and millions died.

This was known as the Great Terror.

The USSR also intensified its efforts to undermine Western democracies.

In the mid-1930s, Russia began a new program of attracting and recruiting spies for so-called Perception Management, or Information Operations. The plan was to attract smart young communist sympathizers from Cambridge and Oxford Universities. The new Russian bureau called *"Cominform"* was opened to attract students to the cause.

The Soviets also spied on the United States. The Soviet intelligence agency, the KGB, sent an army of agents to America.

The Communist Party of the United States grew fastest during the economic catastrophe in the 1930s when many young Americans distrusted capitalism. But success was limited. Most labor unions were resolutely anti-communist, and apart from concentrations of intellectuals and renegade labor leaders in a few urban areas, communism never had much appeal to most Americans.

The Soviets were far more successful in influencing European internal affairs after World War I when communist parties became active in many of the new representative democracies established under the Treaty of Versailles, and again after World War II, when the Nazis were defeated.

Soon after taking control of the USSR in 1924, Stalin portrayed the Western powers, especially France, as warmongers eager to attack the Soviet Union. To aid the triumph of communism, Stalin was intent on weakening the moderate social democratic parties of Europe.

In the early 1930s, Russians even sought to help Adolf Hitler, head of the National Socialist German Workers' Party (NSDAP), later known as the Nazi Party. The *Comintern* ordered the Communist Party of Germany to support the National Socialist German Workers' Party, even though the Nazis were anti-Soviet. The Soviets hoped that the Nazi movement would worsen social tensions, destabilize German democracy, and lead to a communist revolution in Germany. Stalin's election meddling in Germany thus helped bring about Hitler's rise to power in 1933.

Dictators love an aspiring dictator, even if he might later become an enemy. Their common enemy is democracy.

On August 23, 1939, Stalin signed the Molotov-Ribbentrop Pact with Hitler, agreeing not to aid the allies if war broke out. Hitler in turn agreed not to invade the USSR. They also agreed to parcel out Poland, with Hitler giving the Baltic States to the Russians.

Dictators can make peace with other dictators—but only for a while.

A week after signing the pact, Hitler invaded Poland, then invaded France. In 1940, Stalin's troops marched into Russia's "share" of Poland and the Baltic States. Latvia, Lithuania, Estonia, Finland, and parts of Romania would fall to the Russians.

Then the dictators turned on each other.

Hitler broke the pact on June 22, 1941, by invading the Soviet Union. Stalin wasn't prepared, and in three weeks, 750,000 Russians died. By the end of 1941, 4.3 million Russians had died and another three million were captured by the Germans.

In 1942, the Germans marched on Stalingrad. Though the Russians lost more than two million men defending it, Stalingrad held. It was a turning point in the war. The US and Russia were allied for the three and a half years that both countries fought Germany.

Winston Churchill warned FDR about Stalin taking advantage of the allies at the Yalta negotiations, but to little avail. Stalin had a plan for post-war Europe, and he executed it masterfully.

During World War II, the Russians sent the Red Army into Poland, Lithuania, Latvia, Hungary, Czechoslovakia, and other countries to liberate them from the Nazis. Meanwhile, the Communist Party operating in these countries before, during, and immediately after the war collaborated with the Kremlin. Soviet tanks thus reinforced the political interference that the Kremlin has often used to subvert Western democracies.

The result was the dropping of the "Iron Curtain"—as Winston Churchill famously called it —all across Eastern Europe.

The Soviets weren't always successful in their takeovers. Communists attempted to take over Greece, resulting in fighting in the 1940s, but the unsuccessful coup ended in what came close to a civil war.

There were attempts in Italy and other countries, but the communist parties were pushed back.

The communists also firmly believed that the United States would become communist, and that it was their duty to do everything in their power to make this happen.

They insisted there could be no rule of law in a country that espoused capitalism. They insisted that legislators, judges, and all legal establishment in non-communist countries were always dominated by the capitalist class and inherently against the proletariat. Overthrowing this regime—*overturning the rule of law*—was their overriding priority.

The Soviets had very little success gaining a political foothold in the United States, despite our massive overreaction in the Red Scare of the 1920s and again in the McCarthy era of the late 1940s and early 1950s, which we will discuss in Chapter 7.

The Soviets, however, were expert spies.

There was, for example, an espionage attempt in the UN Security Council. Henry Cabot Lodge, the US ambassador to the United Nations, blew the whistle on the Russians. At a press conference, he displayed a wooden reproduction of the Great Seal of the United States. Inside, he said, the Russians had placed a listening and transmitting device. The seal had been presented to the US embassy in Moscow by a Russian citizens' group in 1945. A security sweep at the embassy revealed the spying device. Over the years, more than a hundred such devices were found in American embassies throughout the communist bloc.

The listening device at the US embassy wasn't found until 1952. The Russians had seven years to listen in to American secret conversations.

The Russians also established successful spy rings. In Great Britain, the most famous was Kim Philby's "Cambridge 5." In the United States in the late 1940s, Julius Rosenberg helped a spy ring steal secrets that assisted the USSR to develop the atomic bomb. The guilt of his wife Ethel is still disputed. Both were tried and executed.

For decades the United States waged the Cold War against Soviet communist aggression, ultimately with success, but at a heavy price.

Communism in Russia collapsed in 1991. Immediately afterward, President Boris Yeltsin brought in Western-style representative democracy—and

capitalism. Russia quickly learned about corruption. Without strong democratic institutions or a viable political philosophy, and with a centuries-old
history of brutal authoritarian rule, representative democracy in Russia was
unable to survive the problem of corruption.

With rapid denationalization and privatization of major state-owned
industries came the opportunity for Russian organized crime figures and
other oligarchs to reap billions in profits by currying favor with government
officials. The Clinton administration flew experts to Russia to advise on the
privatization process and the functioning of free markets. Plans were made to
draft a detailed code to regulate Russian stock markets. Some of the American experts came from private industry, including Wall Street banks, seeking
to profit from Russian economic expansion. Others came from academia.
Most did not understand the potential for widespread corruption in Russia's
burgeoning capitalist economy. A relatively weak central government in the
Kremlin made the problem worse.

Some American advisors were themselves corrupt, or they at least had
personal financial conflicts of interest. In an infamous federal court case, the
US Agency for International Development (USAID) sued Harvard University for breach of contract. USAID had sent Harvard law and economics professors to Russia to advise on privatization without screening for or preventing
financial conflicts of interest. The professors—or their spouses—traded in
the newly issued shares of Russian companies. Harvard settled the suit with
USAID in 2005 for $26.5 million.

That American "advisors" couldn't keep their hands out of the Russian
cookie jar made it clear that, without a strong central government, Russia was
ripe for the picking. Russian mobsters and their allies in business and government acted in a far worse way, shooting many of their competitors and political opponents dead on the streets. Russia needed to control the chaos—and
give the economy and culture back to the Russians.

They found their man in Vladimir Putin.

In July 1998, Boris Yeltsin appointed Putin as Director of the Federal
Security Service (FSB), the successor of the KGB, where Putin had prior
experience. In 1999, Putin became prime minister of the Government of the
Russian Federation. By December 1999, Yeltsin had resigned. Before long,

Putin was functionally in control of the Russian government. He has been in charge of Russia now for twenty years.

Only after Putin's election in 1999 did Russia finally change its strategy away from subversion on the political left through communist movements. Russia shifted back toward the traditionalist and intensely nationalist ideology of the czars. Official atheism was abandoned, and the Russian Orthodox Church was brought back to power, adding a religious element to Russian nationalism.

From then on, Russian interference with the affairs of other nations, and attacks on the rule of law, would emphasize the role of the political right—ideally steeped in nationalism and ultra-conservative religion. Russia—after carrying the communist banner for seven decades, losing the Cold War, and abandoning the political left—was finally poised to influence the United States.

It didn't take Russia—or Putin—long to figure out how to hit pay dirt.

CHAPTER 6

The Nazi Assault on the Rule of Law

*If you win, you need not have to explain. If you
lose, you should not be there to explain!*
—ADOLF HITLER

WHAT HAPPENED IN GERMANY WAS THE WORST POSSI-
ble outcome for a representative government. How could a democracy allow a madman to take over the country and reign terror on the world? How could his followers—and the world—allow the slaughter of millions of Jews, Gypsies, gays, and others?

A number of important factors contributed to the Nazi rise to power:

- Anger at Germany's dysfunctional and in some ways corrupt republican government established after World War I;
- An ideology of racial superiority to compensate for Germany's defeat in that war;
- Conservative Catholic and Protestant concern about moral decay and desire for a more orderly society under authoritarian rule;
- "Alternative fact" conspiracy theories blaming Jews for Germany's military humiliation and economic misery;

- The public's willingness to dispense with procedural due process and succumb to the politics of accusation; and
- The Nazis' success in directing public anger at the "fake" news media.

Germany in the 1920s and early 1930s thus was simultaneously confronted with most of the problems undermining the rule of law in a democratic society: religious intolerance, violations of due process, myths and alternative facts, attack on the free press, and corruption.

Meanwhile, the British and French were intent on retaliating, punishing, humiliating, and squeezing reparations out of Germany for the First World War. The German economy was in free fall, and fascist gangs began fighting the fear-mongering communists in the streets.

Another important factor was the Russian interference in the Weimar Republic. Soviet-backed Communists colluded with their ideological enemies—the Nazis—to attack the more centrist parties.

By the middle of 1933, the rule of law—or at least the democratic rule of law—had completely collapsed as Hitler and the Nazi Party took over the country.

Hitler for thirty years had been a ne'er-do-well, until 1919, when he found his purpose in the German Workers' Party, a small group of crazed right-wing radicals.

Hitler was *not* a politician. The first political office he held was Reich chancellor in 1933. He had run for the presidency in 1932, but failed. Once in office as chancellor, he often left the capitol, refused to read the documents he didn't want to read, and rarely held cabinet meetings. A man with no friends, Hitler did all the talking when he met with staff. His relationships with important underlings like Goebbels, Goering, and Himmler were cool and remote. If he read, it was military history. Though poorly educated, he felt he always knew better than anyone else. He would spout half knowledge, made-up ideology, and fake news in front of audiences that knew nothing at all.

Before Hitler, the Nazi Party was obscure and on the fringe. Once he joined, Hitler discovered his ability to charm large crowds. His speeches about halting immigration and making Germany great again, as it was before

World War I, vitalized the party. In the beginning, Hitler was seen as a crank and a fool, but once his brown-shirted thugs began doing his bidding, those who mocked him did so at their own peril.

His Nazi Party preached an extreme nationalist agenda, and as early as 1920, the Nazis proclaimed that "members of foreign nations are to be expelled from Germany." Said Joseph Goebbels, later Hitler's minister of propaganda, "Certainly, we want to build a wall, a protective wall."

Hitler excelled at telling and spreading lies. He said Germany would have won the First World War if only more Jews had been gassed. (Poison gas had been used by both sides, but Hitler later found other even more pernicious uses for it.) In speeches, he called Nazis victims of communist violence, without mentioning that the Nazis were violent themselves.

Most importantly, Hitler excelled in using mass media. On the radio he was spellbinding. Large posters with his slogans were seen in cities and towns everywhere. He became a featured performer in cinemas.

Hitler was not a conservative—his intention was to destroy democracy and the rule of law—but the representatives in the legislature, even those not in the NSDAP, were sure they could control him and use him to forward their agenda.

Hitler spoke out forcefully against the rise of communism in Russia.

But Hitler took a page out of Stalin's playbook, sharing his contempt for democracy, freedom of thought, and a free press.

The Nazis used music and language to emphasize their cultural identity. Religion was important, but it was subverted to national identity. The Nazis didn't care whether you were Protestant or Catholic, only that you were *German* Protestant or *German* Catholic.

As the Communists and the Nazis fought for the soul of the German people, Nazi supporters established a rule of law built on nationalism.

Then there were hateful lies about Jews. Anti-Semitism had anti-globalist overtones including the conspiracy theory that the Jews were always trying to establish an international regime—a world government led by Jewish bankers. Another myth that emerged during this time is that German-Jews were disloyal during World War I, resulting in Germany's defeat. Jews who didn't support Hitler and the Nazis were also called disloyal. European, German, and Nazi anti-Semitism was built upon a foundation of fake news.

The Nazis also hated the Jews because some of the leaders of Marxist-Leninism were Jewish, even though the vast majority of German Jews were not communists. Only the most perverted minds could combine a Jewish bankers' plot with a Jewish international communist conspiracy, but so be it.

The Nazis also had their own—unique—views about the rule of law.

Whereas the communists in the USSR viewed the rule of law solely through the lens of class struggle, the Nazis viewed the rule of law solely through the lens of nationalism. As a result, *the rule of law became relative to the national identity defining it.* Any universal endeavor to understand right and wrong, good and bad, whether based on legal tradition, religion, or secular philosophy, was subordinate to the national cultural context. Great religious leaders such as Martin Luther, great late-nineteenth-century phi-losophers, great writers, and great composers from Bach to Beethoven were great *because* they were German. Thus, the law had to be uniquely German as well.

Principles of law that were generally recognized in international treaties, and principles of right and wrong at the center of religious teachings and secular philosophy for centuries, were shunned by Nazi legal scholars who emphasized instead the importance of an inherently *German* legal system to suit Germany's unique needs, given its place in the world. If Germany was going to be strong, not pushed around by Great Britain, France, and the United States, the rule of law must be undertaken in a *German* way.

Perhaps fair-minded judges in other countries applied legal principles to the facts of individual cases, but Hitler and his sympathizers believed that did not work in Germany. Judges needed to be sympathetic above all else to the nation and to the Nazi Party. Carl Schmitt and other pro-Nazi legal scholars did not trust other legal systems. Not right for Germany. Hitler's most ardent supporters believed that independent judges, particularly Jewish judges, should be removed.

With relative truth, both legal principles and facts lose their importance. Hitler and his propaganda minster Joseph Goebbels made up scary stories to use against their enemies. They created alternative facts. The charge that Jews caused Germany to lose the war was repeated over and over until the large non-Jewish segment of the German populace believed it. If you repeat a lie enough times, it becomes true.

Alternative legal principles + alternative facts = alternative law.

During Hitler's presidential campaign in 1932, he also ramped up his attack on the free press.

Hitler in 1932 was campaigning against Paul von Hindenburg, who was a commander during the second half of World War I before being elected president of Germany. Hitler would fly around in his airplane and make dramatic landings, out of the clouds. He'd give a speech at an airfield and then fly to the next town. He was stirring things up, spreading propaganda, stressing German unity and Aryan supremacy, and attacking the press.

Hitler called the free press of the Weimar Republic "*die lügenpresse*, the lying press," a term coined in 1914 during World War I by Reinhold Anton, who used it to refer to enemy propaganda. In 1918, when news stories appeared about Germany losing the war, the German Defense Ministry released a book titled *The Lügenpresse of Our Enemies*. A decade later, in his presidential campaign, Hitler turned *lügenpresse* into a powerful propaganda slogan to stir hatred against newspapers. Hitler called his critics members of the "*lügenpresse* apparatus."

Hitler lost the 1932 presidential election by a considerable margin, receiving roughly one-third of the popular vote. The results were Paul von Hindenburg (Independent), 53 percent; Adolf Hitler (NSDAP), 36 percent; and Ernst Thälmann (Communist), 10.2 percent.

After this loss, Hitler turned to gaining more seats in parliament for the NSDAP during a series of parliamentary elections. In the election of July 1932, the results for the four largest parties were: NSDAP, 37.27 percent; Social Democrats, 21.58 percent; Communists, 14.32 percent; Centre Party, 12.44 percent. In another election, in November 1932, support for Nazis actually slipped by four percentage points: NSDAP, 33.09 percent; Social Democrats, 20.43 percent; Communists, 16.86 percent; Centre Party, 11.93 percent.

At this point, Hitler consolidated his power and pressured President Hindenburg to appoint him chancellor in January 1933. Hindenburg's government was based on popular support in parliament, so Hindenburg agreed. In March 1933, Germany had yet another "election," and with Hitler now chancellor, the results were even better for the Nazis: NSDAP, 43.91 percent; Social Democrats, 18.25 percent; Communists, 12.32 percent; Centre Party, 11.25 percent.

That was the last election. On February 27, 1933, six days before that election, there had been a fire of unknown origin in the parliament building, the Reichstag. Hitler embraced the fake news story that the fire was part of a plot by the Communist Party, and the next day he persuaded President Hindenburg to sign the Reichstag Fire Decree under emergency powers presumably authorized by Article 48 of the German Constitution. The decree suspended civil liberties including freedom of the press and freedom of assembly. Hitler began mass arrests of communists and other political opponents. Then on March 23, 1933, the Reichstag, with Communist deputies and some Social Democrats in prison rather than voting, passed the Enabling Act, which gave Chancellor Hitler and his cabinet power to enact laws without approval from the Reichstag. Germany was transformed from a constitutional republic to a dictatorship in less than three months.

Hitler vowed to make Germany great again by promising to bring back traditional German moral and cultural values; deal with the lying press; put his political opponents in jail; solve the "problem" created by a religious minority, the Jews; and deal with the foreign powers who had been Germany's enemies abroad. Was Hitler all talk, or would he actually do some of the things that he had wanted to do for years?

HITLER MADE GERMANY GREAT AGAIN—AT LEAST ON THE BIG SCREEN.

Hitler was able to spread his lies largely because he was charismatic. He spoke his mind, and even when he was offensive and belligerent, his audience was captivated. With motion pictures directed by Leni Riefenstahl (known best for *Triumph of the Will* in 1935), the Nazi propaganda machine effectively combined a new form of entertainment (motion pictures) with politics. Purveyors of this Nazi propaganda always insisted it was fair and accurate, but hidden behind the dramatic rhetoric and visual effects was a bevy of alternative facts and falsehoods about what made Germany great (Hitler and the NSDAP), who made Germany weak (Jews, among others), and who were Germany's enemies (the world's democracies).

HITLER BROUGHT BACK "TRADITIONAL" GERMAN CULTURAL AND MORAL VALUES.

"Degenerate" (modern) art was displayed in a government-sponsored exhibition in 1937. Some of the valuable works by better-known artists (Van Gogh, Cézanne, Dalí, Ernst, Klee, Léger, and Miró) were then sold or secretly taken by Nazi officials for personal collections, while less valuable works, and some valuable ones, were destroyed.

Degenerate books were burned. The most famous book burning was at Bebelplatz in Berlin on the evening of May 10, 1933, but there were many more.

Traditional, not modern, German music was glorified. Richard Strauss (the first president of the *Reichsmusikkammer*) was in vogue; Felix Mendelssohn and Gustav Mahler (and other German Jewish composers) were considered "degenerate."

Gay men and lesbians were put in concentration camps where they were forced to wear the pink triangle (men) and black triangle (women).

Left-wing professors were removed from their posts.

Hitler tore apart any semblance of separation of church and state. Conservative theology was celebrated. A nationalist "religious right" emerged within the German Evangelical (Lutheran) Church in the 1920s calling itself the *Deutsche Christen*, "German Christians," and then in the 1930s worked to unify a Protestant "Reich Church," using biblical teaching to support the Nazi regime. Some Catholic bishops also embraced Nazism, in spite of their loyalty to Pope Pius XII, who struggled to address the obvious moral concerns from this dual allegiance.

Opponents of the Nazification of the Protestant and Catholic churches were removed from their posts and imprisoned. Dietrich Bonhoeffer had founded the Confessing Church, an alternative to the government initiative to unify all Protestant churches into a single pro-Nazi Protestant Reich Church. Bonhoeffer was arrested in April 1943 and executed in April 1945.

Minority Christian sects, such as Jehovah's Witnesses, were persecuted and put in concentration camps (Jehovah's Witnesses wore the purple triangle). That persecution continued until Hitler's forces were defeated by the Soviets and Allied forces led by General Dwight D. Eisenhower, who, coincidentally, grew up in a Jehovah's Witness household in Abilene, Kansas.

HITLER WENT AFTER THE PRESS.

When Hitler was appointed chancellor in 1933, 4 percent of the newspapers were controlled by the Nazis. Within six months, that number grew to 96 percent. The "fake news" media was put out of business and the news was whatever Hitler said it was.

HITLER ENDED THE INDEPENDENCE OF JUDGES.

No longer would German law be concerned with individual rights. Now the focus was on the collective identity of Germans. That meant replacing "degenerate" judges with ones who supported traditional German values.

To that end, months after taking office, Hitler disqualified all Jews from being judges. He argued that Jewish judges would be biased in cases involving non-Jewish Germans.

"We can't have biased Jewish judges," Hitler said.

In April 1933, existing Jewish judges were removed from office.

The judges who succeeded them were members of the Nazi Party.

HITLER PUT HIS POLITICAL OPPONENTS IN JAIL.

Soon after Hitler took over as chancellor on January 30, 1933, the Communist Party was dismantled and its real estate holdings were confiscated. Ernst Thälmann, the Communist candidate who had run against Hitler and Hindenburg in 1932, was arrested and held in solitary confinement for eleven years before being shot in 1944.

In early 1933, Hitler began arresting people. Storm troopers raided homes, rounded up citizens, especially communists and Jews, and took them to barracks where they were beaten, tortured, and often killed.

All political opposition was destroyed, and Hitler was free to do as he wished.

HITLER SOLVED THE "PROBLEM" OF GERMANY HAVING A "DANGEROUS" RELIGIOUS MINORITY: THE JEWS.

By April 1933, the Jews had become targets. The editor of Der Stürmer, Julius Streicher, called for a boycott of Jewish businesses. Nazis picketed Jewish stores and told others not to buy from Jews.

On April 7, all civil service workers who weren't Aryan were fired. In Frankfurt, Jewish teachers were banned from universities. Jews were excluded from being lawyers, artists, and farmers.

Later in 1933, ten concentration camps were built in Germany. Dachau, the first, was built to hold political prisoners, especially Jews and gays.

In 1934, the German government hired Adolf Eichmann to be its expert on Jews. He spied on Jewish organizations in Germany.

Hitler then stepped up the fake news. *Der Stürmer* printed the oft-told story that Jews used Christian blood to bake matzoh. It "documented" two years of ritual murders.

When President Hindenburg died on August 2, 1934, Hitler became the head of state. A year later the Nuremberg Laws codified Hitler's blatant anti-Semitism. Only Aryans could be German citizens. Non-Jews could not marry Jews. Jewish-owned property could be confiscated. Jews were banned from serving in the military.

In 1936 the Gestapo was placed above the law. The SS Death's Head division was assigned to guard the concentration camps. In 1937 Jews were banned from many more professional occupations.

In 1938 Germany annexed Austria. Hitler put Eichmann in charge of the Austrian Jews. The Germans built a concentration camp near Linz, Austria. In July, Jewish doctors were prohibited from practicing medicine.

On November 7, 1938, a seventeen-year-old Jewish boy deported to Poland shot and killed Ernst vom Rath, a German official. Rath died on November 9, precipitating Kristallnacht, the breaking of the windows of Jewish-owned stores. The next month Hitler decreed that all business must be Aryan owned. On December 14, 1938, Hermann Goering was put in charge of "the Jewish question."

HITLER WENT TO WAR.

In September 1939, Hitler did what many dictators do to further consolidate their power—he started a war.

Hitler invaded Poland, then the rest of Europe, northern Africa, and finally the Soviet Union. Tens of millions of people died.

By 1941, the organization to murder all the Jews in Germany was in place. In *Der Stürmer*, it was written, "Now judgment has begun and it will reach its conclusion only when knowledge of the Jews has been erased from the earth."

The Wannsee Conference on January 20, 1942, led to the "final solution." Mass killings at Auschwitz began. More camps were built, and the killings went unabated for more than a thousand days until, in April 1945, Auschwitz was liberated. Meanwhile, millions died at other death camps such as Bergen-Belsen, Theresienstadt, and Buchenwald.

By 1945, at least six million Jewish men, women, and children had been murdered.

The lesson that we all must learn is that the breakdown of the rule of law isn't immediate. It's progressive.

We need to listen to candidates for public office. Hitler's rhetoric should have warned the Germans that he was unfit to be chancellor and never should have been appointed to that position.

Another lesson is that it can happen in a representative democracy. Although many dictators rise to power in a revolution or a military coup, the Weimar Republic was a representative democracy—an imperfect one for sure, but a representative democracy. Whereas ancient Rome took decades to transform from a republic into the dictatorship personified by Nero and other ruthless dictators, Nazi Germany in 1933 made that transformation in three months.

And the voters went along with it. Hitler was appointed chancellor after the NSDAP won support from only about a third of German voters in 1933, but other voters and politicians accepted his appointment. Many who did not support him preferred him over a socialist or communist. Hitler took advantage of these divisions to unify the country behind him.

German industry leaders tolerated and sometimes supported Hitler because he helped them make money. Ordinary people also believed he was making them better off because the economy was growing.

Hitler had impressed voters with a wonderful infrastructure plan. He promised a lot of jobs building plans. Two of those projects were the autobahn and train stations. But this infrastructure wasn't really about civilian travel. Rather the roadways were built to transport tanks and soldiers. It wasn't to give German citizens better lives. It was to win a war.

Hitler was also a very good con man, easily able to help his allies in industry separate ordinary Germans from their money.

A new company established by the Porsche family promised every Aryan German citizen an inexpensive car—a German version of Henry Ford's famous Model T in America. In 1938, at a Nazi rally, the Fuhrer declared: "It is for the broad masses that this car has been built. Its purpose is to answer their transportation needs, and it is intended to give them joy." The people heard Hitler's promise and, in a propaganda film, watched a German family having a picnic by the side of the autobahn in their car—the People's Car, or "Volkswagen."

The sales pitch was "*Fünf Mark die Woche musst Du sparen - willst Du im eignen Wagen fahren*" ("five marks per week you must save, if you want to drive your own car"). Middle- and working-class families all over Germany sent in their five marks every week. They waited for their cars.

Hitler arranged with the Porsche family to build this car for the people of Germany.

Volkswagen delivered a specimen to Hitler, then took the people's money to build military vehicles. Few people got a car. Few dared complain.

Lawyers and judges also were Hitler's partners in crime.

After World War II, US authorities held twelve trials in Nuremberg, Germany, that were later known as the Nuremberg trials.

The third trial indicted sixteen German judges and lawyers. Nine were officials of the Reich Ministry of Justice. The others were prosecutors and judges of the People's Court of Nazi Germany.

These judges implemented the German "racial purity" laws. They were accused of crimes against humanity, abuse of the legal system resulting in mass murder, torture, theft of property, slave labor, and membership in a criminal organization—the SS or the Nazi Party.

Twelve were found guilty.

But what about the German people? Why did they go along with this?

The German people who kept Hitler in power believed they were no longer being humiliated by the French and English. He was making Germany great again. Hitler also kept the German people from feeling threatened by the Soviets who were undermining the rule of law in other countries. To protect themselves from Russians interfering with elections, spreading fake news, and using violence, the German people turned to the NSDAP, which did the very same things—only worse.

They felt that Hitler was helping the economy, which actually outperformed many other industrialized countries in the 1930s. The improved economy attracted a lot of support, particularly in the business community.

Why the German people accepted a man like Hitler as a leader, and why even some Jews, who were used to persecution throughout history, did not view the situation as being uniquely dangerous, is one of the mysteries of history.

But Germany is not necessarily unique.

CHAPTER 7

McCarthyism

I will not get into a pissing contest with that skunk [Joseph McCarthy].
—DWIGHT D. EISENHOWER

T HE COMMUNIST PARTY (CPUSA) BEGAN TO GAIN
strength in America at the time of the Red Scare in the 1920s. The party
founded a newspaper, the *Daily Worker*, in 1924. In the early 1930s, some
Americans devastated by the collapse of the stock market and the ensuing
Great Depression felt that capitalism had failed them, and they saw hope in
communism.

The Russians were of course happy to take advantage of the situation.

William Zebulon Foster, a militant, communist union organizer, and
member of the Industrial Workers of the World, ran for president in 1932.
Foster came to prominence as a leader of the bloody 1919 steel strike—an
attempt to organize steel workers in the US. In 1921 the Russians supported
his Foster Trade Union Education League to make inroads in the United
States. Three times Foster ran for president, calling for the end of capitalism
and the rise of a workers' republic. In 1932 he won 102,991 votes. Afterward,
he suffered a serious heart attack and leadership passed to Earl Browder, who
in 1940 ran for president.

By the 1930s there were 65,000 members of the Communist Party in America. The hotbed for support was New York City, as members fought for fair housing for African Americans and the poor. Nightclubs in Greenwich Village owned by communists and communist sympathizers were some of the few places in the country where African American performers like Billie Holiday, Buster Brown and the Speed Kings, Beige & Brown, and Bill "Bojangles" Robinson could perform in front of white audiences.

CPUSA was founded in Chicago, but in 1927 its headquarters was moved to 35 East 12th Street in New York City, two blocks from Union Square. In the 1920s American communists were predominantly immigrants, some of them Eastern European Jews.

But unlike in Weimar Germany, where communists were often more than 10 percent of the vote, the CPUSA was a nothing party. The Socialist Party, which became strong in the 1930s, ran Norman Thomas for president in 1932 and garnered 884,781 votes, almost nine times the 102,991 votes that the Communist William Foster received. Almost all of the nearly 40 million votes in that election were split between the Republican, President Herbert Hoover (39.7 percent), and Democratic challenger Governor Franklin D. Roosevelt of New York (57.4 percent). The Socialists stood at about 2 percent and the Communists at about 0.25 percent.

Hardly a threat to American democracy.

As Stalin took over Russia and murdered millions, American communists put on blinders and pretended it wasn't happening. These misguided idealists rooted for Russia to show the world that socialism and communism were workable systems.

When the Nazis seized power in Germany in 1933, American communists stressed the importance of uniting to defeat the Nazis.

By the late 1930s, a left-wing movement had grown up around the Communist Party. Most people who identified as communists didn't belong to CPUSA. They were "small-c" communists, sympathizing with the party's goals, but not submitting to its discipline. Dozens of organizations rose up to fight for racial equality, unions, and freedom for Spain in the (Spanish) Republicans' civil war against fascist dictator Francisco Franco. Most of these were not actually part of the Communist Party.

By 1938 half the 75,000 members of the American Communist Party lived in New York City.

Communist candidate Pete Cacchione was elected to the city council in 1941, as was Benjamin Davis, an African American from Harlem, in 1943.

In Harlem the Communist Party's commitment to fighting racism helped attract the support of African Americans. Meanwhile, some members of the Teachers Union, the American Newspaper Guild, the Transport Workers Union, and the National Maritime Union expressed their support for the Communist Party. Hundreds of students and professors at Columbia, New York University, Brooklyn College, and the City College of New York signed up for Communist fronts such as the American Youth Congress, but it's unclear how many actually joined.

Most American communists were "fellow travelers." They weren't communists—because they disliked like the party discipline—but they sympathized with at least some of its ideals. During the May Day Parade, marchers with the *Daily Worker* wore baseball uniforms and carried signs that read: END JIM CROW IN BASEBALL.

Even though communists were very few in number, heavily concentrated in New York City and a few other urban areas, and even though they supported civil rights when FDR's Democrats, beholden to Southern politicians, did relatively little, they were perceived as a threat. Although they earned far less than one percent of the vote in presidential elections, they were perceived as dangerous for democracy.

They needed to be investigated.

In 1940 the New York State legislature appointed a committee to investigate teachers and professors in New York City. The committee, headed by two staunch conservatives, Republican state assemblyman Herbert Rapp and Republican state senator Frederic Coudert, sought to curb the influence of the Jewish teachers and professionals. Some of the outrage was also over CCNY's hiring of a black professor, Dr. Max Yergan, who was a member of the Communist Party.

The final straw came when CCNY announced it intended to hire peace activist and leader of the antiwar movement Bertrand Russell.

Within a year, eight hundred public school teachers and college faculty members were targeted. The key informant at City College, William Canning, named more than fifty of his colleagues and got them fired.

Though the teachers were fired solely because they had once been members of the Communist Party, the courts upheld these decisions until 1957, when the Supreme Court finally ruled that such flimsy grounds of dismissal were unconstitutional.

Most of the victims of the Rapp-Coudert investigation never taught again in New York City or anywhere else. Morris Schappes, who acknowledged membership in the Communist Party, was pressed to name other communists he knew, but he only named those he knew who had been killed in the Spanish Civil War. He was charged with perjury and sentenced to fourteen months in "the Tombs" in New York City. The Rapp-Coudert Committee had worked outside the normal prosecutorial and judicial framework—outside of the rule of law—to have an American put in jail.

Perhaps the communists Schappes knew had received support from the Soviet Union. Perhaps. But there were at least three or four degrees of separation between Schappes and the Kremlin's meddling in American elections through the CPUSA, an endeavor that year after year garnered far less than 1 percent of the vote. And this was when the USSR was ostensibly our *ally* in World War II.

Imagine what would have happened back then if people working close to the US president had direct contacts with Russian agents seeking to influence American elections and then lied about it to the FBI. Imagine what would have happened if a presidential candidate urged the Russians to obtain, read, and publicly release the private correspondence of an opposing candidate.

But we're getting ahead of ourselves.

On far more flimsy grounds, leading Democrats were uncomfortable with Vice President Henry Wallace during World War II. Rumors spread that Wallace was more sympathetic to our Soviet allies than the administration officials and congressmen who saw Stalin as a brutal and untrustworthy dictator. That—and various unsubstantiated rumors about Wallace's personal associations with people who might be communists—got him thrown off the Democratic ticket in 1944 and replaced with Harry Truman.

By the end of World War II, the Communist Party had very little influence left. Russia, no longer an ally, almost overnight had become an enemy.

In 1940, Julius Rosenberg had joined the Army Signal Corps Engineering Laboratories at Fort Monmouth, New Jersey, where he worked as an engineer-inspector until 1945. He was fired when the US Army discovered his previous membership in the Communist Party.

Six years later, on March 29, 1951, Rosenberg and his wife, Ethel, were convicted of espionage. They were accused of sharing secrets about the atomic bomb with Russians. They were sentenced to death on April 5 under Section 2 of the Espionage Act of 1917, which prohibits transmitting or attempting to transmit to a foreign government information "relating to the national defense."

Prosecutor Roy Cohn, a shadowy, controversial figure who assisted Joseph McCarthy with his hearings as his chief counsel, later bragged that his influence led to the appointment of US attorney Irving Saypol, who prosecuted the case, and of the judge who ordered the Rosenberg death sentence. Cohn patted himself on the back when he bragged that the judge, Irving Kaufman, had imposed the death penalty on Cohn's personal recommendation.

When the reprisals came, it was open season on anyone who had ever been a member of the Communist Party or one of its many organizations.

The law that gave rise to the anti-communist persecutions in the 1940s and 1950s was written by an anti-labor, segregationist congressman named Howard W. Smith, a Democrat from Virginia. Formally titled the Alien Registration Act, but more widely called the Smith Act, the law made it a federal offense for anyone to "knowingly or willfully advocate, abet, advise or teach the duty, necessity, desirability or propriety of overthrowing the government of the United States or any State by force or violence, or for anyone to organize any association which teaches, advises or encourages such an overthrow, or for anyone to become a member of or to affiliate with any such association."

It was the first statute since the Alien and Sedition Act of 1789 to make a crime out of advocating an idea.

The bill was signed into law by Franklin Roosevelt in 1940.

The first prosecution under the act was against Communist leaders in Minnesota who encouraged the teamsters to strike for better wages. The party was simultaneously campaigning to stay out of the war.

The prosecution used the *Communist Manifesto* and writings by Lenin and Trotsky as evidence. They also called two witnesses who said that some of the defendants had told antiwar soldiers to complain about the food and living conditions.

On December 8, 1941, one day after the bombing of Pearl Harbor frightened the country, the jury handed down its sentences. Twelve defendants got sixteen-month terms, and eleven others received a year in jail.

The framework for the House Un-American Activities Committee, with its platform for hunting out Communists in the 1950s, was established in 1938 with the Dies Committee. The sole function of this body was to "expose" threats to America's way of life. It was supported by liberals such as Congressman Samuel Dickstein, who had become alarmed at the growth of the German Bund and of anti-Semitism. Its focus, however, was anti-communism.

Representative Martin Dies Jr. of Texas originally supported the New Deal, but by the late 1930s he opposed Franklin Roosevelt's New Deal programs, as he had become obsessed with what he saw as the subversive threat from the left. He introduced a resolution calling for a special committee to investigate "un-American propaganda" instigated by foreign countries. His intention was to investigate Communists, Socialists, Trotskyites, and those who held similar beliefs. On May 26, 1938, the House established the committee, and Dies became its chairman. His chief investigator was J. B. Matthews, publisher of Father Charles Coughlin's anti-Semitic book, *Social Justice*.

Dies wanted to go after his political enemies. But there was one roadblock in the way—President Franklin Roosevelt.

As long as Roosevelt was alive, Dies and the committee would be frustrated and blunted. But even Roosevelt couldn't stop them from wreaking some havoc.

The American Federation of Labor (AFL) was battling the Congress of Industrial Organizations (CIO) for control of labor unions. Dies's first witness was John Frey, the president of the Metal Trades Department of the AFL. Frey testified—without any evidence—that the CIO was filled with Communists. He identified as Communists 283 CIO organizers. Dies accepted his testimony, and headlines and firings followed.

The next witness, Walter Steele, a self-appointed "patriot," testified that there were communists in the Boy Scouts and Camp Fire Girls. Reporters rushed to print the allegations but, again, nobody was accused of having *done* anything. *Belonging* to the Communist Party at any point in one's life—or merely having expressed interest in the Party—was enough to find one in the wrong.

The politics of Dies's actions were highlighted when he went after the Federal Theater Project, of the Works Project Association, which employed several thousand writers and actors.

When the director, Hallie Flanagan, was asked about an article she had written about the English playwright Christopher Marlowe (who died in 1593), Congressman Joe Starnes ignorantly questioned, "Is he a Communist?" All across America there were howls of protest—and laughter. Nevertheless, the investigation killed the theater project.

Dies's House Un-American Activities Committee (HUAC) was scheduled to expire in 1938, but he petitioned to keep it going, all the while accusing President Roosevelt of refusing to pursue subversives.

In 1939 Dies went after an organization called the American League for Peace and Democracy (ALPD). It had twenty thousand members, and it presented Dies with yet another opportunity to try to embarrass President Roosevelt.

When the offices of the ALPD were raided, on the list of members were Harold Ickes, the secretary of the interior, and Solicitor General Robert Jackson, who later became a justice of the Supreme Court. The release of 560 names on the list created a firestorm.

President Roosevelt condemned HUAC's action as a "sordid procedure."

Dies pushed to prosecute the organization, but Attorney General Francis Biddle said the ALPD hadn't broken any laws. Nevertheless, the accusation was enough to cause the organization to dissolve.

In 1940 Dies began to investigate the Communist Party itself. Under the law, Dies had to ask the full House for contempt citations. He ignored the law, and he got warrants without approval. Dies brought the hearings to a close without further action.

Then in 1940 Congress passed the Smith Act. The bill passed the House by 382 to 4.

Dies, maniacally pursuing his political agenda, went after Vice President Henry Wallace, accusing him of being too close to the KGB. Then in 1941 he ordered the Justice Department to investigate more than a thousand federal employees accused of "subversive" activities. In all 1,121 were investigated, but Attorney General Biddle fired exactly two. Dies, furious, accused Biddle of dereliction of duty.

Dies released yet another long list of federal employees to be investigated. One employee, William Pickens, who was black, was singled out, and the House moved to cut his salary. An uproar ensued. The resolution to reduce his salary was killed.

When Roosevelt ran for a fourth term in 1944, Dies went after him again. He attacked Sidney Hillman, chairman of the CIO Political Action Committee and close advisor to FDR. The CIO PAC had been campaigning to defeat all the members sitting on HUAC. Dies said that this *proved* they were pro-Communist.

In 1945 Dies, in poor health, announced he would not seek reelection. But HUAC continued on.

The man who saved HUAC was Democratic congressman John E. Rankin, a segregationist from Mississippi. Using his knowledge of procedure, Rankin made HUAC a permanent committee and gave it broad investigative powers.

When FDR died on April 12, 1945, HUAC could operate without its most powerful foe. Harry Truman became president.

In 1945 Rankin went after subversives in Hollywood. None was found guilty of *doing* anything. They were convicted of either contempt or perjury for citing their right to remain silent and refusing to answer the committee's questions. Then in November 1946 Republicans took over control of the House and Senate. One of the new members of HUAC was Republican congressman Richard Nixon of California.

One of President Harry Truman's first requests was to ask Attorney General Tom Clark to identify subversive organizations. The list included all groups for workers' rights and especially civil rights. Said Jack O'Dell, a civil rights activist, "Every organization in Negro life which was attacking segregation per se was put on the subversive list."

In 1947 Truman warned the nation of the Cold War with Russia, saying it was up to the United States to support "free peoples of the world in maintaining their freedom." His approach would be called the Truman Doctrine. The Communist threat now would be seen in global, apocalyptic terms.

On March 21, 1947, nine days after his Truman Doctrine speech, he signed an executive order creating a loyalty program for federal employees.

J. Edgar Hoover's FBI enforced the loyalty program, which meant he had carte blanche to repeat, if not improve on, his performance during the Palmer raids of 1919. He would determine who was loyal and who was not.

Hoover became a lawyer in 1917 by going to night school while working as a messenger at the Library of Congress. He may have been a file clerk at heart, but he had the power to conduct an inquisition. His domain was secret. He used hearsay, rumor, snitching, backbiting, and innuendo. Hoover, moreover, was not above blackmail, even against the nine presidents he served.

Hoover was a Red hunter the way that the Puritans of Salem were witch hunters.

Hoover, a closeted gay man, began attacking Americans' sexuality in the 1920s. He went after those who violated the Mann Act by crossing state lines to have sex. He said it was essential to attack "the problem of vice in modern civilization," and he was not going to rest until America's cities were "completely cleaned up." He also gathered lists of gay people that could easily be used for blackmail.

Hoover talked about communists in sexual terms, calling them "lecherous enemies of American society." He often referred to the left wing as "intellectual debauchery," and warned his agents of the "depraved nature and moral looseness" of student radicals.

Later, the Reverend Martin Luther King Jr. was his special target. Hoover called him a "tom cat with obsessive degenerate sexual urges."

Hoover needed a front man in Congress to help him conduct the witch hunt that he so desperately desired. That man appeared to Hoover quite by accident on February 9, 1950, in Wheeling, West Virginia, at a meeting before the Ohio Country Women's Republican Club. The man was Joseph McCarthy, a senator from Wisconsin who had defeated the incumbent senator, Progressive-turned-Republican Bob La Follette, in the 1946 Republican primary.

During dinner McCarthy discussed his flagging political fortunes with cronies. When he got up to speak, he told the assemblage, "While I cannot take the time to name all of the men in the State Department who have been named as members of the Communist Party and members of a spy ring, I have here in my hand a list of 205 names . . ." McCarthy said that though the secretary of state had their names and knew they were communists, he allowed them to work anyway. In a similar speech in Salt Lake City the next day, McCarthy, perhaps after looking at a bottle of Heinz ketchup, told that assemblage that he had a list of "fifty-seven Communists in the State Department."

It was exactly the fake news that J. Edgar Hoover wanted to hear.

Once the media spread McCarthy's falsehoods, it wasn't long before he convened a Senate committee to launch his infamous witch hunt.

Some tried to stop McCarthy in June 1950. Senator Millard Tydings (D-MD) issued a report on McCarthy's allegations, calling the senator a "fraud and a hoax on the Senate." McCarthy, before seeing the report, undermined the findings by saying any such report would be a "disgrace to the Senate, a green light for the Reds."

When McCarthy pushed on, he was backed by Republicans wanting to give President Harry Truman and the Democrats a black eye. In the next Senate election, Millard Tydings was defeated. The winner, John Butler, had received a potful of money from McCarthy's backers. In the campaign, Butler's henchmen doctored a photo of Tydings standing with Earl Browder, the former head of the Communist Party.

With Tydings out of the way, McCarthy repeatedly demanded Truman be impeached and Secretary of State Dean Acheson be fired. For the next four years McCarthy poisoned America's air. Truman couldn't stop him. The next president, Dwight Eisenhower, decided to remain quiet for political reasons, a mistake he later regretted.

McCarthy undermined the rule of law by bringing people against their will in front of the Permanent Subcommittee on Investigations, which, along with the Senate Internal Security Subcommittee, was a counterpart to the HUAC in the House, to testify about whether they had ever been a member of the Communist Party and to name friends known to be communists.

The committee became McCarthy's real source of power. Those who lied could be tried criminally for lying to Congress. Those who took the Fifth Amendment—refusing to incriminate themselves—ruined their careers.

McCarthyism's rampage was fueled by fear, and the greatest fear came when the Soviet Union tested its first atomic bomb in 1949. That same year,

Mao Zedong took over in China and declared it communist. Americans built bomb shelters to house their families in case the worst occurred. And here was a US senator saying members of the State Department were harboring communists.

Once the inquisition began, the question was not whether you were a communist but, rather, whether you were *not* an *anti*-communist. If you dared criticize McCarthy, you became one of *them*. Throwing away the Constitution, the investigators snooped, accused, and informed as they looked for communists in civil service, unions, industry, universities, local school boards, and churches. We truly *were* back to the bad old days of the Salem witches.

McCarthy scared people, calling anyone who disagreed with him either Communist, pro-Communist, a tool of the Communists, or a "Fifth Amendment Communist." It was hunting season; anyone McCarthy and his minions accused of being a Communist was a dead man. The truth had nothing to do with it.

McCarthy went after intellectuals like former students at City University of New York who had joined the Communist or Socialist Parties in the 1930s. Many were high school and college teachers, and some ended up in Hollywood as directors and writers.

McCarthy's witch hunt had strong anti-Semitic undertones. As in 1940, when the Rapp-Coudert Committee targeted Jewish teachers, ten years later McCarthy in the Senate and his allies in the House on the HUAC came back for a second shot. Never bother with academic freedom or the fact that personal politics has nothing to do with the ability to teach: the way Joe McCarthy and the HUAC witch hunters defined it, anyone who was ever a member of the Communist Party or who refused to testify surrendered the right to teach.

Most of those who were fired had exercised their Fifth Amendment right.

Firings were usually permanent. The victim's name remained on a blacklist that everyone denied existed, and getting another job in the field was impossible.

The McCarthy era only came to an end after he picked a fight with the US Army. McCarthy's lawyer, Roy Cohn, became infatuated with his close friend David Schine, a wealthy heir to a hotel fortune who was brought onto McCarthy's staff and later drafted into the army. After failing to get Schine transferred to a base closer to home and to get him a commission, Cohn did everything he could to make sure Schine lived like a king at Fort Monmouth,

New Jersey, where Schine was stationed. Cohn enlisted McCarthy's help in getting these favors for Schine.

When the army would not do this personal favor for Cohn and McCarthy, the senator and his lawyer used the power of Congress to subpoena and demand testimony, crashing down like a hammer on high-ranking army officials who dared challenge them.

McCarthy decided to investigate whether there were subversives at Fort Monmouth.

The whole thing smacked of blackmail. During the hearings McCarthy attacked Fort Monmouth's commanding officer, General Ralph Zwicker—who had led a key regiment at the Battle of the Bulge—for granting a dentist an honorable discharge even though he had refused to answer questions about being a member of a "subversive organization." McCarthy tried to humiliate Zwicker, a close friend of President Eisenhower, by accusing the general of protecting a Russian spy. The charge, entirely false, was absurd.

Roy Cohn was the legal arm supporting McCarthy. Cohn tried to fit all his boss's actions within the framework of a rule of law (including endless investigations, subpoenas, and witness intimidation) while in fact he and McCarthy were undermining the rule of law.

On the March 3, 1954, episode of his show *See It Now*, moderator Edward R. Murrow aired clips of McCarthy terrorizing witnesses and patronizing the president. Murrow intoned, "The actions of the junior senator from Wisconsin have caused alarm and dismay amongst our allies abroad and given considerable comfort to our enemies. And whose fault is that? Not really his. He didn't create the situation of fear. He merely exploited it, and rather successfully. Cassius was right. The fault, dear Brutus, is not in our stars but in ourselves. Good night—and good luck."

Then the White House released a memo revealing McCarthy's and Cohn's requests for favors for David Schine, listing forty-four counts of improper behavior.

The next day, in one of the most dramatic exchanges of the hearings, McCarthy responded to aggressive questioning from army counsel Joseph Welch, when Welch challenged Cohn to turn over McCarthy's list of 130 subversives in defense plants to the FBI and the Department of Defense "before the sun goes down."

McCarthy suggested that Welch check on Fred Fisher, a young lawyer in Welch's own Boston law firm whom Welch planned to have on his staff for the hearings. McCarthy accused Fisher of once belonging to the National Lawyers Guild, a group Attorney General Herbert Brownell had called "the legal bulwark of the Communist Party."

Welch then reprimanded McCarthy for his needless attack on Fisher.

"Until this moment, Senator," said Welch, "I think I never really gauged your cruelty or your recklessness."

McCarthy, accusing Welch of filibustering the hearing and baiting Cohn, dismissed Welch's dissertation and casually resumed his attack on Fisher, at which point Welch angrily cut him short.

"Senator, may we not drop this?" asked Welch. "We know he belonged to the Lawyer's Guild . . . Let us not assassinate this lad further, Senator; you've done enough. Have you no sense of decency, sir? At long last, have you left no sense of decency?"

It was a line for the ages.

When Welch was finished, the room broke into thunderous applause. It was all caught on national TV. In that one dramatic moment McCarthy became a liability to the Republicans and the cause of anti-Communism.

On June 17, 1954, after thirty-six days of testimony, the army hearings were recessed. Said Arkansas senator John McClellan, the Democrat who led the walkout, "I think this will be recognized and long remembered as one of the most disgraceful episodes in the history of our government."

On December 2, 1954, McCarthy was censured by the Senate, sixty-seven votes to twenty-two. He was finished. Eisenhower vowed never to invite him to state dinners. Worse, reporters stopped writing about him, even when he called press conferences.

Roy Cohn went back to New York to practice law. He became known as one of the meanest lawyers in New York City. Mean and effective enough to be hired in the early 1970s by Queens real estate developer Fred Trump and his son Donald when the Nixon Justice Department sued them for refusing to rent apartments to African Americans. Cohn remained a lawyer for the Trump Organization until he died of AIDS in 1986.

Joe McCarthy died on May 2, 1957, of an acute hepatitis infection. Though he had hepatitis, he didn't stop drinking, and the combination killed him. The far right has never stopped defending, even praising McCarthy. Right-wing publicist Ann Coulter said in an editorial in the Fort Worth *Southern Conservative,* "Joe McCarthy was slowly tortured to death by the pimps of the Kremlin."

After all the hearings and firings, *McCarthy never uncovered one single subversive.* Instead, he just smeared innocent people with impunity. Most of the names, documents, and statistics McCarthy brought were phony. Said historian David Oshinski, "He understood intuitively that force, action, and virility were essential prerequisites for a Red-hunting crusade."

Finally President Eisenhower, his administration, and many Republicans in Congress stood for the rule of law. When the United States Senate censured McCarthy, and when the general counsel of the army gave his famous decency speech, Joe McCarthy was shut down forever.

CHAPTER 8

Race and the Rule of Law

America will not be destroyed from the outside. If we falter and
lose our freedom, it will be because we destroyed ourselves.
—*ABRAHAM LINCOLN*

IN THE MAY 17, 1954, RULING ON *BROWN V. BOARD OF Education*, the Supreme Court determined that separate public schools for black and white students was unconstitutional. The ruling overturned the 1896 Supreme Court case of *Plessy v. Ferguson*, which allowed the discriminatory practice. The court in 1954 was led by Chief Justice Earl Warren, the former governor of California who, ironically, had been instrumental in implementing the wartime internment of citizens of Japanese ancestry only a decade before. Although the public was deeply divided on school segregation at the time, the court's job was to interpret the equal protection clause of the Fourteenth Amendment. It was about the rule of law. The court ruled nine to zero that "separate educational facilities are inherently unequal" and thus unconstitutional.

Enforcement would be wholly another matter. Was the United States to be a country where the executive branch would enforce the orders of the courts, or would Southern governors be allowed to ignore the courts? The

United States Supreme Court has never had an army, and its tiny police force of US marshals only protects the justices. President Eisenhower would have to enforce the court's order against strong opposition in Congress.

The opposition in Congress and from elected state officials, almost all Democrats, was fierce. In Virginia, Senator Harry Byrd organized a movement that closed schools rather than integrated them.

In Texas, John Shepperd, the attorney general, threw up legal challenges to prevent the implementation of school desegregation. In Dallas, the schools integrated one class level at a time per year. White Texans dragged their feet as long as they could, and then they sent their children to new whites-only private schools. In Arkansas, Governor Orval Faubus called the state's National Guard to prevent black students from entering Little Rock Central High School.

In Florida, the state legislature passed a resolution declaring the *Brown v. Board* decision null and void. But Florida governor LeRoy Collins, who had himself protested against the decision, nevertheless refused to sign the resolution into law. He argued that the overturning of *Brown* should only be done legally.

Governor Collins, a segregationist, at least recognized the importance of the rule of law. Unlike some Southern leaders, he was not willing to send the South down the path it had chosen in 1861 to confront the rule of law—in that case the election of Abraham Lincoln—with violence.

President Eisenhower was ready. He had been careful in his public comments on the merits of the case, although his Justice Department had submitted briefs supporting the plaintiffs. Eisenhower understood his role, which was not to decide the case but to enforce the court order. He would have to support the ruling, and subsequent similar rulings, throughout the country, and especially throughout the South, where federal district judges would have to give the orders to desegregate specific school districts. In Arkansas, Eisenhower answered Faubus's challenge by sending members of the 101st Airborne Division from Fort Campbell, Kentucky, to Arkansas. He also federalized the Arkansas National Guard.

If Arkansas wanted to go the route that the South had gone in 1861, Eisenhower, who had been one of the most famed generals in American history, was ready. Governor Faubus backed down.

Mississippi continued to practice school segregation, and no one challenged the practice for nine years for fear of violence by the Ku Klux Klan and the White Citizens' Council. In 1963, Medgar Evers sued to desegregate the Jackson, Mississippi, schools, and he was murdered by White Citizens' Council member Byron De La Beckwith. Many knew De La Beckwith did it, but two trials ended in hung juries. Thirty-one years after the murder, De La Beckwith was finally convicted.

In 1963, when two black students attempted to enter the University of Alabama, Governor George Wallace stood in front of the door of Foster Auditorium to prevent them from entering. He capitulated only when President John Kennedy intervened, and General Henry Graham of the Alabama National Guard ordered him to step aside.

What Eisenhower and Kennedy did was crucially important to the protection of the rule of law. When the Supreme Court decides whether a law is constitutional, that ruling needs to be enforced on both the federal and state levels, and it is the job of the president to enforce it.

It took years to eliminate de jure segregation in the South, and de facto segregation throughout the country remains because school district boundaries are often drawn along segregated neighborhood lines. Housing segregation is instigated by real estate agents, developers, and landlords, including in the 1960s and 1970s in Queens, New York, by Fred and Donald Trump. Bringing these private actors to heel would take additional legislation and decades of investigations and litigation, including the Nixon administration's civil rights litigation against the Trumps.

Many Democrats from other parts of the country and some from the South, including Lyndon Johnson, did not side with the powerful segregationists within Democratic Party ranks. The Democratic Party was soon made to pay an enormous political price for this decision, when alienated white Southern Democrats sought a new political home. Ironically they would find it within the Republican Party that through the 1960s had a comparatively ("comparatively" is the key word here) progressive stand on equality for African Americans from Lincoln through Theodore Roosevelt and Eisenhower.

In 1952 and 1956, many African Americans backed the Republican Party. President Eisenhower gave them good reason. Upon the Supreme Court ruling in the *Brown v. Board of Education* decision, Eisenhower ordered the Washington, DC, public schools to be desegregated. In 1957 and 1959, Eisenhower proposed strong civil rights bills to enforce the long-neglected

Fifteenth Amendment and give Southern blacks the right to vote. However, Southern Democrats in the Senate filibustered the bills and watered down their strongest provisions.

Kennedy was the first Democratic president after *Brown v. Board*. He appointed his brother Robert Kennedy as attorney general (this was before Congress passed an anti-nepotism statute in 1967) and put him in charge of enforcing court-ordered school desegregation. Segregationists through much of the South hated Robert Kennedy.

The president faced a Congress led by segregationist committee heads from his own Democratic Party.

In May 1961, Robert Kennedy was forced to act when a Freedom Rider bus was set on fire in Birmingham. He sent aide John Seigenthaler to Birmingham, where a rioter bashed him over the head with a pipe and cracked his skull, knocking him unconscious.

Eight days later, Robert Kennedy asked the Interstate Commerce Commission to end segregation on interstate buses. The rules ending this type of segregation took effect in November.

In the fall of 1962, Mississippi governor Ross Barnett refused to comply with the Supreme Court ruling demanding integration at the University of Mississippi. In response, President Kennedy addressed the nation on September 30, 1962, and announced that he'd federalized the state National Guard.

In April 1963, civil rights activists started a campaign in Birmingham that included boycotts, lunch counter sit-ins, and a protest at city hall. Birmingham police commissioner Bull Connor turned high-pressure hoses and police dogs on the protesters, including children. The violence, captured on national television, was viewed across the country.

By June President Kennedy was prepared to take a stand.

June 11, 1963 was one of the most notable days of the early civil rights movement. That morning, Alabama governor George Wallace stood at the schoolhouse door in a futile attempt to stop the integration of the University of Alabama.

That evening, Boston's NAACP leaders had their first confrontation with Louisa Day Hicks, the chairwoman of the Boston School Committee, in the battle over segregated schools.

And just after midnight, a white segregationist in Jackson, Mississippi, murdered civil rights leader Medgar Evers.

Another event marked that notable day. President Kennedy surprised everyone when he asked for airtime at 8 PM from the three major TV networks.

He announced that the National Guard had helped enroll two black students at the University of Alabama. He then for the first time spoke of civil rights as a "moral issue." He asked every American, "regardless of where he lives, to stop and examine his conscience." America "for all its hopes and all its boasts, will not be fully free until all its citizens are free."

Kennedy said to the nation, "If an American, because his skin is dark, cannot eat lunch at a restaurant open to the public, if he cannot send his children to the best public schools available, if he cannot vote for the public officials who represent him, if, in short, he cannot enjoy the full and free life which all of us want, then who among us would be content to have the color of his skin changed and stand in his place? Who among us would be content with the counsels of patience and delay?"

Toward the end of the speech Kennedy addressed white Americans, many of whom knew little of the struggle of African Americans for civil rights and who had no idea that a political and cultural revolution was sweeping the land. He invited all Americans to actively support change.

"A great change is at hand," he said, "and our task, our obligation, is to make that revolution, that change, peaceful and constructive for all."

Kennedy announced he would introduce sweeping civil rights legislation and push for faster school desegregation, which had been advancing with glacial slowness for nearly a decade.

Kennedy did as he promised, submitting a strong civil rights bill to Congress. A bombing of a black church in Birmingham, Alabama, that killed four young African American children, added to the pressures to pass such a bill. He pushed for its passage up until November 22, 1963, when he was murdered in Dallas.

President Lyndon Johnson then used his powers of persuasion in Congress and his credibility as a Southerner from Texas the following year to push through this bill, which he signed into law on July 2, 1964 as the Civil Rights Act of 1964.

The act provided, among other things, that it was illegal for private businesses and governments to discriminate on the basis of race in public accommodations, including buses, restaurants, and hotels. This was a dramatic change in the federal government's assertion of power not only over the states but also over individuals and businesses engaged in interstate commerce, who had previously been subjected only to regulation by state governments controlled by segregationist politicians.

The bill passed the House by a margin of 290 to 130. Sixty-one percent of Democrats supported the bill (152 yes and 96 no), and 80 percent of Republicans supported it (138 yes and 34 no). After the longest filibuster in Senate history, the Senate passed the bill 73 to 27. Sixty-nine percent of Senate Democrats supported the bill (46 yes, 21 no), and 82 percent of Republicans supported it (27 yes, 6 no). But in both the House and Senate, the overwhelming majority of members from the South (almost all Democrats) voted against the bill.

President Johnson commented to his chief of staff, Bill Moyers, "I think we just gave the South to the Republicans for your lifetime and mine."

He was right.

LBJ's next move, after considerable pressure was put on him by Martin Luther King, was to enact a law to prevent states from disenfranchising African Americans at the ballot box.

Enforcement of the post–Civil War Fifteenth Amendment, which granted male freed slaves the right to vote, would be a pervasive problem from its adoption until the present day. To facilitate enforcement, Congress also passed the Enforcement Act of 1870, giving the federal government the ability to protect black voting rights by arresting and indicting conspirators like the Ku Klux Klan. But a later Supreme Court decision declared that law unconstitutional.

Without the protection of the Enforcement Act of 1870, Southern states made sure that most blacks didn't vote. In 1874 President Rutherford B. Hayes received the support of three Southern states in exchange for his pledge to refuse to enforce federal civil rights protections. The responsibility of protecting voting rights fell solely on state governments. Federal troops withdrew from the South in 1877, and states passed Jim Crow laws. The eleven Southern states, which were predominantly Democratic, passed poll taxes and literary tests, refused to count black votes, and allowed violence against African Americans who tried to vote.

In 1932 the Democratic Party of Texas instituted a rule that only whites could vote in the primaries. Dr. L. A. Nixon of El Paso, a black man who was denied the right to vote, sued. In *Nixon v. Condon*, the Supreme Court ruled in 1932 that whites-only voting was unconstitutional. In *Grovey v. Townsend*, however, the court in 1935 upheld a reworking of the same essential rule in which only the Texas Democratic Party (which called itself a "private organization") discriminated against black voters. Later, in *Smith v. Allwright* (1944), the court ruled that primaries were an essential part of the electoral process, and *Grovey* was overruled.

The Texas Democratic Party responded by barring blacks from the party nominating conventions and other measures.

Whites-only primaries continued.

For years after the end of the Civil War, Southern blacks also were kept from voting by the use of the poll tax, whereby citizens in some states had to pay a fee to vote in a federal election. It was a fee most blacks couldn't afford.

In 1964, the Twenty-Fourth Amendment to the Constitution was ratified, banning poll taxes, but only in federal elections. The amendment provided that:

Section 1. The right of citizens of the United States to vote in any primary or other election for President or Vice President, for electors for President or Vice President, or for Senator or Representative in Congress, shall not be denied or abridged by the United States or any State by reason of failure to pay poll tax or other tax.
Section 2. The Congress shall have power to enforce this article by appropriate legislation.

In the case of *Harper v. Virginia Board of Elections*, the Supreme Court in 1966 declared the poll tax in state elections also to be unconstitutional.

Annie Harper, a Virginia resident, could not afford the $1.50 poll tax, and she sued. Harper argued the tax violated her rights under the equal protection clause of the Fourteenth Amendment.

In a two-month period following the *Harper* decision, federal courts declared as unconstitutional poll taxes in Texas, Alabama, Virginia, and Mississippi.

In 1965 came the Voting Rights Act. This legislation was designed to provide for African Americans the right to vote already guaranteed to them in the Fifteenth Amendment, which had not been enforced by Congress for almost a century.

The express wording of the heretofore unenforced Fifteenth Amendment was clear:

> **Section 1.** The right of citizens of the United States to vote shall not be denied or abridged by the United States or by any State on account of race, color, or previous condition of servitude.
> **Section 2.** The Congress shall have power to enforce this article by appropriate legislation.

The drafters knew that Section 1 was meaningless unless Congress actually used Section 2 to pass a law to enforce voting rights. With the exception of a few temporary measures taken during Reconstruction, Congress had done hardly anything to enforce Section 1. Segregationist politicians had used methods like poll taxes, literacy tests, and intimidation to keep African Americans from the polls. By 1965, finally, the president and Congress realized it was time for this to change. A rule of law set forth in the Constitution was meaningless unless it was enforced.

The Voting Rights Act of 1965 prohibited state and local governments from imposing any law that would discriminate on the basis of race in national and state elections. The federal government was given oversight powers to enforce the act in specific states (Alabama, Georgia, Louisiana. Mississippi, South Carolina, and Virginia) where the right to vote had been denied. In future years, other states such as Alaska, Arizona, and Texas were added.

On August 6, 1965, with civil rights activists Martin Luther King, Rosa Parks, and John Lewis in attendance, President Johnson signed the bill into law.

The political ramifications of the Civil Rights Act and the Voting Rights Act were swift. When Barry Goldwater ran for president against Lyndon Johnson in 1964, Goldwater boasted that he was one of the few Republicans (only six) in the Senate who had voted against the Civil Rights Act. He was one of the first Republicans to say that such an act violated states' rights and that people should be able to do business (or not) with whomever they chose.

Though Lyndon Johnson won the 1964 election in a landslide, voters in five Southern states fled the Democrats for the Republican Party. The lesson for the Republicans was that even in a terrible election year, appealing to white Southern voters could make inroads on what the Democrats claimed to be their "solid South."

From 1964 on, Republican strategy would hinge in part on attracting Southern white voters. Richard Nixon's Southern strategy, implemented by media advisor Roger Ailes, used coded racist messages to attract former Democratic white voters alienated by President Johnson's civil rights advances.

In 1968, Alabama's Democratic governor, George Wallace, who intoned "segregation now, segregation tomorrow, segregation forever," ran for president as an Independent and was able to win in seven Southern states. Wallace gained forty-six electoral votes and almost ten million votes.

Richard Nixon's 1968 presidential campaign stressed "states' rights" and "law and order." When told by campaign aide Kevin Phillips that "Republicans are never going to get more than ten to twenty percent of the Negro vote," the way to victory for the Republicans seemed obvious. Said Phillips in his book *The Emerging Republican Majority*, "The more negroes who register as Democrats in the South, the sooner the negrophobe whites will quit the Democrats and become Republicans."

In the 1960s and '70s, race was a predominant issue—first school desegregation, then the Civil Rights Act, and the Voting Rights Act. Affirmative action, criminal justice, and a wide range of policies also have had a disparate impact on white and black Americans. Republicans increasingly sided with white Southerners. The price to be paid was a very quick erosion of support for Republicans among African Americans (most of whom had abandoned the GOP by the 1970s), and a more gradual loss of support among more progressive groups of white Americans.

Ironically, after Nixon's Southern strategy helped win him the election, he worked to end desegregation when he appointed a panel led by Vice President Spiro Agnew and Labor Secretary George Schultz to provide federal aid to desegregate the public schools. Nixon was against busing school children away from their neighborhood schools, but when courts ordered it, he enforced the court orders.

Nixon knew that African Americans needed jobs. Soon after taking office, one of Nixon's first tasks was to settle the impasse between civil rights leaders and skilled labor unions that were almost exclusively white.

In his first address to Congress in 1970, Nixon announced the Philadelphia Plan for affirmative action, which imposed goals and timetables for race-based hiring on the city's unions. The act put in place racial preferences and quotas.

After the plan was implemented in Philadelphia, it was enacted in dozens of cities nationwide. Nixon also pushed affirmative action in federal programs. He managed affirmative action in government procurement contacts and applied them to any institution that received federal funds, including universities. Nixon then issued Executive Order 11478, which called for affirmative action in all government employment. Thousands of African Americans were added to the federal payroll.

Nixon's record on race issues, however, was mixed. During his first term, he supported a bill that provided federal tax subsidies for the new charter schools that gave white Southerners an alternative to public school integration. The bill didn't pass, but Republicans advocating for "school choice" gained the sympathies of a generation of Southern white voters.

The Nixon administration—sometimes—enforced fair housing laws, bringing lawsuits against landlords (including Fred and Donald Trump in New York) who refused to rent to African Americans. Nixon, despite all of his flaws, was at least willing sometimes to stand up for the rule of law.

Subsequent administrations—Ford, Carter, Reagan, Bush, Clinton, Bush, and Obama—continued to enforce the landmark civil rights laws of the 1960s with varying degrees of enthusiasm. The Republican administrations from Reagan on generally devoted fewer resources to enforcement and took noticeably more conservative positions on legal issues.

Gerald Ford's administration continued many Nixon policies. Ford appointed William Coleman as secretary of transportation, only the second African American to serve in a presidential cabinet, and the first appointed by a Republican.

Next came Jimmy Carter, a Southerner with experience standing up to racism and segregation.

When Carter was elected governor of Georgia, during his inaugural address he told his audience, "I say to you quite frankly that the time for racial discrimination is over." On January 15, 1973, Carter declared Martin Luther King Day a state holiday. Against the advice of some of his closest aides, Carter hung King's portrait in the state capitol.

In his 1976 presidential campaign, Carter's high-profile backers included Andrew Young and Barbara Jordan, the first black members of Congress from the South since Reconstruction. At the 1976 Democratic Convention in New York, Jordan gave the keynote speech, Young helped nominate Carter, and Martin Luther King Sr., the father of the deceased martyr, delivered the closing benediction.

Carter appointed the first black division head at the Department of Justice, the first black female cabinet member, and the first black ambassador to the United Nations. Carter named more blacks, Latinos, and women to the federal judiciary than all previous administrations combined.

The Reagan era, however, saw a retrenchment on civil rights.

But it was not framed that way. It was framed as a debate over the rule of law.

First, there was the principle that discrimination against *anyone* on the basis of race should be illegal. This interpretation of the Fourteenth Amendment and of civil rights laws meant a rejection of the Nixon-Ford policies on affirmative action.

Second, there were the debates over individual liberty (how much power the government should have over the persons and property of individual Americans) and federalism (the division of responsibility and authority between the federal and state governments).

Individual liberty is one of our founding principles. As Thoreau said in his "Civil Disobedience" treatise, "The government that governs best governs least." Federalism is also one of our founding principles. Many of the founders including the Jeffersonian Democrats preferred a relatively small central government. Decentralized government was believed to be a hallmark of individual liberty, and it still is.

But society also needs some limits on both individual liberty and decentralized government. George Washington's Federalists believed this. So did the first Republican president Abraham Lincoln.

Another very important principle, embodied in the Fourteenth Amendment, is that the states must provide equal protection under the laws. *Brown v. Board of Education* was one of several cases in which the federal courts overrode rights of states that had demonstrated that they would discriminate against their African American citizens. Then came the Civil Rights Act of 1964, the Voting Rights Act of 1965, and more.

The Jeffersonian political philosophy of small central government and individual rights can become an attractive way to frame an agenda on race issues with racially neutral terms.

These issues are hotly debated in organizations like the Federalist Society, a group of conservative and libertarian lawyers formed in the early 1980s. Federalism—the question of how much power to give to the states—has been a very legitimate rule of law question since the founding. If, however, the federal government has a stronger approach to civil rights laws than the states (as it did beginning in the 1960s), federalism also can be used to perpetuate race discrimination. Occasionally it is the states that stand up for the rights of racial and ethnic minorities. (Recently, many state and municipal governments have used sanctuary cities and other measures to oppose federal immigration policy.) Nonetheless, since the Civil War, the federal government has been a better champion of African Americans than many of the states, particularly in the South. This raises the question of whether a federalist vision of decentralized government is sometimes just an intellectual veneer on opposition to civil rights laws.

The answer to that question is not always easy. One side says it is only interested in federalism, while the other says that most federalists are promoting race discrimination.

As these two principles clash and the rhetoric heats up, one wonders whether the rhetoric itself is undermining the rule of law.

When Ronald Reagan ran for president, he opened his campaign at the Neshoba County Fair in Mississippi—not far from where three civil rights workers, Andrew Goodman and Mickey Schwerner from New York City, and James Chaney from Meridian, Mississippi—were murdered by white supremacists in June 1964. In his first campaign appearance, Reagan told the crowd, "I believe in states' rights. I believe in people doing as much as they can for themselves at the community level and at the private level. And I believe that we've distorted the balance of our government today by giving powers that were never intended in the Constitution to be given to that federal establishment."

So far, so good. On the surface, candidate Reagan was espousing the federalist principles of many before him, including Thomas Jefferson. But was there something more to it?

It was odd for Reagan to speak at such a remote area with so few electoral votes, but he was letting Southerners know where he stood on federalism. Was Reagan's speech also a veiled statement on civil rights laws? Even though he never mentioned the murdered Goodman, Schwerner, and Chaney in his speech, he let white Southerners know that he was squarely in their corner.

In 1980 almost a quarter of all Democrats switched and voted for Reagan. In 1984 Reagan got about two-thirds of the white vote. Ninety percent of blacks voted for his opponent, Walter Mondale.

As president, Reagan signed into law a 1982 extension of the Voting Rights Act that he had earlier opposed, vetoed the Civil Rights Restoration Act (a 1988 law that requires recipients of federal funds to comply with civil rights regulations in all areas, not just the program that receives federal funding—Reagan's veto was overridden by Congress), and scaled back some of the enforcement work of the Equal Employment Opportunity Commission (EEOC).

When it came to enforcing key civil rights laws, the administration of President George H. W. Bush brought a mixed bag. In his campaign, he told the country to "leave that tired old baggage of bigotry behind."

In 1990 Bush signed the Civil Rights Act of 1991, which was a watered-down version of an employment discrimination bill that he had vetoed in 1990 because of concerns about affirmative action using hiring quotas.

Bush's appointments of prominent African Americans included Dr. Louis Sullivan, president of Morehouse School of Medicine, as secretary of Health and Human Services, and Colin Powell as chairman of the Joint Chiefs of Staff.

He also appointed conservative lawyer and judge Clarence Thomas to the Supreme Court to replace liberal lawyer and justice Thurgood Marshall. The Congressional Black Caucus opposed the nomination. Representative Major Owens of New York called Thomas a "monstrous negative role model, a Benedict Arnold." Putting him on the Supreme Court, said Owens, "would be a gross insult, a slap in the face of all African Americans." Thomas was confirmed in 1991 even after former employee Anita Hill accused him of sexual harassment when they had worked together at the EEOC.

Thomas has been on the court for twenty-eight years, almost always siding with litigants opposing affirmative action, litigants supporting gerrymandering (as least political gerrymandering that is not overtly racist), and others aligned against positions espoused by African American advocacy groups such as the NAACP.

Bush lost his 1992 reelection try to Arkansas governor Bill Clinton.

Clinton appointed an unprecedented number of African Americans as cabinet secretaries, ambassadors, federal judges, and other administrative positions. He oversaw an agreement to give billions of dollars to black farmers who faced discrimination in the federal government's farm loan program. He ordered HUD secretary Henry Cisneros to increase the homeownership rate for African Americans. The administration devoted more resources to enforcing civil rights laws than the preceding two Republican administrations, and even more importantly, legal positions interpreting those laws shifted in the direction of more aggressive enforcement. The Clinton administration resisted the notion, increasingly popular among conservative Republicans, that affirmative action programs were unconstitutional.

The next president, George W. Bush, had the most ethnically diverse Republican administration ever. General Colin Powell headed the State Department, and Condoleezza Rice followed. Alphonso Jackson and Rod Paige, both African American, headed the offices of Housing and Urban Development and the Department of Education.

The problem again was that the most conservative elements in the Republican Party had gained ascendency in the House and Senate, including many conservative Southern politicians. The administration's legal interpretations of the Civil Rights Act of 1964, the Voting Rights Act of

1965, fair housing laws, and other civil rights laws were at least as conservative as those in the Reagan-Bush years.

Democratic candidate Barack Obama in 2008 again mobilized the African American community to demand progress on civil rights. As a candidate he promised to fight employment discrimination, expand hate-crime laws, end racial profiling, and eliminate criminal sentence disparities. He achieved some of these goals, but no new major civil rights legislation. The focus was on enforcing existing laws.

Then came attention to another civil rights issue—police shootings.

On August 9, 2014, in Ferguson, Missouri, a white police officer shot to death college student Michael Brown, who was unarmed. The officer was not indicted. That same year there were police shootings of unarmed black men in Los Angeles, Chicago, New York, Brooklyn, Madison, Tulsa, and many other cities.

On November 22, 2014, a police officer approached Tamir Rice, an African American twelve-year-old who was playing with a toy gun in a Cleveland playground. Police responding to a 911 call shot the boy dead without warning. The shooting was caught on tape. Nevertheless, the officer was not prosecuted.

Obama's Justice Department investigated these cases, but federal charges rarely are brought. This was a matter left to state prosecutors, who rarely charge police officers for fatal shootings. Support from police unions allows state prosecutors to keep their jobs and also achieve higher office.

Meanwhile, the Supreme Court moved on civil rights in the opposite direction of Obama. The court decided that important parts of the Voting Rights Act were no longer needed. In the case of *Shelby County v. Holder*, the Supreme Court in 2013 decided by a five-to-four-justice margin that the Voting Rights Act had achieved its purpose. The federal government no longer would oversee the fifteen states with histories of voting rights violations: Alabama, Alaska, Arizona, Georgia, Louisiana, Mississippi, South Carolina, Texas, Virginia, Florida, California, Michigan, New York, North Carolina, and South Dakota. These states were essentially now back on their own, trusted to uphold the voting rights of all citizens.

With federal oversight disbanded, voting rights of African Americans and other minorities in some states is once again under attack.

One instrument of attack has been the campaign against voter fraud. Conventional voter fraud (people who vote when or where they are not supposed to vote, or people who vote twice) historically posed a very real threat to the rule of law, but today is very rare. At the same time unjustified fears—or fake news—of voter fraud are used to impose voting restrictions that disproportionately affect minority voters.

In sum, a solution to one problem (voter fraud) has been used to exacerbate another problem by denying some African Americans and other minorities the right to vote.

In 2012, of the 146 million registered voters who voted over the past twelve years, there were 2,068 cases of alleged voter fraud. Of those, only *ten* were cases of voter impersonation. Before the 2016 presidential election, politicians from Arizona, Georgia, Texas, Ohio, and Kansas expressed concerns about voter fraud. According to the *Washington Post*, attorneys general in those states prosecuted thirty-eight cases of voter fraud. A third of those involved nonvoters—election officials or volunteers. None was for voter impersonation.

Said Jennifer Clark of the Brennan Center for Justice, "[Voter fraud] is not a significant concern."

Of the 5.6 million ballots cast in the 2016 presidential election, investigators found exactly fifty-two cases of voter fraud.

The evidence clearly indicates that voter fraud had largely disappeared by the late twentieth century. The days of dead people voting and ballot-box stuffing are gone.

If we stick to paper ballots, voter fraud should not be an issue—with computerized voting machines, and the Russians playing their usual tricks, all bets are off. But computerized voting fraud is not the fraud that voter ID laws are aimed at. And these laws disproportionately discourage minority voters from coming to the polls.

On the very day of the *Shelby v. Holder* ruling, Texas announced it was implementing a new, strict voter ID law. To vote you had to have an approved picture ID.

The Voting Rights Act had been an impediment to voter ID laws because they disproportionately discriminated against minorities, some of whom didn't have driver's licenses, the usual voter ID. Estimates suggested as many as 800,000 voters in Texas lacked an ID. North Carolina passed a similar bill, and so did Alabama, where legislators also passed a law requiring individuals to prove their citizenship.

Mississippi passed a law saying voters had to have driver's licenses. But thirteen counties lacked a motor vehicle bureau office.

Without Section 5 of the Voting Rights Act, it is difficult for the federal government to deter these and other voting law changes. Laws more easily can be passed to prevent a disproportionate number of blacks and Latinos from voting in the fifteen states where the right to vote was once protected by the federal government.

The 2016 Republican platform urged states to require proof of citizenship and photo IDs because "voting procedures may be open to abuse."

According to the Brennan Center for Justice, as of January 2018, lawmakers in eight states had introduced sixteen bills making it harder to vote, and there are thirty-five restrictive bills from fourteen states held over from the year before.

Kris Kobach, who later became chairman of President Trump's now disbanded "Election Integrity Commission," had a long history of defying the law to suppress the black and Latino vote. Before Kobach became the secretary of state of Kansas, a person needed only to swear an oath of citizenship to vote. In 2013, Kobach drafted a law that was passed by the Kansas legislature mandating citizenship documents such as a passport or birth certificate for voter registrations.

Large numbers of citizens, primarily African Americans and Hispanics, had neither, and they didn't have money to acquire one. By December 2015, more than thirty thousand Kansas citizens were disenfranchised.

In May 2016, Kansas federal judge Julie Robinson, who was appointed by George W. Bush, ruled that Kobach's law was illegal.

When Judge Robinson ordered Kobach to register those voters, he refused. Instead, he sent them notices that they could not vote unless they provided citizenship papers.

The day before Kobach was ordered to appear in front of the court on a contempt citation, finally he agreed to comply. He promised the judge he would send postcard notifications telling people that they could vote.

He never sent the postcards. When called on it by the ACLU, Kobach's office said he was under no obligation to send the postcards.

The judge had also ordered him to correct the voting requirements published on the secretary of state's website. He refused to do that as well.

During a contempt hearing in April 2018, Robinson dismissed Kobach's claim that he couldn't force election officials in 105 counties to send out the postcards.

Judge Robinson held Kobach in contempt of court.

Kobach fought back. Arrogantly predicting that he would win his appeal with the US Court of Appeals Tenth Circuit to defend his "proof of citizenship" law, Kobach has announced his candidacy for governor of the state of Kansas in 2020.

In January 2018, the Supreme Court ruled in the case of *Husted v. A. Philip Randolph Institute* that a citizen in Ohio who didn't vote or answer mail could be disenfranchised. The Ohio legislature passed a bill saying if a citizen does not vote in two elections, doesn't return a prepaid notice, and doesn't update their registration over the next four years, they will be stricken from the rolls.

A man named Larry Harmon sued. He hadn't moved. He just chose not to vote in 2009 and 2010. When he showed up to vote in 2015, he was told his registration had been cancelled. He had received no notice of cancellation.

In September 2016 a federal appeals court ruled that this violated the National Voter Registration Act. It said a person can't be taken off the rolls just because they didn't vote.

Ohio attorney general Mike DeWine appealed the ruling to the US Supreme Court, arguing that the state has to be allowed to remove ineligible voters from the rolls. The Supreme Court agreed with him by a five to four vote, with the conservative justices being in the majority.

Said attorney Stuart Naifeh, "Ohio's process targets lower income voters and those of color and penalizes voters who may already face obstacles in exercising the right to vote. It disproportionately harms the most vulnerable voters."

The state-by-state assault on voting rights continues.

With a hostile Congress and Supreme Court, President Obama had an uphill battle to advance civil rights. His most vicious enemy, however, was the right-wing media, whose commentators were often racist.

Right wingers were outraged that an African American might be in the White House. His very existence infuriated them, and in an attempt to delegitimize his presidency, they mounted a campaign to argue that Obama was born in Kenya, not in the United States, and could not hold the presidency under the Constitution. This was the so-called "birther movement." Only a few years into the Obama presidency, the birther movement found a new champion, the same New York real estate developer who had viciously fought the Nixon Justice Department's lawsuit against him for housing discrimination: Donald J. Trump.

Long before he announced his run for the presidency, Donald Trump would attend rallies, where his battle cry was, "Show us your birth certificate."

We would end our pre-Trump story about racism and civil rights here, but it is appropriate to report one more development in the Supreme Court concerning voting rights that extends into the Trump administration.

The Supreme Court in 2019, with two new Trump-appointed justices, Gorsuch and Kavanaugh, abdicated responsibility for judicial oversight in gerrymandering cases. Federal courts have barred at least some explicitly racially motivated gerrymandering. But political operatives quickly replaced it with politically motivated gerrymandering. Gerrymandering is accomplished when congressional district maps are drawn in such a way as to concentrate one party's voters in a few districts, leaving the majority of a state's congressional districts to be controlled by the other party. Whichever political party controls the state legislature controls the gerrymandering game and gets to choose a disproportionate share of the state's delegation in the US House of Representatives. A similar game can be played to draw legislative district maps in a manner that perpetuates a party's control over the state legislature.

And when racial minorities are far more likely to support one political party than the other, politically motivated gerrymandering often is de facto racial gerrymandering.

This is happening as overwhelming numbers of African American voters support Democrats. Hispanic voters, particularly after the rise of Donald Trump, have also preferred the Democratic Party.

Would a Supreme Court that was willing to intervene in racially motivated gerrymandering also rule that politically motivated gerrymandering in at least some cases was unconstitutional?

The answer the Supreme Court gave in *Rucho v. Common Cause* and *Lamone v. Benisek*, decided on June 27, 2019, by a five to four vote was no.

The federal courts could not interfere. Even though extreme partisan gerry-mandering could be unconstitutional, this was still a nonjusticiable "political question," and it was up to state legislatures to rule on it. (Strange, since state legislatures are creating the gerrymandering problem to begin with.) Alter-natively, Congress under the elections clause of the Constitution could solve the problem. (House members whose own seats may be in gerrymandered districts have shown no interest in doing this.)

Without the supervision of the courts, the rule of law is undermined by political operatives armed with sophisticated computer models that carve up states into oddly contorted districts so a political party can win the majority of a state's congressional delegation while getting less than 50 percent of the vote in the state. School districts drawn this way to avoid *Brown v. Board* would likely run into trouble with the federal courts, but state legislatures can gerrymander legislative districts with impunity, provided they say that the motivation is politics, not race.

CHAPTER 9

The Phony War: Science vs. Religion

Nearly half of Republicans, 45 percent, believe
that God wanted Trump to be president.
—*THE* WASHINGTON POST, *FEBRUARY 14, 2019*

CONFLICT BETWEEN SCIENCE AND RELIGIOUS CONVEN-tion is a centuries-old problem. Science does not preclude belief in a higher being, and there is very little in the core beliefs of most religions that requires a categorical rejection of observations made through science. But all too often the two are pitted against each other, with tragic consequences for the rule of law.

For decades the USSR and other communist countries used scientific discoveries and Marxist theories of social science as excuses to persecute religion. Religion, they said, was inconsistent with scientific advancement and with social and economic progress. Religious Russians were subjected to discrimination, and those who dared to teach religion to others were often imprisoned and sometimes killed.

Through much of human history, however, it has been the other way around. Religion, often cloaked with the authority of the law, has been used to persecute and silence those who believe in science.

117

Galileo was persecuted and even tortured by the Catholic Church for suggesting that the earth wasn't flat. It didn't matter that the "flat-earth" theory lacked scientific evidence. Church leaders had convinced themselves that a flat-earth theory was the only scientific theory consistent with religion, and they steadfastly held to that position—until the scientific evidence in Galileo's favor became so overwhelming that the Church risked badly losing face.

EVOLUTION AND EDUCATION

With the nineteenth century came Charles Darwin's theory of evolution. At first Darwin faced near uniform rejection. The Church of England, the Catholic Church, and just about every denomination denounced his theory.

Then, once again, strong opposition receded in the face of overwhelming scientific evidence, as the Anglican Church, Catholic Church, and other denominations reconciled biblical accounts of creation with scientific revelations about how we and the earth evolved.

In America, pockets of resistance remained into the twenty-first century. The drama—like the 1690 drama in Salem, Massachusetts, over the superstitious belief in witches—would again play itself out in the courtroom. It wasn't just a battle between scientific ideas and religious beliefs, but it was a battle over the rule of law.

No one would be hanged as in Salem, but courts would have to decide whether religious viewpoints still held by some denominations, as opposed to generally accepted scientific viewpoints, would be taught in the public schools.

The battle between modern science and myth reared its head in March 1925 after the Tennessee legislature passed the Butler Act, making it a misdemeanor punishable by fine to "teach any theory that denies the story of the Divine Creation of man as taught in the Bible, and to teach instead that man has descended from a lower order of animals."

A month later John Scopes, a public schoolteacher, was arrested for teaching evolution. The case became headline news. Two of the most famous lawyers of the day took part: Clarence Darrow championed the teacher's right to teach science, and William Jennings Bryan, a four-time Democratic presidential nominee and leader in the anti-evolution movement, spoke for the state of Tennessee.

Bryan argued that the biblical word of God took priority over all human knowledge.

Clarence Darrow retorted, "We find today as brazen and as bold an attempt to destroy learning as was even made in the Middle Ages."

The judge ruled for the prosecutors when he banned expert testimony from scientists. Bryan agreed to join the prosecution's team, and Darrow called him to the stand to testify as a biblical expert.

He asked Bryan whether he really believed a whale had swallowed Jonah, and whether Adam and Eve were really the first humans. Did all languages emanate from the Tower of Babel?

"I accept the Bible absolutely," said Bryan, though he conceded that the six days described in the Bible were probably not literal days.

Darrow concluded his examination by saying, "I am examining you on your fool ideas that no intelligent Christian on earth believes."

The jury convened for nine minutes and fined Scopes one hundred dollars.

Bryan died in his sleep five days later.

The next year Mississippi also passed a law banning the teaching of evolution in public schools. Arkansas followed a year later.

Tennessee's Butler Act was repealed in 1967. A year later the Arkansas and Mississippi laws were struck down by the courts. The back-and-forth process of regulating these teachings and then changing course continued in other states. In 1973 Tennessee passed a bill saying that the account in Genesis had to be given equal weight when evolution was taught. Two years later, a federal appeals court declared the law unconstitutional.

Not surprisingly, evolution is still a controversial subject even though the Catholic Church and most Protestant denominations have accepted the science.

Next came a national debate over prayer in public schools. In April 1962 the Supreme Court heard *Engel v. Vitale*. A group of parents in New Hyde Park, New York, complained that the official prayer written by the state board of regents to "Almighty God" contradicted their religious beliefs.

Steven Engel, who was Jewish, challenged the constitutionality of the state prayer in the public schools. He was supported by groups including the ACLU. They argued that the prayer violated the establishment clause of the First Amendment, which says in part, "Congress shall make no law respecting an establishment of religion." They also argued that the Fourteenth Amendment imposed these same restrictions on the states.

In a six-to-one vote, the Supreme Court ruled that the promotion of religion by persons exercising governmental authority in a public school setting violated the Constitution.

The ruling didn't sit well with religious groups in Southern states, who have been fighting to bring back prayer in public schools ever since.

In a rally in Hartsville, South Carolina, in September 2014, Pat Gibson-Hye Moore, a school board member, complained, "We're taking God out of everything. We are taking the creator, the one that created everything, we're just trying to kick Him out and He's not happy with that."

Those who demanded prayer in public schools argued that since the *Engel* decision, the schools have replaced morals and values with sex education. Some even argued that the removal of religion from the classroom has led to violence. "Should we be surprised that schools become places of carnage?" asked Mike Huckabee, former governor of Arkansas, who is also a minister. Huckabee didn't mention guns, or the fact that just about every Catholic diocese and mainline Protestant denomination in the United States has called for stricter gun laws to protect children. For him the relevant issue was school prayer.

The public school prayer debate wasn't fought between believers and nonbelievers. Rather, much of the debate was between those who belonged to denominations that dominated local government (these are almost always Christian denominations, although most Christian denominations do not support public school prayer) and persons of other faiths (Jews, Muslims, Unitarians, and others) who prefer to pray with family at home or in religious institutions. Many Christians also believe that Sunday school, church groups, private schools, and homes are the best places for a child to pray without forcing a particular religious viewpoint on other children.

Another constitutional debate focuses on public support for private schools, usually religious schools. Some religious conservatives—having abandoned public schools over both racial integration and removal of school prayer—seek government funding for their private religious schools. Such funding is not unheard of elsewhere; for instance, some European countries provide for it. But the establishment clause of the United States Constitution prohibits any government endorsement or financial support for particular religions and creates a serious impediment to public subsidies for religious schools.

We will not summarize the political and legal battles over public subsidies for religious schools here, but this issue, which was first championed by the Catholic Church and has been taken up by evangelical Protestants, continues to challenge the rule of law in America to this day.

CONTRACEPTION AND ABORTION

The battle between scientific advancement and religious principles next shifted to human reproduction. Because of the disparate impact of contraception and abortion laws on women, this debate involves equal protection considerations as well as the influence of religious principles on the law. It also involves government intrusion on personal privacy, a right not explicitly guaranteed under the Constitution but implicit in the due process clause of the Fourteenth Amendment, which forbids the government from taking away a person's "liberty" without due process of law. Laws requiring women to have children when they don't want to raise all of these concerns.

The battle started with contraception.

"Birth control" was first advocated by Margaret Sanger, who opened a family planning and birth control clinic at 46 Amboy Street in the Brownsville section of Brooklyn in 1916. Sanger had ten siblings, and she observed how without birth control women were helpless to direct their lives as they wished. As a nurse she saw women who gave themselves abortions with coat hangers and ended up very ill or dead. She vowed to do something to prevent this.

Sanger created a firestorm. Not only was it illegal to *teach* women about contraception, religious conservatives considered it obscene.

Nine days after she opened her clinic, she was arrested, and the clinic was closed. Bail was set at five hundred dollars. She returned to the clinic and was arrested again, charged with running a public nuisance. Sentenced to thirty days in jail, she went on a hunger strike and had to be force-fed.

At trial, the judge declared that women did not have "the right to copulate with a feeling of security that there will be no resulting conception."

But in 1918, the New York Court of Appeals ruled that doctors could legally prescribe contraceptives.

Sanger, the founder of Planned Parenthood, remained a target of some religious conservatives long after her death, but it wasn't until 1960, when the FDA approved birth control pills, that the legal battle heated up. "The pill," invented by Carl Djerassi, quickly became popular with the public, and also a target of restrictive birth control legislation and enforcement.

The Catholic Church, a powerful force in American politics, has been a primary opponent of contraceptive measures. The battle over birth control also reflected long simmering social tensions between mainline Protestants, the most powerful religious group in American society and politics from the founding up through much of the twentieth century, and Catholics, who arrived as immigrants beginning in the nineteenth century and then acquired considerable political power in the Northeast and Upper Midwest.

Most mainline Protestant denominations embraced birth control in the 1950s once it was found to be safe, whereas the Catholic Church to this day rejects it.

Who controlled the law on this subject became a test for whose religious ideas would hold sway. Lost in the power struggle—which also included ethnic dimensions—was the idea that in a country without an established church, one person's religion should not hold sway over another's personal decisions.

In an article in 1939, Father Francis Jeremiah Connell, a highly respected priest and professor of dogma theology, said this about birth control:

> [W]hen husband and wife deliberately and positively frustrate the procreative purpose of sexual intercourse, they prevent the order of nature and thus directly oppose the design of nature's Creator. And since the reproductive function is so vital to the upkeep of the race, and since any exception to this law would be multiplied indefinitely, every act of contraception frustration is a gravely immoral act, or, in Catholic terminology, a mortal sin.

By the 1960s, the Catholic Church was deeply embedded in a fight to keep contraceptives from people who wanted them.

In Connecticut, an 1879 law said that "any person who uses any drug, medicinal article, or instrument for the purposes of preventing conception shall be fined not less than forty dollars or imprisoned not less than sixty days." The law provided that anyone who "assists, abets, counsels, causes, hires or commands another to commit any offense may be prosecuted and punished as if he were the principle offender."

Estelle Griswold, the executive director of Planned Parenthood League of Connecticut, and Dr. C. Lee Buxton, a doctor and a Yale professor, were both arrested and found guilty of providing contraception. They were fined one hundred dollars each.

The US Supreme Court in *Griswold v. Connecticut* in 1965 reversed the decision. Judge William O. Douglas declared that married couples had a right to privacy. He said their use of contraception was a "fundamental right."

In 1972, in the case of *Eisenstadt v. Baird*, the court extended this right of privacy to all women, married or not.

In some ways the *Eisenstadt* case was as important as *Griswold*. Before 1972, unmarried women had difficulty obtaining contraceptives from anyone other than a registered physician or pharmacist.

William Baird gave a lecture at Boston University on April 6, 1967, and invited members of the audience to come forward to take contraceptive materials including a vaginal spermicide. Baird was then arrested for violating the law that allowed only doctors and pharmacists to pass out contraceptives. In court he was found innocent of presenting contraceptive items but guilty of distributing them. He faced a three-month prison sentence. When the US Court of Appeals for the First Circuit found his conviction to be unconstitutional, he was released.

Then came the battle over abortion. Many of the same considerations underlying the contraception battle were relevant here as well (science vs. religious belief, privacy, and equal protection). The scientific component, however, became more complex as science also could be used to form opinions about, if not to determine, whether and when a human life begins inside the womb.

This battle escalated quickly after the 1973 Supreme Court decision in *Roe v. Wade*.

The debate was not just about science, religion, and personal privacy, but also about the law's equal protection of women.

In 1965 illegal abortions comprised one-sixth of pregnancy-related deaths. A survey conducted in the 1960s revealed that eight in ten poor women in New York City who had an abortion did it by themselves.

In 1970 two University of Texas School of Law graduates brought a lawsuit on behalf of a pregnant woman, "Jane Roe" (real name Norma McCorvey). Roe claimed that Texas's law criminalizing abortions except to save the life of the mother violated her constitutional rights. Though her life wasn't in danger, Roe didn't have the money to travel out of state to get an abortion in a safe medical facility. The suit was filed against Henry Wade, the Dallas County district attorney. When a Texas court ruled for the plaintiff, Wade appealed to the US Supreme Court.

By a seven to two decision, the court in an opinion by Justice Harry Blackmun ruled that the Texas law violated "Roe's" right to privacy. The court ruled that the Constitution's First, Fourth, Ninth, and Fourteenth Amendments protected her "zone of privacy" against state laws. The court said that a statute that did not take into consideration the stage of pregnancy or interests other than the life of the mother violated the plaintiff's due process.

The court considered the physical, psychological, and economic issues a pregnant woman must endure. The court also considered three reasons to ban abortions, but dismissed the first two—discouraging illicit sex and protecting women's health—as irrelevant. The third reason—protecting prenatal life—was by far the more complex question. The court examined a wide range of scientific evidence, and centuries of religious and philosophical teachings going back to the ancient Greeks. No field of inquiry—philosophy, religion, or science—gave definitive answers.

But the court reached a conclusion and ruled that the unborn fetus during the first trimester was not a person under the law, and thus that protecting the fetus at this stage was not a sufficient justification for a state to prohibit abortion. Despite all of the criticism that *Roe v. Wade* has received over the years, the decision was unique in its use of science, religion, and philosophy to answer a very difficult question: At what stage of pregnancy is a human life worthy of legal protection, at substantial cost to the mother who does not want to give birth? The court implicitly rejected two alternative approaches—one that would allow state legislators to decide this question for pregnant women, even at the very beginning of pregnancy, as well as the other extreme of always allowing women and their doctors to make these decisions without any state regulation, regardless of the stage of pregnancy. The court held that the right to abortion during the first trimester was near absolute. Abortions during the second trimester could not be made illegal if the abortion was needed to protect the life of the mother.

The court that decided this case was all male. Only one of the justices, William Brennan, was Catholic, and he voted with the majority. The opinion was written by Justice Blackmun who had been appointed by a Republican president, and three of the other justices in the majority—Burger, Stewart, and Powell—had been appointed by Republican presidents. One Democratic appointee, Justice White, and one Republican appointee, Justice Rehnquist, dissented.

It is too often said that a jurist's gender, religion, and political party determine case outcomes. In this seminal decision, that didn't happen. The rule of law need not turn upon the religious or other identity of lawmakers or the judges who interpret the laws. It turns on our ability to put aside our own identity—whether gender, religion, or political party—and call the shots as we see them. That's what the *Roe* court did.

The outcry was immediate. Religious conservatives claimed the court was allowing the murder of unborn children. Groups like TFP (Tradition, Family, Property) Student Action, which was founded in 1973, protested abortion clinics. The TFP on May 15, 2009, in a paper, cited ten reasons why abortion is "evil and not pro-choice." The rationales behind all ten reasons were either religious (abortion is "evil") or the premise that human life begins at conception ("abortion is murder").

Other critics of legalized abortion were much more scholarly in their approach.

John Noonan, a judge on the US Court of Appeals for the Ninth Circuit and professor of law at the University of California, Berkeley, was staunchly pro-life and anti-abortion. He wrote an essay titled "The Morality of Abortion: Legal and Historical Perspectives" that concluded with an argument against taking the life of the unborn.

"The perception of humanity of the fetus and the weighing of fetal rights against other human rights constituted the work of the moral analysts," he wrote. "But what spirit animated their abstract judgments? For the Christian community it was the injunction of the Scripture to love your neighbor as thyself. The fetus as human was a neighbor; his life had parity with one's own. The commandment gave life to what otherwise would have been only rational calculation."

The backlash against *Roe v. Wade* brought protests to abortion clinics nationwide by Catholic and other religious organizations. Planned Parenthood, a provider of women's health and reproductive care including abortions, became a prime target nationally.

Most protests were peaceful, but the movement had its violent side. Some people, convinced that human life begins at conception, believed not only that abortion is murder but that violence was justified to prevent it. The threat to our democracy and the rule of law was twofold: first the violence itself, and second, the ideological obsession that became so intense that individuals ignored all other aspects of the rule of law. The rule of law has worked when people who violently attack abortion clinics or doctors have been prosecuted and convicted. The threat to the rule of law is that we have such cases to begin with.

But this raises the question of how far others are willing to go without using such extreme violence. What are abortion opponents willing to give up to have a president who will appoint a Supreme Court that will reverse *Roe*? For example, if a staunch abortion opponent had to choose between a "pro-choice" president whose loyalty to the United States is not in question, and a "pro-life" president likely beholden to Russia or some other hostile power, which candidate would the abortion opponent choose?

SEXUAL ORIENTATION

In 1969 it was illegal in New York City for a man to solicit sex from another man. Police patrolled areas where gay people congregated for the purpose of harassing and intimidating them. To avoid the glare of the cops, many gays who lived in Greenwich Village went to the Stonewall Inn, a safe haven for gay, lesbian, and transgender people.

It was early in the morning of June 28, 1969, when nine policemen raided the bar. They arrested the bartenders for selling liquor without a license, ordered the bar cleared, and physically assaulted the patrons. They arrested three who weren't wearing "gender-appropriate" clothing.

It was the third raid on the Stonewall Inn in a month.

Bystanders and those in the bar had usually been passive, but this time the anger about police harassment and social discrimination erupted spontaneously and forcefully. More than four hundred gays and lesbians rioted. Police called in reinforcements, fights broke out, and someone tried to set the place on fire.

In the context of the civil rights and women's movements, the uprising at the Stonewall Inn became a symbol of resistance to what gays, lesbians, bisexual, and transgender people had long recognized was unfair social and political discrimination.

The uprising at the Stonewall Inn was the catalyst for the formation of many powerful gay rights organizations, including GLAAD (Gay and Lesbian Alliance Against Defamation), PFLAG (Parents, Families and Friends of Lesbians and Gays), and Queer Nation. In the years after the Stonewall Inn incident, June became Gay Pride month, and the LGBTQ community has held celebratory parades in cities across America.

Since the Stonewall riots, gay men, lesbian women, and transgender and bisexual people have come out of the closet by the millions. They insisted that the state recognize same-sex marriages to be just as legitimate as marriages between a man and woman.

Science once again was on the side of change. According to scientific evidence, people who are attracted to members of the same sex develop their orientation before they are born. This is *not* a choice. In 2014 researchers confirmed the connection between same-sex orientation in men and a specific chromosomal region. This was thought to be a scientific fact as early as 1990.

Scientific studies also showed the psychologically harmful effects of trying to deny one's orientation. Studies showed that keeping one's sexual orientation hidden ("in the closet") and dealing with the social stigma of homosexuality can result in severe depression or even suicide.

On the other hand, there are the religious institutions that often fight against—but in some instances fight for—equal legal treatment of gays and lesbians, whether the battle be over repeal of sodomy laws or the approval of civil unions and same-sex marriage. Once again different denominations disagree in their approach. Before the late 1980s, most religious denominations agreed to varying degrees to condemn homosexuality, even if they differed in their view of sodomy laws, police harassment, and discrimination against gays and lesbians. Beginning in the 1990s, a growing number of denominations accepted gay and lesbian parishioners, then gay and lesbian clergy and church leaders, and finally same-sex marriage. Other denominations remained steadfastly opposed to equal rights for gays and lesbians inside the church, and yet other denominations were eager to continue discrimination against gays and lesbians in society as a whole.

Among those strongly opposed to gay and lesbian rights in at least some of these areas have been the Catholic Church, Orthodox Jews, Southern Baptists, and other evangelical Protestant denominations. Mainline Protestant denominations and liberal Jewish congregations were the most supportive of gay rights. Many have accepted same-sex marriage, allowing their religious leaders to perform same-sex weddings, including Reform and Conservative Jews, Unitarians, Episcopalians, many Presbyterians and Lutherans and the Congregationalists in the United Church of Christ.

Hawaii made the first move.

In 1993, the Supreme Court of Hawaii ruled in *Baehr v. Lewin* that it was unconstitutional for the state to interfere with marriage on the basis of sex.

Immediately other states rushed to pass laws to *prevent* same-sex marriage. Opponents attempted to show that defining marriage as a union between a man and a woman preserves family values and traditional ethical notions.

Pushed by the religious conservatives in September 1996, Congress passed the Defense of Marriage Act (DOMA). Both chambers had Republican majorities for the first time since the 1950s. The Republicans passed the bill, and President Clinton signed it, despite voicing some reservations. The law allowed states to refuse to recognize same-sex marriages granted in other states. The spouses could not be legally recognized as such for all federal purposes, including insurance benefits for government employees, social security survivors' benefits, immigration, bankruptcy, and the filing of joint tax returns.

Then federal courts stepped in, recognizing the serious equal protection problems with such laws.

This judicial intervention started with sodomy laws.

Four states were still enforcing sodomy laws against gay men when a Houston resident named John Geddes Lawrence was arrested after police raided his apartment complex in response to a weapons disturbance. They found him having sex with another man and arrested both men, charging them with violating the Texas homosexual conduct law.

After they were convicted and fined, Lawrence appealed. He argued that his arrest and conviction were violations of the right to privacy and the equal protection clause of the Constitution. A Texas appeals court affirmed the conviction, and the *Lawrence v. Texas* case went to the US Supreme Court, which reviewed it in 2003.

Justice Anthony Kennedy ruled the law was unconstitutional and, with a majority of the justices on his side, overturned the conviction. The court ruled the law violated the Fourteenth Amendment's due process clause. The men, the court ruled, were entitled to privacy in their home. The court reversed its own 1986 decision in *Bowers v. Hardwick,* which had upheld a Georgia anti-sodomy law.

Meanwhile, polls showed that public support for same-sex marriage nationwide rose above 50 percent for the first time in 2011. In 2012 the NAACP supported same-sex marriage for the first time. While poll numbers should not be used to interpret and apply the law (the rule of law sometimes requires that judges be willing to make unpopular decisions), the unavoidable reality is that changing social attitudes are continually shaping the rule of law in America.

In the year 2013, the DOMA statute that limited the federal definition of marriage to one man and one woman was struck down in the Supreme Court case of *United States v. Windsor.* Edith Windsor had been required to pay $363,000 in estate taxes after her wife died because the federal government didn't recognize the marriage. The court found DOMA to be unconstitutional and recognized Windsor's marriage under federal law. Despite the ruling, states were not forced to recognize same-sex marriages made in other states.

After the *Windsor* decision, thirty-six states legalized same-sex marriage through laws, court rulings, and voter petitions.

Pressure was mounting to make same-sex marriage legal nationwide, and in 2015 the United States Supreme Court heard *Obergefell v. Hodges.* Represented were plaintiffs from four states—Michigan, Ohio, Kentucky, and Tennessee. In a five to four decision written by Justice Anthony Kennedy, the court rejected the reasoning in *Baker v. Nelson,* a 1971 case in which the Minnesota Supreme Court had ruled that a state law limiting marriage to persons of the opposite sex did not violate the US Constitution. The US Supreme Court would not hear an appeal of *Baker* in 1971, because there was "no federal question," but forty years later it was abundantly obvious that there *was* a federal question that needed to be resolved—in favor of a constitutional right to same-sex marriage.

Among the reasons for the decision, the court said, "The right to personal choice regarding marriage is inherent in the concept of individual autonomy." The court held that because "marriage is a keystone of our social order," preventing same-sex couples from marrying unconstitutionally denies them countless benefits of marriage for no justifiable reason.

"No longer may this liberty be denied," Justice Kennedy wrote.

Kennedy opined that the decision wouldn't harm religious liberty, but in his dissent, Justice John Roberts said that "people of faith can take no comfort in the treatment they receive from the majority today."

Justice Antonin Scalia, one of four conservatives on the court to dissent, went further. He said the decision represented "a threat to American democracy."

Justice Kennedy, who was the deciding vote in both the *Lawrence v. Texas* sodomy case and the *Obergefell* marriage case, has retired. He has been replaced by his former clerk Justice Brett Kavanaugh, who has yet to rule on these questions.

RELIGIOUS LIBERTY

Despite these rulings on contraception, abortion, and same-sex marriage, pushback from religious conservatives continues unabated. Religious liberty—or the right not to follow generally applicable laws because of religious conscience—is now a focal point of legal and political debate. For years pacifists and others made "religious liberty" arguments to avoid military service, sometimes successfully and with support from some political liberals. Now religious conservatives use that argument in very different contexts.

In 2014 in the case of *Burwell v. Hobby Lobby Stores, Inc.*, the US Supreme Court ruled that David and Barbara Green, the founders of Hobby Lobby, did not have to provide four types of contraception in their employees' health plan, because of their strong religious beliefs.

In a similar case in Colorado in 2012, Jack Phillips, a baker, refused to bake a cake for Charlie Craig and David Mullins, a same-sex couple, because of his deeply held Christian beliefs and was sued. In a seven to two decision handed down in November 2017, the US Supreme Court in the case of *Masterpiece Cakeshop v. Colorado Civil Rights Commission* ruled that Phillips had faced religious discrimination in a Colorado proceeding. (The narrow ruling did not address his core religious liberty claim but instead the discriminatory conduct of the Colorado tribunal that had heard his case. Such a case has yet to be decided on its merits. Whether the baker has a First Amendment right to refuse to bake the cake has yet to be resolved.)

The United States was founded as a country where the government would neither establish nor interfere with religion. We are now a country of many religions. Science continues to inform many religious belief systems. The growing alarm and activism in many churches and other religious organizations over climate change illustrates that scientific and theological understandings of God's creation and our stewardship of the earth are compatible and can reinforce each other. Nonetheless, hostility in some religious denominations—particularly some very conservative Evangelical denominations—to climate-change science shows that the tensions of the 1925 Scopes Monkey Trial are still with us, and with consequences for humanity even more severe than Tennessee schoolchildren not being taught about evolution.

Religious traditions that staunchly oppose scientific findings also can come into conflict with the rule of law if the legal system is used to impose religious views on others. The battle between particular sectarian perspectives on religion and the rule of law has been an important part of our history and will continue.

The question remains of how Americans will fight this battle. Will we allow religious wars to destroy representative democracy in the United States just as religious wars destroyed much of Europe in the centuries before the United States was founded? Will identity politics rooted in religion—whether beliefs in a particular religion or dislike of someone else's religion—be so important that Americans forget loyalty to our country and the principles upon which it was founded? To return to an earlier question, would we really choose an unqualified man to be president of the United States—a man with a sordid business and personal life and who was perhaps even beholden to a hostile foreign power—so long as that man claimed to agree with us on abortion?

CHAPTER 10

The Stain of Vietnam

The war in Vietnam is going well and will succeed.
—ROBERT MCNAMARA

JOHN KENNEDY WAS A VERY INSPIRING PRESIDENT FOR many people. He advanced the civil rights movement and other reforms at home while drawing a very hard line against Soviet expansionism. The Kennedy approach to the Soviets came out in the debates in which Kennedy accused the Eisenhower-Nixon administration of allowing a "missile gap" between the USSR and the United States. After Kennedy won the election, Eisenhower was sufficiently worried about escalating military commitments overseas and a spiraling defense budget that in his January 1960 farewell address, he emphasized the threat of a growing "military-industrial complex" controlling the US government.

After Kennedy took office, the USSR tested him by putting missiles in Cuba in October 1962. Kennedy stood down the Soviets in the Cuban Missile Crisis, and he remained determined to counteract Soviet expansionism and meddling in foreign politics anywhere on the globe.

One of those places was Vietnam.

The tragedy of the Kennedy administration and the subsequent Lyndon Johnson administration was Vietnam.

The war began toward the end of World War II when Japan occupied the French colony of Indochina. Ho Chi Minh, a communist leader, took control of much of Vietnam in August 1945. The French then sought to reclaim the colony, and the two sides fought until 1954, when Minh defeated the French at the battle of Dien Bien Phu. The French left Vietnam, but Vietnamese who did not want to live under Soviet-style communism formed a government in the south.

The United States had become involved to stop the spread of communism. Most of the American foreign policy and defense establishment from the 1940s on believed in the domino theory, which posited that if one country fell to Soviet-style communism, the countries surrounding it would also fall. The long-standing Soviet practice of meddling in other countries' politics (continued by post-Soviet Russia to the present day) made this prospect even more fearsome.

The fall of China to communist rule had been an enormous blow in 1949. Then came the Korean War. Americans were vigilant—in hindsight *too* vigilant—in Southeast Asia as well.

As early as 1950, the US military had sent advisors and money to the French to take over the forces trying to stop Ho Chi Minh, and then in 1956 the Eisenhower administration sent advisors to train the army of South Vietnam.

The Geneva accords signed in July 1954 were supposed to separate North Vietnam and South Vietnam forces for two years. South Vietnam, led by Prime Minister Ngo Dinh Diem, was established with US help to be a free and independent democracy. Sabotaging his efforts were thousands of communist subversives from the north. In 1954, a coup by the army against Diem was thwarted with help from the CIA.

South Vietnam was bankrupt and without leadership, and Diem began filling important government posts with relatives and friends. Diem's brother, Ngo Dinh Nhu, who had known fascist sympathies, oversaw the creation of the Army of the Republic of Vietnam (ARVN), which at its peak became the fourth-largest army in the world.

By 1956 it was clear that the Diem regime was antidemocratic and corrupt. Elections were rigged. Freedom of the press was curtailed. Thousands of suspected communists were arrested and jailed. A decree was passed allowing the execution of anyone who belonged to the Viet Minh, the North Vietnamese independence faction. The Diem regime, however, was the enemy of the communists in the north. For a United States fearful of the spread of communism, the enemy of our enemy was our "friend."

In 1959 the Diem government in Saigon began a program of massive resettlement, similar to Soviet farm collectivism. Thousands of South Vietnamese citizens—mostly peasants—were displaced. By 1961 the CIA was helping Diem with his resettlement program. Peasants were supposed to be compensated, but the corruption was so great that most money ended up in the hands of government officials. Meanwhile, the United States bolstered South Vietnam's military with over $1 billion in military aid.

On December 11, 1961, President Kennedy sent aid, money, weapons, and supplies to Diem. An aircraft carrier with thirty-three helicopters and four hundred crewmen arrived in Saigon. The first American died ten days later. When Americans began dying in action in Vietnam, a critically important question arose: At what point would the rule of law require the informed consent of Congress to proceed?

Eisenhower didn't need permission from Congress to send advisors to South Vietnam, but as we began to send more and more troops, the rule of law should have required that Congress consent to further US involvement.

In Article 1, Section 8, Clause 11 of the United States Constitution, which is often referred to as the war powers clause, Congress is vested with the power to declare war. The exact wording is: *[The Congress shall have Power . . .]* "*To declare War, grant Letters of Marque and Reprisal, and make Rules concerning Captures on Land and Water.*"

President Kennedy never went to Congress to get any war powers in Vietnam. His successor, Lyndon Johnson, did not go to Congress about Vietnam until 1964. Moreover, Congress was lied to, making any "consent" it gave morally, if not legally and constitutionally, invalid.

In 1963 Diem went after the Buddhists, accusing them of harboring NLF (National Liberation Front, what we knew as the Viet Cong) guerrillas. On

June 11 a Buddhist monk set himself on fire for the world to see, but that didn't stop Diem, who sent his forces to arrest and murder hundreds of Buddhists. Diem was hardly the type of foreign leader the United States wanted to support to counter Soviet expansionism.

By August 1963 President Kennedy was discussing ways to remove Diem. In late October, Kennedy was informed that members of the army were planning a coup against Diem, and he signaled he would not interfere. On November 1, Diem and his brother Nhu were seized by special forces. The generals promised them safe conduct, but Diem and Nhu were brutally murdered.

By early November 1963 it appears that President Kennedy began to have second thoughts and believed that getting involved in Vietnam was a bad idea. He pulled out one thousand American troops, and he then signed an order that contemplated withdrawing the rest by 1965.

Then on November 22, 1963, Kennedy was assassinated.

US military intervention that had begun on Kennedy's watch would plague the administration of his successor Lyndon Johnson to the very end. We will never know whether Kennedy would have reversed course and extracted the US from Vietnam.

On August 4, 1964, while cruising in heavy weather in the Gulf of Tonkin, American warships received radar, radio, and sonar reports that signaled a North Vietnamese attack. Taking evasive action, they fired on numerous radar targets. But, after the incident, the captain was not sure whether his ships had been attacked.

Subsequent research and declassified documents have shown that the information the Defense Department gave about this incident in the Gulf of Tonkin wasn't accurate. Thus began a pattern of misinformation that would continue throughout the long, drawn-out war as General William Westmoreland and other government officials who knew what was really happening evaded the truth.

In retaliation for the "attack," President Johnson ordered air strikes on the Viet Cong. He addressed the nation about the Gulf of Tonkin attack.

He asked that Congress pass the Southeast Asia (Gulf of Tonkin) Resolution giving him the power to use military force in the region without requiring a declaration of war.

Johnson promised he would not seek a "wider war," but that he would "continue to protect national interests."

The resolution was approved on August 10, 1964, and Johnson rapidly escalated American involvement in the Vietnam War.

The Gulf of Tonkin Resolution, which Congress passed with overwhelming support from both houses on August 14, 1964, was based on untruths— faulty intelligence reports distorted into sound bites of fake news. It authorized the president to take any necessary measures to repel attacks and prevent aggression against US forces in Vietnam.

Without a formal declaration of war, with a congressional resolution based on misinformation, and with subsequent military action exceeding authorization, warfare in Vietnam became an ever-more serious breach of the rule of law.

Only years later did we learn that Secretary of Defense McNamara apparently misled LBJ by failing to mention critical information about the Gulf of Tonkin attack. By deliberately withholding information, McNamara usurped President Johnson's constitutional power of decision on the use of military force.

Johnson suspected that he was being misled by overly hawkish foreign-policy and military leaders. For months he refused to bomb North Vietnam, despite calls to do so from both the CIA and the military. McNamara pushed for commando raids near the North Vietnamese coast, hoping another incident would persuade Johnson to act. When it looked like Johnson was getting ready to pull out of Vietnam, McNamara and McGeorge Bundy, the national security advisor, wrote Johnson a letter in late January 1965 making it clear that responsibility for US "humiliation" in South Vietnam would rest squarely on his shoulders if he continued his "passivity."

After LBJ's top advisors—McNamara, Maxwell Taylor, and Dean Rusk—recommended escalating the war, Johnson, afraid that his critics and the public would blame him for the loss of South Vietnam, began bombing North Vietnam.

By 1969, more than 500,000 US military personnel were stationed in Vietnam. Meanwhile, the Soviet Union and China poured weapons, supplies, and advisors into the north, which in turn provided support, political direction, and regular combat troops for the campaign in the south.

The Vietnam War destroyed Johnson's presidency, and by 1968 he had declared his intention not to seek reelection. Bobby F. Kennedy, a fierce opponent of the war that had started on his brother's watch, ran for president on an antiwar platform but was assassinated in June 1968. Vice President Hubert Humphrey, who out of loyalty to LBJ—or conviction—expressed support for most of Johnson's Vietnam policy, won the Democratic nomination in 1968. He was beaten by Republican Richard Nixon whose "dirty tricks" (see Chapter 11) included encouraging the South Vietnamese not to enter a peace agreement being pursued by the Johnson-Humphrey administration during the 1968 presidential campaign.

The costs and casualties of the growing war proved too much for the United States to bear, and US combat units were withdrawn by 1973. In 1975 South Vietnam fell to a full-scale invasion by the north.

Before the Vietnam War was over, official statistics put the number of American military personnel who died in or as a direct result of the war at 58,307. Millions of Vietnamese were killed and hundreds of thousands of American soldiers were wounded or suffered from post-traumatic stress disorder (PTSD). (In 2019 a survey showed that 67,000 former soldiers who fought in Vietnam were homeless.)

The Vietnam War itself was a breakdown in the rule of law. Congress should have been consulted and provided accurate information, and the military operations should only have gone to the extent authorized by Congress. On top of this, the United States confronted serious questions about whether the conduct of the Vietnam War conformed to international law and the terms of the UN charter. (The UN had authorized intervention in the Korean War but never authorized any country to intervene in Vietnam.)

What followed at home was a different breakdown in the rule of law. Many Americans—both Republicans and Democrats—also opposed the war, and some participated in public demonstrations. Most demonstrators were peaceful, including those led by clergy who believed the killing in Vietnam violated a higher law. But backlash against the war was sometimes violent. One group, SDS, the Students for a Democratic Society, vehemently protested the war. Some campuses had riots. And violent demonstrations led to violent police responses.

After President Johnson escalated the war, University of Wisconsin students protested against recruiters from Dow Chemical, the maker of napalm, in the fall of 1967. SDS and other antiwar groups coordinated a series of demonstrations against the draft. On October 21, 1967, more than a hundred thousand marched on the Pentagon.

The SDS began nighttime raids on draft offices to destroy records. A million students boycotted classes on April 26, after the SDS organized "Ten Days of Resistance" on college campuses.

By 1969 the organization had split into several factions, and the protest movement in some places focused on issues besides the war. The most notorious of these was the Weathermen, or the Weather Underground, which employed terrorist tactics. The group embraced violent revolutionary force. FBI investigations and criminal prosecutions followed.

Another divide brought on by the Vietnam War was far less violent but far more important. The war caused a rupture among religious groups—some opposing the war and others supporting it.

In May 1968 five men, including a Presbyterian minister and the Yale University chaplain, William Sloane Coffin Jr., were charged with conspiracy for encouraging Americans to evade the draft.

Some of Coffin's followers were motivated by moral outrage at the war, others by the mounting evidence that despite what our political leaders said, the United States appeared to be losing.

Younger ministers and divinity school students returned their draft cards. Other students soon followed. Some publicly burned their draft cards, incensing even more public outrage.

In the 1950s, 1960s, and 1970s, religious progressives in the vein of Martin Luther King Jr. and William Sloan Coffin appeared to have formidable influences on American democracy, injecting concepts of higher law into political discourse. Their causes included civil rights, fighting poverty, and opposing the war in Vietnam.

Conservative evangelical Protestant clergy and their parishioners, who had supported the war throughout, were horrified by their more liberal counterparts. They looked for a way to bring their own religion into politics. They were ready to take to the streets for their own cause. Photos of Vietnamese children running down the street covered with burning napalm did not move them. But photos of fetuses inside the womb did.

Finally, for young men called to war, there was a moral dilemma. Their three main options:

1. Protest the war and refuse to serve, risking jail and loss of future employment
2. Feign an illness to avoid serving, enjoy life, and remain silent while other men serve
3. Serve

Reverend William Sloan Coffin encouraged young men at Yale and others to choose the first option.

Donald Trump chose the second. Diagnosed with "bone spurs" by a foot doctor who happened to lease space from Trump's father, he stayed in Manhattan. Two decades later he brought up Vietnam in a 1997 radio interview with Howard Stern when asked how he avoided contracting STDs when having sex:

"It's amazing, I can't even believe it," he said. "I've been so lucky in terms of that whole world, it is a dangerous world out there. It's like Vietnam, sort of. It is my personal Vietnam. I feel like a great and very brave soldier."

Robert Mueller and his St. Paul's School hockey teammate John Kerry went to Vietnam.

Navy pilot John McCain went to Vietnam and was captured, imprisoned for six years, and tortured. When McCain returned on crutches, President Nixon greeted him as he deplaned. Forty years later in 2016, Donald Trump said of McCain, "He's not a war hero. He was a war hero because he was captured. I like people who weren't captured."

Several hundred thousand young Americans went to Vietnam. Over fifty thousand of them never returned.

CHAPTER 11

Tricky Dick and Dirty Tricks

Never forget, the press is the enemy. The establishment is
the enemy. The professors are the enemy. Professors are the
enemy. Write that on the blackboard and never forget it.
—RICHARD M. NIXON

MUCH HAS BEEN WRITTEN ABOUT NIXON AND WATERgate. We will point out highlights of Nixon's egregious assaults on the rule of law, and how Congress responded by opening an impeachment inquiry and voting on articles of impeachment before he resigned the presidency in August of 1974.

Richard Nixon made his political career with McCarthyism. In 1946, Nixon, a former navy officer, ran for the House of Representatives against incumbent Jerry Voorhis, a liberal Democrat who had supported Franklin Roosevelt's New Deal. Nixon's campaign stressed that Voorhis, a staunch anti-communist, had "radical left-wing views." Voorhis accused the Nixon campaign of making anonymous phone calls to voters alleging that he was a communist. Nixon won by 15,000 votes.

Nixon joined the House Un-American Activities Committee, and he gained notoriety going after a state department official named Alger Hiss.

Intelligence experts and historians to this day dispute whether Hiss was a Russian spy. What we do know is that the Hiss case propelled Richard Nixon to the front ranks of politics.

In 1950 Nixon ran against Democratic candidate Helen Douglas to become one of California's US senators. It was a dirty race filled with nasty name-calling and character assassination. Nixon referred to her "communist sympathies"; questioned the loyalty of her Jewish husband, actor Melvyn Douglas; and printed her votes in Congress on a pink sheet.

When Douglas appeared at USC, members of the Skull and Dagger fraternity doused her with water and threw hay at her (some members of this same fraternity—Donald Segretti, Gordon Strachan, Dwight Chapin, and Herb Kalmbach—were later part of the team of "dirty tricksters" who helped Nixon with his presidential campaigns).

The Nixon campaign made 500,000 phone calls calling Douglas a communist.

Douglas referred to Nixon as "Tricky Dick," a nickname that stuck for the rest of his political career. During a campaign speech, Douglas called Nixon "a young man with a dark shirt," a sly reference to the Nazis.

Nixon's response: "I'll castrate her."

In subsequent rallies Nixon repeated that Douglas was "pink right down to her underwear." Through the final days of the campaign, Nixon continually accused her of being soft on communism.

Nixon defeated Douglas by 59 percent to 41 percent.

Nixon was President Eisenhower's vice president from 1953 to 1961 and won the Republican nomination to run for president in 1960. Nixon narrowly lost to John F. Kennedy in 1960. After Kennedy was assassinated and Lyndon Johnson became president, Nixon had a second chance at the presidency when Johnson announced he would not run for a second term because of the criticism he was getting over Vietnam.

By 1968 the war had been going strong for four years, and the backlash was growing. Johnson decided to open up peace talks.

Nixon knew that if Johnson ended the war before the election, Democratic candidate Vice President Hubert Humphrey would probably win. Nixon set out to make sure that didn't happen.

He told the American public he had a "secret plan to win the war," and then through a fund-raiser named Anna Chennault, he sent a message to South Vietnam president Nguyen Van Thieu. If Thieu waited until *after* the election, he, Nixon, could get Thieu a better deal for South Vietnam.

Thieu, who figured he could make a deal with either candidate, at the last minute backed out of the peace talks.

President Johnson was alerted by NSA wiretaps of Nixon's enticement to Thieu, but he didn't want Thieu to know the NSA had been listening in to his conversations, so he didn't call him on it. Johnson told Humphrey what Nixon had done, but Humphrey was so certain he'd win the election that he saw no need to accuse Nixon of violating the Logan Act during the campaign. The Logan Act prohibits a private citizen without authorization from conducting diplomacy on behalf of the United States.

At the same time Nixon was criticizing Johnson for not making more progress with peace negotiations.

After winning the election, Nixon revealed that his plan to win the war was to escalate bombing in the north and expand the war into Laos and Cambodia.

This extension resulted in the deaths of over 22,000 additional Americans and more than a million Vietnamese.

Johnson's national security team had written a classified dossier about Nixon's actions. Walt Rostow, Johnson's national security aide, was ordered to hide the dossier. When Nixon found out about the document from FBI Director J. Edgar Hoover, he ordered White House chief of staff H. R. "Bob" Haldeman and Henry Kissinger to find it. They were unsuccessful, and the possibility that one day the public might find out about the trick weighed on his mind when, in June 1971, the *New York Times* published the first installment of the *Pentagon Papers*.

These papers had originated with President Johnson's secretary of defense Bob McNamara, who requested that a team working for the Department of Defense put together a highly classified analysis of the American political and military involvement in wars from the end of World War II to 1969.

The study was completed in 1969 and was bound in forty-seven volumes. Three thousand pages of material showed beyond a doubt that the military brass had been lying to the public about the Vietnam War since the beginning.

One of the men who worked on the report was Daniel Ellsberg, a Marine Corps officer employed by the RAND Corporation and the Department of Defense. By 1969 Ellsberg, knowing the truth, felt the war was unwinnable. He decided he would show the American people why it was unwinnable, and after he secretly photocopied large swaths of the report, he approached several members of Congress, who brushed him off. Frustrated, he gave parts of it to Neil Sheehan, a *New York Times* reporter.

Starting on June 13, 1969, the *Times* published these excerpts on the front page. After the third article ran, the Justice Department got a restraining order to stop further publication. The *Washington Post* joined the *Times*, arguing that under the First Amendment they had every right to publish the information. The Supreme Court voted six to three in their favor.

Americans were horrified to see how much they had been misled about the conflict in Vietnam in the Truman, Eisenhower, Kennedy, and Johnson administrations. However, no president had wanted the information from the *Pentagon Papers* quashed more than Richard Nixon, because in those papers was the story of how Nixon had sabotaged a peace summit just so he could be elected president.

One of Nixon's aides believed the dossier was hidden in a safe at the Brookings Institution, a center-left think tank in Washington. Nixon ordered a break-in at the institute to find that dossier.

And Nixon went after Ellsberg.

"Get Colson in," Nixon instructed his chief of staff in a taped meeting in the Oval Office on June 17, 1971. "He's the best. It's the Colson type of man that you need."

To assist him in "nailing" Ellsberg, Charles Colson, a top Nixon aide, recruited a retired CIA operative and novelist named E. Howard Hunt. Hunt teamed up with former FBI agent G. Gordon Liddy and a group of right-wing Cuban émigrés to burglarize the office of Ellsberg's psychiatrist Lewis Fielding and gain information about the man who leaked the *Pentagon Papers*.

To make sure no one found the dossier, they planned to firebomb the Brookings Institution. John Dean, the White House counsel, said he heard

Nixon "literally pounding on his desk, saying, 'I want that break-in at the Brookings [Institution].'" Colson suggested that while firefighters tried to douse the fire caused by a bomb, operatives could rush in and seize the papers.

John Ehrlichman, White House domestic affairs advisor, told John Dean, "Chuck Colson wants me to firebomb the Brookings [Institution]."

Replied Dean, "John, this is absolute insanity. People could die. This is absurd."

The firebombing was scrubbed, but the dossier has still never been found.

When it came time, Nixon vowed he would do anything to make sure his reelection would be a runaway. The Nixon campaign earmarked hundreds of thousands of dollars for an extensive undercover campaign to hurt the reputations of the more centrist—and electable—Democratic candidates including Edmund Muskie. The best example of the sabotage was a letter to the editor of the New Hampshire *Union Leader* saying that Muskie condoned the use of the word "Canucks," a racial slur on French Canadians. The letter was published two weeks before the New Hampshire primary, prompting Muskie to call a press conference in front of the newspaper's office in which he began to cry, ending his chances to be president. Later, Ken Clawson, deputy director of White House communications, admitted writing the letter. He subsequently denied it.

Nixon's dirty tricksters sent a mass mailing to Democrats in New Hampshire urging them to write in Ted Kennedy as their presidential candidate. They also sent a mass mailing to Democratic voters in Florida claiming Muskie was for forced busing, against FBI Director J. Edgar Hoover, and was against the space shuttle.

Federal investigations found that at least fifty of Nixon's men, working under assumed names as part of Nixon's "security offensive," followed Democratic candidates' families and compiled dossiers of their private lives; forged letters and distributed them under the candidate's letterhead; leaked false items to the press; seized confidential campaign files; and investigated dozens of Democratic campaign workers. They also sent provocateurs to demonstrations at both the Democratic and Republican conventions. Nixon and his White House chief of staff H. R. Haldeman even discussed sending campaign contributions to Jesse Jackson, a prominent African American minister who had marched with Martin Luther King, in an attempt to get him to run for president as an independent.

All this took place even *before* the Watergate incident, when on June 17, 1972, security guard Frank Wills of the Watergate Hotel in Washington, DC, discovered that the Democratic headquarters had been broken into. The police arrested five men recruited by E. Howard Hunt: James McCord, a former FBI and CIA agent, who was security coordinator for the Republican National Committee and the Committee to Re-elect the President; Virgilio Gonzales, a locksmith from Miami; Frank Sturgis, who had CIA connections; Eugenio Martinez, who had CIA connections; and Bernard Barker, a former CIA operative. The five men were arrested in the Watergate complex and charged with attempted burglary and attempted interception of telephone and other communications.

The FBI discovered a connection between cash found on the burglars and a slush fund used by the Committee to Re-elect the President. On September 15, 1972, the five burglars were indicted by a grand jury along with Liddy, a former FBI agent, treasury official, and counsel to the Committee to Re-elect the President, and Hunt, a former White House consultant and CIA employee.

More investigations ensued, which were largely the result of reporting by Bob Woodward and Carl Bernstein in the *Washington Post*.

Congress stepped in, exercising its right and indeed duty under the Constitution to oversee activities in the executive branch. Although Congress was controlled by the Democrats, most Republicans did not try to sabotage the investigation. Many Republicans participated in the investigation, and while many of them were skeptical about claims of presidential wrongdoing, and some spoke in defense of the president, political attacks on the investigation were relatively few—and *nobody* dared attack the FBI.

In February 1973, the Senate established a committee to investigate the Watergate scandal. In July, evidence mounted against the president's staff, including testimony provided by former staff members. The Senate's investigation revealed that Nixon had a secret tape-recording system in his offices and that he had recorded his conversations.

It almost didn't happen. The man who told the committee about the tapes, Alexander Butterfield, had ordered the Secret Service to install a voice-activated taping system in the Oval Office in February 1971. When the Senate committee published the list of people it intended to question, Butterfield's name wasn't on it. Butterfield had left the White House and was heading the Federal Aviation Administration, relieved that he wasn't going to be called.

Then in July 1973 he was called for a pre-interview. A Republican, he didn't want to tell them about the tape recorder, but he didn't want to lie. He volunteered that he knew about the Dictaphone machine of Rose Mary Woods, Nixon's secretary.

"Were there ever any recording devices other than the Dictaphone system you mentioned?" he was asked.

"Yes," he said.

That one word changed the course of American history.

In front of the Senate select committee on national TV, Butterfield testified that Nixon had a taping system in the Oval Office. Eight months later, he was fired from the FAA.

Archibald Cox had been appointed the special prosecutor to look into whether the president was involved in the break-in, and in July 1973 he issued a subpoena to get Nixon to turn over the secret tapes.

Nixon refused, invoking executive privilege. He was so sure he would win, that when it was suggested that Nixon burn the tapes, he refused. He wanted to use them for memoirs.

Cox went to the court of appeals, which ruled on October 12, 1973, that the president had to turn them over.

At this point, a cornered Nixon wanted Cox gone. On October 15, 1973, Nixon tried to make a deal with Cox's boss, Attorney General Elliot Richardson. He said he would fully disclose the contents of the tapes to a federal judge. John Stennis, a Democratic senator from Mississippi, would corroborate.

Four days later Nixon appealed to the public, saying this was a reasonable compromise.

"I believe that by these actions I have taken today America will be spared the anguish of further indecision and litigation about the tapes," Nixon wrote.

The next day, October 20, 1973, Richardson was called to a meeting at the Justice Department. Nixon had ordered him to fire Cox. He refused. He said he would resign as attorney general.

It now fell to Deputy Attorney General William Ruckelshaus to fire Cox, and Ruckelshaus also refused.

Said Ruckelshaus to Alexander Haig Jr., White House chief of staff, who made the request on behalf of Nixon, "Not if I think he's fundamentally wrong, which I do. Then my obligation is higher than just him."

"Your commander in chief has given you an order," said Haig.

But Ruckelshaus told himself he would fire Cox only for gross improprieties or malfeasance in office, and Cox had done neither.

Ruckelshaus wrote a letter saying his conscience would not allow him to fire Cox.

Conflicting reports questioned whether Ruckelshaus had resigned or was fired.

Ruckelshaus chose to say he had resigned.

The next in line to fire Cox was Robert Bork, the US solicitor general, and he carried out Haig's orders. (When Bork was nominated for the Supreme Court in 1987, the Senate refused to confirm him, in part because of this involvement.)

The events of the evening would become known as "the Saturday Night Massacre."

That night, Cox issued a statement: "Whether ours shall continue to be a government of laws and not of men is now for Congress and ultimately the American people."

The issue of whether Nixon had to turn over his tapes went to the United States Supreme Court, which ruled unanimously in favor of the federal investigators. The tapes proved that Nixon had attempted to cover up his role in the break-in and foil the investigation itself.

Faced with impeachment in the House of Representatives and a conviction in the Senate, on August 9, 1974, Nixon resigned as president. A month later his successor, Gerald Ford, pardoned him.

The overlooked story in the glare of the Watergate scandal was how the modern Justice Department was founded. Two idealistic men, Edward Levi and Griffin Bell, the first two attorneys general appointed after Watergate—Levi by Gerald Ford and Bell by Jimmy Carter—decided that they would change the department, making it more apolitical and independent of the executive branch.

Levi saw that Nixon, like other presidents, used his power to weaponize the Justice Department against his enemies. Bell saw how J. Edgar Hoover had used his power to go after leaders of the civil rights movement, especially Martin Luther King. Hoover had bugged King's phone conversations and used them to try to destroy King's marriage.

Levi and Bell wanted to keep the White House from being able to get involved in criminal prosecutions. They were largely successful, the legacy of their work lasting for over forty years.

Not until the Trump administration has a president again used the Justice Department as a weapon to protect his friends or to pursue political enemies. In a few short months in 2019, however, much of the work of Levi and Bell to depoliticize the Justice Department was undermined by Attorney General William Barr, a story that we tell in Chapter 29.

There were some other things we didn't have to worry about in 1974. At least the corrupt politicians during the Vietnam and Watergate era were loyal enough Americans that they did not collude with hostile foreign powers. Many of them had used hostility to the USSR—and public fear of Russian schemes to undermine Western democracies—to propel themselves to the top of the political heap. We didn't have to worry about them colluding with the Russians.

Nixon's dirty tricksters did everything possible to sabotage Senator Edmund Muskie and other electable centrist candidates to prevent them from getting the 1972 Democratic nomination. But the president never got on the phone with a foreign leader asking for an investigation of Muskie or of anyone else. Dirty tricks were domestic tricks.

The Watergate break-in was a third-rate burglary motivated by the corrupt political operation determined to reelect President Nixon, but at least it was not a KGB break-in job.

Nixon was a crook, but at least he was *our* crook.

CHAPTER 12

Iran Contra

We need an independent media to hold people like me to account.
—GEORGE W. BUSH

AFTER PRESIDENT NIXON RESIGNED, VICE PRESIDENT Gerald Ford was sworn in that same day. Ford had been named vice president eight months earlier after Spiro Agnew was forced to resign. Agnew had been accused of extortion, bribery, and income tax violations going back to when he was governor of Maryland. He took more than $100,000 in illegal payments from contractors both as governor and as vice president. With Nixon in line for impeachment, it would not have looked good to have an indicted Agnew succeed him.

Agnew's lawyers argued his innocence and that a sitting vice president could not be indicted, that the only way he could be removed was impeachment. But prosecutors made a compelling argument that he *could* be indicted, and on October 10, 1973, after a secret plea-bargain, Agnew copped to one count of income tax evasion and resigned. He paid a fine and was on unsupervised probation for three years.

Gerald Ford, who Nixon named to replace Agnew, was the only man in history to serve as president *and* vice president without ever being elected.

Ford had always said he never wanted to be president. He had spent twenty-four years in the House and never wanted to leave. He was chosen to replace the disgraced Agnew because Congress wanted an honest and admired man. Ford, the minority leader in the House, was highly respected. After the turmoil of the Nixon and Agnew presidency, Ford brought the country integrity and honesty.

One of Ford's first acts upon assuming the presidency was pardoning Richard Nixon for his criminal enterprise. The pardon was absolute. Nixon could not be tried for his crimes.

As a result of the Watergate investigation, forty government officials were either indicted or imprisoned. Those jailed included Nixon's right-hand men H. R. Haldeman and John Ehrlichman, his White House counsel John Dean, attorney general John Mitchell, and two men involved in the break-in, Howard Hunt and G. Gordon Liddy.

Had Ford not pardoned him, Nixon well might have stood trial for his crimes. He would have been held responsible for obstructing justice and perhaps other violations.

Most important for us today—a Nixon trial for obstruction of justice in the 1970s would have provided an answer to that very question that faced Robert Mueller in 2019 when Attorney General Barr told him that President Trump could not be criminally charged for obstruction of justice. When can a president, as head of the executive branch, lawfully obstruct an investigation in the executive branch? Does the "unitary executive" theory or any other sweeping concept of presidential power make it impossible to ever charge a president with obstructing a federal investigation? Or is such a theory of executive power inconsistent with the founders' intent that no man—not even the president—should be above the law?

Nixon was never tried, so the federal courts never had to give an answer.

Robert Mueller's 2019 report, which we discuss in Chapter 30, strongly suggests that a president *can* be criminally charged for obstructing a Justice Department investigation by abusing his presidential power, but it reaches no definitive conclusion on that question because Mueller was required to defer to Attorney General Barr on that other open question raised in the 1973 Spiro Agnew case—whether a sitting president or vice president can be charged for any crime before leaving office. A trial of Richard Nixon after he left office at least would have addressed the "obstruction of justice" question, and a Nixon criminal conviction might have served as a warning to future presidents not to abuse their power in this way.

But because of Ford's pardon, the Nixon trial never happened.

In the end, Ford granted Nixon a pardon because, as he said, he wanted the national nightmare of Watergate to be over.

Ford didn't want to polarize the public, but the pardon probably lost him the presidential election to Jimmy Carter in 1976.

Carter was very open about his Christianity. He emphasized morality and ethics, and he tried hard to live up to expectations. But even his administration had some pitfalls.

One of his appointees, Bert Lance, his director of the Office of Management and Budget, was indicted for financial improprieties in running a Georgia bank. He resigned. At trial Lance was found not guilty.

The biggest crisis of Carter's presidency wasn't of his own doing. The seeds of the Iranian crisis had been planted years before.

Mohammad Reza Pahlavi, the shah of Iran, an American ally since he took over the country in 1941, had gradually become a tyrannical dictator. The Russians during World War II occupied parts of Iran. So did Allied forces. Both the Russians and the Allies agreed to withdraw from Iran within six months after the end of the war. However, when this deadline came in early 1946, the Soviets stayed, and local pro-Soviet Iranians proclaimed a separatist People's Republic of Azerbaijan. In late 1945, the Republic of Mahabad also was formed by Kurdish separatists.

A crisis in Iran occurred in 1953 when the shah attempted to fire Prime Minister Mossadegh, who was in the thrall of the Russians. Mohammad Mossadegh was popular, and his supporters tried to throw the shah out. Not a week later, American and British forces staged a coup against Mossadegh, returning the shah to power as the sole leader of Iran.

In an attempt to make his country more Western, the shah in 1963 began a government program that included infrastructure development, land reform, women's suffrage, and illiteracy reduction. His "White Revolution" was virulently criticized by ultra-conservative mullahs, the Islamic leaders. Ruhollah Khomeini, a Shiite cleric, called for the overthrow of the shah. The shah exiled Khomeini to neighboring Iraq.

As religious discontent grew in Iran, the shah became more repressive. He used his secret police, SAVAK, which was formed under CIA guidance in 1957 and trained by Israel's Mossad.

In 1978, public demonstrations against the shah broke out in major cities in Iran, and on September 8, 1978, the shah's security guards fired on a crowd of protesters, killing hundreds and wounding thousands. Two months later, the people rioted, destroying symbols of the West including banks and liquor stores.

On December 11, 1978, a group of soldiers mutinied, attacking the shah and his security forces. The shah fled.

On November 4, 1979, Islamic militants stormed the US embassy and captured the fifty-two Americans inside. With Khomeini now in charge of the country, the militants demanded in exchange for the Americans the return of the shah so he could stand trial for his crimes.

President Carter refused to negotiate, and the situation escalated when Carter allowed the shah to come to the United States to be treated for cancer.

On April 24, 1980, Carter tried to free the American hostages. He sent the aircraft carrier USS *Nimitz* into Iranian waters. Eight attack helicopters landed in a remote desert in Iran. The pilots weren't informed of a severe sandstorm, and two of the helicopters were disabled. When a third helicopter experienced hydraulic system failure, the mission, which was already in jeopardy, was called off. As the remaining helicopters refueled, one ran into a C-130 cargo plane, killing eight servicemen and injuring several others.

When the failure became public, Khomeini said it was the work of God. President Carter went on television and explained what had gone wrong, probably ending any chances for his reelection.

The captured Americans remained prisoners for 444 days while Carter continued to negotiate for their release, and Khomeini refused to let them go so long as Carter was president.

On January 20, 1981, as Ronald Reagan gave his inaugural address to the nation, Khomeini put the hostages on a plane in Tehran and allowed them to leave.

What followed was a conspiracy theory that Ronald Reagan had conspired with Khomeini to influence the American presidential election. Jimmy Carter called for an investigation, but no evidence of collusion was found.

The collusion theory was allowed to die.

Then in 1986, the Iran-Contra scandal broke. The Reagan administration was accused of doing what it denied in 1981. It was reportedly selling arms to Iran at inflated prices and taking the profits to arm the Reagan- and CIA-backed Contras in Nicaragua against the socialist Sandinista regime. The Sandinistas, named after Augusto César Sandino, a Nicaraguan general and rebel leader, assassinated President Anastasio Somoza and took control of the Nicaraguan government in 1979. The Contras, backed by the United States, fought them for control during the 1980s.

No part of the arms-for-the-Contras deal was in any way legal. Arms sales to Iran were prohibited, and it was illegal to fund the Contras above congressionally set limits.

After Congress in 1984 approved the Boland Amendment, barring military aid to the Contras, Reagan administration officials didn't hide their disdain for the law. Oliver North, a National Security Council staff member, was in charge of arranging "private" funding for the Contras. North had drafted a memo to bypass the Boland Amendment, and Reagan approved the request.

North then recruited John Singlaub, a former general, to raise the money. Two former CIA officers, Donald Gregg and Nestor Sanchez, also were involved.

A Beirut weekly newspaper revealed that National Security Advisor Robert McFarlane was meeting with Iranian representatives to sell them anti-tank weapons. (Meanwhile, the Reagan administration accused Iran of sponsoring terrorism.)

When Reagan confirmed the McFarlane meeting, reporters immediately saw the connection between that meeting and the sales of arms to the Contras.

The United States was secretly selling arms to Iran and using the proceeds to fund the Contra war in Nicaragua.

The Reagan administration had broken the law.

Reagan's reputation suffered, and Oliver North became a household name. Senator John Kerry led an investigation that proved that Contra gunrunners were also smuggling drugs to the United States.

Eleven members of the Reagan administration were convicted of criminal charges. Among them, Secretary of Defense Caspar Weinberger was indicted on five counts of perjury and false statements about a secret shipment of Hawk missiles to Iran. He was sentenced to five years in prison for each count and fined $250,000.

Oliver North was charged and found guilty on twelve felony counts. He was sentenced to a three-year suspended prison term, two years' probation, $150,000 in fines, and 1,200 hours of community service.

John Poindexter, national security advisor to the Reagan administration, was found guilty of five criminal charges including conspiracy, false statements, and destruction and removal of documents. He was sentenced to six months in prison on each count to be served concurrently. A year later the verdict was reversed in appellate court, and the indictment dismissed.

McFarlane pleaded guilty to four counts of withholding information from Congress. Elliott Abrams pled guilty to two counts of the same. Clair George was found guilty of two felony charges of making false statements to Congress. Richard Miller pled guilty to one felony count of conspiracy to defraud the United States.

Maj. Gen. Richard Secord was charged in the Iran-Contra affair in 1987 and on March 16, 1988, was indicted on six felony charges. Secord pled guilty to one felony count of false statements to Congress and was sentenced to two years' probation. In 1992 the Federal District Court for the District of Columbia expunged the conviction on the grounds that the US Supreme Court had earlier found the underlying indictment to be illegal and without effect. The Justice Department did not oppose the matter. For Secord, the Iran-Contra brouhaha was over.

After his indictment, Secord started a legal defense fund. Shortly thereafter, an Iranian arms dealer transferred $500,000 from a secret Swiss bank account into the fund.

In a congressional investigation, Secord said he wasn't sure exactly where the funds had come from but said they were from acquaintances outraged by what the committee was doing to him.

Noel Koch, a former Pentagon anti-terrorism expert, resigned because of the mysterious windfall. He told a congressional committee investigating the Iran-Contra affair he didn't know who made the contribution or whether Secord had any connection to the Swiss bank account. But, he said, the money "had a peculiar odor to it."

CIA Director William Casey undoubtedly would have been criminally charged, but he died in 1987 before charges could be brought.

In his book, *Under Fire*, published in 1991, Oliver North wrote that "Ronald Reagan knew of and approved a great deal of what went on with both the Iranian initiative and private efforts on behalf of the contras and he received regular, detailed briefings on both." North also wrote: "I have no doubt that he was told about the use of residuals for the contras, and that he approved it. Enthusiastically."

In response, Reagan denied any knowledge of the Iran-Contra scandal.

"I cannot recall virtually any specific details of the affair," Reagan said in a deposition.

On Christmas Day 1992, President George H. W. Bush, who had succeeded Reagan as president in 1989, pardoned six of the Iran-Contra defendants (some already convicted and some awaiting trial) including Elliott Abrams, Robert McFarlane, and Caspar Weinberger. President Bush issued the pardons on the advice of Attorney General William Barr (the same William Barr who again was appointed as attorney general in 2019 by President Trump).

Independent prosecutor Lawrence Walsh saw the pardons as a way for Bush to keep himself from being implicated. Walsh charged that despite several requests, then–Vice President Bush had refused to turn over his diaries and other notes.

"The Iran-Contra cover-up, which has continued for more than six years, has now been completed," said Walsh bitterly.

Bush complained that the Walsh investigation and prosecution reflected "a profoundly troubling development in the political and legal climate of our country: the criminalization of political differences."

He concluded, "The proper forum is the voting booth, not the courtroom."

Bush said he pardoned the men "to put the bitterness behind us."

In a statement, independent counsel Walsh commented, "President Bush's pardon of Caspar Weinberger and other Iran-Contra defendants undermines the principle that no man is above the law. It demonstrates that powerful people with powerful allies can commit serious crimes in high office—deliberately abusing the public trust without consequence."

CHAPTER 13

The Clinton Impeachment

*This great nation can tolerate a president who makes mistakes, but it cannot
tolerate one who makes a mistake and then breaks the law to cover it up.*
*—ORRIN HATCH, AFTER PRESIDENT BILL CLINTON WAS
ACCUSED OF LYING UNDER OATH*

IN NOVEMBER 1992 THE COUNTRY ELECTED AS PRESIDENT
Bill Clinton, the Democratic governor of Arkansas.

One of his most important initiatives, the Clinton healthcare proposal,
failed in a Democratic-controlled Congress in 1993 and 1994. Instead of consulting with powerful members of Congress early on (including Massachusetts
senator Ted Kennedy who tried several times to be president himself), Clinton put First Lady Hillary Clinton in charge of drafting a healthcare bill. Her
team kept Congress in the dark during much of the process. This approach
alienated powerful Democrats as well as Republicans, giving the insurance
industry a chance to mount an aggressive advertising campaign against what
would become known as "Hillary Care." And so the demonization of Hillary Clinton—a nonstop barrage of attacks mostly but not exclusively from
right-wing media outlets—began, and continues to this day.

Republicans took control of both houses of Congress only two years into the Clinton presidency in 1994 by gaining eight Senate seats and fifty-four House seats. It was the first time since 1954 that control switched parties in both chambers.

When Newt Gingrich became the Speaker of the House, he set the new Republican majority on a platform of confrontation. No longer would Republicans and Democrats try to find common ground. With Gingrich in the lead, this was *war* for the heart of America. Every day, every week, and every month of every year was to be treated as if it were Election Day. Governing was an afterthought.

In 1990, a conservative organization called GOPAC issued a memo entitled "Language: A Key Mechanism of Control." Gingrich wrote the introduction. The premise was to teach Republicans to "speak like Newt," using "optimistic positive governing" language to describe Republican policies—words like truth, courage, reform, prosperity, crusade, family, challenge, and opportunity—while using negative language to describe what the Democrats believed: words like failure, crisis, destroy, sick, pathetic, liberal, and decay.

According to the memo, the ideas and language had been tested in focus groups.

What set Gingrich apart was his penchant for anti-establishment rhetoric. This was nihilistic talk that harkened back to earlier populists whose goal was to destroy the status quo and take over. He also became adept at disinformation. Gingrich was much more like Louisiana Democratic senator Huey Long in the 1930s than the Republican leaders who had preceded him: Eisenhower, Nixon, Reagan, George H. W. Bush, and earlier Republican politicians.

Gingrich, a former college professor, loved to quote from philosophers Clausewitz and Camus, but it was his penchant for lobbing grenades at his enemies that propelled him through the Republican ranks.

In a 1985 Indiana House election, Gingrich ratcheted up the rhetoric with comparisons to the Holocaust.

"We have talked a lot in recent weeks about the Holocaust, about the incredible period in which Nazi Germany killed millions of people and, in particular, came close to wiping out European Jewry," Gingrich said. "Someone said to me two days ago, talking frankly about the McIntyre affair [in which Democrats refused to seat the winner of a House race until they'd conducted a recount] and the efforts by the Democratic leadership not to allow the people of Indiana to have their representative but, instead, to impose upon them somebody else, something in which he quotes [German poet Martin] Niemöller, and I have never quite until tonight been able to link it together—Niemöller, the great German theologian, said, 'When the Nazis came for the Jews, I did nothing . . . and when the Nazis came for me, there was no one left.'"

In 1987, when the Democrats had the majority in the House, Gingrich took to the podium and declared: "After the first five months of this Congress, I must report to my fellow citizens that this one hundredth Congress may be the most irresponsible, destructive, corrupt, and unrepresentative Congress of the modern era . . . In future weeks, I will make a series of speeches outlining the threats of corruption, of communism, and of the left-wing machine which runs the House."

Two years later he said of the Democrats, "The left-wing Democrats will represent the party of total hedonism, total exhibitionism, total bizarreness, total weirdness, and the total right to cripple innocent people in the name of letting hooligans loose." He also said of congressional Democrats, "These people are sick. They are so consumed by their own power, by a Mussolini-like ego, that their willingness to run over normal human beings and to destroy honest institutions is unending."

If the Democrats weren't stopped, he warned, "We may literally see our freedom decay and decline."

A year later, the GOPAC memo was published.

Gingrich's most telling comment came when he said, "People like me stand between us and Auschwitz. I see evil all around me every day."

Of course, he was talking about his political opponents—the Democrats and moderate Republicans who loathed his demagoguery.

With control of the House, Gingrich and the Republicans sought to discredit President Clinton in any way they could. Clinton's careless approach to personal and government ethics gave Gingrich and his allies plenty of ammunition.

Soon after Bill Clinton became president, in May 1993, First Lady Hillary Clinton apparently wanted to replace seven members of the White House travel office with her own people. The travel office handled arrangements for the press corps. In any other political climate, the switch would have gone unnoticed, but nothing was too small for anti-Clinton Republicans to investigate. Following the complaints of those fired, the FBI interviewed Hillary Clinton and had Independent Counsel Robert Ray investigate whether to bring perjury charges. The "Travelgate" firings were unwise, but hardly illegal.

The pursuit of Hillary Clinton was classic. First she was accused of wrongdoing for a foolish act that was not illegal. The allegations made headlines, and her pursuers spoke of possible criminal wrongdoing. She was grilled, having to answer embarrassing questions under oath. The intent was to catch her in a misstatement, no matter how trivial, so she could be accused of lying. The tactic was part of Gingrich's take-no-prisoners strategy.

Hillary Clinton was forced to hand over more than 55,000 pages of documents. She denied having any role in the firings, and the independent investigator could not find evidence to prove she had lied.

The government had spent six years and $60 million trying to build a case against her. It would not be the last time that the FBI would clear Hillary Clinton of wrongdoing in an investigation that also successfully smeared her.

Other scandals followed that reflected bad judgment by Clinton administration officials but were greatly exaggerated by Clinton's opponents.

The gunshot death of White House aide Vincent Foster in Fort Marcy Park in Virginia in July 1993 had conservative interest groups screaming that Bill and Hillary Clinton had probably murdered him to keep him from testifying about Travelgate and other "scandals."

Robert Fiske Jr., a moderate Republican, was named special counsel by Attorney General Janet Reno, and his investigation involved 4 lawyers, 5 physicians, 7 FBI agents, 89 subpoenas, approximately 125 witnesses; also DNA tests, microscopes, and lasers.

All that effort resolved many of the lingering mysteries surrounding Foster's death. Vince Foster had committed suicide. The Clintons had no involvement in the tragedy, regardless of the wishful thinking of conspiracists.

But the largest mystery remained: Why did the slings and arrows of Washington life prove fatal for Vincent W. Foster Jr.?

Foster's note left in his briefcase offered an answer: "I was not meant for a job or the spotlight of public life in Washington. Here ruining people is considered a sport."

The Whitewater "scandal" started as an investigation of a real estate deal and ended in Bill Clinton's impeachment for something entirely different. The story is so convoluted and circuitous that a novelist who made it up would be mocked.

This real estate scandal went back to the time when Bill Clinton was attorney general of Arkansas and then governor. Hillary Clinton was an attorney in the Rose Law Firm in Little Rock. While investing in cattle futures, she made $100,000 in less than a year. An investigation into her trades found no evidence of any violations. In that same year, 1978, Bill and Hillary formed the Whitewater Development Corporation with James and Susan McDougal. The plan was to buy and sell off 230 acres of riverfront land for vacation homes. James McDougal was an old friend, and Bill didn't have to put up any money up front. McDougal paid $203,000 for the land. McDougal and Clinton jointly took out a loan for $180,000. McDougal took out a second loan to make the down payment.

The land was on a swamp, and the investment was a disaster. James McDougal bought a small savings and loan association, which he named Madison Guaranty, and he defrauded both the bank and a small business investment firm of $3 million.

The president of Capital Management Services, that small business investment firm, claimed Bill Clinton was in on the conspiracy. James McDougal himself would allege they were in on it together.

The McDougals were found guilty of fraud, as were thirteen other people. But after months of investigation, independent investigator Robert Fiske Jr. could not establish wrongdoing by either Bill or Hillary Clinton.

Robert Fiske Jr., who was also the independent counsel in the Travelgate case, investigated the Whitewater case for six months. His report at the end of that case said there was "no evidence that issues involving Whitewater, or other personal legal matters of the president or Mrs. Clinton, were a factor in Foster's suicide."

At this point the Republicans howled that Fiske was "unfit for the job."

Years later Fiske said that had he not been replaced, he would have pursued a case against Bill Clinton from testimony by David Hale, a former municipal judge and the owner of the small-business lending company. Hale claimed that Clinton, while Arkansas governor, had pressured him to make a fraudulent $300,000 federally backed loan to a marketing company owned by Susan McDougal that was really intended to pay off the Whitewater real estate investment debt.

"My name can't show up on this," Hale claimed Clinton told him, an account that President Clinton later denied.

Defenders of the Clintons have long depicted Hale as an inveterate liar in the pocket of the Republicans.

Hale was also a confessed felon who had pleaded guilty to defrauding the government.

"Standing alone, nobody was going to bring a case based on what he was telling us," Fiske said. He needed corroboration.

"But from what we had seen of him, we thought the story was plausible and was certainly worth pursuing," said Fiske.

Cries of foot-dragging brought an end to Fiske's investigation. Fiske was replaced by an activist conservative, a former federal appeals judge named Kenneth Starr.

In December 1997, Starr closed down the Whitewater investigation for lack of evidence. A month later, he reopened it with a different focus: Bill Clinton's long-standing reputation for lurid sexual conduct.

Republicans thus took a page from the handbook of the Clarence Thomas–Anita Hill battle and Democrats' efforts to make sexual harassment a political issue in the 1992 elections. As soon as Bill Clinton was put at the top of the Democratic ticket in 1992, Republicans knew they would have a field day alleging sexual harassment, which can be a political weapon.

Clinton's enemies—those in the private sector led by, among others, Pittsburgh billionaire Richard Mellon Scaife, and those in the independent counsel's office led by Ken Starr—intended to use sexual harassment allegations to destroy Clinton's presidency.

Paula Jones, an Arkansas clerk, filed a lawsuit against Bill Clinton in federal court in Little Rock, accusing him of sexual harassment and asking for

$700,000 in damages. Jones claimed that when Clinton was governor, he sexually harassed her and then defamed her after she went public with her accusations.

Susan Carpenter-McMillan, a California conservative commentator, became her press spokesperson. Carpenter-McMillan wasted no time bringing the issue to the press, calling Clinton "un-American," a "liar," and a "philanderer" on *Meet the Press, Crossfire, Equal Time, Larry King Live, Today, The Geraldo Rivera Show, Burden of Proof, Hannity & Colmes, Talkback Live*, and other shows.

"I do not respect a man who cheats on his wife, and exposes his penis to a stranger," she said.

Paula Jones's lawsuit was financed by Scaife, a billionaire Republican and economic libertarian. Scaife's $1.8 million gift to *The American Spectator* funded investigations into Whitewater and Bill Clinton's personal life, including David Brock's notorious "Troopergate" exposé, which led to Paula Jones's sexual harassment suit.

In that article, Brock interviewed four Arkansas state troopers who spoke in detail about covering up Governor Bill Clinton's affairs. The revelations included the first accusations from Paula Jones.

Scaife's "Arkansas Project" not only accused Clinton of financial and sexual indiscretions, it also spun wild conspiracy stories about a drug-smuggling operation with the CIA. Clinton's lawyers filed a motion saying Jones couldn't sue him because he was the president. A federal judge said that Jones would have to wait until after Clinton's term of office had ended, but she appealed and took her case to the Supreme Court.

Her Supreme Court brief was written in part by George T. Conway III, a prominent conservative lawyer at Wachtell, Lipton, Rosen & Katz in New York, who later married a well-known Republican pollster named Kellyanne Fitzpatrick. Conway did this work without charge, leading to some consternation among his law firm partners, many of whom were Democrats.

Clinton ended up paying Paula Jones a lot of money to end her lawsuit, and that should have been the end of the story, but it wasn't, as we know. President Clinton was impeached because he had lied in a deposition in the Jones case, and his lie was exposed by a woman working at the Pentagon named Linda Tripp.

Sometimes friends can't be trusted, something Monica Lewinsky learned the hard way. Lewinsky came to Washington, DC, on an unpaid internship in the White House Office of Legislative Affairs, and she was working there when she and President Clinton started fooling around. Her superiors noticed that the two were spending a lot of time together, so they transferred her to work as the assistant to chief Pentagon spokesman Kenneth Bacon. Even so, the relationship continued.

While at the Pentagon, Lewinsky became friends with Tripp. Lewinsky was unaware that Tripp, something of a prude, was horrified by the apparent lovefest between Lewinsky and the president. She felt that public officials weren't telling the truth about what she was seeing. After reading retired FBI agent Gary Aldrich's book, *Unlimited Access,* she decided to write a book herself. In the summer of 1996, she called Lucianne Goldberg, a literary agent. Goldberg hooked her up with Maggie Gallagher, a conservative columnist who interviewed her for twenty hours. The two pitched a book proposal based on her life under George H. W. Bush and Bill Clinton. Regnery Publishing passed on it.

Soon afterwards, Monica Lewinsky began telling Tripp about her affair with President Clinton. For more than a year Tripp kept her confidences.

Then came the Paula Jones accusation. *Newsweek* reporter Michael Isikoff was told of a "sexual incident" that Clinton had with a woman whose husband committed suicide. That woman was Kathleen Willey, and he went to see her. Willey told Isikoff that Linda Tripp could back up her story.

After four visits, Isikoff finally got Tripp to tell him about the Willey incident. Trying to protect Clinton, she told him that Willey had thoroughly enjoyed the tryst and that Clinton hadn't harassed her in any way.

At the last minute Tripp got cold feet and asked that her name *not* be used in the story.

Had Isikoff agreed, we never would have known about Monica Lewinsky.

But in the published story Tripp was quoted about the Willey incident. In response, Clinton's lawyer, Robert Bennett, said that Tripp was not believable.

Her honesty under attack, Tripp was furious. She went on the offensive. Tripp told Lucianne Goldberg what she knew about Clinton and Monica Lewinsky. She also got back in touch with Isikoff—to tell him about Lewinsky and the president.

Goldberg told Tripp that to be believed, she needed to tape-record her conversations with Lewinsky. No one is sure how Paula Jones's lawyers found out about Tripp, but she finally opened up to them, as well.

On December 19, 1997, Lewinsky was subpoenaed by Paula Jones's attorneys. On January 7, 1998, she stated she never had a sexual relationship with the president. But Lucianne Goldberg had found Tripp a new lawyer who sent her to see independent investigator Kenneth Starr. On January 12, 1997, Linda Tripp gave him more than twenty hours of recordings, including conversation with Lewinsky about her affair with the president. The next day Tripp met with Lewinsky with the FBI listening in secretly.

Tripp, who had worked for Vince Foster, also talked about the removal of Foster's documents, including those related to the Whitewater affair after he was found dead. She discussed how lax the Clinton administration was with background checks. She revealed that Hillary Clinton had broken the law by reading security clearance documents of current and former government employees, including some top Republicans. She talked about Travelgate and Whitewater, and she was able to bring Starr evidence of Lewinsky's affair with Clinton.

On January 16, 1998, the court of appeals, responsible for supervising the investigation under the post-Watergate independent counsel statute, gave Starr the okay to add the Clinton-Lewinsky allegations to see whether she or the president had lied under oath.

On January 17 Bill Clinton testified in a deposition and denied the affair. Four days later, the conservative Drudge Report published that Lewinsky had kept a "garment with Clinton's dried semen."

On January 26 President Clinton went on TV and uttered the infamous words, "I did not have sexual relations with that woman, Miss Lewinsky."

Hillary Clinton, on national TV, dismissed the allegations as "a vast right-wing conspiracy that has been conspiring against my husband since the day he announced for president."

On January 19, a US District Court judge ruled that the Lewinsky scandal had nothing to do with the Paula Jones case and couldn't be included. On February 10 Starr went after the dress with semen on it. Starr questioned Lewinsky's mother, Marcia Lewis, for three days, granting her full immunity in exchange for the dress.

On national TV, Kathleen Willey said Clinton had groped her. In the next two weeks a flight attendant and a former Miss America made the same claim.

Starr's legal staff prepared a detailed analysis of the allegations against Clinton. Starr aide Brett Kavanaugh, a conservative Washington lawyer who would twenty years later become a justice of the United States Supreme Court despite his own sexual misconduct allegations, drafted detailed questions for the independent counsel's office to ask President Clinton about ejaculation and oral sex. At the cost of millions in taxpayer dollars, Starr pursued this questioning.

In July 1998 Clinton was subpoenaed. On July 29, he agreed to testify to a grand jury.

On August 3, 1998, a semen sample was taken from the blue dress for DNA testing. On August 17 Clinton testified for four hours on camera. He admitted to "inappropriate intimate contact" but said he had not lied in January. That evening, on TV, he admitted to his affair with Lewinsky.

"Indeed, I did have a relationship with Miss Lewinsky that was not appropriate. In fact, it was wrong. It constituted a critical lapse in judgment and a personal failure on my part for which I am solely and completely responsible."

That could have been the end of it. He had been caught having an affair and admitted to it on national TV. But on September 9, after spending four years on the $52 million dollar investigation, Kenneth Starr was not about to let it go. He issued a 445-page report that cited eleven impeachable offenses.

On September 11, 1998, Starr's report became public. Denied the chance to impeach him on Whitewater, Starr focused on the Lewinsky affair.

The report was pornographic.

It read: "According to Ms. Lewinsky, she performed oral sex on the president on nine occasions . . . On all nine of those occasions, the president fondled and kissed her bare breasts. He touched her genitals, both through her underwear and directly, bringing her to orgasm on two occasions. On one occasion, the president inserted a cigar into her vagina. On another occasion, she and the president had brief genital-to-genital contact."

The country became obsessed with Bill Clinton's penis.

Newt Gingrich immediately announced that he would give a speech on the moral turpitude of Bill Clinton every day on the floor of the House until the elections were held. It didn't work. The Republicans lost five House seats in the 1998 elections, the first time since 1934 in which the president's party gained seats in the House.

To this day, twenty years later, there is still debate about whether voters in 1998 were aghast at the idea of impeaching any president without overwhelming evidence of serious crimes in office or whether the sexual nature of the accusation made voters dismissive of Gingrich's impeachment charade. Some say the loss of those Republican seats, and Gingrich's loss of the speakership, haunt the current Democratic Speaker of the House Nancy Pelosi as she considered impeachment of President Trump in 2019.

On November 13, Clinton settled the Paula Jones suit, paying her $850,000 and admitting nothing.

On December 11, 1998, the House Judiciary Committee voted to recommend impeachment, approving two articles related to perjury. Clinton was accused of lying to a grand jury and obstructing justice.

On December 19, the House of Representatives approved the two articles of impeachment proposed by the Judiciary Committee. In a response, Clinton vowed he would remain in office until "the last hour of the last day of my term."

That day his approval rating was more than 64 percent, an all-time high.

Before that, only President Andrew Johnson had been impeached by the House. Now there were two.

That same day, Bob Livingston of Louisiana, who had been picked to replace a toppled Newt Gingrich, announced that he was resigning his seat.

He too had had an extramarital affair.

Helen Chenoweth, a populist Republican congresswoman from Idaho and vocal Clinton critic, revealed she had carried on a six-year affair with a rancher in neighboring Oregon. Senator Henry Hyde, a Republican from Illinois, the chairman of the House Judiciary Committee that recommended impeaching Clinton, disclosed a five-year affair with a married woman with three kids. The affair broke up the woman's marriage.

Newt Gingrich, the man who stood for "family values," left his wife dying from cancer in the hospital for a younger woman. Shortly after remarrying, Gingrich started an affair with a House staffer whom he married after divorcing his second wife.

Kenneth Starr would go on to become the president of Baylor University. In May 2016 he was fired for his poor handling of sexual assault charges brought by six women against several of Baylor's football players.

As 1998 came to an end, *Time* magazine noted that the war between the Republicans and Clinton had taken a serious toll on our democracy.

"All around the city," said *Time*, "there was a feeling that brutal, lasting damage had been done to an already threadbare culture of political accommodation, that impeachment would be not the end of something but the beginning. And that it would be something bad."

Three weeks later the Senate found Clinton not guilty.

Lying about a blow job—even under oath—did not meet the definition of "high crimes and misdemeanors."

CHAPTER 14

W

You must remember that some things legally right are not morally right.
—ABRAHAM LINCOLN

G EORGE W. BUSH BECAME OUR FORTY-THIRD PRESI-
dent after one of the most contested presidential elections in US history.
Al Gore won the popular vote, but Bush won the Electoral College after winning Florida by a few hundred votes.

The Florida ballot was a mess. The so-called butterfly ballots were printed
in such a way that some people who wanted to vote for Al Gore ended up
voting for conservative candidate Pat Buchanan, or for *both* Gore *and*
Buchanan. The voter also had to hand-punch a hole in the ballot to choose
a candidate, but the design was faulty, and sometimes the punched-out piece
remained bent but attached. These so-called hanging chads weren't counted
when the votes were tallied.

The final total was 2,912,790 for Bush and 2,912,253 for Gore. A difference of 537 votes.

Then came a legal battle over the recount. Which ballots would be
recounted in which counties and how many recounts would there be? The
Gore and Bush legal teams each pushed a preferred approach. Some election

experts have observed that in retrospect the Gore team should have pushed for a statewide manual recount rather than just focusing on Democratic strongholds. Other experts say that the result would not have changed, no matter how many recounts there were. Nobody knows for sure.

On November 21, 2000, the Florida Supreme Court ruled that the deadline for a recount of votes from Miami-Dade County would be extended five days. Republicans organized to make sure it didn't happen.

The recount was being held in a conference room on the eighteenth floor of the Stephen P. Clark Government Center in Miami. In front of the building Bush supporters, many of them Hispanic, protested the recount. Among them was a band of young Republican congressional aides wearing suits and ties. Republican political operative Roger Stone—who had worked for President Nixon and would later work for President Trump—sent these disruptors into the room where the ballots were being counted to keep the counters from finishing their task. The rioters created so much chaos that the recount stopped. Because of the disruptors' attire, this was later known as the "Brooks Brothers riot."

Meanwhile, the Bush legal team complained to the Supreme Court that the protracted recounting process violated the Fourteenth Amendment.

On Tuesday, December 12, 2000, the Supreme Court released its decision. The court voted five to four to stay the recount, in effect ordering the Florida Secretary of State to certify the election in Bush's favor. Five conservatives on the court voted for Bush: Chief Justice William Rehnquist, Anthony Kennedy, Antonin Scalia, Clarence Thomas, and Sandra Day O'Connor. The four liberals voted for Gore: John Paul Stevens, Stephen Breyer, Ruth Bader Ginsburg, and David Souter.

Said Justice John Paul Stevens in his dissent, "Although we may never know with complete certainly the identity of the winner of this year's Presidential election, the identity of the loser is perfectly clear. It is the Nation's confidence in the judge as an impartial guardian of the rule of law."

Counterfactual historians will always wonder who would have won the election if the Supreme Court had ruled the other way. We do not enter that debate here. Regardless of the answer to that question, the rule of law is jeopardized by the fact that under the Electoral College system mandated by the

Constitution, a presidential election can turn on the results in a single state, and that state does not have a trustworthy voting system.

When the courts get involved, elected state court judges, who are often allied with one political party, order recounts (the Florida courts at the time were narrowly dominated by the Democrats). When a candidate complains to the federal courts, the United States Supreme Court (then, as now, narrowly dominated by Republicans) becomes the arbiter. At least in retrospect both Bush and Gore supporters should be able to agree on one thing—such a legal morass surrounding an election should never be allowed to happen again.

Sadly, very little has been done to prevent it from occurring again. Butterfly ballots and hanging chads are gone, but many of the other problems we saw in 2000 remain. And nobody stopped to think that the debacle advertised to the world the potential for electoral chaos in the United States, the world's strongest representative democracy. With the blue-state/red-state divide so predictable, and presidential elections likely to be very close for the foreseeable future, some foreign adversary just might see for itself an opportunity to make mischief in a future election.

George W. Bush's presidency would not be an easy one.

Only nine months later, on September 11, 2001, an organized group of terrorists that had been in the United States planning its attack for well over a year hijacked four airplanes. There were nineteen hijackers, all affiliated with Al Qaeda. Fifteen were citizens of Saudi Arabia, and the others were from the United Arab Emirates, Egypt, and Lebanon. The hijackers flew two planes into the twin towers of the World Trade Center in New York City, and one into the Pentagon building in Washington, DC. When the fourth group of hijackers was overpowered by passengers, the plane crashed to the ground in rural Pennsylvania, killing all on board.

Osama bin Laden, leader of Al Qaeda, was the mastermind of the attack. It was his second try to bring down the Twin Towers. His men had been much less successful on February 26, 1993, when they detonated a bomb in the underground garage of the north tower of the World Trade Center, killing six people. Al Qaeda had also launched an attack later during the Clinton administration when the USS *Cole* was bombed on October 12, 2000. We were still not prepared for 9/11.

Saudi Arabia, where Al Qaeda originated, was never accused of complicity. The United States, continuing a pattern that predated the first Gulf War under President George H. W. Bush, sought to approach Saudi Arabia as an ally in the Middle East rather than an adversary. What the Saudi government knew about Al Qaeda before the attack may never be known. Yet our close relationship with Saudi Arabia, often shrouded in secrecy, continues to this day, despite the autocratic, dictatorial king ruling the country.

The United States within months invaded Afghanistan, which under the Taliban had been harboring the Al Qaeda terrorists who had, among other things, used that country for a training ground. Pursuing bin Laden and the terrorists into Afghanistan made sense in theory. Keeping American ground forces in Afghanistan over a protracted period of time, however, had risks that any student of world history would recognize. Three great military powers—Macedonia under Alexander the Great, the British Empire, and the Soviet Union—have all tried to invade and hold Afghanistan. All failed. Entering Afghanistan required an exit strategy. Almost twenty years later, we are still there.

Then there was Iraq, which was a problem entirely unrelated to the 9/11 attacks. Iraq was led by a cruel dictator, Saddam Hussein, who had violated international law by invading Kuwait in 1990 and was driven out by a broad-based coalition led by the United States and NATO. He used poison gas on his own people. In 1993 Hussein had made an unsuccessful assassination attempt on George H. W. Bush while Bush was visiting the Persian Gulf region. Several times during his presidential campaign, George W. Bush had talked of removing Hussein from power. But Hussein had no connection to the Al Qaeda terrorists, and *none* of the 9/11 attackers had any connection to Iraq.

The strongest argument for invading Iraq was the fact that Hussein *might* have been in possession of weapons of mass destruction.

How this "might" became enough of a certainty to justify a US and UK invasion of Iraq was one of the more serious intelligence failures in American history. That failure was not a defect in raw intelligence as much as it was a failure in how facts reported by reliable sources are interpreted by career professionals in intelligence agencies and then by political appointees seeking a certain conclusion. At some point along the way, hard facts became conjecture or even alternative facts, and they no longer reflected the reality on the ground as much as the perception of that reality in the mind of some politically appointed government official thousands of miles away. Officials then used the intelligence to make decisions and recommendations or to support those that had already been made.

This happened in Vietnam under LBJ and Nixon. It happened again with Iraq. And it would happen yet again in 2016 when intelligence officials were asked a simple question: Did the Russians interfere in our presidential election?

In sum, *myths*—or alternative facts—can again and again undermine the rule of law when facts are mingled with politically motivated interpretations of those facts.

The opening salvo in the campaign to convince the public that Hussein was a danger to America came on August 26, 2002, when Vice President Cheney announced, "Simply stated, there is no doubt that Saddam Hussein now has weapons of mass destruction." He continued, "There is no doubt he is amassing them to use against our friends, against our allies, and against us."

According to Anthony Zinni, the former commander in chief of the United States Central Command, there was *no* credible evidence that Hussein had such a program.

On March 30, 2003, Secretary of Defense Donald Rumsfeld told the press, "We know where [Iraq's WMDs] are. They're in the area around Tikrit and Baghdad and east, west, south, and north somewhat."

No such weapons were ever found.

One debunker, Joseph Wilson, had gone to Niger only to find that the story that Iraq was importing uranium from Niger was pure fiction. To that end he wrote an op-ed piece in the *New York Times* on July 6, 2003.

Wilson wrote, "If my information was deemed inaccurate, I understand. If the information was ignored because it did not fit certain preconceptions about Iraq, then a legitimate argument can be made that we went to war under false pretenses."

Days later, someone told conservative columnist Robert Novak that Wilson's wife, Valerie Plame, was a covert CIA agent. Novak said the information had come from "two White House officials." When Novak printed the information, he was putting Plame's career in jeopardy.

Novak's column outing Wilson's wife clearly was retaliation for Wilson's criticism of the Iraq War. When the Justice Department investigated, John Ashcroft, the attorney general, recused himself from the case because of his close involvement with the White House. James Comey, who had just been appointed deputy attorney general three weeks earlier, took over the case. Comey named Patrick Fitzgerald to be the special counsel. A grand jury was convened, and though no one was indicted for outing Plame, I. Lewis "Scooter" Libby, Vice President Cheney's top aide, was indicted for lying to the grand jury and obstructing justice. He was sentenced to thirty months in prison and two years of probation.

President Bush commuted his sentence but let the conviction stand. Libby would later be pardoned by President Trump. Lying to protect the president, after all, is not that serious an offense, and perhaps in the eyes of President Trump, it is something that should be encouraged.

The "intelligence" about weapons of mass destruction (that were never found) was used to get congressional approval to invade Iraq. This was similar in some ways to what happened with the Gulf of Tonkin Resolution in 1964 when the Lyndon Johnson administration told Congress what it wanted to hear to get permission to escalate our involvement in Vietnam. This time, once again, Congress asked some questions but took the intelligence reports at face value. Congress overwhelmingly—with many Democrats including Senator Hillary Clinton voting yes—authorized the invasion of Iraq.

Another important aspect of the Iraq War was that some of the billions spent by the US Treasury went to corporations as the private sector took on more and more of the responsibility for the war. In addition to paying Halliburton and other large contractors to rebuild Iraq, the administration hired a firm called Blackwater as the new private fighting force abroad. Founded by Erik Prince, a former member of the Navy SEALs, Blackwater grew from a small company providing shooting ranges in rural North Carolina for police departments and the military into a global security contractor for the State Department and the CIA.

In Iraq the Blackwater militia had a reputation for recklessness and criminal behavior. Iraqis reported that they were impolite and showed no respect for Iraqi civilians. Iraqis said that the contractors often would shout at them if they got too close. Blackwater militiamen were accused of shooting into the streets, running cars off the road, and even killing civilians.

On September 16, 2007, a convoy of Blackwater contractors guarding State Department employees entered a crowded square near the Mansour District in Baghdad. According to Baghdad police, when a small car driven by a couple with a small child wouldn't get out of their way, the contractors opened fire on them. Iraqi police and the Iraqi military retaliated, and other Blackwater forces raced over.

Twenty Iraqi civilians were killed in the firefight, including the couple in the car and their child.

The Iraqi government was furious. Iraqi prime minister Nouri al-Maliki called the killings a crime. The Blackwater militiamen, however, were never prosecuted. Because contractors are not subject to court martial, and their crimes took place outside the United States, prosecution under United States law was difficult. Prosecuting them under Iraqi law was politically and legally unworkable at a time when Iraq was dependent upon US military personnel and contractors for security and basic services.

The massive outsourcing of military operations has created a dependency on the private sector that seriously threatens the rule of law. These men from Blackwater were lone wolves acting under their own rule of law. They weren't answerable to the leaders of our armed forces, only to Erik Prince. And because Iraqi Prime Minister Nouri al-Maliki was dependent upon American forces for his own protection, he could not insist upon prosecution.

Then came the question of what to do with captured enemy combatants and noncombatants who were suspected terrorists.

After ending Saddam Hussein's reign in Iraq, the CIA took over the Abu Ghraib prison on the outskirts of Baghdad.

American soldiers made reports of waterboarding—pouring water over a prisoner's head to simulate drowning. Another military log stated, "All three detainees reported separately that they received an electric shock to different parts of their body. Detainee ##### reported that an Iraqi policeman (1) held a knife to his throat and (2) placed a pistol to his head and pulled the trigger. He further alleged that American forces (1) punched him and hit him with weapons, (2) threw urine on him, and (3) applied electric shocks to his body."

To justify "enhanced interrogation" techniques in some situations, John Yoo, a UC Berkeley law professor serving as the deputy assistant attorney general, and other Department of Justice lawyers, wrote a series of memos that distorted the law to justify the enhanced interrogation methods. What they were really talking about was torture.

Was it worse than what sometimes has happened in big-city police stations with criminal defendants? Probably not, but it was still horrible. The difference was that *lawyers*—and that's the key—said it was okay. (Police officers using excessive force during interrogation don't get explicit approval from prosecutors, but that is essentially what happened when the Department of Justice approved torture as an interrogation method.)

This was the first time lawyers at the highest level of our government said, "Torture is okay."

Not believing in an objective concept of right and wrong is nihilism. We can argue about the role of nihilist theories in abstract philosophy, but in the political realm nihilism means that *everything* is reduced to power and that *any* means is justified. Political nihilists don't believe in normative values of right and wrong. Torture for them is not necessarily wrong.

Nihilists in charge of interpreting laws are dangerous to our democracy. When John Yoo wrote that torture memo, he twisted federal statutes, the Constitution, and the United Nations Convention Against Torture to get the result he wanted. He threw in a ludicrous common-law "self-defense" argument for good measure. By doing so, he basically substituted power for the rule of law.

And to achieve nothing. Experts quickly pointed out that torture has no purpose and doesn't lead to valuable information. The Senate Select Committee on Intelligence in 2014 issued a report that found that CIA detainees subjected to "enhanced interrogation techniques" either produced no intelligence or "fabricated information," which resulted in faulty intelligence. The report refuted CIA claims that waterboarding Abu Zubaydah 83 times and Khalid Sheikh Mohammed 183 times produced useful intelligence. All useful information came from traditional nonviolent questioning.

"Waterboarding produced nothing further of value," said the report.

Not to mention the terrible consequences for American military personnel and civilians captured by hostile forces. Torture is a practical and moral disaster.

In the world of *actual facts*, not anger-driven conclusions, torture doesn't work. The rule of law was tragically destroyed to achieve nothing.

One last "scandal" really wasn't a scandal at all. Between 2003 and 2009, more than twenty-two million private emails of the Bush administration disappeared. The Bush White House used a private email server owned by the Republican National Committee and failed to keep the emails, as required by law. When a congressional investigation sought to subpoena them, they couldn't be found.

In 1978, Congress had passed the Presidential Records Act, which declared that all presidential and vice-presidential records created after January 20, 1981, be preserved. The public, not the president or vice president, owned the records. In the end, the Bush administration admitted it "lost" up to twenty-two million emails. Then in 2009, after Bush was out of office, they were found. They had been "mislabeled."

White House aides Karl Rove and Josh Bolton were held in contempt of Congress for refusing to comply with subpoenas for those emails, but the matter was not pursued. Losing emails was *not* a criminal offense, said the Senate Investigative Committee. Nobody was going to call the FBI. At the Democratic National Convention in the summer of 2008 nobody yelled: "Lock them up." The matter simply went away. When Barack Obama was elected, he didn't pursue it.

CHAPTER 15

"But Her Email . . ."

My identity might begin with the fact of my race, but it didn't,
couldn't end there. At least that's what I would choose to believe.
—*BARACK OBAMA*

SENATOR HILLARY CLINTON WAS THOUGHT TO BE THE front-runner for the presidency when she announced her candidacy in 2007. Clinton was a strong candidate, but her opponents now blamed her for the scandals of the Clinton years. She was, through her husband's and her own fundraising, also associated with the enormously effective Democratic Party money machine, which had very close ties to Wall Street and titans of the high-tech industry.

Political corruption, worsened enormously by our campaign finance system, is a serious threat to the rule of law. Indeed our campaign finance system may be the single greatest threat that will remain with us long after the departure of Donald Trump. But in 2008 it was all too easy to pin corruption on the people who had been at the head of the Democratic Party since 1992: Bill and Hillary Clinton.

A new US senator from the state of Illinois (elected only four years earlier in 2004) entered the presidential race, promising to end the war in Iraq, increase our energy independence, and especially to reform our healthcare system. He also talked about corruption in government. Barack Hussein Obama came on the scene like a whirlwind, crisscrossing the country with his message.

Obama won the Democratic nomination and chose Delaware senator Joe Biden as his running mate. Obama and Biden ran against Republican war hero and senator John McCain, who made the unfortunate choice of Alaska governor Sarah Palin, a far-right Republican, to be his running mate. It was a fatal mistake.

Said Nicolle Wallace, Palin's advisor during the presidential campaign, "There was a moment shortly after I met her that I realized that she realized that she was in over her head."

Voters saw how shallow Palin was when Katie Couric asked her to name a newspaper that she read regularly, and she couldn't name one.

> Couric: And when it comes to establishing your worldview, I was curious, what newspapers and magazines did you regularly read before you were tapped for this—to stay informed and to understand the world?
> Palin: I've read most of them again with a great appreciation for the press, for the media—
> Couric: But what ones specifically? I'm curious.
> Palin: Um, all of them, any of them that have been in front of me over all these years.
> Palin: I have a vast variety of sources where we get our news.

Kellyanne Conway may have coined "alternative facts" in 2016, but Sarah Palin demonstrated a remarkably similar attitude in 2008. She was a tragic choice for McCain, who not only had suffered years of imprisonment and torture as a prisoner of war in Vietnam, but had a remarkable career in the Senate, often breaking with Republican leaders on critically important issues such as campaign finance reform.

During one interview with Fox News on November 1, 2008, Palin said, "We're confident that we're going to win on Tuesday, so from there, the first one hundred days, how are we going to kick in the plan that will get this economy back on the right track and really shore up the strategies that we need over in Iraq and Iran to win these wars?"

Critics quickly pointed out that we weren't at war with Iran.

In another interview she suggested that the media's criticisms of her were unconstitutional, or at least not protected by the First Amendment.

She said, "If [the media] convinces enough voters that that is negative campaigning, for me to call Barack Obama out on his associations then I don't know what the future of our country would be in terms of First Amendment rights and our ability to ask questions without fear of attacks by the mainstream media."

Obama won the presidency with 365 electoral votes to McCain's 173.

In 2009 Obama faced the worst financial crisis since the Great Depression. Banks were going under, and the stock market was dropping fast. Unemployment rose to 10 percent. The Bush administration had stabilized Wall Street and provided a rescue package for financial institutions the previous fall, but the economy was sinking. In February 2009 Congress approved Obama's $787 billion economic stimulus package. It cut some taxes and raised others, extended unemployment benefits, and funded public works projects.

To avoid another financial crisis, Congress passed the Dodd-Frank Wall Street Reform Act of 2010. The law regulated the riskiest investments—derivatives, credit default swaps, and commodities futures. The law also regulated consumer finance. Obama wanted to install Harvard Law professor Elizabeth Warren as head of the newly created Consumer Finance Protection Bureau, but banks and other lenders hated her, and Republican opposition in Congress made her confirmation impossible. Instead, she advised the president on consumer finance for two years and then ran for the Senate.

Obama's most significant and most controversial legislative achievement was the passage of the Affordable Care Act (ACA). Healthcare is roughly one-seventh of our economy, and people who did not like the ACA had plenty of incentive to oppose it.

Then there were the continuing military operations in Iraq and Afghanistan.

On May 1, 2011, Navy SEALs attacked Osama bin Laden's compound in Pakistan and killed him. Later that year Obama removed American troops from Iraq. Getting out of Afghanistan was a difficult task that, after two terms and eight years in office, Obama couldn't accomplish.

Obama tried to reduce the number of US troops abroad and use high-tech substitutes for military ground operations. This meant unarmed drones and the political and legal problems that come with them. Obama authorized 506 drone strikes in the Middle East that killed 3,040 terrorists and 391 civilians. Human Rights Watch revealed as many as twelve civilians were killed in December 2014 when a US drone targeted vehicles that were part of a wedding procession going toward the groom's village outside the central Yemeni city of Rad'a. Sometimes the drones were aimed at anonymous targets who appeared to be associated with Al Qaeda or the Taliban through their behavior. That those deploying the drones didn't always know who the target was became obvious when eight Americans were killed by drones.

Using drones was probably a better alternative than reliance on ground troops to find and kill terrorists, but it came at a steep political cost and subjected the United States to legitimate criticism from human rights organizations.

The Obama years saw heightened political rhetoric from Republicans. Many (but not all) Republican officeholders stuck to policy differences and avoided getting personal.

That being said, there was at times a noticeable drop of decorum in Congress during the Obama years.

During his first State of the Union address, as Obama mentioned that the Affordable Care Act would not mandate coverage for undocumented immigrants, there was a shout from the audience: "You lie." It was Republican congressman Joe Wilson from South Carolina. Later in the speech when Obama mentioned that there were still significant details to be worked out, a group of Republicans in the audience actually laughed derisively.

Such scenes are familiar in the House of Commons in the United Kingdom, where the opposition routinely shouts down the prime minister. But rules of decorum in the United States House and Senate have traditionally demanded more respect, particularly during the president's State of the Union address. Until Obama showed up. We can agree or disagree about the rules on the floor of a legislature (whether catcalls are allowed), but when the rules of decorum change, we have to wonder why.

Admittedly this incident during Obama's State of the Union was not as egregious as what happened over 150 years earlier on May 22, 1856, in the United States Senate when Representative Preston Brooks, also a congressman from South Carolina, attacked Senator Charles Sumner of Massachusetts with a cane because Senator Sumner supported the abolition of slavery. The question is whether Wilson's motivations in 2010 weren't that much different from Brooks's 150 years earlier. Was Wilson's outrage about the Affordable Care Act, or about our having an African American president?

Criticism from the right-wing media was even worse. Collective hatred for Obama was evident even when he first began running. Those protesting his candidacy called him a traitor, a socialist, a communist, a Muslim, or an Arab. None of the adjectives were true, but the name-calling never stopped, even after he was elected.

One of Obama's severest critics was right-wing pundit Dinesh D'Souza. D'Souza started his career as a pundit writing for the ultra-conservative (some said racist) *Dartmouth Review* as a student at Dartmouth College. D'Souza became a Twitter troll saying terrible, scurrilous things about President Obama. Once, D'Souza tweeted a photo of Obama with the caption "Obama's dad dumped him at birth & his mom got rid of him at the age of 10—did they know something we didn't when we signed up this guy?"

On another photo, D'Souza wrote, "THEY CAN TAKE THE BOY OUT OF THE GHETTO . . . Watch this vulgar man show his stuff while America cowers in embarrassment."

D'Souza for five years was President Obama's most vocal hater, writing three books, *The Roots of Obama's Rage, Obama's America,* and *America: Imagine a World Without Her.* He filmed companion documentaries for the last two.

Most of D'Souza's findings in the books and documentaries were widely discredited by scholars, journalists, and those who rely on facts. The film *Obama's America* still became a hit among Obama haters. It grossed $33 million, making it the highest-grossing political documentary after Michael Moore's anti-Bush *Fahrenheit 9/11.*

In May 2014, D'Souza pleaded guilty to a campaign-finance violation after he was caught getting two straw donors to contribute to the campaign of his old friend Wendy Long, who was running against Kirsten Gillibrand in the US Senate race in New York. D'Souza faced up to two years in prison but ultimately got eight months in a halfway house, plus community service, and a $30,000 fine.

On May 31, 2018, President Trump pardoned D'Souza, who continues to spew his venom on right-wing media.

Meanwhile, Republicans took over Congress in 2010, largely because of a backlash against the ACA and the enormous government economic stimulus spending that had spurned a successful "Tea Party" movement. This movement promised lower taxes and less regulation as a path to economic prosperity and individual liberty.

The connection between small government and the original Boston Tea Party of 1773 was unclear (especially to anyone who understands history). But that did not stop participants from showing up in eighteenth-century costumes and railing against Obama and the Democrats as our forbearers had railed against the British. It was a period theme party and a political party in one.

Then the racists showed up. Racist comments about Obama were made in chat rooms and at impromptu "tea party" meetings around the country.

In April 2011, during Obama's first term, there was a call to see President Obama's birth certificate. The request came on *The View*, from the New York City real estate developer and reality TV star Donald Trump.

Obama released his full-form birth certificate on April 26, 2011. It stated he was born at Honolulu's Kapiolani Hospital on August 4, 1961.

"We do not have time for this kind of silliness," said the president.

Even after this, Trump and his followers refused to accept its legitimacy—or Obama's. In speeches, Trump praised himself for making Obama produce the birth certificate.

Besides this cruel injection of racism (yet again) into American politics, another separate threat to the rule of law, the injection of money into politics, was about to get a lot worse. Corruption would accelerate with a vengeance.

In 2009 the United States Supreme Court heard *Citizens United v. Federal Election Commission*. The case, decided five to four by the conservative majority, overturned a federal statute, the McCain-Feingold Act, that prohibited independent political expenditures by corporations.

Corporations are people, ruled the court. This gave corporations the First Amendment right to spend money on communications about candidates as they please. A cornerstone of the bipartisan campaign finance legislation drafted by Senator John McCain—President Obama's opponent in 2008—and signed by President Bush in 2001 was thrown out in 2009 by five justices of the Supreme Court who themselves had never been elected to any public office. People across the political spectrum were—and still are—outraged. Polling data continues to show that Americans of all political viewpoints are disgusted by the role of money in politics.

By 2012 Republicans hoped to use some of this anger to oust Obama. Said Mitch McConnell, the Senate majority leader, "The single most important thing we want to achieve is for President Obama to be a one-term president."

They didn't succeed. In 2012 Obama defeated Mitt Romney and his running mate Paul Ryan, but it wasn't as big a victory as his first election. Obama amassed 65,446,032 votes to Romney's 60,589,084. Obama won 332 electoral votes, Romney 206.

Republicans vowed not to let Obama pass a single bill in his second term. Obama resorted to issuing executive orders to further his agenda.

Here, yet another issue crucial to the rule of law arose, one recognized by the founders but not fully addressed in the Constitution. Should the president have the power to act unilaterally without the consent of Congress? The party that controls the White House almost always supports expanded use of executive orders, and the party that controls Congress almost always opposes it. When the playbooks switch, their positions switch, although their sheer hypocrisy is apparent to anyone with a memory.

The executive orders Obama signed protected the environment, including addressing climate change; promoted diversity and inclusion in the federal workforce; promoted rehabilitation of prisoners; provided aid to students to get more affordable loans; normalized relations with Cuba; provided for job training for workers; allowed children of undocumented immigrants to remain in this country at least temporarily (DACA); provided for admission to this country of refugees; and much more. Democrats were thrilled with many of these policy initiatives. The "rule of law" question was rarely discussed by Democrats. They chose not to discuss what might happen with executive orders if a Republican were in the White House. They would soon learn.

Conservative commentators jumped all over Obama's executive orders, taking legitimate arguments about presidential power way overboard. They even fantasized that he intended to issue an executive order allowing himself a third term. None of that was true.

Republican members of Congress then jumped in.

"President Obama has cemented his legacy of lawlessness," declared House Speaker John Boehner. Charles Krauthammer, the conservative pundit, said this was "an impeachable offense."

President Obama did observe some limits. He never declared a "national emergency" under the National Emergencies Act to spend money on a project that had been proposed to Congress and rejected. Obama used executive orders to the extent he could get away with it (he sometimes won in court and sometimes lost), but he did not call any of his policy priorities or campaign promises a "national emergency." He understood that there were at least some limits on executive power.

Obama never called the right-wing press that criticized him the "enemy of the people" or questioned freedom of the press under the First Amendment.

The Obama years saw a resurgence of another threat to the rule of law: gun violence. Assassins did not target prominent political leaders as they had in the 1960s with the deaths of John F. Kennedy, Robert Kennedy, and Martin Luther King. Now, forty years later, assassins took the lives of schoolchildren.

On December 14, 2012, twenty-year-old Adam Lanza walked into the Sandy Hook Elementary School in Newtown, Connecticut, and gunned down twenty small children and six adults, including teachers, with an assault rifle. The wailing around the country was loud, but Congress refused to do anything about gun violence. Many Republican lawmakers cried that the Democrats were trying to take away guns in violation of the Second Amendment.

Gun proliferation and the campaign finance problem were not unrelated. The National Rifle Association usually supported Republican candidates, but it also threatened to support an opposing primary candidate if any Republican supported any kind of gun legislation. The NRA had the money to do this as one of the largest spenders in political races—often GOP primaries.

This happened to Debra Maggart, a Republican leader in the Tennessee House of Representatives. A lifetime member of the NRA with an A-plus rating, she refused to support a 2012 bill that would permit Tennessee residents to keep guns inside locked cars. In her primary run for reelection, the NRA spent $155,000 to defeat her. They ran ads linking her with President Obama concerning gun control.

She lost badly.

The message was clear: We will help you get elected and protect your seat from Democrats. We will spend millions on ads that make your opponent look worse than a liquor store robber. In return, we expect you to oppose any laws that regulate guns. If you don't comply, we will load our weapons and direct everything in our arsenal at you.

For the GOP it was an NRA protection racket.

Some Democrats in rural districts—including Democratic congresswoman Kirsten Gillibrand of New York—also took substantial amounts of money and support from the NRA. The NRA message to them was also clear: oppose gun laws or lose your seat to a Republican. Many of these Democrats only had a "change of heart" about guns when they were appointed or ran for statewide office and had to appeal to a different electorate.

For the 2012 election, the NRA spent more than $19 million to defeat Democrats and stray Republicans who supported gun control. As *Citizens United* showed us, big money in politics has become the single most important aspect of our elections. When Russian agents interfered in the 2016 elections in the United States, establishing connections with the NRA to meet top Republican politicians was one of their subversion strategies.

The Sandy Hook school shooting also brought about a resurgence of another age-old problem going back to the Salem witch trials—myth or what we call today "fake news."

Alex Jones, the founder of InfoWars, which publishes false and often dangerous conspiracy theories and other alt-right talking points, posted on his website that the Sandy Hook massacre was a hoax—a "staged event." Jones also claimed that the Oklahoma City bombing and Boston Marathon bombing were staged by actors. (He has also said that the government puts fluoride in the water to turn people gay.)

As a result of Jones's postings, family members of the Sandy Hook victims received harassment, death threats, and even physical attacks from Jones's followers.

At least six relatives of the deceased Sandy Hook children have sued Jones for defamation.

Jones made up the outrageous story that the New York Police Department, while searching Congressman Anthony Weiner's emails, discovered a pedophilia ring linked to the Democrats. The ring, Jones blared, participated in satanic ritual abuse. One Twitter user, following his "story," wrote that "cheese pizza" was code for child pornography. Another said the ring operated out of the Comet Ping Pong pizza parlor in Washington, DC. The story spread as far as Turkey, appearing in pro-Erdoğan newspapers.

The owners of the Comet Ping Pong pizza parlor received hundreds of threats. An armed man appeared in front of the restaurant and was arrested.

Jones has gotten rich spouting his inflaming nonsense. His YouTube channel has 2.3 million viewers. He rakes it in.

In 2015 Trump, then a Republican candidate, appeared on Jones's show. "Your reputation is amazing," said Trump. "I will not let you down."

Meanwhile, Obama was angering the man who would arguably be the most decisive factor in determining the next president of the United States: Vladimir Putin.

His administration passed the Magnitsky Act in December 2012 in retaliation against the human rights abuses suffered in Russia by Sergei Magnitsky, a Russian lawyer and whistle-blower who untangled a web of tax fraud and graft involving twenty-three companies and $230 million linked to the Kremlin and persons close to Putin. Magnitsky was beaten and jailed, and he died just before he was to be released.

The law kept eighteen Russian government officials and businessmen from entering or banking in the United States.

Two weeks after Obama signed the bill, Putin signed a bill in Russia blocking the adoption of Russian children by American parents. Magnitsky was also declared guilty of all the crimes he was accused of.

Getting in a fight with Russia—or rather standing up to human rights abuses and Russian military aggression—for President Obama and his first-term secretary of state Hillary Clinton, may have been a political mistake even if it was the right thing to do.

Obama intended for ethics to be a strong point of his presidency, and he largely succeeded. His first full day in office, January 21, 2009, he signed an executive order, drafted by his chief ethics counsel Norman Eisen, that substantially narrowed the conflicts of interest in the revolving door from the private sector into government. He wanted to set a higher bar and he did.

The Obama presidency still had its share of scandals, although less than his predecessors'. The most discussed scandal was Secretary of State Hillary Clinton's cavalier insistence that she use a personal email server for State Department business. She should not have done that. State Department lawyers should not have allowed her to do that because it potentially violated the Presidential Records Act.

Karl Rove did something similar with his email, using a Republican National Committee server in the Bush administration, and he had been subjected to a congressional investigation by angry Democrats when his emails were lost. State Department security officials should have made absolutely certain that, if Secretary Clinton insisted on using the private server, the records would be retained and nobody would use it for classified information. The private email server was bad judgment on multiple levels, but not criminal.

Unless of course Republican members of Congress wanted to try to make it criminal in order to win the presidency in 2016. And of course that's exactly what happened.

Meanwhile, the rhetoric on policy heated up as well. Let's listen to some Republican members of Congress. Keep in mind that these are members of Congress, not right-wing radio talk show hosts.

"This administration has so many Muslim Brotherhood members that have influence that they just are making wrong decisions for America," said Texas congressman Louie Gohmert. Gohmert also warned that the hate crimes bill would lead to Nazism and the legalization of necrophilia, pedophilia, and bestiality.

Michele Bachmann, a former congresswoman from Minnesota, said in 2014:

"The gay community thinks that they've so bullied the American people and they so intimidate politicians that politicians fear them, and so they think that they get to dictate the agenda everywhere."

The right-wing media was even worse.

Fox News commentator Sean Hannity invited his guests to bring their hatred to the fore. He once said that "all Muslims are barbaric terrorists that need to be hunted down and killed."

Laura Ingraham, a Fox radio host, stated she hates government, Planned Parenthood, immigrants, and the poor. Ann Coulter hates soccer moms. Ingraham hates soccer. She once said, "Liberal moms like soccer because it's a sport in which athletic talent finds so little expression that girls can play with boys. No serious sport is coed, even at the kindergarten level."

Rush Limbaugh has been mocking women, especially liberal women, for years. He once said, "Feminism was established so as to allow unattractive women access to the mainstream of society."

Limbaugh had an equal amount if not greater contempt for President Obama, going as far as telling his listeners that "Obama hates this country."

Then he paused, and went on, "He is trying—Barack Obama is trying—to dismantle this country brick by brick, the American Dream. There is no other way to put this. He was indoctrinated as a child. His father was a communist. His mother was a leftist. He was sent to prep and Ivy League schools where his contempt for the country was reinforced.

"This is what we have as a president: a radical ideologue, a ruthless politician who despises the country and the way it was founded and the way in which it has become great.

"He hates it."

The GOP, the party of Lincoln, had more and more people trying to turn it into the party of hate.

Enter Donald Trump.

CHAPTER 16

Who Is Donald Trump?

Better to remain silent and be thought a fool than
to speak out and remove all doubt.
—ABRAHAM LINCOLN

THIS BOOK IS NOT A BIOGRAPHY OF DONALD TRUMP before he campaigned for president. Bookshelves of such biographies have been written; four of the best are *The Trumps*, by Gwenda Blair; *Never Enough: Donald Trump and the Pursuit of Success*, by Michael D'Antonio; *Donald Trump: 45th US President*, by Dominick Reston; and *Donald J. Trump: A President Like No Other*, by Conrad Black.

We will, however, briefly discuss aspects of Trump's personal and business life that have had a profound impact on his campaign and presidency.

First: Trump has always seen himself as an outsider, and he is very insecure about not being accepted. This came partly from his father Fred Trump's outsider status in New York business circles, with a real estate enterprise focused in Queens, rather than Manhattan. Fred Trump's business reputation was not particularly good. (Fred's father, Friedrich "Fritz" Trump, emigrated from Germany after dodging the draft, and he ran hotels in Washington State and Alaska that were rumored to provide prostitution services on the side.) Fred Trump was skittish around White Anglo-Saxon Protestant (WASP) and Jewish businessmen who ran in Manhattan circles. The Trumps may have been Protestants, but old money WASPs often looked down on them as typical nouveau riches. (Trump's name has been noted in society pages for its absence in the Social Register.) The Trumps' German ancestry made them feel so insecure that Fred Trump pretended the family was Swedish in the years after World War II.

As the Trumps acquired more wealth, they were not the type to be invited to join country clubs. Once Donald took over the family real estate business, the Trumps built their own country clubs. They didn't try to buy an apartment and gain admission to snobbish Upper East Side co-ops, which often discriminated against prospective buyers for a range of reasons. They built their own co-ops and condos.

Those who wanted to get along with the Trumps would join a Trump country club, live in a Trump building, or both—that is how Kellyanne Conway first met Donald Trump.

Social climbing for Donald Trump was not climbing someone else's ladder but instead perching himself atop a pedestal, lowering a ladder from it, and inviting others to climb up the ladder *toward* him.

Perhaps there is something admirable in this singular focus on dictating one's own definition of status and success rather than striving to meet someone else's definition. But if anyone wonders where Donald Trump's self-centeredness comes from, this is part of the story. Equally significant was his very deep suspicion of the establishment, whether it be establishment businessmen, social circles, country clubs, parties, or charitable boards of large Manhattan cultural institutions that he almost never joined. If America could ever create a billionaire who even in times of great business success (he had some) was still an anti-establishment outsider, Donald Trump was it.

Second: Trump never had to work for anybody else but himself, and very briefly for his father. He avoided the draft during Vietnam (the unsubstantiated foot maladies). He became a very rich businessman (at times) and worked hard (at times), but he never had to work for an organization or play by someone else's rules.

He worked for his father at a very young age, but within years of graduating from college, he was given millions in "start-up" capital (apparently about $15 million) and a great deal of autonomy to put together real estate deals in new places where his father had done very little business—at first mostly Manhattan, which his father had always avoided.

Most successful businesspeople have at some point worked in organizations where others make the rules. Law firms and investment banks have partners or managing directors. (Former New York City mayor and billionaire Michael Bloomberg was an employee and then a partner of Salomon Brothers before setting up his own company in midlife.) Corporations have boards of directors that hire and fire top officers. Most organizations—including all public corporations—are bound by disclosure rules requiring that financial books and records be available to investors, and often to the public. Under federal securities laws, executives can be imprisoned for inaccurate records. Accountability and transparency are required.

How well these transparency and accountability rules are enforced for public companies is arguable, but with private family-owned companies such as the Trump Organization, there are no such rules. Business records, including financial statements and the names of foreign and domestic investors and lenders, are kept private. The business owner runs the show.

It is not surprising that a TV reality show such as *The Apprentice* would have a private company head as its star. Public company CEOs can hire and fire people in their organization but they don't have absolute power. The public company CEO may very well be told by the board of directors "you're fired." By contrast, nobody can fire Donald Trump from a company wholly owned by Donald Trump.

For someone aspiring to be president of a constitutional republic, a résumé showing no experience with transparency and accountability to others is not a good sign. For someone aspiring to head a country such as Russia or Saudi Arabia or North Korea, that résumé might work, but in the United States not so much.

Third: Trump has never particularly liked playing by the rules. His singular experience with rigid enforcement of rules was apparently not a happy one. When it came time for young Donald to go to prep school, there is no record that he even applied to the prominent day schools and boarding schools favored by New York City's elite. He did not enter one of New York

City's many good public high schools. He was instead enrolled by his father, seemingly against his will, in New York Military Academy (NYMA), an institution marketing itself to wealthy parents with difficult-to-manage sons. The typical advertisement—in the back pages of the *New York Times* Sunday magazine section—invariably featured a photo of a boy with short hair wearing a military uniform. It does not appear that young Donald learned much about rules, except that brute force is needed to make and enforce them.

The *Washington Post* ran an article describing young Trump as a bully who rode through his Queens neighborhood on a bike, shouting and cursing loudly, throwing rocks at others, and beating up smaller kids.

As a seventh grader, he and a friend would sneak out of his Jamaica Estates mansion, take the subway to Manhattan, and walk around. He bought stink bombs, hand buzzers, fake vomit, and switchblades to be like the gang members from *West Side Story*.

When Fred Trump found the knives and learned of his son's secret jaunts, he enrolled him at the military academy in Cornwall-on-Hudson, sixty-five miles away. Observers felt this response much too severe for a boy who hadn't gotten arrested and wasn't involved in any real mischief. When young Donald suddenly disappeared from the neighborhood, his friends were dumbfounded.

At NYMA, separated from his cook and butler, Trump rebelled, but then fit in very well, getting good grades (presumably—his transcript is a closely guarded secret), and shining on the football and baseball teams. He had a temper, and once after a classmate struck him with a broom, he tried to push his assailant out a second-floor window, only to be stopped by two other students.

During his senior year he was promoted to captain of A Company, but a month into his reign, a platoon sergeant shoved a plebe too hard against a wall, and Trump was accused of not being strict enough with the leaders under him. He was reassigned.

Paul Schwartzman and Michael Miller related this incident in their *Washington Post* article. After many phone calls, they visited the home of the former NYMA cadet who had replaced Trump as Company A captain. Reluctantly he told them of Trump's demotion. After the story was published,

Trump reacted as all narcissists would to public embarrassment. Three times Trump called the *Post* to say the writers had done "a lousy interview."

Trump verbally attacked the interviewee, saying the former cadet's account was "a fiction" and accusing him of telling the story to get "himself a little bit of publicity."

Trump insisted he had not been demoted.

"It was a promotion for me," declared Trump, "and it was a demotion for him."

Trump called the *Post* twice more to argue the point.

"I was promoted," he said. "Promoted. Mark it down."

Fourth: Trump grew up in the 1960s, and his background and his life experiences could not be more different from the "religious right" he now courts. Trump's hedonism and materialism gave rise to a lifestyle that was a cross-section perhaps of that described and practiced by famous novelists Kurt Vonnegut and Norman Mailer. Combine that with the free flow of money, and we have a rich-man's world reminiscent of F. Scott Fitzgerald novels (minus the booze that Donald Trump apparently avoided after his brother tragically suffered from alcoholism).

Trump did not grow up with a Catholic education, and it is not clear that his Protestant family attended church regularly. Fred Trump does not appear to have embraced conspicuous displays of wealth as much as Donald has, but money appears to have been an important part of the family relationship. We learned from a 2018 *New York Times* story that Fred Trump, with some assistance from Donald and perhaps Donald's sister Maryanne, spent decades engineering intrafamily wealth transfers to avoid estate taxes.

Trump's mother was apparently very passive, leaving him with no forceful female role model. He did not experience either the influence of an intellectually engaged professional woman or the domineering societal matriarch that many other wealthy young men had.

Even though his own sister Maryanne later moved beyond this mold to become a federal judge, Donald Trump had very little experience with women being in charge of anything at all, whether a business, a charitable organization board of directors, or even a debutante cotillion. At some early point he formed the opinion that women existed primarily for the pleasure of men, particularly rich men like himself.

Fifth: Donald Trump has always been far more honest than many men about some things, and much more dishonest about others. He is most honest about his own feelings and prejudices.

The "stiff upper lip" of the WASP Society crowd is nowhere to be seen with Donald Trump. If you offend his ego, he lets you know it. Thin-skinned is an understatement. His racial and religious prejudices are laid bare.

The contrast of Trump with other presidents is striking. Everyone knows from the White House tapes that Richard Nixon disliked Jews (except for a few such as Henry Kissinger, his secretary of state). But Nixon did not talk that way publicly. Trump by contrast, forty years later when prejudices are far less socially acceptable, will very publicly say what he thinks of Muslims and Mexicans. His long history of race-baiting African Americans sets him apart from most Americans, including those who harbor similar prejudices but are less open about it.

He even wears his attitude toward women on his sleeve, not only in the infamous interview with Billy Bush ("grab them by the pussy"), but even more notoriously in radio interviews with Howard Stern in which he talked of the sexual attractiveness of his own daughter Ivanka. Shocking people—with brutal honesty about his own prejudices and hedonism—was a part of Donald Trump's mantra long before he went into politics.

For conventional politics (typified by the genteel mannerisms of the late George H. W. Bush or Barack H. Obama), Trump's candidacy for any office for this reason alone should have been a nonstarter. For unconventional politics and appealing to a "base" of voters willing to support any candidate bold enough to voice their own disdain for the establishment, minorities, and women, he was the *perfect* candidate.

In business, by contrast, Trump learned that lying pays off. Because he has never worked for a public company and thus has not been subject to at least some of the legal prohibitions on lying (particularly to investors), business for him is similar to a poker game. Lots of bluff—and also some cheating.

Trump has attracted more lawsuits than just about any other New York businessman, but here also he learned that fighting back with dirt was the way to win. When he and his father needed a lawyer to defend against Nixon Justice Department lawsuits alleging housing discrimination against blacks in the 1970s, Trump retained a notorious lawyer whom he had reportedly met in a nightclub: Senator Joe McCarthy's former chief counsel Roy Cohn who, entirely apart from his red-baiting at the McCarthy Army hearings, was known as one of the nastiest lawyers in New York. Cover-ups were a Cohn method that Trump admired. (According to the 2019 Mueller Report, Trump criticized his White House lawyers for taking notes that could be used against him, saying that "Roy Cohn never took notes.")

Lie. If that doesn't work, lie again and then sue. That became Trump's way of doing business.

THE UNITED STATES FOOTBALL LEAGUE

If you're looking for an example of Trump's business history, look no further than the New Jersey Generals of the United States Football League (USFL).

After the first season of the USFL, thirty-seven-year-old Donald Trump in 1983 bought the Generals from J. Walter Duncan for $10 million, even though Duncan's asking price was $8.5 million. The USFL played in the spring. The owners felt there would be room for a football league playing when the NFL wasn't.

Trump's office was on the twenty-sixth floor of the Trump Tower in Manhattan, and those wishing to meet with him found it curious that before they met, they had to sit through an eight-minute film describing his greatness. The video called him a "visionary builder" and included a sales pitch for Trump Tower.

The video wasn't optional. If you wanted to see him, you had to sit through the video.

Though Trump had bought a USFL franchise, he had no interest in the success of the USFL. He wanted to get a professional football franchise for himself and take it to the prestigious National Football League (NFL). First he failed to get a number of star NFL players to switch leagues, and then he failed to hire legendary Miami Dolphins coach Don Shula. He publicly announced that Shula was close to signing, angering Shula, who decided to stay in Miami.

Embarrassed, Trump lied to save face, saying he hadn't signed Shula because the negotiations were too complex and time-consuming.

Despite his public failures, Trump was grabbing headlines. The other owners were furious and felt that he was trying to steamroll them to take over the league. They weren't wrong.

Not long after he bought the team, Trump angered the other owners when he announced he wanted to move their games from the spring to the fall to compete head-to-head with the NFL. He talked of his Generals playing in the NFL in a new Trump Stadium in Manhattan.

The other owners, who knew it was suicide to switch to the fall, were furious. In a meeting, Trump demanded they schedule the move—now.

"I don't want to be a loser," he told them. "I've never been a loser before . . . and I'm not going to be a failure."

The USFL could have succeeded if Trump had allowed their original plan to play in the spring. But Trump was insistent, even though his desire to play in the fall wasn't based on anything but his gut and his ambition, as he ran roughshod over the other owners.

"He understood nothing about football," said TV producer Mike Tollin. "He knows less than the average fan."

"He was great entertainment," said Charley Steiner, the announcer for the Generals, "but he was also poisonous. He didn't care about the league, about his players. He cared about one person, and one person only. He cared only about Donald J. Trump."

Trump bullied the owners to move to the fall. He told them that he was the richest owner, that this was his intention whether they liked it or not. He disparaged USFL commissioner Chet Simmons, who saw Trump clearly for what he was: a huckster. Trump became known as a "charlatan, dead set on getting his way."

Independently, Trump asked the top executives at CBS and NBC *if* the networks would carry the USFL if they played in the fall. They said yes.

Trump then lied to the owners, saying that the network execs told him they *preferred* that the USFL played in the fall.

"He held sway, even when his sway made no sense," said author Jeff Pearlman.

Trump billed himself as the savior of the USFL when the USFL might well have succeeded if he hadn't steered them toward oblivion.

When the *New York Times* quoted Trump saying that the USFL was going to play in the fall because it was "the only logical way for the league to continue," Tampa Bay Bandits owner John Bassett said, "[The story] is absolute nonsense. I hate to see [the *Times*] used by a con man. At this point there is absolutely no basis to [the story] whatsoever."

Trump arranged a secret meeting with NFL commissioner Pete Rozelle but didn't let Rozelle get a word in. At the end of the meeting, Rozelle told him, "Mr. Trump, as long as I or my heirs are involved in the NFL, you will never be a franchise owner in the league."

The USFL paid $600,000 for a report that said its best chance for its survival was to play in the spring. Trump immediately called the report "bullshit." He threatened to quit if the league played in the spring. He and Eddie Einhorn, owner of the Chicago team, bullied the others into agreeing they would play the next season in the fall.

Trump had overwhelmed his peers to do his bidding. Sharon Patrick, who conducted the study, told the owners that playing in the fall meant sure death to the league. The owners voted with Trump anyway.

In the end the league folded. Ticket sales across the league plummeted. Owners closed up shop. Trump insisted he would find new owners.

The league was down to eight teams for the 1986 fall season. More than seventy-five USFL players switched to the NFL.

Meanwhile, Trump asked the other USFL owners to trust him. He insisted the USFL sue the NFL for being a monopoly and hired Roy Cohn to represent them. Trump promised that the suit would bring down the NFL. (Trump's use of antitrust laws to attack his enemies has been a reoccurring theme in his presidency, including an antitrust suit brought in 2017 against Time Warner, the corporate owner of CNN.)

When Cohn became ill with AIDS (he died in 1986), Trump hired a new lawyer, Harvey Myerson. Said Jeff Pearlman, "He was the personification of slime." Attorney Myerson was unduly beholden to Trump, and he was a disaster.

The trial took eleven weeks. The USFL sued for $1.69 billion, plus punitive damages. Myerson didn't call a single USFL owner except Trump. The litigation was essentially between Trump and the NFL.

"Donald wanted to be the star of the trial," said Pearlman.

The NFL's lawyers made it clear that the USFL had failed because Trump insisted on a fall schedule. Trump said NFL Commissioner Pete Rozelle had asked him to own an NFL franchise. Rozelle did no such thing.

Wrote Richard Hoffer in the *Los Angeles Times*, "[NFL lead attorney Frank] Rothman characterized Trump as the worst kind of snake who was selling his colleagues down the river so he could effect a merger of a few rich teams."

Said one of the jurors about Trump, "He was not believable in anything he said. He came off as arrogant and unlikeable."

On July 29, 1986, the jury ruled that the NFL was guilty of being a monopoly. The USFL had won.

The jury then awarded damages. The USFL was to get exactly *one dollar*.

Which was tripled, because it was an antitrust violation.

When the verdict was announced, New York Giants owner Wellington Mara handed a one-dollar bill to Donald Trump.

Thanks to Donald Trump, the USFL was officially dead.

Trump since then has done all he can to get back at the NFL. When Colin Kaepernick in 2015 knelt to protest the number of African Americans shot and killed by white policemen, Trump declared that Kaepernick was dishonoring America by kneeling during the national anthem. This was Trump's revenge for the NFL refusing to allow him to become a team owner as much as it was yet another opportunity for him to engage in race-baiting the African American community.

More importantly, Trump's disastrous leadership showed how his lust for power, insistence on making decisions by the seat of his pants, and inability to be swayed by logic and research could lead to total disaster.

OTHER TRUMP VENTURES

Separating investors from their money has made Trump rich. One of many disastrous ventures was Trump University, in which students put up as much as $35,000 to learn how to become rich selling real estate. The come-on was that these students would learn from "Trump's hand-picked instructors," when in fact Trump had little to do with the instructors.

Trump University shut its doors after five years in 2010, leaving thousands of tuition-paying students in the lurch. Students sued, and in one case Trump countersued, a favorite strong-arm tactic of his, demanding $1 million from the student. (The countersuit was thrown out.) Trump was accused of using Trump University to cheat thousands of people out of millions of dollars.

Before the lawsuits were settled, Trump in 2016 launched an attack on the federal judge, Gonzalo Curiel, saying that because the judge was "Mexican," he couldn't be impartial. He said Curiel made "bad rulings" and said he had been "treated very unfairly." Curiel was born in Indiana.

In November 2016 Trump agreed to settle all the lawsuits for $25 million.

It could have ended far worse for Trump if law enforcement had stepped in, but the Florida attorney general saved the day. A raft of Floridians who were scammed by Trump University contacted Florida attorney general Pam Bondi. Bondi said she was considering whether to join the lawsuit filed by New York State attorney general Eric Schneiderman, when Bondi called Trump and asked him for a $25,000 donation to her campaign. He complied. Bondi's office dropped the inquiry.

Before becoming president, Trump was accused of violating antitrust laws, entering into deals with known mobsters and other criminals, refusing to pay workers and contractors, hiring undocumented workers at all three casinos, and operating a phony charitable foundation. He was also accused and fined for housing discrimination and paid a settlement to tenants who accused him of intimidation when he tried to evict them and charge higher rents.

One of his biggest moneymaking schemes was hatched in 2006. In the 1990s he had paid $2 million for 436 acres north of New York City with the idea of building a golf course. When he couldn't get past the environmental restrictions, he sought to sell it. Four years later he donated the land to New York State for a park named after him.

During the dedication of the Donald J. Trump State Park, a reporter asked him the value of the land.

"People have told me about $100 million," he said.

A town official said it was worth closer to $15 million.

The question arose whether Trump claimed a $100 million charitable deduction in his income tax return of 2006. Did he lie about the $100 million valuation? Did he cheat the government with a $100 million valuation?

Only his tax returns can tell us.

THE APPRENTICE

The Apprentice, the reality show that made Donald Trump nationally famous, was the brainchild of Mark Burnett, who made his reputation with the *Survivor* franchise.

Burnett needed to find a host—someone "bigger than life and very colorful, someone who would be likeable, tough, and fascinating enough to interest an audience for a full season."

In 2002 Burnett found what he was looking for when he rented the Wollman Rink in Central Park for a live broadcast of the Season 4 finale of *Survivor: Marquesas*. Donald Trump, who had leased the rink in 1986, was in attendance with girlfriend Melania Knauss.

Burnett noticed that TRUMP was plastered all over the ice-making machine and the walls of the rink. By 2002 The Donald was a local celebrity, a real estate mogul, and the author of *The Art of the Deal*, a book written largely by Tony Schwartz that stayed at the top of the *New York Times* bestseller list for thirteen weeks.

Burnett immediately saw in Trump the host for his new show. To get him to sign on, Burnett told Trump the premise—teams of job seekers would vie for his approval—and he told Trump that the show would showcase his helicopter, jet, Mar-a-Lago, his casinos, fancy apartment, and all that splendor. Trump would be The Boss. He would be judge, jury, and executioner in a weekly contest to see which desperate go-getter would work in one of Trump's businesses for $250,000 a year.

Trump worried the show would take up too much of his time. Burnett promised him it would only take three hours a week and would be filmed in Trump Tower.

On impulse, without doing any research or talking to consultants, Trump shook hands with Burnett to become equal partners. The show was ingenious. It was about "what makes America great"—contestants fighting to become rich. Trump, the quintessential New York tycoon, would pick the winner after each session.

Burnett knew how to treat his new partner. Burnett flattered Trump as often as he could, knowing how much he liked flattery. Trump often told people that the two had invented the show together, and Burnett never corrected him. Burnett saw the importance of never upstaging him. Trump used the show to advertise his properties. The contestants stayed at Trump Tower, did events at his Trump National Golf Club, and sold various Trump products.

Trump saw how the show would promote his brand and how it would allow him to rebrand his image.

Twenty million viewers tuned into the first episode of *The Apprentice.*

When the show began, Trump was deeply in debt, but it didn't take long for Trump to be seen as someone who had fought his way back to respectability.

At the start of the first show, Trump's voice-over intoned, "I own buildings all over the place. Model agencies, the Miss Universe pageant, jetliners, golf courses, casinos, and private resorts like Mar-a-Lago . . . I've mastered the art of the deal and have turned the name Trump into the highest-quality brand. And as the master, I want to pass along some of my knowledge to somebody else."

Trump never read a script. He wasn't always coherent, but editors removed the worst of his garbled syntax and malapropisms. On air he was bombastic, overbearing, and clearly in charge. The final lines of each show, "*You're fired*," weren't in the script. He just blurted it out. The line became a symbol of Trump's toughness.

"*The Apprentice* offered a promise not only of enrichment," wrote David Frum, "but of justice, at a time when Americans craved that fantasy even more than usual."

By the end of the first season *The Apprentice* was the highest-rated show of the week. It had twenty-seven million viewers. Trump would be liked for his honesty, the way he told bad contestants to take a hike. He was blunt. Sometimes he'd humiliate a contestant. Viewers ate it up.

"Above all," wrote Michael Kranish and Marc Fisher in *Fortune* magazine, "*Apprentice* sold an image of the host-boss as supremely competent and confident, dispensing his authority and getting immediate results. The analogy to politics was palpable."

The Apprentice ran for fourteen seasons. With his newfound fame, Trump began to talk politics. He appeared on the *Imus in the Morning* show every week, and he talked with Don Imus about the possibility of running for president one day.

When Trump made his grand entrance down the gold-colored escalator to the atrium of the Trump Tower to announce his candidacy in 2015, it was choreography that Burnett had used often for *The Apprentice*. Those who cheered his speech that day were extras paid fifty dollars for the event.

Burnett also tried to market a reality show starring Vladimir Putin. The show was to be called *Destination: Mir*, and the idea was that the winner each week would be launched into space. When Russia shut down the Mir space station, Burnett scuttled the idea. In 2015 Burnett again brought up the idea of a reality show starring Putin. It would be a hymn to the glory of Russia, he said.

On August 12, 2015, NBC announced that Donald Trump, then a Republican candidate for president, had been fired from *The Apprentice*. After Trump made negative comments about Mexican immigrants, NBC cut their ties. It also cancelled its airing of the *Miss USA* pageant, which Trump owned.

"Due to the recent derogatory statements by Donald Trump regarding immigrants, NBC Universal is ending its business relationship with Mr. Trump," NBC said in a statement, adding, "At NBC, respect and dignity for all people are cornerstones of our values."

In response, Trump blasted NBC, saying it was "so weak and so foolish to not understand the serious illegal immigration problem." He has never let go of his anger at NBC.

In sum, there is one aspect of business that Trump is extraordinarily good at: sales. Trump is the consummate salesman. He can usually sell just about anything to anybody. He *can* close the deal. Some observers have argued that without help from his father, Trump never would have been successful in business, but that is probably not true—even starting at the lowest levels selling any product, he most likely would have been a successful salesman.

At a certain point a sales pitch becomes so "convincing" and "compelling" that it becomes a fraud. Most salespeople who become con artists get sued or perhaps go to jail. Once again Trump, because of family circumstances, was protected from this aspect of the real world. He had the political connections—and tough lawyers including Roy Cohn and Michael Cohen—to fight allegations, plaster over lies with more lies, and get away with it.

The salesperson unchecked by the long arm of the law at some point becomes a con artist. Many businesspeople (in addition to the holders of some $900 million in Trump casino bonds in the mid-1990s) believe that is exactly what happened with Donald Trump.

CHAPTER 17

A Man of Many Assets
or a Foreign Asset?

*You can fool all the people some of the time and some of the people
all the time, but you cannot fool all the people all the time.*
—*ABRAHAM LINCOLN*

A S WE SAID, THIS BOOK IS NOT A FULL ACCOUNT OF THE
virtues and vices of Trump's early years. In the previous chapter we
discussed the personality traits that we believe are most relevant to his presidency. In this chapter we discuss some of the highs and lows of his personal
and financial life that define Trump and make him more vulnerable than any
past president to the influence, and perhaps even control, of a foreign power.

TRUMP'S PERSONAL LIFE

Trump's personal life is, and always has been, colorful. He has had two ugly
divorces. He talked on the *Howard Stern Show* about his many affairs and
the physical attractiveness of his daughter Ivanka. He has made bizarre sexist

comments such as, "Bad press doesn't matter as long as you have a sexy girl-friend," "A woman must be hot in order to be a journalist," and "All women hate prenups because they are gold diggers."

Trump bragged about how he could grab women by the private parts and get away with it, and shortly before the election, he paid the *National Enquirer* to buy and then bury stories of a porn star and a model who accused Trump of sexual abuse, just to keep the evidence of his bad behavior from the public.

But enough with the Trump sex stories. Entire books have been written about that. The upshot is that Trump's sex life is far more salacious than any previous president's, including Warren Harding and Bill Clinton, the most promiscuous presidents in modern American history. (We suspect that at least half the other presidents had affairs outside of marriage as well, but with far less publicity.)

In most representative democracies, sexual promiscuity is not a serious obstacle for an elected leader, but since the days of the Puritans, memorial-ized by Nathaniel Hawthorne's book *The Scarlet Letter*, American mores have been affected by an intersection of our quest for perfection with our hypocrisy. Keeping sexual promiscuity under wraps is, in America more than in most other countries, important for political success.

On one side we have the preachers of the "religious right," some of whom preach as often as they fornicate. On the other side we have politicians and political commentators who purport to strive to correct imbalances in rela-tions between men and women by politicizing sexual harassment and assault, while keeping their own hypocrisy under wraps. For example, Senator Ted Kennedy was one of the most senior Democrats on the Judiciary Committee for the confirmation hearing when Judge Clarence Thomas was nominated to the Supreme Court. President Clinton used the Anita Hill allegations in his 1992 campaign, before his own reputation was marred by sexual harassment allegations in Arkansas. Everyone is eager to hang upon someone—usually a political rival or opponent—the scarlet letter.

There's an endless list of instances in which Americans have torn them-selves apart over sexual misconduct allegations that would be minimized or even ignored elsewhere in the world.

What is important for this book is not the fairness of our more puritanical—and some would say righteous—approach to sexual misconduct. It's the *effect* on our political life when candidates and elected officials are involved in misconduct. Candidates use sexual misconduct as a weapon against each other in America far more easily than in other countries. After the release of the Billy Bush tape in 2016, the first thing Trump did was invite Paula Jones to attend his debate with Hillary Clinton in an attempt to humiliate her. It worked.

More ominously, foreign powers that obtain evidence of sexual misconduct can use it to hold high-ranking American officials—and perhaps even our entire government—hostage.

The gravest risk from Trump's personal life is blackmail. Religious conservatives, with their extreme sensitivity to sexual immorality, have limits to what they will tolerate. Granted, they have tolerated a lot of Trump's bad behavior, including his admission that he can "grab them by the pussy." A videotape of Trump actually performing or witnessing a perverted sex act would likely be too much. Evidence of his ever having paid for an abortion would be even worse. It remains to be seen whether the religious right will decide to pull the plug on this president and replace him with one of their own: Vice President Mike Pence. So far that doesn't seem apt to happen.

But if Vladimir Putin has a tape of Trump's sexual activity in Russia—a "pee-pee tape" or any other—as private investigator Christopher Steele suggests he might, the blackmail risk is a near certainty. Same if Putin has evidence of anything else that could make the religious right turn on Trump.

Voters from other powers, especially France, would probably laugh off evidence of sexual misconduct by an elected leader. After what happened to President Clinton in 1998, however, Russia and other adversaries know that in America sexual conduct can create a constitutional crisis. They also know that an elected leader will do anything to avoid being exposed.

We'll talk more about Russia taking advantage of this in our discussion of hacked emails. The focus here is on Donald Trump.

In sum, the problem for the United States and our national security is not so much what Donald Trump has done in his personal life—history is filled with examples of promiscuous and even perverted world leaders—but the combination of puritanical responses and what foreign adversaries with sophisticated intelligence operations, particularly Russia, can do with it.

Is Trump being blackmailed by Russians?

His behavior certainly has made him vulnerable.

His bromance with Vladimir Putin also begs the question.

TRUMP'S BUSINESS ASSETS (AND LIABILITIES)

Even more troubling and complex than Trump's personal life is his financial life, which makes him vulnerable to the influence and control of foreign powers.

It's clear that Donald Trump decided to run for president for the opportunity to expand his wealth. He didn't think he would win, but he saw a campaign as a great way to promote himself and his businesses. When he did win, he found more ways to accomplish the same objective.

Donald Trump took his extraordinary sales talent (or conmanship) into the family business of real estate. It's a business that very much depends upon borrowed capital. The developer invests some of the developer's own money—ideally no more than 10 percent to 20 percent—borrows the rest with a note and mortgage of the land and buildings, and then, hopefully, takes all the profits and pays off the loan. In boom times such as the 1980s, the developer makes an extraordinary amount of money (80 percent or more of the capital comes from the lender, but the developer gets all of the profits). The seasoned developer with good judgment knows to keep enough cash on hand for bad times.

If the market collapses, the developer can be stuck with the building, a sluggish rent roll, and a mortgage coming due. At that point it's decision time: whether to keep paying the mortgage out of personal funds, even if the building is "underwater" (worth less than the loan), or to give the bank the keys and walk away.

Developers who choose the latter option usually don't get to borrow again for a while, if ever.

For large-scale projects, this can be done not only with banks, but with bonds. Securities can be sold to public or private investors with the help of Wall Street investment bankers, and the proceeds can be used to buy land and construct a project. In boom times it is win-win for the bondholders and the developer, although the developer gets the lion's share of the profits and the bondholders only get interest. In bad times the developer has to decide whether to inject more funds into the project to make payments on the bonds until the economy improves, or to simply walk away and allow the bonds to go into default.

In the late 1980s, Trump insisted his major qualification to build a new casino in Atlantic City was that he wouldn't need to use junk bonds. Then he used junk bonds to build the Trump Taj Mahal at a cost of nearly $1 billion.

When his company couldn't keep up with the interest payments, it declared bankruptcy in 1991. Trump sold his yacht, his airline, and half his ownership in the casino.

A year later another of Trump's Atlantic City casinos, the Trump Plaza, went bust after losing more than $550 million. He gave up his financial stake and managed to avoid personal losses while remaining CEO. His debt exceeded $900 million.

By 2004 Trump Hotels & Casino Resorts was $1.8 billion in debt. The company filed for bankruptcy and became Trump Entertainment Resorts. In 2009, after the real estate collapse, Trump Entertainment Resorts went bankrupt. Donald Trump resigned from the board and had to sue to take his name off the building.

When these defaults on bonds and other loans began in the early 1990s, Trump ruined his relationship with New York's financial establishment. Both commercial bank lenders and investment banks shunned him. He was always insecure in New York society and business circles, but he was now persona non grata. *Nobody* with large amounts of money to lend would deal with him (or at least nobody on this side of the ocean).

To make matters worse, bondholders believed not only that Trump had been extraordinarily reckless with their money, but they also believed he had lied to them. They sued. In a high-profile case—*In Re Donald J. Trump Casinos Securities Litigation*—the United States Court of Appeals for the

Third Circuit in 1993 made a highly controversial decision that has been the subject of securities law seminars and law school courses ever since.

In establishing the so-called "bespeaks caution" doctrine, the court held that the bond issuer and its officers, here Donald Trump, could not be sued. Even if Trump did lie, said the court, there were enough other disclosed facts to make it clear that Trump couldn't pay off the bonds like he said. In other words, the bondholders had trusted Trump, but they should have known that his word wasn't worth the paper it was printed on.

Richard Painter, one of the authors of this book, has frequently lectured about the *Trump Casino Securities Litigation* case, criticizing the court's opinion because the federal securities laws were intended to provide investors with more protection than the old adage "buyer beware." Yet the court, in a nutshell, was telling investors:

People who trust what Donald Trump promises to do, and make decisions based on those promises, get what they deserve.

The country should have paid attention, but few Americans outside of New York City and the banking community knew much about Trump's business reputation.

So where did Trump get the money he needed to recover financially and restore his business reputation?

There is scant record of Trump having any significant relationship with any large American financial institution since the mid-1990s. He has had a relationship with Deutsche Bank, Germany's largest bank with a major office in New York and other cities worldwide, including Moscow. Deutsche Bank has lent the Trump Organization a lot of money, and hundreds of millions of dollars of those loans are still outstanding. It is not clear where Deutsche Bank got that money, whether Deutsche Bank is really taking the risk associated with those loans, or whether there has been a guarantee and perhaps even a deposit to secure that guarantee from some other place.

Very little is known about the Trump Organization's finances, particularly its debt and equity capital, because it is a private company that doesn't have to file reports with the SEC. You cannot look up its balance sheet and profit and loss statement online. The only people who know are Donald Trump and those who work for him.

As a presidential candidate or even as president, Trump does not have to disclose any of this. The financial disclosure form 278 only requires reporting of *his* personal assets and debts (and Melania's). His personal assets are his ownership interest—often 100 percent—of dozens of separately incorporated entities that make up the "Trump Organization." He simply reports their names and descriptions (golf courses, hotels, condos, real estate, etc.). He is not obligated to say where these entities get their money. In sum, all of the borrowing, equity investments by other people, and joint corporate ventures need not be disclosed. Only if Donald Trump personally guarantees a debt does it have to go on the "liabilities" schedule on his form 278.

As the holders of $900 million in casino bonds found out in the early 1990s, Donald Trump does not like to personally guarantee much of anything.

We have known very little about where Trump gets his money for over twenty years, but we do know that hundreds of millions in capital were required for the projects that bear his name around the globe. We also know that in the mid-1990s he had relatively little money, a few million at best, to call his own. We also know where Trump has been expanding his business, and something about the people and projects he's been involved with.

Except for some parts of the United States and Scotland, Trump has generally avoided countries that could be characterized as long-standing representative democracies. He has taken a position (even if he has not invested his own money) in enormous projects in authoritarian regimes including Saudi Arabia and China, titular representative democracies with "elections" (Russia and most of the former Soviet republics), or actual democracies that are moving in a decidedly undemocratic direction including Turkey and the Philippines.

Going into the presidential election of 2016, Trump was involved with 144 companies doing business in twenty-five countries. His interests ranged from management deals with golf courses in the United Arab Emirates (UAE), branding agreements with real estate projects in India, and companies that have been involved with beverage sales in Israel.

Trump was doing business in Argentina, Bermuda, India, Indonesia, Canada, UAE, Scotland, China, Brazil, Panama, Saudi Arabia, St. Martin, Azerbaijan, Saint Vincent, Ireland, Israel, Qatar, Dominican Republic, Egypt, Georgia, Mexico, Philippines, South Africa, Turkey, and Uruguay.

Trump created multiple companies to handle his deals, and much of his foreign business involved licensing agreements. The Donald J. Trump collection of clothing had shirts made in China, Bangladesh, Honduras, Vietnam, and South Korea. His sport coats were made in India. Trump eyeglasses were made in China. The Trump home brand of luxury furniture had production facilities in Turkey and Germany. Trump china was made in Slovenia. His vodka was distilled in the Netherlands and Israel.

His Make America Great Again hats, however, were made in Southern California.

Donald Trump has in the course of these business dealings met a lot of foreign dictators and oligarchs. Almost all of these he says he likes. The autocrats in his circle include Anar Mammadov, a millionaire playboy in Azerbaijan, a country known as the "world's most corrupt regime." In 2015 Anar and his father, "the Corleones of the Caspian," helped finance the Trump Towers Istanbul. Turkey's government apparently had a hand in the project as well, as acknowledged by Ivanka Trump in April 2012 in a Tweet saying: "Thank you Prime Minister Erdogan for joining us yesterday to celebrate the launch of #TrumpTowers Istanbul!"

Speaker of the House Nancy Pelosi and her colleagues in the House leadership had finally seen and heard enough. On September 23, 2019, Pelosi announced that the House would initiate a formal impeachment inquiry against President Trump. The House formally voted to approve the impeachment investigation, making it very likely that Trump would soon be charged in articles of impeachment with betraying his oath of office and the nation's security, and perhaps also extortion and soliciting a bribe, when he sought to enlist the president of Ukraine to dish dirt on political rival Joe Biden in exchange for US military aid to Ukraine. Other charges—particularly with respect to the Mueller investigation—might be included as well.

"Mr. Trump must be held accountable," Pelosi said. "No one is above the law."

Since his election in 2016 Trump has tried to convince his followers to disregard the overwhelming evidence that the Russians had helped him win. He has done this advancing a patently false conspiracy theory—spread by Fox News and other right-wing media outlets—that the Ukranians had helped Hillary Clinton in that election. Getting the Ukrainian president to announce he was investigating this fake charge about the 2016 election would be Trump's way of making it more real. Getting Ukraine to investigate Joe Biden and his son Hunter would also help Trump in 2020. To get President Zelensky to conduct both investigations, Trump was willing to withhold American aid when Ukraine desperately needed that money to fight rebels backed by the Russians. Trump was willing to withhold US military aid to commit extortion and solicit a bribe (help for his 2020 political campaign) from a foreign power. Even more reprehensible, Trump was enlisting White House officials, State Department officials, and even persons not employed by the United States Government—mostly notably his "Sancho Panza" Rudy Giuliani—in his illegal scheme.

When a whistleblower (identity unknown as this book went to press) let the world know what Trump was doing, and this story was corroborated by multiple witnesses, Pelosi, the Democrats, and most of the country had all had enough. It was time to hold this rogue president accountable.

The House Impeachment Committee called twelve witnesses, who testified one after another that Trump had been behind a scheme to try to force the Ukranian president to broadcast two phony conspiracy theories, about Ukraine interfering in the 2016 election and about the corruption of the Bidens. If Ukraine didn't do this, no US aid would be forthcoming. It was only the whistleblower's report—the fact that Trump had been caught red handed—that moved Trump to release the aid.

One after another, the witnesses, proud long-time professionals from the State Department and armed services, spoke about Trump's Ukraine scheme and their opposition to it. These State Department stalwarts were implementing a longstanding US policy of trying to protect Ukraine from domination by Russia, all while Trump was trying to get the Ukrainian president to become a part of his own corrupt campaign for re-election.

"I couldn't believe what I was hearing," said Lt. Col. Alexander Vindman, the National Security Council's Ukraine expert. An Iraq war combat veteran who appeared in his Army dress uniform covered with ribbons, Vindman told the House Impeachment Committee that what Trump wanted President Zelensky to do would have "significant implications for US national security."

Sitting next to Vindman was Jennifer Williams, a career diplomat on Vice-President Pence's national security staff. She said that Trump's phone call to President Zelensky asking for dirt on the Bidens was "unusual and inappropriate."

Both said that Trump was holding up the $391 million that Ukraine needed to defend itself against the Russians. No national security official supported holding up that aid, they said.

Some Republicans on the Intelligence Committee, toeing the line that Trump had done nothing wrong, went after Vindman with a vengeance. When Representative Jim Jordan questioned Colonel Vindman's judgment, the officer brought out a performance evaluation by his boss Dr. Fiona Hill.

"Alex is a top 1 percent military officer and the best Army officer I have worked with in my fifteen years of government service," he read with pride.

That shut Jordan up, at least for a while.

Colonel Vindman decried the smears on government officials called to testify.

"The vile character attacks on these distinguished and honorable public servants is reprehensible," he said.

The next day the star witness was wealthy hotel owner Gordon Sondland, who had made a $1 million contribution to President Trump's inaugural fund. As a reward he had been appointed as ambassador to the European Union. Sondland was eating at a restaurant in the Ukraine when President Trump called him to ask whether he had spoken to Ukrainian President Zelensky about announcing his investigations into the 2016 election and into the Bidens. Trump spoke so loudly that the conversation was overheard by several diplomats.

When asked by Democratic counsel Daniel Goldman whether American aid was contingent on Zelensky doing as Trump was asking, Sondland responded, "Was there a quid pro quo? As I testified previously, with regard to the requested White House call and White House meeting, the answer is yes."

Sondland was making it clear that Trump, not just Rudy Giuliani, was behind the extortion. Sondland later said, "We all understood that if we refused to work with Mr. Giuliani, we would lose an important opportunity to cement relations between the United States and Ukraine. So we followed *the president's orders.*"

In this testimony from a high-ranking Trump political appointee, the House Intelligence Committee had a smoking gun.

Dr. Fiona Hill, the White House's former top expert on Europe and Russia, was present during meetings in which Ukrainian officials were pressed to announce investigations to help President Trump. When she was called to testify, she pleaded with Republicans to stop trying to spread the phony conspiracy theory that Ukraine had interfered in the 2016 election to help Hillary Clinton.

Russia's "goal is to weaken our country," said Hill. Spreading phony conspiracy theories plays into Vladimir Putin's hands. "These fictions are harmful even if they are deployed for purely domestic political purposes."

Dr. Hill added, "In the course of this investigation, I would ask that you please not promote politically driven falsehoods that so clearly advance Russian interests." She said that "right now Russia is seeking to interfere in the 2020 election. We are running out of time to stop them."

Republicans on the Committee made it clear that they would not vote to impeach Trump. It appeared that they would follow Trump to the end—whatever that end might be.

Said Paul Krugman in an op-ed piece in the *New York Times*, "Anyone imagining that the mountainous evidence of Trump's malfeasance will lead to a moral awakening, or that Republicans will return to democratic political norms once Trump is gone, is living in a fantasy world.

"The big question is whether America as we know it can long endure when one of its two major parties has effectively rejected the principles on which our nation was built."

Will House Republicans—and more importantly Senate Republicans—adhere throughout 2020 to this stubborn support for Trump, notwithstanding the overwhelming evidence against him? Or will we reach the point we reached in August 1974, when Senate Republicans finally called President Nixon to tell him that the game was over? As evidence mounts in a scandal far more egregious and far more dangerous for our national security than Watergate, we can only hope that the answer to this latter question will be in the affirmative.

In November 2004 Trump paid $41 million for a 62,000-square-foot mansion in Palm Beach named the Maison de L'Amitie, and in the summer of 2008 he sold it to forty-one-year-old Russian billionaire Dmitry Rybolovlev, who spent a year in a Russian prison on murder charges but who was acquitted. Rybolovlev paid $100 million for the property.

In 2013, Trump partnered with the Russian real estate mogul Aras Agalarov to bring the Miss Universe pageant, which Trump owned at the time, to Moscow. Trump later boasted that "all the oligarchs" attended the event. While in Moscow, Trump discussed plans for real estate projects there.

In the fall of 2015, Trump was introduced via satellite to a crowd of people attending the Yalta European Strategy (YES) conference. The conference was set up by Ukrainian billionaire philanthropist Victor Pinchuk. During his twenty-minute teleconference, Trump referred to Pinchuk as his friend, and afterwards Pinchuk made a $150,000 donation to the Donald J. Trump Foundation.

Trump's love for foreign dictators is amazing—troubling but amazing.

Trump in 2018 said of China's president Xi Jinping, "He's now president for life. President for life. No, he's great. And look, he was able to do that. I think it's great. Maybe we'll have to give that a shot someday."

In September 2016, while Barack Obama was still president, Trump said about Vladimir Putin, "If he says great things about me, I'm going to say great things about him. I've already said, he is really very much a leader." Comparing Russian's political system to ours, Trump concluded, "He's been a leader, far more than our president has been a leader."

Philippines president Rodrigo Duterte had boasted about killing suspected drug dealers. Commented Trump in April of 2017, "I just wanted to congratulate you because I am hearing of the unbelievable job on the drug problem."

Trump also heaped praise on Turkish president Recep Tayyip Erdoğan, whose crackdown on the Turkish people, the media, and especially his opponents, was brutal. In September 2017, Trump said of Erdoğan, "Frankly, he's getting very high marks. He's also been working with the United States. We have a great friendship and the countries—I think we're right now as close as we've ever been—a lot of that has to do with a personal relationship."

Another dictator, Egyptian president Abdel Fattah el-Sisi, gained power in a coup after Egypt flirted with democracy following its Arab Spring. El-Sisi quickly suppressed civil liberties and crushed all opposition under the pretext of fighting terrorism. Said Trump about el-Sisi, "We agree on so many things. I just want to let everybody know in case there was any doubt that we are very much behind President el-Sisi."

Trump has similarly kind words for North Korean dictator Kim Jong-Un, particularly when Chairman Kim strokes his ego or insults American Democrats such as Joe Biden.

Trump has also praised earlier dictators Benito Mussolini, Saddam Hussein, and Muammar Gaddafi. He also commended China for its crackdown on protestors in Tiananmen Square in July 1989.

"It shows you the power of strength," Trump said.

In sum, Trump has broken his financial relationship with American bankers and investors beyond repair and needs to turn elsewhere. But we have no idea where. He has extensive business dealings abroad, mostly in dictatorships. And he loves foreign dictators.

So what happens when a businessman with this portfolio and these attitudes moves into the White House?

We have never experienced this before, but imagine what it would have been like in the 1940s when Western civilization faced its greatest threat in history if the President of the United States had substantial foreign financial interests.

Before World War II, many American businesses and banks had millions of dollars invested in Nazi Germany. John Foster Dulles, a New York lawyer, managing partner of Sullivan & Cromwell, and future secretary of state, had a thriving Berlin practice and an office in Berlin late into the 1930s. Money invested in Germany would be lost if Germany were to be bombed or invaded by the allies. Millions down the drain. Many American businessmen supported the America First movement, dedicated to keeping the United States out of the war. Pacifism was the proclaimed rationale, but financial interests (and in the case of Henry Ford, a strong dose of anti-Semitism) were part of the explanation. Many American businessmen supported neutrality as did many newspapers, particularly the Hearst chain. Money was on the line.

But not for FDR. His administration constantly pushed back against America Firsters. At least our president at the time, and presumably many of the people working for him, did not have great financial exposure to Germany and the rest of Europe. When Lend Lease of military equipment was being arranged with Churchill in 1940 and 1941, and later when the Japanese attacked us on December 7, 1941, there were no "Roosevelt Towers" in Berlin and Frankfurt or "Roosevelt casinos" in Rome and Paris. American voters would not have accepted such blatant conflicts of interest, even if they supported neutrality.

But then was then and now is now. The world is still a dangerous place, but today, eighty years later, are such global financial conflicts of interest for our leaders presumably acceptable?

President Trump's financial conflicts of interest, his closeness to foreign oligarchs, and his admiration for dictators were issues during the campaign. But these were not issues that the Hillary Clinton campaign chose to emphasize, in part because the Clinton Foundation had its own alleged conflicts of interest, and Hillary Clinton was unwilling to promise to close or hand over the foundation to others outside her family, even if she were elected president.

Trump's financial conflicts of interest were *enormous*. And he refused to do anything about them.

In November 2016, two weeks after the election, Director of the Office of Government Ethics Walter Shaub urged Trump, like every other recent president, to divest himself of conflict-creating business holdings and put the sale proceeds either in a blind trust or conflict-free assets such as mutual funds. Many billionaires appointed to high-ranking government jobs have done just this. They have sold conflict-creating assets and invested sale proceeds in a way that avoids conflicts of interest.

In his November 2016 speech, OGE Director Shaub simply asked Donald Trump to do the same.

Trump refused. He insisted on holding on to his hotels, clubs, and real estate and licensing interests at home and around the world. In doing so he also retained his financial ties all over the globe, many of which have not been disclosed.

Trump's response to critics was a blanket "the president cannot have a conflict of interest," an attitude more fit for a kinglike ruler such as King George III than for a president.

Even if Trump's moral argument on conflicts of interest is vacuous, he does have a *technical* legal argument, and it is there that he hangs his hat (where no recent president before him has done so). There is no specific law that directly prohibits the president from owning assets—of any kind—that conflict with his official duties. The criminal conflict of interest statute, 18 US Code 208, does not technically apply to the president even if his business holdings in fact create massive conflicts of interest.

His conflicts are so serious that if Trump were in any executive branch position other than president or vice president, they would be *criminal* offenses. This long-standing provision of the United States criminal code specifically states that it is a crime for a federal executive branch employee to participate "personally and substantially" in any "particular matter" affecting their or their spouse's financial interest, whether a company they hold stock in, a hotel or golf club they own, or any other financial interest.

A treasury secretary may not own Goldman Sachs stock while regulating Wall Street. A Health and Human Services secretary may not own healthcare stocks; an Energy Department secretary may not own oil company stocks; an Education Department secretary may not own for-profit education stocks, unless they recuse themselves from any and all government matters that have a predictable effect on those stocks. Otherwise they risk indictment and even jail.

Given that choice, most government officials sell the stocks and put the sale proceeds in diversified mutual funds, other conflict-free assets, or a blind trust. That was exactly the advice given to incoming Bush administration officials by one of the authors of this book (Painter), and that must be given to executive branch officials.

Perhaps because members of Congress did not want to apply this law to themselves, however, they chose not to apply it to any *elected* official, including the president. 18 USC 208 does not apply to the president, the vice president, or members of Congress.

There's a potential problem in prosecuting presidents for a financial conflict of interest while they are fulfilling their constitutional duties. Prosecution of a president or vice president under the financial conflict of interest statute could be unconstitutional. The Department of Justice Office of Legal Counsel came to this conclusion in the mid-1970s. However, this does not mean that the president "cannot have a conflict of interest," as Trump claims. It means that the criminal code is not used to penalize this conflict of interest. It is up to Congress, and ultimately voters, to penalize a president in this circumstance.

When Trump looked for examples of previous presidents with financial conflicts of interest, he had to look very far back because recent presidents have avoided such conflicts. Herbert Hoover had some modest mining interest, but Trump dismissed that. (Hoover is not often associated with a strong economy.) So Trump went farther back, to George Washington and Thomas Jefferson at the founding of our nation. Trump repeatedly claimed that his holdings in the Trump Organization were perfectly fine because they both owned plantations, Mount Vernon and Monticello, while they held office.

These two presidents could not possibly be "unethical," Trump argued, so neither was he.

Washington and Jefferson were indeed two of our greatest presidents. But they had flaws. Their flaws—and those of so many other wealthy men of their time—were the most tragic flaws in United States history. Their plantations made Washington and Jefferson fabulously wealthy, but they used slave labor, as did many other wealthy business owners throughout the South, many of whom served as representatives, senators, governors, and even presidents, including Presidents Madison and Monroe.

Conflicts of interest of high-ranking government officials have consequences. Trump's repeated references to these presidents and their plantations shows not only how tone deaf he is to the legacy of slavery and racial injustice, but what contributed to that tragedy: financial conflicts of interest of very wealthy men in Washington.

Fast-forward to more recent times. Financial conflicts of interest of elected officials—even if not banned—have consequences, whether those interests include real estate, healthcare, fossil fuels, the defense industry, banks, or any other. While perhaps not criminal, it is *unacceptable.*

Financial conflicts of interest on an international scale can be a direct threat to our national security.

As we pointed out, Donald Trump does not invest heavily in democracies. He prefers wealthy but non-democratic countries in the Middle East and Asia, including Russia and the former Soviet Republics. He is the first president in American history to have enormous financial exposure in nations outside the United States, on top of the fact that most of the countries he has financial relationships with are not our close allies.

Some are long-standing adversaries.

The consequences could be catastrophic. An international crisis involving one or more of these countries where he has financial exposure, even if not as big as the crisis we faced with Germany and Japan in the early 1940s, could end disastrously for the United States. Donald Trump has been known to put himself first. Indeed that may be something he has never been known *not* to do.

As pointed out in a *Washington Post* op-ed written by one of this book's authors (Painter) with former US ambassador to the Czech Republic Norman Eisen:

> Even more serious [than his domestic conflicts of interest] are the questions raised by Trump investments abroad. Those relate to some of the United States' most important—and most sensitive—relationships, among them ones with Russia, China, India, South Korea and Turkey. When the United States must support or confront those nations, or their adversaries, would Trump act to benefit the national interest, or his and his family's investments? Moreover, who are the foreign individuals with whom he has had financial ties, and how would those relationships affect his decisions? As the electorate considers those questions, it is entitled to more information.

American voters never got to see the information. Trump—with help from Russia, where he may have business dealings—won anyway.

Furthermore, a subset of Trump's investments, revenue streams, and sources of financing is illegal. The profits and benefits he derives from *foreign governments and entities controlled by foreign governments* are specifically prohibited under the foreign emoluments clause of the Constitution unless Congress provides explicit consent. (It hasn't.) Profits and benefits from dealings with individual states within the United States are also prohibited by the domestic emoluments clause of the Constitution, but the foreign government emoluments present the gravest risk to our national security. Donald Trump is the first president in US history to come into confrontation with this clause.

Before Trump, most Americans, including most lawyers, had *never heard* of the emoluments clause. It was not taught in constitutional law classes and was almost never discussed in the media. Until 2018, when a federal district court issued a ruling against the president in *District of Columbia and Maryland v. Trump*, no federal court had ever interpreted the clause.

Things are very different now.

First the problem. Again, as Painter warned in the *Washington Post* op-ed written with Ambassador Eisen:

> Because of Trump's seeming unwillingness to set up a true blind trust, and the difficulty of his doing so, his potential foreign conflicts could raise immediate legal issues. Most federal ethics rules, surprisingly, do not apply to the president. But Trump would be covered by bribery laws and the Constitution's emoluments clause, which broadly prohibits the president from accepting gifts "from any King, Prince, or foreign State." The emoluments clause has been interpreted by the Justice Department to include any payment from a foreign government, except with the consent of Congress. Every time there was a financial transaction between a foreign government—or a company controlled by a foreign government—and any Trump entity, there would be a potential for favorable treatment that could violate this limitation, as well as the anti-bribery laws.

The point of the emoluments clause is to prevent a crime that is often impossible to prove—bribery.

In the case of foreign governments, our Constitution prohibits *any* emoluments (profits and benefits) to a federal office holder. It doesn't matter whether there is quid pro quo bribery, which is extremely difficult to prove. Avoiding these risks was so important to the founders that they made the ban on foreign government emoluments absolute unless Congress gives consent. The clause applies to every single United States government employee, and unlike the financial conflict of interest statute, it applies to the president.

How extensive are Trump's emoluments from foreign and state governments? Very. As Painter noted in a December 2016 paper for the Brookings Institution co-authored with Norman Eisen and Laurence Tribe:

> As things already stand, that risk is higher than it has ever been. By way of illustration, consider these examples of all the ways in which Mr. Trump's global business empire creates the conditions for his ongoing violation of the

Emoluments Clause to surface in obviously dubious transactions—transactions casting doubt on the ability and inclination of a President Trump to conduct himself with a singular focus on the Nation's interests and of foreign leaders dealing with him to treat his motives as public-spirited:

- Mr. Trump has recently completed the Trump International Hotel, a major new project in Washington, D.C. and a new hot spot for foreign diplomats.
  - ◇ As a former Mexican ambassador to the United States has candidly remarked, "The temptation and the inclination will certainly be there. Some might think it's the right way to engage, to be able to tell the next president, 'Oh, I stayed at your hotel. '"
  - ◇ Speaking on the Senate floor, Senator Ben Cardin noted, "One diplomat was recorded as saying 'Why wouldn't I stay at his hotel blocks from the White House, so I can tell the new president, *I love your new hotel!* Isn't it rude to come to his city and say, *I am staying at your competitor?*'"
  - ◇ Indeed, with lots of public fanfare, the Kingdom of Bahrain already has decided to mark the seventeenth anniversary of King Hamad bin Isa Al Khalifa's accession to the throne by hosting a reception at the Trump International Hotel.
- Since Mr. Trump's election, long-delayed Trump projects have suddenly jump-started around the world, including in Argentina and Georgia. This may be especially noteworthy in light of Mr. Trump's acknowledgment that he has raised business issues on calls with foreign officials.
- Mere weeks before Mr. Trump spoke by phone with the president of Taiwan, dramatically altering American foreign policy, a businesswoman claiming to be associated with Mr. Trump's conglomerate arrived in Taiwan and made inquiries about major new investments in luxury hotels.
- Shortly before the election, President Duterte of the Philippines named Jose E.B. Antonio, a business partner of Mr. Trump and founder of a company behind Trump Tower Manila, as a special envoy to the United States.
- After Mr. Trump spoke of banning Muslim immigrants, President Erdoğan of Turkey demanded that Mr. Trump's name be removed

from Trump Towers in Istanbul, but that demand abruptly ceased after Mr. Trump defended President Erdoğan's brutal crackdown on Turkish dissidents.

⋄ Indeed, while running for President, Mr. Trump openly admitted during a radio interview that "I have a little conflict of interest because I have a major, major building in Istanbul."

• The Industrial and Commercial Bank of China—owned by the People's Republic of China—is the single largest tenant in Trump Tower. Its valuable lease will expire, and thus come up for re-negotiation, during Mr. Trump's presidency.

• Even as debates rage over American/Russian relations and Russian cyber-attacks on U.S. interests and even on the recent presidential election, it has been reported that Russian financiers play a significant (albeit concealed) role in Mr. Trump's organization.

• Mr. Trump's businesses owe hundreds of millions to Deutsche Bank, which is currently negotiating a multi-billion-dollar settlement with the U.S. Department of Justice, a settlement that will now be overseen by an Attorney General and many other appointees selected by and serving at the pleasure of Mr. Trump.

That's *a lot* of emoluments, most of them probably unconstitutional. Even if only *some* of these business relationships involve money from a foreign government, as opposed to money from a politically connected foreign oligarch, that's still a lot of unconstitutional emoluments.

This we knew back in 2016 even without tax returns from Trump or his organization, and without any public financial disclosure statements from the Trump Organization. As mentioned earlier, Trump's own financial disclosure, form 278, which he files every April as president, does not list any of the financial relationships, contracts, debts, or other arrangements of the private companies he owns. Form 278 simply lists the companies he owns. Dozens of line items report that Trump owns a 100 percent interest in Trump Partnership or LLC ABC without any information about where those companies get their money.

Trump is required to report personal debts and contractual arrangements, but as we know, Trump does not like to borrow money in his own name, or be legally liable to pay it back—so he doesn't have many debts to disclose. The money moves in and out of the Trump Organization entities and from there the profits (emoluments) move up to the owner of these entities—Donald Trump.

The economic reality behind all of these entities, however, is clear. Trump *owns* them. He can put his sons or someone else in charge, but he still *owns* them. He can create all sorts of new trusts and other entities with the details in documents hidden in brown envelopes proudly displayed on a table before television cameras. But the economic interest is still *his*. And when a foreign government provides profits and benefits (emoluments) to one of these entities, or several of them, the money goes to Donald Trump.

Also as mentioned, once he became president on January 20, 2017, these profits and benefits became unconstitutional unless Congress granted consent. The Republican-led Congress didn't consent, but it also didn't do anything about them. The Congress members, sworn to uphold the Constitution, have failed to do their job.

Thus far, three lawsuits have been filed against Donald Trump alleging violations of both the foreign and domestic emoluments clauses from revenue streams including room and ballroom rentals in Trump hotels, purchases of condominiums in Trump buildings, joint ventures, and probably Trump's undisclosed sources of financing.

The first suit was dismissed by the federal district court in New York City, not on the merits, but because the court determined that the plaintiffs, including a private organization, Citizens for Responsibility and Ethics in Washington (CREW), did not have standing to sue the president. According to the ruling, not every concerned citizen or group can sue the president for violating the Constitution; a special nexus with the facts of the case must be established.

That decision was appealed, and the second circuit reversed the holding below, saying that some of the plaintiffs, groups of hotels and restaurants that compete with the Trump Organization, did have standing to sue for the emoluments clause violations. Discovery in that case is pending.

Two other groups of plaintiffs also sued. The District of Columbia and the state of Maryland sued in federal court in Maryland arguing that some of these emoluments clause violations disadvantaged Maryland and DC businesses and cost these governments tax revenue and other losses. The Justice Department defended Trump in this lawsuit as well, but the court rejected the DOJ's argument that the plaintiffs lacked standing. Even more important, in its decision the court interpreted the emoluments clause essentially the same way as the plaintiffs did, and as did CREW earlier. Unfortunately the Fourth Circuit Court of Appeals later dismissed this suit, not disagreeing with the district court's interpretation of the emoluments clause, but disagreeing with allowing the state attorneys general the standing to sue.

A third suit has been brought by Senator Richard Blumenthal of Connecticut leading a group of Democrats in the Senate and House arguing that they have standing to sue Trump under the emoluments clause because it specifically prohibits the emoluments "without the consent of Congress." Trump, likely totally in the dark as to constitutional restraints, never even asked Congress for its consent, even when both chambers were controlled by Republicans. Perhaps even the Republicans would have wanted to see his tax returns and other records before giving consent to foreign emoluments. The Justice Department defended this lawsuit as well, this time in the federal district court in the District of Columbia.

The district court rejected Trump's motion to dismiss and held that these members of Congress had standing to sue. That suit was set to proceed to discovery. Perhaps this discovery would finally yield tax returns and other records answering that mysterious question: Where does Donald Trump get his money? Once again, however, Trump appealed that decision and the court of appeals stayed discovery while it considers whether the plaintiffs—in this instance members of Congress—have standing to sue.

The House of Representatives is also investigating foreign government money in the Trump Organization. Subpoenas of Trump financial records have been issued to private organizations including the Trump Organization itself, and the Treasury Department has been asked to turn Trump's tax returns over to Congress. Thus far Trump himself has ordered his staff—in the Trump Organization and the federal government—to refuse to cooperate. He is using Justice Department lawyers at taxpayer expense—just as he did in defending the emoluments clause lawsuits—to fight the subpoenas. Thus far the federal courts are siding with the House, holding that most of these subpoenas must be complied with. In a 2 to 1 ruling (with Trump appointee Neomi Rao dissenting), the US Court of Appeals for the District of Columbia Circuit upheld a federal district court ruling that Trump Organization accountants must turn over eight years of records in response to congressional subpoenas. Trump has appealed to the Supreme Court, which will decide the case by June 2020.

The bottom line is that Donald Trump does not want anyone to know what he owns, and more importantly, what he owes, and to whom.

Finally, Robert Mueller investigated Trump's financial ties with at least one foreign power, Russia. Trump got very upset about the Mueller investigation, threatening to fire Mueller when he looked into the Trump finances. Perhaps Mueller was getting warm.

There is little information about that in the unredacted portions of the Mueller Report, but the redacted portions of the report likely tell at least part of this story. Reasons for the redactions include respect for personal "privacy," ongoing grand jury investigations, and possible future criminal indictments. (See more in Chapter 30.) Congress has asked to see the redacted portions of the Mueller Report behind closed doors, but the Justice Department, headed by Trump's second attorney general, William Barr, has refused.

We also know that a lot of Trump associates (including lawyer Michael Cohen, campaign manager Paul Manafort, and deputy campaign manager Rick Gates) have had a lot of financial dealings in Russia. Trump asked Cohen to lie to Congress about his plans for a Trump Tower in Moscow. Half a dozen Trump associates have been criminally convicted in the Mueller investigation.

The bottom line is that Donald Trump has *a lot to hide* when it comes to Russia, not to mention other authoritarian regimes. The founders anticipated this danger when they drafted the emoluments clause, but enforcement in the courts has advanced at a snail's pace, and Congress continues to do next to nothing about it. The American public remains in the dark about the extent of the problem.

The great danger for our national security and our democracy is that Vladimir Putin or some other foreign ruler knows more than we do.

CHAPTER 18

Draining the Swamp

Sorry losers and haters, but my IQ is one of the highest—and you all know it! Please don't feel so stupid or insecure. It's not your fault.
—DONALD TRUMP

ON THE CAMPAIGN TRAIL DONALD TRUMP WOULD BEL-low, "Lock her up," which would arouse his base of Hillary Clinton haters. His other signature call was "Build the wall," meant to signal to racists and nativists that he wasn't going to put up with hordes of "dangerous criminals" crossing into the United States, even though most people seeking asylum are frightened parents and children.

The third plank of Trump's platform to "Make America Great Again" was his promise to "drain the swamp" of lobbyists and career government employees whom he associated with President Obama and the Clintons. His "promise to stop the gravy train for government consultants and to keep Wall Street insiders from getting away with murder" was music to the ears of his supporters, many of whom were suffering financially and felt alienated from DC politics.

Draining the swamp turned out to be just another blatant lie. In fact, he did the opposite. He has brought as many lobbyists into his government as any other administration, and probably more. Meanwhile, the part of the "swamp" that Trump really hates is the least corrupt part of our government, the career civil servants with invaluable expertise. These civil servants serve from administration to administration, protected by civil service laws dating back to the era of Teddy Roosevelt. Trump, however, is determined to get rid of them, shifting power in agencies as much as possible to his political appointees at the top. He has gutted the State Department, as dozens of longtime civil servants have resigned or been pushed out. Intelligence agencies have lost some of their most talented career officers. For cabinet and sub-cabinet appointments he chose men and women more apt to destroy departments than run them. Many of the best career civil servants in this environment don't need to be fired. They simply quit.

Moreover, whatever Trump did to "drain the swamp" of lobbyists and corruption (next to nothing, unless the "corrupt" government officials were Democrats) was overwhelmed by the massive "swamp backfill" that he imported into Washington from New York City, New Jersey, or wherever else he could find it. The fact that almost none of Trump's political appointees remotely resembled the economic profile of Trump's many lower-middle-class supporters was irrelevant.

Rather than rid his campaign of lobbyists and insiders, Trump filled his transition team with hundreds of them. He hired men and women who had formerly worked for defense contractors, oil and gas companies, General Electric, Choice Hotels, Dow Chemical, T-Mobile, the American Beverage Association, and the National Asphalt Pavement Association.

As president, Trump hired people like Timothy Clark as White House liaison at the Department of Health and Human Services. Clark was formerly president of Clark Strategy Group, a firm that represented Pharmaceutical Research and Manufacturers of America.

Another example is Jeffrey Gerrish, whom Trump hired as deputy US trade representative to Asia, Europe, the Middle East, and industrial competitiveness. He had been a lobbyist for US Steel.

A report, prepared by the offices of senators Elizabeth Warren (D-MA) and Sheldon Whitehouse (D-RI), listed 160 identified lobbyists working for the transition team and in the White House.

Making things cozier for the lobbyists was Executive Order 13770, which weakened ethics rules put in place by President Obama. Under Obama, former lobbyists couldn't work at agencies they had contacted as lobbyists. Under the new rule, at least twenty-five lobbyists did just that. For example, Taylor Hansen, a lobbyist for for-profit colleges, was hired by the Department of Education as the special assistant to the secretary of the Department of Education. Tara Bradshaw, a lobbyist for the New York Life Insurance Company, who had lobbied the Treasury Department, was hired by the Treasury Department as secretary Steven Mnuchin's nominations advisor.

When Trump commissioned a Drug Pricing and Innovation Working Group, he chose Joe Grogan, a lobbyist for Gilead Sciences, to lead the group. Gilead's hepatitis C drug had recently risen to $1,000 a pill. Grogan was hired as the associate director of health programs for the Office of Management and Budget.

Meanwhile, Trump administration proposals give the pharmaceutical industry everything it asks for, including strengthening monopoly rights for pharmaceutical companies overseas and curbing discounts that pharmaceutical companies are required to give to hospitals and clinics that serve the poor.

Trump hired Geoffrey Burr, a former lobbyist for Associated Builders and Contractors, to the Labor Department transition team. Burr lobbied for years against the OSHA rules and regulations. One of his goals was to allow beryllium and silica back into construction, even though they have been proven to cause various lung diseases. The building industry wins. Workers affected by the dangerous materials might lose their lives.

The list goes on. Byron Anderson, the former lobbyist for Transamerica, served as special advisor to the Department of Labor, which had a rule requiring retirement plan advisors to act in the best interests of their clients when providing investment advice. Trump's Department of Labor delayed implementation of the rule, putting the interests of financial advisors such as Transamerica over the interests of retirees.

Trump hired lobbyists for the energy industry to infiltrate the EPA. Gas and oil companies have been given a green light to build pipelines and to drill on public lands including lands that used to be national parkland. Andrew Wheeler, confirmed by the Senate in February 2019 as the head of the EPA, lobbied for coal companies. As EPA head, he makes the rules that regulate coal companies. His predecessor, Trump's first EPA administrator Scott Pruitt, had used his earlier position as Oklahoma attorney general to advance the agenda of various Koch brothers' energy interests and worked closely with the Koch-led American Legislative Exchange Council.

Andrónico Luksic, a billionaire from Chile, has wanted to open an environmentally dangerous copper and nickel mine in Minnesota's Boundary Waters for decades, and he leases the proposed mine site from the federal government. The Obama administration refused to renew the lease in 2016, saying that a sulfide mine in that location would destroy one of the most pristine waterways in the country. As soon as Trump won the election, Luksic bought a $10 million mansion in Washington, DC, where Jared Kushner and Ivanka Trump wanted to live while working in the White House. Luksic now leases the house to them. The Trump administration meanwhile reversed the Obama administration's decision and approved Luksic's lease of the federal land in Minnesota, and he is going forward with his plans to seek regulatory approval for the sulfide mine.

In appointing Steve Mnuchin as secretary of the treasury, Trump found someone who not only had expertise in mortgage-backed securities and hedge-fund management, but who had made enormous amounts of money trading in those securities after the 2008 financial collapse. In addition to safeguarding Trump's tax returns, Mnuchin's job at Treasury apparently includes rolling back as much as possible of the 2010 Dodd-Frank Act regulations. The 2008 financial collapse worked out well for Mnuchin (and anyone else who knew when to buy and when to sell), so he may not appreciate the danger of doing it all over again. Most Americans presumably beg to differ.

But what's most remarkable, what marks the Trump administration as one of the *worst* in American history when it comes to the rule of law, is the number of Trump team members who ended up indicted and convicted of serious crimes. Not since Watergate have we seen so many close associates of a president headed off for prison.

The list of indicted and convicted Trump associates began with General Michael Flynn, who was suspected of making secret contacts with the Russians when he was national security advisor. Others include Trump's campaign manager Paul Manafort; deputy campaign manager Rick Gates; former personal lawyer Michael Cohen; and even the campaign "coffee boy"

George Papadopoulos, who regularly met with a Russian handler called "the professor."

Indicted—and convicted of seven counts of lying to Congress—is the infamous Roger Stone, of the 2000 Brooks Brothers riot during the Florida Bush-Gore recount. Stone is not only a close Trump associate but was a loyal supporter of Richard Nixon. Stone has a tattoo of Nixon etched on his back that he should perhaps remove if he joins the other Trump associates in prison.

Moving along, we meet the lesser sinners in this new Hades that is Trump's Washington. These are the men and women whose ethics violations are plentiful and disgraceful, but who have not—yet—been charged with criminal offenses.

The list is long.

1. Health and Human Services Secretary Tom Price resigned after just eight months on the job after spending as much as $400,000 on private jets to conduct government business. Before joining the Trump administration, Price had been buying and selling (mostly buying) healthcare company stocks while working on healthcare legislation in the House of Representatives (most of it designed to water down Obamacare and enrich healthcare companies).

2. Interior Secretary Ryan Zinke came under at least fifteen investigations, including inquiries into his connection to a real estate deal involving a company that Interior regulates, a $412,000 trip to deliver a speech celebrating a new NHL team in Las Vegas, whether he bent government rules to allow his wife to ride in government vehicles, and whether he allowed a security detail to travel with him on a vacation to Turkey at considerable cost. After the accusations became public, Zinke was forced to resign.

3. Treasury Secretary Steven Mnuchin, the former Wall Street mogul, came under scrutiny for using a $25,000-an-hour military plane for his European honeymoon and later using a government jet to fly to Fort Knox to view a solar eclipse, all at taxpayer expense. The House Intelligence Committee, moreover, is looking into a

deal Mnuchin struck with US billionaire Leonard Blavatnik, an associate of Oleg Deripaska, who has strong ties to Vladimir Putin. According to the committee, Mnuchin sold his shares in RatPac-Dune Entertainment to Blavatnik for around $25 million. When the US lifted sanctions against Deripaska in February 2019, members of Congress noted that Mnuchin had been involved in the move and wondered whether there was a quid pro quo. At best, it appeared to be a flagrant conflict of interest.

4. Scott Pruitt, administrator of the Environmental Protection Agency, had been the attorney general of Oklahoma who filed lawsuit after lawsuit opposing the EPA and its environmental policies. Pruitt, a climate-change denier, urged Trump to pull out of the 2015 Paris climate agreement. Before he resigned, Pruitt was the subject of at least thirteen federal investigations. Pruitt allegedly paid $43,000 for a soundproof telephone booth at the EPA (perhaps for private phone calls with polluters), made lavish expenditures for foreign travel, and went on a trip to Morocco arranged by a lobbyist even though the EPA had no connection to Morocco. Pruitt rented his living quarters in Washington, DC, for fifty dollars a night from a "friend" who was an energy lobbyist. Pruitt also had a fondness for vanity clothing including $3,000 "tactical pants" purchased with taxpayer dollars. His unethical behavior became so pronounced that even Laura Ingraham, the ultra-conservative talk show host on Fox, tweeted, "Pruitt is the swamp. Drain it."

5. Wilbur Ross, the commerce secretary, has often been accused of conflict of interest violations. Among the stock he held was that of Navigator Holdings, which has a partnership with a Russian energy company owned by oligarchs with close ties to Vladimir Putin. Ross sold some stock worth more than $10 million after the Office of Government Ethics alleged that he had not divested himself of the stock in a timely manner. It is not clear what conflicts he continues to have.

6. Counselor to the President Kellyanne Conway used an official interview with Fox News to advertise Ivanka Trump's clothing

brands. When the Office of Government Ethics wrote the White House a letter explaining that this violated ethics rules about misuse of official position, the White House "ethics lawyer" responded that the OGE ethics rules did not apply to the White House staff (the exact opposite of what one of your authors told Bush White House staffers in 2005–07). Later, Kellyanne Conway twice violated the Hatch Act by using her official position—in television interviews on the White House lawn—to attack Doug Jones, the Democratic candidate for US Senate in Alabama. Jones nonetheless won because the GOP—at Steve Bannon's urging—had nominated a former state supreme court justice who had twice been suspended from the bench and later was accused of soliciting girls for sex. The Office of Special Counsel (OSC) wrote the White House that Conway's actions clearly violated the Hatch Act, but the letter was ignored. In June 2019, after Conway yet again violated the Hatch Act, this time attacking presidential candidate Joe Biden on the White House lawn, the OSC wrote another letter stating that Conway should be fired. This letter also was ignored.

Combine this with the long list of resignations and firings, and it's not hard to see that the Trump administration has been the most chaotic in American history. In no particular order, there were the resignations of the top national security advisor Michael Flynn; press secretaries Sean Spicer and Sarah Sanders; communications directors Mike Dubke, Hope Hicks, and Anthony Scaramucci (who has turned against the president and now urges his removal from office); chief strategist Steve Bannon; Deputy Chief of Staff Joe Hagin; Secretary of Defense James Mattis; Reince Priebus, the first chief of staff; John Kelly, the second chief of staff; Nikki Haley, the US ambassador to the UN; Don McGahn, the first White House counsel; Tom Bossert, the first homeland security advisor; H. R. McMaster, the second national security advisor; John Dowd, Trump's first lead lawyer; Gary Cohn, the first director of the National Economics Council; and Rob Porter, the first White House staff secretary, accused of sexual assault. There were also the firings of FBI Director James Comey; David Shulkin, the first secretary of veteran's affairs; Andrew McCabe, the first deputy director of the FBI; Rex Tillerson, the first secretary of state (for among other things referring to Trump as a "moron"); Steve Goldstein, the first undersecretary of state for public diplomacy and affairs; Attorney General Jeff Sessions (for refusing to stop the Mueller investigation); and Homeland Security Secretary Kirstjen Nielsen (for refusing to order DHS employees to engage in illegal conduct at the southern border). And then there was the mysterious departure of Keith Schiller, Trump's longtime bodyguard who was appointed the first director of Oval Office operations; and the unpleasant departure of White House senior aides Steve Bannon and Sebastian Gorka, in the wake of the racial unrest in Charlottesville, Virginia, presumably because of their extreme right-wing views (the White House was also embarrassed by the World War II–era medals from a Hungarian Nazi sympathizer organization that Gorka had worn to the inaugural ball). Bannon's and Gorka's close ideological ally—extreme xenophobe Stephen Miller—remained at the White House to coordinate Trump's immigration policy.

What is remarkable is not only the extent of corruption but the complete lack of congressional oversight before January 2019 when the Democrats took control of the House of Representatives, and since then the continued resistance to oversight by Trump's allies in the House and the Republican-controlled Senate.

Just one example is the congressional response to shocking testimony by Michael Cohen, who for ten years was Donald Trump's lawyer and "fixer." On February 27, 2019, Cohen appeared before the House Intelligence Committee. Sentenced to three years in prison for lying to the committee, he came this time to make amends.

During seven hours of testimony, Cohen told Congress that Trump knew in advance about the WikiLeaks dump of Hillary Clinton's emails, that Cohen had arranged payments of hush money to hide Trump's affairs, that Trump was involved in a Moscow real estate project even while running for president and Cohen was told to lie about it. He told Congress that Trump had him threaten schools the future president had attended, to keep Trump's grades from being released; and that Trump once confided in Cohen about getting a medical deferment to avoid serving in Vietnam even though Trump's doctor hadn't examined him.

"I am ashamed that I chose to take part in concealing Mr. Trump's illicit acts rather than listening to my own conscience," said Cohen.

When a string of Republican congressmen, led by minority leader Jim Jordan and Congressman Mark Meadows, repeatedly called Cohen a liar and sought to undermine Cohen's credibility, Cohen finally snapped, "I did the same thing that you're doing now. For ten years—I protected Mr. Trump for ten years . . . The more people that follow Mr. Trump—as I did blindly—are going to suffer the same consequences that I'm suffering."

Commented *New York Times* op-ed columnist Timothy Egan, "The creepy criminal world that surrounds Trump is not off-putting to many Republicans . . . They are headed for a reckoning. In years to come as Representative Elijah Cummings, the committee chairman, put it, people will ask, 'What did we do to make sure our democracy is intact?' For Trump's new fixers, Cohen gave them an answer: 'I did the same thing you're doing now.'"

The day before Cohen was scheduled to testify, Matt Gaetz, a Republican representative from Florida, tweeted, "Hey @MichaelCohen212—Do your wife & father-in-law know about your girlfriends? Maybe tonight would be a good time for that chat. I wonder if she'll remain faithful when you're in prison. She's about to learn a lot."

Gaetz had been one of Trump's most ardent supporters, but for most of the country he had gone too far. His tweet appeared to be an attempt to cow Cohen into not testifying. It seemed like a move out of *The Godfather.*

Walter Shaub, the former director of the Office of Government Ethics, replied to Gaetz's tweet with the federal statute about tampering with a witness. Gaetz apologized.

When Trump was campaigning, he pledged to drain the swamp. Instead his administration has been a deep cesspool of corruption and incompetence. Congress not only tolerates it (including the Republicans who now control the Senate, if they do not convict him), but some members of Congress even go as far as Representative Gaetz did to threaten witnesses who appear before their own committees.

The checks and balances that the founders believed would constrain corruption and abuse of power by the executive branch are ineffective because Congress simply won't do its job.

CHAPTER 19

The Steele Dossier and More: The Trump-Russia Connection

The government you elect is the government you deserve.
—THOMAS JEFFERSON

O N JANUARY 5, 2017, PRESIDENT OBAMA AND President-Elect Trump were briefed by US intelligence officials. They were told that the Russians said they had compromising personal and financial information on Trump.

When part of this briefing became public, Trump immediately tweeted, "FAKE NEWS—A TOTAL POLITICAL WITCH HUNT!"

Then came BuzzFeed's thirty-five-page report of the contents of what would become known as the Steele dossier. The report said that Russian officials fed Trump information damaging to Hillary Clinton. Michael Cohen, Trump's lawyer, had met secretly with Kremlin officials in Prague. Carter Page, Trump's advisor on foreign affairs, had met with the head of Russia's state-owned oil company and a senior Kremlin internal affairs official in Moscow. It talked of Trump's attempts to make real estate deals with

Russians in Moscow. Most headline making was a report that Trump had hired prostitutes to "perform lewd acts such as golden showers" on a bed in the presidential suite of the hotel where President Obama once stayed. The report said that the Russian security services, FSB, had "arranged and monitored" what went on and were holding it as leverage against Trump.

The information was based on memos compiled by a former British intelligence operative, whose past work US intelligence officials considered credible.

That former British operative was Christopher Steele, who had served in the MI6, the British equivalent of the CIA, since the end of the Cold War. The MI6 was so secretive that the British government for many years didn't acknowledge its existence. Steele was a spy in Moscow and Paris. His expertise was in all things Russian, and he was assigned to investigate the murder of Alexander Litvinenko, a former Russian spy whose tea was poisoned with radioactive polonium-210 during a meeting with two other Russian agents in London. Litvinenko had been a member of Russia's FSB, defected to London in 2000, and wrote two books, including one describing how the FSB's violence had helped bring Putin to power. After a British inquiry, on which Steele worked, the British concluded that the FSB was responsible for Litvinenko's murder and that Putin had "probably approved" it.

Steele left the MI6 in 2009 and founded Orbis Business Intelligence Ltd. The London-based firm specialized in investigations and intelligence gathering. Steele was hired by the US Department of Justice in 2015 to investigate the corruption of FIFA, the international governing body of soccer. Several members of FIFA's ruling executive committee were indicted on bribery charges as part of a far-reaching corruption investigation headed by the FBI and Department of Justice.

Steele had remarkable Russian sources, many close to Russian intelligence, and he was hired by anti-Trump conservative groups to get background information on Trump and his connections with Russia. After Trump won the nomination, the Hillary Clinton campaign used Steele and similar investigations for much the same purpose. The result was the "Steele dossier."

When this information was first offered to the *New York Times* and the *Washington Post* during the run-up to the 2016 presidential election, the papers declined to publish the story because the information wasn't verified by another source.

The Steele dossier, it turned out, became a key issue.

The dossier was first made public by CNN, which reported that the contents had been sent to both President Obama and to President-Elect Trump. The rogue entertainment and news site BuzzFeed published the Steele report ten days before Trump's inauguration.

Because some of the information in the dossier, especially the more sordid revelations, hasn't been proven with second sources, Trump and the Russians have been able to scream that it was a report with "no factual bases." Even so, no one has yet disproven what Steele's dossier says about Trump's deep ties to the Russians.

Below is a transcript of the first part of Steele's dossier.

SUMMARY

Russian regime has been cultivating, supporting, and assisting Trump for at least five years. Aim endorsed by Putin has been to encourage splits and divisions in Western Alliance. So far Trump has declined various sweetener real estate business deals offered him in Russia in order to further the Kremlin's cultivation of him. However, he and his inner circle have accepted a regular flow of intelligence from the Kremlin including on his Democratic and other political rivals. Former top Russian intelligence officer claims FSB (formerly the KGB) has compromised Trump through his activities in Moscow sufficiently to be able to blackmail him. According to several knowledgeable sources his conduct in Moscow has included perverted sexual acts, which have been arranged or monitored by the FSB. A dossier of compromising material on Hillary Clinton has been collated by the Russian Intelligence Services over many years and mainly comprises bugged conversations she had on various visits to Russia and intercepted phone calls rather than any embarrassing conduct. The dossier is controlled by Kremlin spokesmen Deskoff directly on Putin's orders. However it is not yet been distributed abroad including to Trump. Russian's intentions for its deployment are still unclear.

DETAIL

1. Speaking to a trusted compatriot in June 2016 sources A and B, a senior
    Russian foreign ministry figure and a top level Russian intelligence officer
    still active inside the Kremlin respectively, the Russian authorities have
    been cultivating and supporting a U.S. Republican and Presidential
    candidate Donald Trump for at least five years. Source B asserted that the
    Trump operation was both supported and directed by Russian President
    Vladimir Putin. Its aim was to sow discord and disunity both within
    the United States itself but most importantly within the TransAtlantic
    Alliance, which was viewed as inimical to Russia's interests. Source C,
    a senior Russian financial official, said the Trump operation should be
    seen in terms of Putin's desire to return to 19th Century Great Power
    politics, anchored upon country's interests rather than the ideals based
    on international order established after World War II. She or he had
    overheard Putin talking in this way to close associates on several occasions.
    [He wants nationalism, which is also what Trump wants. America first and
    the hell with NATO.]

2. In terms of specifics Source A [identified as Konstantin Kilimnik, once
    an intelligence officer working for the GRU and a close friend of Paul
    Manafort] confided that the Kremlin had been feeding Trump and
    his team valuable intelligence on his opponents including Democratic
    presidential candidate Hillary Clinton for several years. This was
    confirmed by Source D, a close associate of Trump, who had organized
    and managed his recent trips to Moscow. And who reported in June 2016
    that this Russian intelligence had been "very helpful." The Kremlin's
    cultivation operation on Trump also had compromised, offering him
    various lucrative development business deals in Russia, especially in
    relationship to the ongoing 2018 World Cup soccer tournament. However,
    so far, for reasons unknown, Trump had not taken up any of these.

3. However, there were other aspects to Trump's engagement with the
    Russian authorities. One which had borne fruit for them was to exploit
    Trump's personal obsessions and sexual perversions in order to obtain
    suitable kompromat on him. According to Source D (a close associate of
    Trump) where she or he had been present, Trump's perverted conduct in

Moscow included hiring the Presidential Suite of the Ritz-Carlton Hotel, where he knew President and Mrs. Obama, who he hated, had stayed on one of their official trips to Russia. And defiling the bed where they had slept by employing a number of prostitutes to perform a "golden showers" show in front of him. The hotel was known to be under FSB control with microphones and concealed cameras in all the main rooms to record anything they wanted to.

4.   The Moscow Ritz-Carlton episode involving Trump reported above was confirmed by Source E [the rest of the line is blacked out] who said that she or he and several of the staff were aware of it at the time and subsequently she or he believed it had happened in 2013. Source E provided an introduction for a company ethnic Russian operative to Source F, a female staffer at the hotel where Trump had stayed, who also confirmed the story. Speaking separately in June 2016, Source B, the former top level Russian intelligence officer (one who was arrested and killed perhaps) asserted that Trump's unorthodox behavior in Russia over the years had provided the authorities there with enough embarrassing material on the now Republican Presidential candidate to be able to blackmail him if they so wished.

5.   Asked about the Kremlin's reported intelligence feed to Trump over recent years and rumors about a Russian dossier of 'kompromat' Hillary Clinton (being circulated), Source B confirmed that the files existence. S/he confided in a trusted compatriot that it had been collated by Department K of the FSB for many years, dating back to her husband Bill's presidency and comprised mainly of eavesdropped conversations of various sorts rather than details or evidence of unorthodox or embarrassing behaviors. Some of the conversations were from bugged comments Clinton had made on her various trips to Russia, and focused on things she had said which contradicted her current positions on various issues. Others were most probably from phone intercepts.

6.   Continuing on this theme Source G, a senior Kremlin official, confided that the Clinton dossier was controlled exclusively by chief Kremlin spokesman Dmiti Cheskov [Dmitry Chesnokov], who was responsible for compiling and handling it on the explicit instructions of Putin himself. The dossier, however, had not as yet been made available abroad, including

to Trump or his campaign team. At present it was unclear what Putin's intentions were in this regard.

20 of June 2016

Perhaps to feed a public appetite for the most lurid details, the headlines buried the most important information about Russian interference in the 2016 presidential election and the hacking of the emails of the Democratic National Committee. The newspaper, radio, and TV news headlines focused on what is perhaps the most bizarre accusation ever made against an American president. Donald Trump was accused of hiring several prostitutes to come to a ritzy Moscow hotel, where former president Barack Obama and his wife once had slept, and urinate all over the bed. Not only that, but the Russians took pictures! Vladimir Putin supported Trump's blanket denial when, during a press conference, Dmitry Peskov, Putin's spokesman, told the audience, "The Kremlin has no compromising dossier on Trump. Such information isn't consistent with reality and is nothing but an absolute fantasy."

Buoyed by Putin's echoed denial, Trump tweeted, "Russia just said the unverified report paid for by political opponents is 'A COMPLETE AND TOTAL FABRICATION, UTTER NONSENSE.' Very unfair! . . . Russia has never tried to use leverage over me. I HAVE NOTHING TO DO WITH RUSSIA—NO DEALS, NO LOANS, NOTHING! . . . I win an election easily, a great 'movement' is verified, and crooked opponents try to belittle our victory with FAKE NEWS. A sorry state! . . . Intelligence agencies should never have allowed this fake news to 'leak' into the public. One last shot at me. Are we living in Nazi Germany?"

When FBI Director James Comey later asked Trump whether Steele's claim was true, Trump denied even spending a single night in Moscow. Both Bloomberg News and Politico were able to obtain the flight records of Trump's plane, owned by casino mogul Phil Ruffin, and the flight records showed that Trump's plane had landed at Moscow's Vnukovo International Airport, and he had been in Moscow from Thursday through Sunday night, when the jet took off at 3:58 in the morning.

Trump apparently lied to the FBI director about his trip to Moscow.

A year later, in a rambling conversation with *Fox and Friends,* Trump finally admitted he had stayed "one or two days" in Moscow that weekend.

For liars, keeping one's story straight is always a serious problem.

During a news conference at Trump Tower, Trump for the first time opined that the election-related hacking was conducted by Russia. He also said, "If Putin likes Donald Trump, I consider that an asset, not a liability, because we have a horrible relationship with Russia." Trump told the *Wall Street Journal* that he was open to lifting the sanctions on Russia if "Russia is really helping us":

"If you get along and if Russia is really helping us, why would anybody have sanctions if somebody's doing some really great things?"

Here, we must ask ourselves a very important question: What if it turns out everything or even a part of the Steele dossier is true? What if Putin had spied on Donald Trump for five years and learned enough incriminating information to blackmail him? What would Putin ask President Trump to do?

If the Steele dossier is a fabrication, why were four Russian sources for the dossier murdered or arrested?

Oleg Erovinkin, a key aide to Igor Sechin, who was named in the dossier, was murdered. Erovinkin, a former general in the KGB, was found dead in the back of his car in Moscow. He had been shot twice in the head. Steele wrote about "a source close to Sechin who had links between Trump supporters and Moscow." Erovinkin was that source. Russian officials later claimed he had died of a heart attack.

Other Steele sources—Russian cyber experts allegedly involved in hacking Clinton's emails—also were killed, disappeared, or imprisoned. Sergei Mikhailov, the head of the Center for Information Security, a part of the FSB, and Ruslan Stoyanov, the lead researcher with Kaspersky Lab, disappeared and were presumed murdered. According to the newspaper *Novaya Gazeta,* during a meeting of intelligence officers, a bag was thrown over Mikhailov's head and he was dragged away, never to be seen again.

In addition, five other Russian diplomats died under mysterious circumstances. They were not directly connected to the hacking scandal or Trump's interference in the election, but their unexpected deaths—some violent—raised the possibility that somebody wanted them rubbed out to make sure they didn't talk.

In January 2017, a Ukrainian businessman named Alex Oronov, who had arranged a meeting at the Loews Regency on Park Avenue in Manhattan between Michael Cohen, Trump's attorney, and Felix Sater, a Russian-born Brooklynite and associate of Trump's with ties to the Russian mob, died suddenly. Cohen reportedly was bringing Trump's "peace plan" aimed at helping Putin gain control over Crimea. Oronov, who was the father of Cohen's brother's wife, lived in one of Trump's buildings. He also was said to have died of a heart attack, an all-too-common occurrence for prominent Russian businessmen and government officials who get too close to sensitive situations.

Russia's ambassador to the UN, Vitaly Churkin, died in New York on his way to work.

Mikhail Lesin, a Putin aide, dropped dead in a DC hotel room. He had been bashed over the head. Sergei Krivov, a Russian intelligence agent, was found dead in the Russian consulate in New York on Election Day. His head had also been bashed in.

Russian diplomat Andrey Malanin was found dead in his Athens apartment. The Russian ambassador to Turkey, Andrei Karlov, was murdered by a policeman on the same day that another diplomat, Peter Polshikov, was shot dead in his apartment in Moscow.

That's a lot of dead Russians.

Some Americans also had short lives.

Peter Smith, a GOP operative who reportedly told the Russians to turn over the stolen Clinton emails to WikiLeaks, committed suicide in a hotel room in Rochester, Minnesota. Smith had been a focus of Robert Mueller's investigation. He was an ally of Trump campaign advisor Michael Flynn.

Smith, a wealthy businessman, had been hounding the Clintons for years. He had offered to pay Arkansas state troopers to get dirt on Bill Clinton. He had been behind the Troopergate allegations that Bill Clinton used them to arrange trysts with women. Smith also looked into a trip that Bill Clinton made to the Soviet Union in 1969 as a student. In a conversation with the *Wall Street Journal*, Smith said he began his search for Hillary Clinton's missing emails in September. He contacted known hacking groups, including two in Russia, who told him they had the emails. Smith told them to pass the emails on to WikiLeaks to make sure they were genuine and not fakes.

Smith said that in his attempt to obtain Clinton's emails, he worked with Trump associates Steve Bannon, Kellyanne Conway, and Michael Flynn.

Bannon naturally said he had never even heard of Smith.

Ten days after his conversation with the *Wall Street Journal,* Smith killed himself by pumping helium into a plastic bag and placing the bag over his head.

Police found a helium tank, an obituary, and a suicide note.

We should also ask ourselves, why didn't the FBI take action after receiving the Steele dossier in July 2016? According to Steele, the New York office of the FBI appeared to be devoting its time to Hillary Clinton's email transgressions. Steele said that some of the agents had a long-standing relationship with Rudy Giuliani—then part of the Trump campaign—and as we know, just days before the election in November 2016, FBI Director James Comey announced that Clinton was facing another investigation into the use of her emails.

Two days earlier Giuliani mentioned "a surprise or two you're going to hear about in the next few days. We've got a couple of things up our sleeves that should turn things around." In other words, the FBI was focused on election eve announcements about Clinton's email, not on the Steele dossier.

In addition to the allegations in the Steele dossier, there are other disturbing facts about Trump's relationship with the Russians.

First, there is the question of whether Trump could be indebted to the Russians or have profits and benefits tied to the Russians. We raised this earlier with the discussion of the Constitution's emoluments clause in Chapter 17.

Second, there were a remarkable number of contacts between Russian operatives and senior Trump campaign officials during the campaign, his transition team, and then senior Trump White House officials during the beginning of his presidency. Almost nobody is willing to tell the truth about those contacts.

Third, there is an alignment between Trump's foreign and economic policies in several areas (both his promises as a candidate and his actual policies as president) and what Russia wants. Quid pro quo relationships between politicians and patrons are always difficult to prove, but the circumstantial evidence of a pro-Russia bias in the Trump administration is strong.

Fourth, there is the secrecy surrounding meetings that President Trump has with Putin, from which other top US officials are often excluded.

Fifth and perhaps most telling is the extreme sensitivity that Trump has to any allegations related to Russia. Trump has been accused of sexual assault, racism, violations of the emoluments clause, and other financial conflicts of interest, but the allegations that set him off most arise from the Russia "witch hunt." Something is indeed rotten in the United States of America, and in this tragic play within a play, it is Trump who "doth protest too much, methinks."

Some of the many specifics follow (this book would be thousands of pages long were we to list them all).

BUSINESS DEALS WITH THE RUSSIANS

Trump has suspicious financial relationships with oligarchs aligned with Vladimir Putin.

In addition to the mysterious financial arrangements we pointed our earlier, Trump apparently owes as much as $560 million to the Blackstone/Bayrock group, which is owned by Russian billionaires, many of whom owe their position and wealth to Putin. Men who have borrowed from Bayrock claim that owing money to them is like owing to the Russian mob; they ask for favors.

Bayrock, founded by Tevfik Arif, a former Soviet-era commerce official originally from Kazakhstan, partnered with Trump on a series of real estate deals between 2002 and 2011, the most prominent being the troubled Trump SoHo hotel and condominium in Manhattan. Trump lent his name to a number of Bayrock projects for large fees. In return, Bayrock took money from foreign investors—apparently including money launderers—for projects in Iceland, Belgium, France, and England. Trump testified in 2017 that he met Bayrock officials in Trump Tower to discuss deals in Moscow.

"It's ridiculous that I wouldn't be investing in Russia," Trump said in that deposition. "Russia is one of the hottest places in the world for investment."

One of Bayrock's principals, Felix Sater, was implicated in a stock-manipulation scheme involving Mafia figures and Russian criminals inflating stock prices on Wall Street. Around 2001 Sater joined Bayrock. Sater proposed erecting building complexes with Trump's name. They apparently discussed buildings in Phoenix, Los Angeles, Ukraine, and China.

In 2005 Trump and Bayrock joined to develop a project in Moscow. Sater said he had Russian investors and a site for a luxury high-rise—a shuttered pencil factory named for American radicals Nicola Sacco and Bartolomeo Vanzetti.

"I showed [Trump] photos, I showed him the site, showed him the view from the site," said Sater. "It's pretty spectacular."

Sater handled all the negotiations, but the deal fell through.

Another Bayrock principal was Salvatore Lauria, who brokered a $50 million investment in Trump SoHo and three other Bayrock projects by an Icelandic firm. According to a lawsuit against Bayrock by Jody Kriss, a former executive, the firm was funded by wealthy Russians close to President Vladimir Putin. Another Bayrock investor was Alexander Mashkevich, a Russian billionaire once charged in a corruption case in Belgium.

Kriss accused Bayrock of being a front for money laundering. In the lawsuit he said that Bayrock occasionally received unexplained infusions of cash from accounts in Kazakhstan and Russia. In addition to laundering money, Kriss said Bayrock executives skimmed cash, dodged taxes, and cheated him out of millions of dollars.

After Sater left Bayrock, he was given office space in Trump Tower and Trump Organization cards that identified him as a "senior advisor to Donald Trump."

In November 2013 Trump in a deposition denied knowing both Arif and Sater.

When asked about Arif, he said, "I mean, I've seen him a couple of times. I have met him." As for Sater, he said, "If he were sitting in the room right now, I really wouldn't know what he looked like."

An unlikely story.

There was also the Trump Tower Moscow project that, although never consummated, Trump contemplated as late as 2015. Former Trump attorney Michael Cohen has already acknowledged lying on multiple occasions to hide Trump's involvement with this project.

During his presidential campaign, Trump had been attempting to make a deal with Russian oligarchs and Putin's government to build what would have been the tallest building in all of Europe and Asia. The Moscow Trump Tower was to be a dazzling one-hundred-story glass skyscraper offering ultra-deluxe residences, hotel rooms, and his famous name.

Trump always contended that the plans never got very far, but reporters showed that it had gone quite far. Trump's lawyer Michael Cohen worked to convince Russian developer Andrey Rozov to use Trump's completed design.

On September 15, 2015, Rosov wrote to Cohen, "The building design you sent over is very interesting and will be an architectural and luxury triumph. I believe the tallest building in Europe should be in Moscow, and I am prepared to build it."

Rozov signed a letter of intent that he sent to Cohen. Trump countersigned on the same day as his third presidential debate with Hillary Clinton.

As part of the deal, the spa was to be named "The Spa by Ivanka Trump," and Vladimir Putin was to receive his personal penthouse worth $50 million. The idea was brought to Trump by Felix Sater, who pitched it to Dmitry Peskov, Putin's press secretary. According to Sater, giving Putin the penthouse would lure other oligarchs to buy apartments in the building.

On November 3, 2015, Felix Sater emailed Michael Cohen to outline the idea of having Vladimir Putin attend a ribbon-cutting ceremony for the tower.

"I will get Putin on this program and we will get Donald elected," Sater wrote. "I know how to play it and how to get this done. Buddy, our boy can become president of the USA and we can engineer it . . . I will get all of Putin's team to buy in on this. I will manage this process."

Cohen met with the Russians at least ten times in 2016 to discuss the project, but in the end Trump Tower Moscow was never built. Russian real estate experts said that Cohen and Sater's choice for the developer, Rozov, lacked the clout and reputation to take the project to its conclusion.

Trump at times has denied knowing anything about these projects in Russia during the presidential campaign.

Every time he was lying.

Trump Tower Moscow would have been Donald Trump's highest business achievement.

SECRET CONTACTS WITH THE RUSSIANS

The number of Trump officials who have lied about contact with Russians is shocking. By May 2019, information gathered by the FBI, court records, and reporters stated that, during the 2016 presidential campaign and transition, seventeen Trump campaign officials and advisors had interacted with Russians and with WikiLeaks more than a hundred times. These contacts are the subject of the entire first part of the Mueller Report (much of which is still redacted by Attorney General Barr). See more in Chapter 30.

We provide specifics here about a few of the many contacts with the Russians immediately after the election.

While President Obama was still in office, several of Trump's top aides, including his son-in-law Jared Kushner, apparently established a back channel for communications with the Russians without the knowledge of the State Department. This was a violation of the Logan Act, which requires diplomatic contacts made on behalf of the United States government to go through official channels. (Because of First Amendment and other considerations, the Logan Act is extremely difficult to enforce but at a minimum it establishes the widely recognized rule that Americans do not engage in freelance diplomacy. We have *one* president at a time.)

Kushner and the other officials apparently didn't care.

During the final week of January 2017 we learned that Michael Flynn, Trump's choice as national security advisor, had his own connections with Russia. US counterintelligence agents accused Flynn of secretly meeting with Russian ambassador Sergey Kislyak to discuss the impact of President Obama's promise of additional American sanctions of Russia. Flynn told the Russians that when Trump became president, he would have those sanctions lifted. Flynn denied this twice in discussions with the FBI. Sean Spicer, Trump's spokesman at the time, also denied that Flynn had talked about sanctions.

Acting Attorney General Sally Yates called White House counsel Don McGahn and told him that Flynn was lying. That same day, Yates and McGahn met again, at McGahn's request.

The next day Trump fired Sally Yates. The reason given was a smoke screen. She was fired ostensibly for refusing to enforce Trump's travel ban against Muslims. But she had also called out Flynn's lying in the Russia investigation, incurring Trump's wrath.

The *Washington Post* then reported that Flynn had indeed discussed US sanctions with Ambassador Kislyak. Flynn resigned and is now a convicted felon.

PRO-RUSSIA POLICY

As for policy changes that Russia wanted, the Trump administration, and even more so Trump himself, has displayed a pro-Russia tilt.

As a candidate, Trump early on signaled his sympathy for Russia even if he had no idea what he was talking about.

One of Putin's aggressive moves as Russian president was his plan to annex Crimea. In an interview on ABC, candidate Trump discussed the annexation and supported Putin. "But you know," Trump said, "the people of Crimea, from what I've heard, would rather be with Russia than where they were. And you have to look at that, also."

Critics knew Trump was ignorant of world affairs. They wondered, *Did Trump make up that assessment on the spot out of thin air? From whom did he form that opinion?* They suspected Putin or one of his aides had said this to him.

Trump's first pick for secretary of state was well liked by Putin. Rex Tillerson, the former head of ExxonMobil, had previously done a lot of business in Russia. If Trump could get rid of the sanctions imposed on Russia after the Ukrainian civil war, Tillerson could help Putin extract Russian oil at a significant cost savings. And Russia needs revenue from oil exports to fix its struggling economy.

Undermining NATO, which was founded to contain Russian aggression during the Soviet era, was another issue important to Putin, who wished to return to Russia's nationalist ways and to regain some of the territory it lost after the collapse of the Iron Curtain and the Soviet Union. If Putin could regain his access to the Balkan countries, he could ship millions of cubic feet of natural gas and oil into Eastern Europe. NATO stood in the way.

For whatever reason, Trump has gone out of his way to tear asunder as much as possible the relationship between the United States and NATO. Trump has even gone so far as to describe some NATO members as being hostile to the United States. Deterioration, if not the formal breakup, of the

NATO Alliance may very well be the crowning achievement of both the Trump and Putin presidencies.

Although Congress, including Republicans, has made it clear that economic sanctions against Russia will not be lifted any time soon, the Treasury Department has used its authority to shorten and in some ways alleviate the sanctions against key Russian oligarchs, including Putin ally Oleg Deripaska.

On February 2, 2017, the United States added sanctions to Russia for their annexation of Crimea. Nikki Haley, the UN ambassador, vowed that the "US Crimea–related sanctions will remain in place until Russia returns control over the peninsula to Ukraine." The Trump administration had no choice; congressional Republicans in early 2017 made it clear that they needed the administration to at least feign a strong stance against Russia. (Several leading Republicans, including Senator Lindsey Graham, would later change their hawkish stance.)

Two days after these sanctions were announced, Trump made clear his personal views when, instead of condemning the actions that triggered the sanctions, he defended Putin. He told Fox News, "I do respect him," and when asked about the atrocities Russia had brought to the war in Ukraine, Trump replied, "What, you think our country is so innocent?"

His statement made a lot of people wonder: *Why is our president taking the side of a foreign adversary, comparing its culpability favorably with that of the United States? What hold does Putin have over him?*

The checks and balances in our constitutional framework, particularly the power of Congress, have somewhat limited Trump's ability to help Russia. But it is clear that, compared with all of his post–World War II predecessors, Trump's sympathies lie with Russia, a country that has helped him get where he is today.

Trump has favored the Russians despite the hostility to Russia in Congress and the considerable power Congress has to limit Trump's actual Russia policy. Where he has the power to act unilaterally to help Russia, Trump has used it. He has picked multiple quarrels with our longtime allies in NATO, knowing that undermining the NATO alliance has been a Russian priority since the end of World War II. Where possible, his administration has gone easy on the economic sanctions imposed on Russia because of its 2016 election meddling. In 2019, Trump withdrew US forces from Syria, abandoning Syria to Russia and Turkey, and inviting the slaughter of many of our Kurdish allies. Some Republicans in Congress are furious at these developments, but not so much as to acknowledge the fundamental problem—the divided loyalties of the president of the United States.

SECRET TRUMP-PUTIN MEETINGS

Trump very much seems to enjoy meeting secretly with Vladimir Putin.

Trump has had five secret meetings with Putin since the 2016 election. They've had at least nine phone calls. The first time they met, during a G20 economic summit in Hamburg, Germany, Trump and Putin talked for two hours. The other people in the room were Secretary of State Rex Tillerson and Russian foreign minister Sergey Lavrov. That day it was revealed that Donald Trump Jr., Jared Kushner, and various Russians had met in Trump Tower to discuss dirt on Hillary Clinton. Tillerson said that Trump and Putin had a long talk about Russian hacking. After the meeting Trump took the interpreter's notes and ordered the interpreter not to reveal their conversations. At dinner that night, Trump sidled over to Putin and they talked—alone. Putin's translator handled the conversation.

When questioned afterward, Trump said that three times he had asked Putin whether Russia hacked Clinton's emails, and three times Putin said he hadn't. Trump said that Putin told him, "If we did, we wouldn't have gotten caught because we're professionals."

"I thought it was a good point," said Trump, "because they are some of the best in the world [at hacking]."

On the flight back to Washington that night, Trump told reporters that at the June 2016 Trump Tower meeting, his campaign officials were talking about adoptions.

National security experts questioned out loud whether Trump and Putin were both hiding what they had said and done.

Marina Gross, a translator, was the only other American in the room when President Trump for two hours met privately with Russian president Putin in Helsinki in July 2018. All other Americans were excluded.

On June 26, 2019, Trump bluntly told reporters that what he and Putin said to each other is "nobody's business."

TRUMP'S EXTREME DEFENSIVENESS ABOUT RUSSIA

Finally, Trump is so defensive about the Russia investigation that he appears to be psychologically disturbed whenever he discusses it.

It could take hundreds of pages to reproduce all or even a substantial portion of Trump's tweets and other statements about the Russia investigation, James Comey, Robert Mueller, or congressional Democrats investigating Russian interference. A very few examples follow (see Chapter 30 for more).

On February 15, 2017, CNN reported that both President-Elect Trump and President Obama had been briefed on the ongoing investigation of Russian interference in the election. The *New York Times* also had reported the story the day before. In response Trump called the Russian controversy "fake news" and said the *Times* story was "a joke."

"I have nothing to do with Russia," said Trump. "I told you, I have no deals there; I have no anything. Now, when WikiLeaks, which I had nothing to do with, comes out and happens to give, they're not giving classified information."

Trump added, "I didn't do anything for Russia. If we could get along with Russia, that's a positive thing. I would love to be able to get along with Russia. If we have a good relationship with Russia, believe me, that's a good thing, not a bad thing."

When Trump was asked if anyone advising his campaign had contacts with Russia during the campaign, he said, "No. No. Nobody I know of."

Likely story.

That same day George Papadopoulos, a member of Trump's campaign staff who had several meetings with Russian officials, was being interviewed by the FBI. A week later, the *Washington Post* reported that Jeff Sessions had spoken with Russian ambassador Kislyak during the campaign. Sessions had "forgotten" about this meeting in his confirmation hearing when Senator Al Franken (D-MN) asked if he had any contacts with Russians. When Democrats called for Sessions's resignation, Trump declared he had total confidence in his attorney general.

On this day Sessions announced he could not be impartial with respect to the collusion charges against the Trump campaign, and thus he would recuse himself from the investigation. The assistant attorney general, Rod Rosenstein, would take over.

Trump was furious. Going on the offensive, Trump posted an old photo of Chuck Schumer eating donuts with Putin and posted an article of a meeting Nancy Pelosi had with Putin.

"I hereby demand a second investigation, after Schumer, of Pelosi, for her close ties to Russia, and lying about it," Trump wrote.

Clearly rattled, Trump then made up a whopper of a story to deflect the heat being directed at him. He accused President Obama of tapping his phones at Trump Tower during the campaign in a series of tweets: "Terrible! Just found out that Obama had my 'wires tapped' in Trump Tower just before the victory. Nothing found. This is McCarthyism! . . . Just out. The same Russian Ambassador that met with Jeff Sessions visited the Obama White House 22 times, and 4 times last year alone . . . Is it legal for a sitting President to be 'wire-tapping' a race for president prior to an election? Turned down by court earlier. A NEW LOW! . . . How low has President Obama gone to tap my phones during the very sacred election process. This is Nixon/Watergate. Bad (or sick) guy!"

Americans at this point, if not before, had good reason to worry about the psychological stability of the president of the United States.

The "spying" accusation was false. Obama would have had to petition the Justice Department to get permission for such a wiretap. There are long-standing laws and procedures to ensure that presidents cannot wiretap rivals for political purposes. There is no evidence that Obama spied on anyone in the Trump campaign.

"A cardinal rule of the Obama administration was that no White House official ever interfered with any independent investigation led by the Department of Justice," said Kevin Lewis, a spokesman for Mr. Obama. "As part of that practice, neither President Obama nor any White House official ever ordered surveillance on any US citizen."

Trump, it turned out, based his accusation on an article in Breitbart News, famed for its outrageous conspiracy theories and ridiculous accusations against those not on the far right. Trump jumped on the made-up story to deflect criticism coming his way.

At about the same time, Counselor to the President Kellyanne Conway backed up Trump's claim about Obama spying on him. She suggested that domestic spying could be accomplished in many ways, even through microwave ovens. Memes of President Obama holding binoculars leaning out of a microwave oven went viral. Amid all the insanity, there had to be some humor.

On March 20, 2017, FBI Director James Comey announced that the FBI was looking into the Russian government's efforts to interfere in the 2016 presidential election.

That day Trump tweeted, "This story is FAKE NEWS and everyone knows it! . . . The Democrats made up and pushed the Russian story as an excuse for running a terrible campaign. Big advantage in Electoral College and lost!"

Two days later CNN reported that Trump's associates communicated with suspected Russian operatives to possibly coordinate the release of information damaging to Hillary Clinton's campaign. This was the reason for Comey's investigation.

Trump tweeted, "Trump Russia story is a hoax. #MAGA." He asked why the FBI wasn't looking to see whether Hillary Clinton had ties to Russia.

On April 1, 2017, Trump brought up the fake wiretapping charge again.

"When will Sleepy Eyes Chuck Todd and @NBCNews start talking about the Obama SURVEILLANCE SCANDAL and stop with the Fake Trump/Russia story? . . . A total scam."

On April 25, 2017, the Senate voted ninety-four to six to confirm Rod Rosenstein as deputy attorney general. With Sessions having recused himself, Rosenstein would now oversee the investigation looking into Trump's ties to Russia.

On May 8 Trump tweeted, "The Russia-Trump collusion story is a total hoax, when will this taxpayer funded charade end?"

For over three years, followers of the president's Twitter page have been exposed to daily, often hourly, rants about the Russia "hoax" and just about everything to do with Russia.

With respect to all topics Russia, President Trump has lost it.

CHAPTER 20

Russia Hacks the World

These most deadly adversaries of republican government might
naturally have been expected to make their approaches from
more than one quarter, but chiefly from the desire in foreign
powers to gain an improper ascendant in our councils.
—*FEDERALIST NO. 68 (attributed to Alexander Hamilton)*

WHEN BORIS YELTSIN NAMED VLADIMIR PUTIN TO BE Russia's prime minister in 1999, the country was weak. A year earlier Russia had defaulted on its debt. Government workers and pensioners were paid months late. Oligarchs ran the place. The Russian army lost a war in Chechnya, and former Warsaw Pact allies were joining NATO.

Russia moreover was not able to stand by its allies. One of these was Serbia, which Russia had rushed to defend in 1914, precipitating World War I. In 1999 Serbia was bombed for seventy-eight days by US and other NATO forces in an effort to stop the internment and ethnic cleansing of thousands of Albanians. Many Russians, including Vladimir Putin, never forgave President Bill Clinton and NATO for conducting these military operations against Serbia in Russia's backyard when Russia, under Boris Yeltsin, was powerless to stop them.

Putin announced policies to restore domestic stability and Russia's rightful place in world affairs. He would make Russia great again. When Yeltsin stepped down as president, he appointed Putin to take his place.

Putin sent in troops to regain Chechnya, and though thousands died, he had secured Russia's territorial integrity and prestige.

At home Putin crushed the most powerful oligarchs. He first went after those who controlled the media, taking over Russian television and radio. Then he cracked down on independent journalists and businessmen who opposed him. Some were jailed. Others were killed or disappeared. In 2003 Mikhail Khodorkovsky, the richest man in the country, was arrested, and the state took over his oil company.

Putin ended any notion of fair elections. In 2003 Putin and his allies won two-thirds of the Duma, Russia's parliament, a result he trumpeted as a step towards "strengthening democracy."

He brought back the Soviet national anthem and Russian pride.

In just four years the mother country was his.

His goal had been simple: *to make Russia great again.* And he was doing it.

Putin, with contempt for the economics, politics, values, and structures of the West, has also done everything in his considerable power to destabilize the West and democratic leanings all over the world. Putin is against globalization. Among his goals are the breakup of the European Union and NATO.

The Cold War isn't over. For Putin it has hardly begun. He has plenty of missiles, planes, and troops, but the weapons he actually uses are the tools of propaganda and cyber warfare. He and his talented cyber warriors targeted the 2016 US presidential elections, but that was only one in a string of dozens of elections that Russia has reportedly meddled in since 2004.

During each election, Russian hackers, trolls, and bots have promoted an antidemocratic agenda, spreading hatred of immigrants, xenophobia, intolerance of dissent, suspicion of international cooperation, and disdain for the rule of law. In some ways it was similar to the misinformation campaigns conducted by the Soviet Union when Putin was a KGB agent, only the targeted audience was now mostly on the right wing of the political spectrum rather than the left.

In testimony before the US Senate Select Committee on Intelligence, Constanze Stelzenmüller, a senior fellow at the Brookings Institution, noted that by striking at the United States and Europe simultaneously, "the interference appears to be geared towards undermining the effectiveness and cohesion of the Western alliance as such."

She noted that Putin wants to disrupt the West as a "normative force upholding a global order based on universal rules rather than might alone."

Putin's ultimate goal is to disrupt Europe and the US so they're no longer effective counterweights to Russia.

Stelzenmüller noted that Putin's ultimate goal has been to "dismantle decades of progress toward building a democratic Europe that is whole, free, and at peace." Most experts agree that the Kremlin's goal is not necessarily to help a candidate or party to victory, but to delegitimize the democratic process.

The extent of Putin's meddling in governmental affairs is stunning.

UKRAINE

One of the worst cases of Russian interference occurred during the presidential elections in Ukraine in 2014. Ukraine was looking to join NATO, something Putin was dead set against. In May 2014 pro-Russian hackers launched cyberattacks that disrupted the Ukrainian presidential election. Embarrassing hacked emails were released. An hour before the polls closed, malware posted a graphic declaring far-right candidate Dmytro Yarosh to be the winner. Channel One Russia declared Yarosh the winner.

Putin's infiltration of the Ukrainian election caused riots in the streets of Kiev, and ultimately President Petro Poroshenko, who won with 54 percent of the vote, shied away from joining NATO and turned to Putin and Russia instead.

In March 2014 Russia, in violation of international law, annexed the peninsula of Crimea, which had been Ukraine territory since 1954. The United States declared sanctions on Russia for this action.

Although Hillary Clinton had left her post as secretary of state in early 2013, Putin was as angry at her as at any Obama administration official. Clinton had stood firmly on the side of democracy movements in the Ukraine, and since her husband's leadership of the NATO bombing on Serbia in 1999, she had supported strong action against Kremlin-backed strongmen in Eastern Europe.

In 2019 Ukraine held another presidential election in which comedian and entertainer Volodymyr Zelensky defeated incumbent president Petro Poroshenko by a wide margin. It was unclear what Russia did, if anything, to try to interfere in the 2019 election. Ukraine, however, was as vulnerable vis-à-vis Russia as ever before, particularly with US president Donald Trump being so sympathetic to Putin and Russia. When Trump called Zelensky to congratulate him on assuming the presidency, and Trump asked that Ukraine investigate Joe Biden and his son Hunter Biden, Zelensky was in a difficult spot. More on this story in Chapter 31. If interference in US elections is what US presidents demand for United States friendship, is a country as vulnerable as Ukraine in a position to say no?

FRANCE

Russia in 2017 interfered in the French presidential election, using the same tactics Putin used to disrupt the American election. Putin expressed his preference for far-right candidate Marine Le Pen. Her party, the National Front, received a loan from First Czech-Russian Bank to bankroll her campaign. Before the election, Le Pen had flown to Russia to meet with Putin. She held pro-Russian positions, including opposition to NATO. She supported leaving the European Union and supported Russian intervention in Syria.

The Kremlin-controlled news outlet Sputnik released polls showing that François Fillon, a candidate friendly to Russia, was in the lead.

Emmanuel Macron, the candidate most critical of Moscow, was the victim of most of the cyber and propaganda attacks. Russia claimed that Macron was an agent of the United States and was funded by Saudi Arabia. Few took the claims seriously.

Two days before the election, Russian hackers leaked nine gigabytes of Macron's private emails. Macron managed to win the election anyway.

Not even a year after defeating Pen's reactionary National Front, Macron issued a warning against France's rising fascination with antidemocratic and illiberal ideas.

Right before the election, Facebook shut down thirty thousand fake accounts that had been spreading false information in French politics.

Despite Macron's win, the influence of the Russians was deeply felt in France.

"They've still fragmented the electorate," said Clint Watts, a senior fellow at the Foreign Policy Research Institute. "You now have an angry population that undermines the mandate of the winner, and they're now supporting Russian positions."

President Trump has never acknowledged the Russian attack on Macron.

AUSTRIA

In late 2016 Norbert Hofer, the far-right Freedom Party candidate running for president of Austria, almost won with the help of Russian interference. In the first round of elections, Hofer, a strong backer of Putin and Russia, received 35 percent of the vote, marking the best showing the right-wing Freedom Party ever achieved in Austria. During the election process Putin sought to align Austrian and German pro-Russian political players, citizens groups, and the media in an attempt to oust President Alexander Van der Bellen.

In the second round of elections, Van der Bellen defeated Hofer by the thinnest of margins—50.3 percent to 49.7 percent. A scandal arose over the mishandling of postal votes. Malfeasance by the Freedom Party was suspected. A second vote took place on December 4, 2016, and Van der Bellen won by a significantly larger margin.

The Freedom Party was once aligned with Nazis. Though the party has renounced that past, Jews in Austria and Israel have called for a boycott of elected Freedom Party officials. Russia, however, apparently thinks otherwise.

GERMANY

The Germans also held elections in 2017, and Russia used many of the same tactics it employed in the United States to influence that outcome. Germany's chancellor, Angela Merkel, has stood up to Putin. It was no surprise that Putin sought to humble her.

Before the election, Chancellor Merkel warned Putin not to meddle in Germany's elections. She noted that since the annexation of Crimea, the Russians had stepped up their trolling in German social media.

Three German-language media outlets—RT Deutsch, Sputnik Deutschland, and News Front auf Deutsch—are owned by the Kremlin or the Russian secret services, and they circulated fake news prior to the election along with other far-right and anti-immigrant media outlets. They railed against Muslim immigrants, the decadent West, and sometimes against Jews.

In January 2016 the Russians made up a story that three Muslim or Arab men abducted and raped a Russian-German girl. The story was false, but hundreds demonstrated in cities across Germany. For days Russian television railed in indignation about the failure of German authorities to go after the (nonexistent) perpetrators. Sergey Lavrov, the foreign minister, accused the Germans of obstruction of justice. Many Germans eventually saw through the Russian attempt at manipulating them.

The Russians planted another similar story that German soldiers raped a young girl while stationed in Lithuania as part of a NATO mission. One fake story had refugees destroying the oldest church in Germany. The Russians put out a video contending that Merkel was mentally ill. More than a million people viewed it.

As in America, the efforts at disinformation prompted the mainstream German journalists to investigate, fact-check, and protect their country from fake news and the Russian propaganda.

Not all of the Russian efforts were aimed at the media. A pro-Russian hacker group in January 2015 attacked German government computers during the Ukrainian prime minister's visit. In April and May 2015 the German legislature came under attack by hackers for several weeks. More than five thousand computers were infected, including those in Chancellor Merkel's office. Their network was disabled for four days. The attack was linked to Russia's Fancy Bear network, which is connected to military intelligence. A report said that the attack was ordered by President Putin.

These efforts, however, were not enough to derail the chancellorship of Germany's Angela Merkel. How much confusion and doubt was sown remains to be seen.

GREAT BRITAIN

First came Brexit, the push by populists for Britain to leave the European Union.

The role of Russian operatives in promoting support for Brexit has never thoroughly been proven or investigated. Certainly Brexit fits within the broader Russian agenda of promoting nationalist movements in Western Europe over a strong European Union that excluded Russia and was making considerable inroads into formerly communist countries in Eastern Europe.

The English populists who wanted out of the European Union swore that the Russians were *not* involved in the referendum, but in June 2018 it was revealed that Arron Banks, who had financed the Brexit referendum with eight million British pounds—the largest donation in British history—had had four secret meetings with Russian businessmen who offered him the opportunity to invest in the consolidation of six Russian gold mines that could have netted Banks more than a billion dollars.

Banks, whose wife is Russian, denied he had had any part of the deal, but it turned out his business partner and fellow Brexit supporter James Mellon was involved in other lucrative deals with Russia. Mellon had bought stocks in a diamond mine at a discount, and his firm, Charlemagne Capital, cleaned up.

In August 2016 Banks discussed the Trump campaign with the Russian ambassador over lunch. After Trump's victory, emails revealed that they'd discussed what role Jeff Sessions, then a senator, might play in the cabinet.

Denying he had anything to do with the Russians, Banks asked, "What could the Russians possibly have wanted from me?"

The answer was obvious: they wanted Banks to finance Brexit efforts—helping Vladimir Putin achieve one of his most important goals: the breakup of the West.

Then came the 2017 election in Great Britain. Curiously this is one of the few Western elections in which post-Soviet Russia has preferred the left-wing candidate, perhaps because they saw him as a destabilizing force for Britain's conservative government.

In April 2017 Prime Minister Theresa May surprised Great Britain by calling for a general election in June. With the Brexit negotiations coming up, she wanted a stronger mandate as she went into the talks with the other European nations.

Her opponent, Jeremy Corbyn from the left wing of the Labour Party, hammered May for her lack of charisma. The Russians apparently preferred Corbyn. For three years, RT UK television supported him, and it was revealed that the Russians used trolls to sow division in Great Britain. There was evidence of Russian cyberattacks, as there also had been in the 2015 election.

British cyber experts found evidence of Twitter accounts linked to the Internet Research Agency, a Russian cyber factory based in St. Petersburg. The trolls praised RT for its truthfulness while blasting the BBC and other British news agencies. The firm has nine hundred trolls working for it and is owned by a government contractor who is close friends with Putin.

A white supremacist troll, @ProudPatriot101, tweeted at Justice Secretary David Gauke after he called RT a "propaganda station": "Reputable politicians? I have never, not once in my life come across one . . . They don't exist . . . RT tells the truth, is that why you don't like them?"

The Russians, British cyber experts said, were behind the tweet.

Other trolls sent him similar pro-RT tweets.

In 2015, RT—funded by the Russian state headed by Putin—and Sputnik, the Russian news agency, backed Corbyn. In 2017 they supported him again. They also wrote editorials attacking May during the election campaign.

Then there was a murder.

On March 4, 2018, Putin and the Russians were accused of poisoning British immigrants Sergei Skripal, a former Russian spy, and his daughter, Yulia, using a lethal nerve agent developed by the Russian military. They were found slumped on a bench outside a shopping center in Salisbury. Theresa May's outcry was immediate. Only Jeremy Corbyn warned against rushing to judgment. He was criticized by some of his party members for his lax stance on what many were sure was an attack much like the poisoning of FSB agent Alexander Litvinenko, who was living in London when he was murdered during a meeting with another FSB officer.

Putin publicly denied having anything to do with the poisoning of the ex-spy and his daughter.

Putin then quickly turned around and accused the British of meddling in Russia's elections. Later that month, Vladimir Putin gained 76.7 percent of the vote in a general election. More than 56 million Russians voted for him, ten million more than in 2012. Whatever the British did to influence that Russian election, if anything, was insignificant.

Right after the results were announced, Putin's campaign head thanked Great Britain for antagonizing and mobilizing Russian voters with the outcry about the attack on the ex-Russian spy and his daughter.

Said Putin, "Right now the turnout numbers are higher than we expected. We need to thank Great Britain for that because once again they did not consider the Russian mentality. Once again we were subject to pressure at just the moment when we needed to mobilize."

Putin thus said—yet again—that Russians were victims of Great Britain and other Westerners who "pressured" Russians to bend to their ways. Putin's popularity was a test of Russian pride and independence from the West. It was the West that was interfering with Russian elections instead of vice versa.

Putin's "turning of the tables" and rhetorical attacks on the British in 2018 were remarkably similar to the rhetoric Donald Trump used when he said repeatedly that it was the Democrats, and Hillary Clinton, who with the help of the Russians sought to steal the 2016 election from him.

CHAPTER 21

Putin Crowns Our President

It is a sin to be silent when it is your duty to protest.
—ABRAHAM LINCOLN

RUSSIAN PRESIDENT VLADIMIR PUTIN MEDDLED IN OUR 2016 presidential election. That is a fact. Seventeen American intelligence organizations agree. The Russian interference into the election was the worst attack on our country since September 11, 2001, and perhaps the most devastating threat to our independence since the Japanese attack on Pearl Harbor on December 7, 1941.

This didn't bother President-Elect Trump in the slightest. Vladimir Putin was someone Trump looked up to, even idolized. Perhaps there was a reason. A good case can be made that, but for Putin, Trump would not be president.

The public Trump-Putin flirtation may very well have been initiated by Trump. We have no idea what has gone on between the two men in private, or between Trump- and Putin-allied oligarchs, because Trump's business dealings, including his tax returns, remain a mystery. But the public Trump-Putin friendship began when Trump was seriously considering the presidency in late 2013.

From news reports, court documents, and unclassified reports, Trump's fascination with Vladimir Putin began in November 2013 when the Miss Universe pageant, which Trump owned and ran, was broadcast live from Russia.

Tweeted Trump, "A big deal that will bring our countries together." Later that day he tweeted, "Do you think Putin will be going to The Miss Universe Pageant in November in Moscow—if so, will he become my new best friend?"

Trump said on the David Letterman show, "I've done a lot of business with the Russians. They're smart, and they're tough."

The location of the Miss Universe pageant was gained through licensing fees of nearly $20 million paid by a Moscow real estate development firm, Crocus Group, whose president was billionaire oligarch Aras Agalarov. His son, Emin, a pop singer, was vice president of the firm. During his stay in Moscow, Trump went to Aras's birthday party.

The next time Trump commented on Russia was on October 14, 2015, when American intelligence determined that Russian-backed separatists were responsible for the downing of a civilian airliner, Malaysia Airlines Flight 17.

Trump, trying to clear Putin of involvement in such a villainous act, cast doubt on the assessment. Here was a presidential candidate willing to believe Vladimir Putin over our own intelligence services.

"That's a horrible thing that happened," said Trump. "It's disgusting and disgraceful, but Putin and Russia say they didn't do it, the other side said they did, no one really knows who did it, probably Putin knows who did it. Possibly it was Russia but they are totally denying it . . . But they're saying it wasn't them. The other side says it is them. And we're going to go through that arguing for probably fifty years and nobody is ever going to know. Probably was Russia."

A month later as Trump debated GOP opponents, he bragged about his relationship with Putin.

Trump said he got to know Putin "very well because we were both on *60 Minutes*. We were stablemates, and we did very well that night." He then said, "If Putin wants to go and knock the hell out of ISIS, I am all for it, one hundred percent, and I can't understand how anybody would be against it."

By now it was time for Putin to return the favor with some praise for Trump.

Russia Today (RT), the government-owned television network, celebrated its tenth anniversary on December 10, 2015. Sitting just two seats from Putin was Michael Flynn, who was later chosen to be Trump's national security advisor. Flynn was paid to speak at the dinner. A week later at a news conference, Putin praised Trump, who was leading in the polls to be the Republican presidential candidate.

Said Putin, "He is a very flamboyant man, very talented, no doubt about that. But it's not our business to judge his merits, it's up to the voters of the United States." He added, "He is an absolute leader of the presidential race, so we see it today. He says that he wants to move to another level of relations, a deeper level of relations with Russia. How can we not welcome that? Of course we welcome it."

Trump responded in a statement, "It is always a great honor to be so nicely complimented by a man so highly respected within his own country and beyond. I have always felt that Russia and the United States should be able to work well with each other towards defeating terrorism and restoring world peace, not to mention trade and all of the other benefits derived from mutual respect."

On February 17, 2016, Trump bragged about Putin's praise for him. In a stump speech in South Carolina, Trump crowed to the crowd, "Putin called me a genius."

He repeated the line three times in April, once in May in an interview with CNN, once in June during a rally in California, twice in July, and once in August at a town hall meeting in Ohio.

He wasn't bragging about the praise of Ronald Reagan, George H. W. Bush, George W. Bush, or any other Republican leader. No, he was bragging that Russia's strongman Vladimir Putin was saying great things about him. Why was he so beholden to Putin?

We would soon learn why.

In March 2016, Russia hackers tricked an employee of the Democratic National Committee into changing his password, giving the Russians access to and control over thousands of emails of John Podesta, presidential candidate Hillary Clinton's campaign manager.

Two days later George Papadopoulos, a member of the Trump campaign, met with a professor living in London who had connections to Russian government officials. The professor, Joseph Mifsud, honorary director of the London Academy of Diplomacy, introduced Papadopoulos to a woman he said was the niece of Vladimir Putin. The woman, Olga Vinogradova, told Papadopoulos she would arrange a meeting between her uncle and Trump.

"As mentioned we are all very excited by the possibility of a good relationship with Mr. Trump," she wrote to Papadopoulos in an email. "The Russian federation would love to welcome him once his candidature would be officially announced."

Papadopoulos emailed Trump's campaign supervisor and other members of Trump's foreign policy team to tell them he had arranged a meeting with Russian leadership to discuss US-Russian relations under President Trump.

"Great work," replied the campaign supervisor.

When it turned out that Vinogradova was not Putin's niece, American experts suspected she was a Russian "cut-out," a woman assigned to troll for American contacts who could be blackmailed in the future. Papadopoulos's emails did not state who Vinogradova worked for, where she lived, or what her connection was to Mifsud. She was really Olga Polonskaya, a wine company manager. Vinogradova was her maiden name.

A week later, Papadopoulos told Trump's foreign policy advisors he could arrange a meeting between Trump and Putin.

In mid-April 2016, the professor in London sent Papadopoulos an email from someone connected to the Russian Ministry of Foreign Affairs to set the groundwork for a meeting between members of Trump's team and the Russian government.

Papadopoulos emailed a senior advisor to the Trump campaign: "The Russian government has an open invitation by Putin for Mr. Trump to meet him when he is ready."

On April 26 Papadopoulos met with his professor contact in London, who told him the Russians had obtained dirt on Hillary Clinton.

"They have thousands of emails," the professor told him.

Putin had stolen Hillary Clinton's emails and wanted Trump to know he was about to use them to help defeat her.

The next day Trump gave a foreign policy address in Washington. Russian ambassador Sergey Kislyak sat in the front row as Trump called for better relations with Russia.

There was more evidence of Trump's attempted collusion with the Russians when in May 2016, Paul Erickson, a member of the National Rifle Association and a conservative activist, sent an email to Rick Dearborn, one of Trump's campaign advisors, with a subject line: "Kremlin Connection." In the email Erickson said he wished to advise Dearborn and Senator Jeff Sessions—then Trump's foreign policy advisor—how to proceed in arranging a back-channel meeting between Trump and Putin.

"[Russia is] quietly but actively seeking a dialogue with the U.S.," wrote Erickson. He said the Russians would use the NRA's annual convention in Louisville to make "first contact."

"Putin is deadly serious about building a good relationship with Mr. Trump," Erickson wrote. "He wants to extend an invitation to Mr. Trump to visit him in the Kremlin before the election. Let's talk through what has transpired and Senator [Jeff] Sessions advice on how to proceed."

In another email, Erickson made the same pitch to Jared Kushner, Trump's son-in-law.

Sessions denied ever being contacted by Erickson.

In an email to Dearborn, Erickson wrote, "The Kremlin believes that the only possibility of a true reset in this relationship would be with a new Republican White House. Ever since Hillary compared Putin to Hitler, all senior Russian leaders consider her beyond redemption."

Erickson was close to the Right to Bear Arms organization, a Russian guns-rights group. The group hosted Erickson in September 2014 in Moscow. Members of the Russian organization attended the US NRA conventions in 2014 and 2015.

On June 9, 2016, during the infamous secret meeting at Trump Tower, Donald Trump Jr., campaign manager Paul Manafort, and Jared Kushner met with Natalia Veselnitskaya, a Russian lawyer who promised dirt on Hillary Clinton.

Ten days later Papadopoulos sent an email to a Trump campaign official, offering to travel to Russia to meet with Russian officials if Trump himself couldn't go.

Days before the Republican National Convention, three Trump security advisors, Carter Page, J. D. Gordon, and Walid Phares, met in Cleveland with Russian ambassador Kislyak. During a Republican National Convention event, Senator Jeff Sessions, as head of Trump's national security advisory committee, met with Kislyak and several other ambassadors.

What were they talking about? Clinton's emails? Perhaps. But with Russian ambassador Kislyak there, it's also a good bet they were discussing lifting the sanctions President Obama put on Russia for annexing Crimea. The Russian strategy was to help Trump win the presidency and hope that Trump would reciprocate by lifting the sanctions. The extent of Russia's help in winning the presidential election was wide.

One of the goals of the Russians as they spread fake news through Facebook, Twitter, Instagram, and other social media companies, including Reddit, YouTube, Tumblr, Pinterest, Vine, and Google+, was to suppress the turnout among Democratic voters.

According to the Senate Intelligence Committee report, the Russians continue their destructive activity to this day.

The Russian operation was run by the Internet Research Agency, owned by businessman Yevgeny Prigozhin, a close ally of Vladimir Putin. In February 2017, Prigozhin and a dozen of his employees were indicted by Robert Mueller for their interference in the 2016 election.

The Internet Research Agency, said the report, created accounts under fake names on almost every social media platform.

The Russians, said the report, put up posts connecting Trump with Jesus, and Hillary Clinton with Satan.

The Russians even used American-sounding email accounts to contact African Americans to raise their ire over racism and racial conflict in the United States. They posted content sympathetic to the Black Lives Matter movement, as the Russians sought to make racial tensions worse.

The Russians, in their attempt to help Trump get elected, focused on getting followers of Jill Stein and Bernie Sanders *not* to vote for Hillary Clinton. They wanted Stein and Sanders followers either to vote for Stein or Sanders or stay home.

The Senate Intelligence Committee report said 187 million Instagram users either "liked" or "shared" the Russian content. On Facebook there were 76.5 million similar engagements.

After the election, the Russians made seventy posts on Facebook and Instagram mocking the claims that the Russians had interfered in the election.

All through July and August 2016 there were reports that Russia was helping Trump win the election through both email hacks and a covert Russian operation designed to sow public mistrust in the upcoming presidential election and particularly in Hillary Clinton. Trump was briefed on this but said nothing about it. On September 7, 2016, once again Trump praised Putin while making a nasty crack about President Obama.

Noting that Putin's approval rating was 82 percent, Trump said, "He's been a leader far more than our president has been a leader." In an interview with CNN the same day vice-presidential candidate Mike Pence repeated what Trump had said.

"It's inarguable that Vladimir Putin has been a stronger leader in his country than Barack Obama has been in this country."

First Trump and then Pence spoke of the Russian dictator favorably in comparison with the sitting president of the United States.

The next day, September 8, 2016, Jeff Sessions, Trump's future attorney general, met with Russian ambassador Kislyak. That day Trump, in an interview with the Russian-owned TV station RT, declared that "it's probably unlikely" Russia is interfering with the election.

"I think the Democrats are putting that out," he said.

During the first presidential debate on September 26, 2016, Trump continued denying that Russia was responsible for the hacked emails from the Democratic National Committee.

"I don't think anyone knows it was Russia that broke into the DNC," he said. "She's saying Russia, Russia, Russia, but I don't—maybe it was, I mean, it could be Russia, but it could also be China. It could also be lots of other people. It could also be someone sitting on their bed that weighs four hundred pounds, okay? You don't know who broke into the DNC."

It would be another week before Julian Assange and WikiLeaks would release John Podesta's emails. Before that, Roger Stone, a political consultant to Trump, tweeted, "I have total confidence that @wikileaks and my hero Julian Assange will educate the American people soon #LockHerUp."

The very next day Assange announced on video that he would publish new information on the presidential election "every week for the next ten weeks."

Three days later Assange released thousands of John Podesta's emails. The timing was perfect. It came hours after Trump was seen talking to Billy

Bush on an *Access Hollywood* bus about his ability to sexually assault women and get away with it. What wasn't known at the time was that Assange had gotten Clinton's emails from the Russian government.

On October 7, 2016, Barack Obama, who was in the final months of his presidency, complained bitterly about the Russians hacking into the presidential election. James Clapper, the director of national intelligence, accused two Russian organizations, DCLeaks and Guccifer 2.0, along with WikiLeaks, of being behind the operation.

During the second presidential debate, Hillary Clinton repeated Clapper's suspicions about the Russians being responsible for hacking Democratic Party emails.

Responded a gaslighting Trump, "She doesn't know if the Russians are doing the hacking. Maybe there is no hacking. But they always blame Russia. And the reason they blame Russia is because they think they're trying to tarnish me with Russia. I know nothing about Russia. I know—I know about Russia, but I know nothing about the inner workings of Russia. I don't deal there. I have no businesses there. I have no loans from Russia."

Sheer nonsense.

The next day at a rally in Pennsylvania, Trump told the crowd, "I love WikiLeaks."

His comment brought raucous applause.

Two days later Roger Stone bragged of being in communication with Julian Assange. Realizing he was confessing to collusion with a foreign government, quickly Stone made a clarification, denying he ever spoke or met with Assange.

During the third debate, Hillary Clinton commented that Putin was backing Trump because "he would rather have a puppet as president of the United States."

"No puppet, no puppet," Trump replied. "You're the puppet."

The American public was not presented with a smoking gun, but we certainly had lots of clues that the Russians were trying to steal the election for Trump. Nevertheless, on November 8, 2016, Donald Trump was elected president of the United States. Though Hillary Clinton gained over three million more votes than Trump (65,853,506 to 62,984,805), Clinton lost swing states Florida and Ohio as well as three important states that Democrats have usually won: Pennsylvania, Wisconsin, and Michigan. All of these states had been targeted by the Russians.

After the Electoral College votes were counted, Trump was declared the winner, 306 to 232. Regardless of how much discretion the drafters of the Constitution intended to give the electors when they created the Electoral College (this is a question of considerable debate among constitutional law scholars), the GOP electors in 2016 bowed to pressure from the GOP to rubber-stamp the vote in their respective states. They did so despite the irregularities in the election, the nationwide popular vote, and the manifest unfitness of the "winning" candidate.

Upon learning of Trump's victory, the Russian parliament burst into applause.

Meetings between Trump team members and the Russians continued. In December Jared Kushner met with Ambassador Kislyak. Around the same time, Vladimir Putin went on TV to once again praise Trump.

"Trump was an entrepreneur and a businessman," Putin said. "Because he achieved success in business, it suggests that he is a clever man."

A week later Putin sent Trump a letter expressing hope that Trump would "restore the framework of bilateral cooperation in different areas as well as bringing our level of collaboration on the international scene to a qualitatively new level."

Eight days later Trump made the contents of the letter public.

"I hope both sides are able to live up to these thoughts," he said. "We do not have to travel an alternative path."

Three days later, on December 28, 2016, President Obama in his last days in office signed an executive order sanctioning Russia for its interference in the presidential election. The sanctions took place the next day. Obama also tossed thirty-five Russian diplomats out of the country and imposed sanctions on the two Russian intelligence services identified in the hacking.

"All Americans should be alarmed by Russia's actions," Obama said in a statement. He added that the US moves follow "repeated private and public warnings" to Moscow.

"These actions are not the sum total of our response to Russia's aggressive activities," Obama said. "We will continue to take a variety of actions at a time and place of our choosing, some of which will not be publicized."

That day Michael Flynn, Trump's appointee as United States national security advisor, received a series of phone calls from Russian ambassador Kislyak, who railed at America's actions, then threatened retaliation.

Flynn reportedly told Kislyak to calm down, implying that when Trump took office, he would get rid of the sanctions.

When asked about this conversation in late January 2017, Flynn lied to the FBI.

But Flynn had gotten his point across to the Russians. When Putin was asked to comment, he calmly said he would not retaliate with similar expulsions, even though his foreign minister, Sergey Lavrov, had recommended it.

Said Trump on Twitter, "Great move on delay (by V. Putin.) I always knew he was very smart!"

The next day Trump again refused to blame Russia for hacking the Democratic Party emails.

"Hacking is a very hard thing to prove," he said.

That same day Kislyak called Flynn, letting him know that Russia didn't retaliate because Flynn had asked him not to. After talking to Kislyak, Flynn told Trump's transition team about his conversation with Kislyak.

On January 4, 2017, Trump taunted the Democrats about their hacked emails. He tweeted, "Julian Assange said a fourteen-year-old could have hacked Podesta—why was DNC so careless? And said Russians did not give him the info!"

On January 6 the Office of the Director of National Intelligence released a report that the CIA, the FBI, and the NSA concluded that DCLeaks, Guccifer 2.0, and WikiLeaks all obtained documents from hackers backed by the Russian government. James Clapper, FBI Director James Comey, and CIA Director John Brennan that day gave Trump their findings.

Democracy in the United States had been violated as never before, but our new president cared only about the election's result. He had won, and he didn't care how. Pretending he had won fair and square was more important to his ego than blowing the whistle on the Russian hackers, tweeters, and bots who made his victory possible.

More sinister, there was reason to be concerned that Trump and/or people in his organization could have been involved. Whatever involvement the Trump campaign and the Trump Organization had with the Russians needed to be discovered, whether it was legal collaboration (some collaboration with outsiders including foreign countries is legal) or a criminal conspiracy with the Russians. Knowing what happened was critically important for our national security (we could not have anyone compromised by Russia in the highest reaches in our government). Knowing what happened was also important for public confidence in the new administration. A thorough investigation was necessary. A sensible president-elect in Trump's position, particularly an innocent one, would have recognized that and allowed an investigation to proceed while he prepared for the presidency.

But not Donald Trump. He condemned the whole idea of an investigation from the outset.

Trump told the *New York Times*, "The Russian controversy is a 'political witch hunt.'" He then issued a statement saying, "The hacks had absolutely no effect on the outcome of the election."

With Russia's help, Trump had been swept into office. Because the House and Senate were controlled by Republicans, there would be *no* meaningful congressional investigation and *no* inquiry into the Russian hacks—at least not for a while. Trump would do everything he could to stop an investigation by the Justice Department and FBI.

He had won the election fair and square with no help from Russia, and that was the end of it. Or so he said.

Of Vladimir Putin, said Trump, "He means it. I believe him."

CHAPTER 22

Lies, Alternative Facts, Fake News, and the Free Press

*He who permits himself to tell a lie once, finds it much easier to
do it a second and third time, till at length it becomes habitual;
he tells lies without attending to it, and truths without the world's
believing him. This falsehood of the tongue leads to that of
the heart, and in time depraves all its good dispositions.*
—*THOMAS JEFFERSON*

*If you tell a lie big enough and keep repeating it, people will eventually
come to believe it. The lie can be maintained only for such time as the
State can shield the people from the political, economic and/or military
consequences of the lie. It thus becomes vitally important for the State to
use all of its powers to repress dissent, for the truth is the mortal enemy of
the lie, and thus by extension, the truth is the greatest enemy of the State.*
—*JOSEPH GOEBBELS*

I N THESE QUOTES, THOMAS JEFFERSON ACKNOWLEDGES that lying is at the heart of personal and political corruption. Joseph Goebbels, Hitler's propaganda minister, explains its usefulness.

And we all know the old, apocryphal story about George Washington and the cherry tree.

"I shall not tell a lie," said young George.

Donald Trump, our forty-fifth president, however, appears to be *incapable* of telling the truth about anything except his own prejudices and emotions.

The *Washington Post* tallied more than two thousand lies during Trump's first year in office. After three years, his lie total was more than five thousand. By late April 2019, the tally of his lies passed the ten thousand mark.

We can criticize these statistics by arguing about what constitutes a knowing "lie" as opposed to just a stupid or ill-informed statement, but by any definition of "lie" Trump's score is remarkably high.

The irony, of course, is that Trump the serial liar projects his own dishonesty onto others. During the presidential campaign, Trump called Senator Ted Cruz "Lyin' Ted" and called Marco Rubio an "even bigger liar" than Cruz. He said Jeb Bush was "as bad a liar" as Cruz and called Dr. Ben Carson a "pathological liar."

But by far the biggest liar in the Republican primary was Trump himself.

During the primary he continually lied about not taking money from others for his campaign. He lied about Trump University, saying it got an A from the Better Business Bureau. He lied when he said students raved about the courses. (He would later pay $25 million to former students to settle a lawsuit.) He lied about how much his father helped him get started in business. During the campaign he said he always was against gambling in Florida. (He had actually tried to build a casino in Florida.) And he continued to lie about President Obama's birth certificate.

Trump lies because his supporters, and often his cowed opponents in the GOP, let him get away it.

Trump knew he was going to win the nomination when his main opponent, Ted Cruz of Texas, dropped out. This came after Trump made an outrageous claim that Cruz's father, Rafael, an evangelical preacher, had aided Lee Harvey Oswald in the murder of President John Kennedy. This claim came from a fake news article in the *National Enquirer*, which supported

Trump for president in almost every issue (Trump had personal financial ties to the publisher).

After Cruz dropped out, Trump praised Cruz's "whole beautiful family."

One would have thought that Ted Cruz would have been furious with Trump. But Trump was the Republican candidate and later president. Cruz, tamed, seemed to be all for him. Cruz later wrote:

> President Trump is a flash-bang grenade thrown into Washington by the forgotten men and women of America. The fact that his first year as Commander in Chief disoriented and distressed members of the media and political establishment is not a bug but a feature.
>
> President Trump is doing what he was elected to do: disrupt the status quo. That scares the heck out of those who have controlled Washington for decades, but for millions of Americans, their confusion is great fun to watch.

Cruz was willing to heap praise on someone who only a year earlier had falsely accused his father of being involved with murder.

Trump's lies come streaming down like the waters of Niagara Falls. Members of Trump's circle are expected to lie or at least nod in affirmation when Trump lies.

After Trump contended falsely that the crowd at his 2017 inauguration was the biggest crowd ever (it wasn't; Obama's was bigger), his first spokesman, Sean Spicer, repeated the lie. Later, Sarah Huckabee Sanders would continue the trend of lying constantly to appease a crass and uncivil boss before she left the White House in 2019 to join Fox News (of course). White House counselor Kellyanne Conway makes lying or, as she describes it, telling "alternative facts" on behalf of the president, her full-time job.

When Chuck Todd of MSNBC interviewed Kellyanne Conway, the first question he asked was why Spicer had gone on national TV to "utter a falsehood" about the size of Trump's inaugural crowd.

Conway's response was, "Chuck, if we're going to keep referring to our press secretary in those types of terms, I think we're going to have to rethink our relationship here."

Todd, undeterred, again asked her why the president asked the White House press secretary "to come out in front of the podium for the first time and utter a falsehood. Why did he do that? It undermines the credibility of the entire White House Press Office on day one."

"No, it doesn't," Conway replied. "You're saying it's a falsehood, and Sean Spicer, our press secretary, gave *alternative facts* to that."

At this point Todd wanted to know, "What are alternative facts?" He noted that Spicer had uttered five statements, and four of them were untrue.

"Look," Todd said, "alternative facts are not facts. They're falsehoods."

Spicer a day later then went on the offensive, blasting the press for "a constant theme" in the media to "undercut the tremendous support" for Trump.

"The default narrative is always negative," he complained, calling the press coverage "demoralizing" and "frustrating." Spicer, Conway, and President Trump went after CNN, one of those outlets that showed that Trump's inaugural crowd was smaller than Obama's. On January 25, 2017, Trump tweeted, "Congratulations to @FoxNews for being number one in inauguration ratings. They were many times higher than FAKE NEWS @ CNN—public is smart."

Angry at how the inaugural crowd had been described, on January 26, 2017, Trump spoke with Fox's Sean Hannity and complained, "What I'm saying, Sean, is this: the media, much of the media, not all of it, is very, very dishonest. Honestly, it's fake news. It's fake. They make things up."

Really?

The size of the inaugural crowd is perhaps a small thing to lie about, but as Thomas Jefferson observed, people who permit themselves to lie once very soon lie about everything. Kellyanne Conway, Sean Spicer, and the rest of the White House staff were preparing to continue a decades-old Trump trade: lying.

The rule of law depends upon two things: knowledge of both the law and the facts. By distorting the law, facts, or both, one can convince the public that the law requires the opposite of what it actually does. Slick trial lawyers know this but are often held in check by other lawyers and judges. Slick political operatives are often only held accountable by their political opponents and a free press.

Liars of course hate the free press.

Trump and his administration haven't taken over TV stations and newspapers the way Putin has done, but Fox News has done the job of state television for him. He has rewarded Fox News with interviews, supportive tweets, and administration job offers for Fox News anchors and other employees. Never before has a White House had such a cozy relationship with a single news organization. This relationship with Fox News only turned sour in 2019 as the impeachment investigation intensified and Trump became frustrated that the network would, occasionally, allow its anchors or guests to say something critical of Trump.

This hostility to the press was evident during the presidential campaign. A recurring theme for Trump was vitriol towards journalists who disagreed with him, or even dared to ask him questions and expect answers. At a rally in Grand Rapids, Michigan, on December 21, 2015, Trump was confronted with the reality that Russia's Vladimir Putin kills journalists.

"They say he's killed reporters," said Trump, "and I don't like that. I'm totally against that. And by the way, I hate some of those people. But I would never kill them. I hate them. Some of them are such lying, disgusting people. It's true."

As Trump said journalists were "lying, disgusting people," his supporters laughed and cheered.

Then he pondered whether, like Putin, he would kill them.

"Uh, let's see, uh?" he said to the crowd, his voice rising. "No, I would never do that."

Unlike Richard Nixon, who complained about the press in private, Trump expressed his enmity to the world. During rallies he called the press scum, slime, disgusting, dishonest, and said the political press was "the worst types of human beings on earth" or the "enemy of the people." Each time his supporters cheered and jeered.

Freedom of the press, as expressed in the First Amendment to our Constitution, means absolutely nothing to Trump.

No president in history had ever openly attacked reporters the way Trump did during the presidential campaign. When ABC news reporter Tom Llamas asked Trump why he misled people about how much money he had raised for veterans, Trump called him a sleaze. During a press conference in which Trump railed about "the dishonest media," CNN's Jim Acosta was trying to ask him a question when Trump sneered, "Excuse me. Excuse me. I've watched you on TV. You're a real beauty."

He called Fox's Megyn Kelly a "bimbo" and MSNBC's Katy Tur "little Katy, third-rate journalist."

He suggested that Megyn Kelly was having her period when she challenged him during a debate. "There was blood coming out of her eyes, blood coming out of her wherever."

When caught in a lie, Trump blunts the fact-checkers by asserting over and over again that the nation's best newspapers such as the *New York Times* and *Washington Post* only deliver "fake news." Trump cried "fake news" at least 153 times during 2017 alone. His constant attacks reinforce this notion that objective truth is political, that conservatives should get their "truth" from Breitbart and Fox News while liberals get their "fake news" from MSNBC and the "failing *New York Times.*"

During a rally in Fort Worth, Texas, on February 26, 2016, Trump told a crowd of supporters that he wanted to change the libel laws so he can more easily sue news organizations. He ranted against both the *New York Times* and *Washington Post*, saying they were "dishonest" and "losing money." He then threatened them if he were to win the presidency.

"One of the things I'm going to do if I win, and I hope we do and we're certainly leading, I'm going to open up our libel laws so when they write purposely negative and horrible and false articles, we can sue them and win lots of money. We're going to open up those libel laws. So when the *New York Times* writes a hit piece which is a total disgrace or when the *Washington Post*, which is there for other reasons, writes a hit piece, we can sue them and win money instead of having no chance of winning, because they're totally protected."

"If I become president, oh, do they have problems," he said.

Trump for decades had a rocky relationship with the press, but his all-out war began in June 2016 when, during a news conference set up to announce he was giving $5.6 million to veterans groups (a lie), he spent most of the time insulting reporters, calling them "dishonest," "not good people, sleazy, and among the worst human beings I have ever met."

At his inauguration President Trump kept regional newspapers with Washington correspondents from covering the event by turning away reporters who tried to pick up their Secret Service credentials.

At the end of January 2017, Trump announced his Muslim ban (which his lawyers had persuaded him to call a "travel ban"). His ban barred residents of seven Muslim-majority countries including Iraq from immigrating to the United States. To support Trump's reasoning, Kellyanne Conway did interviews with *Cosmopolitan* and *TMZ* and one with Chris Matthews on MSNBC in which she contended that the "Bowling Green massacre" was one justification for the ban.

There was only one problem: there was no "Bowling Green massacre." Nobody in Bowling Green, Kentucky, has ever heard about it (except on Fox News), and there is no Bowling Green anywhere that has suffered a terrorist attack.

Conway contended it was a slip of the tongue, that she was referring to an incident in 2011 in which two Iraqi immigrants were caught sending money and weapons to Al Qaeda in Iraq. The two had never attacked anyone in the United States, and most important there was nobody massacred in a place called "Bowling Green."

But Conway *had* talked about the Bowling Green massacre on other occasions. Said the *Washington Post*, "She doesn't appear to have misspoken at all."

Said Samantha Schmidt in the *Post*, "Conway has taken 'alternative facts' to a new level."

Trump, through his spokesperson Conway, addressed his populist base when she attacked the media for being educated and, therefore, out of touch.

Conway said, "America didn't go to the fancy Ivy League schools like many of the media did. America doesn't—there are some people in the media, their latte and dry cleaning bill for the year is basically what people earn in some of these districts and counties where Donald Trump won . . . "

In a democracy the truth is cherished in the face of falsehoods. For an autocrat, the free press becomes the enemy. The press was Trump's enemy.

On February 19 Reince Priebus, appearing on *Face the Nation*, went so far as to accuse the media of being "an enemy of the American people." He told moderator John Dickerson the media should "stop with this unnamed source stuff."

Priebus defended Trump by complaining about "bogus stories."

Two days later at a press briefing, Glenn Thrush of the *New York Times* tried to interrupt Spicer with a question. Spicer told him, "This isn't a TV program . . . You don't get to just yell out questions. We're going to raise our hand like big boys and girls."

A day later, on February 24, 2017, Spicer held a press gathering exclusively for Breitbart and other right-wing outfits, barring the *New York Times, CNN, and Politico*.

Trump repeated his "enemy of the people" charge at a meeting of CPAC, the Conservative Political Action Conference. He said that some reporters are "terrible, dishonest people" and the "fake news," meaning the media, "doesn't tell the truth and doesn't represent the people."

That same day in an interview with Breitbart, Trump again said the media was the enemy of the people, complaining that the *New York Times* "is so evil and so bad, because they write lies."

What made Trump's attack on the First Amendment and on the press even worse was that his political allies refused to call him on it. On March 1 when Vice President Mike Pence was asked when Trump was going to end his war on the media, Pence waffled. He said what Trump was doing was "calling out the media when it played fast and loose with the facts." Pence claimed that the media was pursuing "baseless and fabricated stories."

On April 1 Trump again trotted out his made-up story about Obama wiretapping Trump Tower. He tweeted, "When will Sleepy Eyes Chuck Todd and @NBCNews start talking about the Obama SURVEILLANCE SCANDAL and stop with the Fake Trump/Russia story?"

Trump's war on the freedom of the press ranged from the general to attacks on specific reporters. On April 5, 2017, in an interview with the *New York Times*, Trump called NBC's Andrea Mitchell "Hillary Clinton's PR person." On April 21 he complained to the Associated Press, "I used to get great press. I get the worst press. I get such dishonest reporting with the media. That's another thing that really has—I've never had anything like it before. It happened during the primaries, and I said, 'You know, when I won, I said, "Well the one thing good is now I'll get good press."' And it got worse. So that was one thing that [was] a little bit of a surprise to me. I thought the press would become better, and it actually, in my opinion, got more nasty."

He continued, "I have learned one thing, because I get treated very unfairly, that's what I call it, the fake media. And the fake media is not all of the media. The fake media is some of you. I could tell you who it is. One hundred percent. Sometimes you're fake, but—but the fake media is some of the media. It bears no relationship to the truth. It's not that Fox treats me well, it's that Fox is the most accurate."

Trump loved Fox. On April 28 of that year he patted himself on the back to news anchor Martha MacCallum for his "high" approval numbers, saying that "Fox has been fair, but every network you see hits me on every topic, made up stories like Russia."

On May 10, 2017, Trump hit a new low in his dealing with the media and democracy when he barred the American press from his Oval Office meeting with Russian foreign minister Sergey Lavrov and Russian ambassador Sergey Kislyak. However, he allowed in a photographer from TASS, the Russian state-run news agency.

That same day Health and Human Services Secretary Tom Price was at the West Virginia state capitol when Dan Heyman of the Public News Service tried to ask him about the Republicans' attempt to repeal the Affordable Care Act.

Price had Heyman arrested. Heyman was charged with willful disruption of government processes, a misdemeanor, and released on $5,000 bond after being held for almost eight hours.

On May 11, the next day, Trump in an interview with *Time* praised Fox News and went after three of his favorite targets. He said that Chris Cuomo of CNN looked like "a chained lunatic," that CNN's Don Lemon is "perhaps the dumbest person in broadcasting," and that CBS *Late Show* host Stephen Colbert is a "no-talent guy who is filthy."

Two days later Trump threatened to end his daily press briefings. In an interview with Judge Jeanine Pirro on Fox News, he said he could replace them with "a piece of paper with a perfectly accurate, beautiful answer" handed out to reporters.

In early October 2017, there were reports from multiple outlets that Secretary of State Rex Tillerson had called Trump "a fucking moron." Trump was both embarrassed and furious that the reports had been printed. Trump tweeted, demanding a Senate Intelligence Committee investigation of "Fake News Networks." (Tillerson was later fired by Trump.)

When Donald Trump ran for president, his biggest and most important ally was Fox News, controlled by Rupert Murdoch. As soon as Trump detailed his platform, which included building the wall on the US and Mexican border, keeping Muslims from entering the country, and getting rid of NAFTA, Fox commentators echoed his talking points. Every time Trump talked about the "lying press" or told a lie, Fox commentators repeated Trump's claims with great seriousness and force.

Another favorite of Trump is Sinclair Broadcast Group, which is controlled by the family of its founder, Julian Sinclair Smith.

Trump's war to control the message and spread propaganda ratcheted up to a new level when in early April 2018 the executives of the Sinclair Broadcast Group issued an ultimatum to its TV anchors across the country to read a script echoing Trump's calling out of "fake news."

The Sinclair news anchors and commentators accused the mainstream media outlets—CNN, ABC, NBC, CBS, and MSNBC—of publishing "irresponsible, one-sided, and fake news stories that just aren't true, without checking facts first for political reasons. Unfortunately, some members of the media use their platforms to push their own personal bias and agenda to control exactly what people think." So said the script read by scores of Sinclair news anchors that night.

"This is extremely dangerous to our democracy," they concluded.

The news anchors had been made into soldiers in Trump's war on the media and, more importantly, on the First Amendment. The video was viewed more than 7.5 million times. Trump then tweeted, "Sinclair is far superior to CNN and even more to Fake NBC, which is a total joke."

Had he lived to see this, George Orwell would have said, "1984 came over thirty years later than I thought it would, but I told you so."

The Sinclair broadcasters had no choice. The executives of the company made it perfectly clear that their newspeople better do as they were ordered. When their Washington bureau chief last year spoke out with his concern about Sinclair's media bias, he was fired—that day. The company then forced him to pay his unemployment benefits back to the state of Maryland.

The lesson had its impact. Not one of the employees ordered to recite the Sinclair and pro-Trump party line refused.

Sinclair, which is headquartered in Hunt Valley, Maryland, owns 193 television stations across the country and is attempting to buy more. It's seen in over a hundred markets that cover 40 percent of the country, mainly in the South and Midwest. Before the forced reading, there were already fears that Sinclair was working with the Trump administration to consolidate its power in the industry. Sinclair had tripled the number of TV stations it owned since 2010 and was seeking to add forty-two more stations with the purchase of Tribune Media. Here's the rub—Sinclair probably needed permission from the Federal Communications Commission (FCC) to make the deal (the other alternative was to go to court against the FCC and probably lose). Who better than the president of the United States to push the sale through? When Trump tweeted approval of Sinclair's national propaganda blast, he signaled to FCC regulators that they needed to approve Sinclair's $3.9 billion acquisition of Tribune Media:

"The Fake News Networks, those that knowingly have a sick and biased AGENDA, are worried about the competition and quality of Sinclair Broadcast. The 'Fakers' at CNN, NBC, ABC & CBS have done so much dishonest reporting that they should only be allowed to get awards for fiction!"

For a president of the United States to attack the press so publicly, viciously, and constantly is bizarre and troubling. His desire to use the FCC to favor a news organization that supports him politically (and to disfavor news organizations "worried about competition" from Sinclair Broadcast) is potentially illegal.

But it gets worse.

President Trump also sought to hurt people and companies he dislikes. Two of his more obvious targets are CNN and the *Washington Post*.

On March 29, 2017, President Trump threatened to raise postal rates on Amazon, founded and headed by Jeff Bezos, who also owns the *Washington Post*. He charged that Amazon uses the post office as its "delivery boy."

Trump tweeted, "While we are on the subject, it was reported that the U.S. Post Office will lose $1.47 on average for each package it delivers for Amazon. That amounts to billions of dollars. The Failing N.Y. Times reports that 'the size of the company's lobbying staff has ballooned,' and that does not include the Fake Washington Post, which is used as a 'lobbyist' and so should REGISTER. If the P.O. 'increased its parcel rates, Amazon's shipping costs would rise by $2.6 Billion.' This Post Office scam must stop. Amazon must pay real costs (and taxes) now!"

"Only fools, or worse, are saying that our money losing Post Office makes money with Amazon. This will be changed."

Neither charge was true, of course, but his tweet spooked investors and Amazon's stock dropped like a rock, losing $35 billion of its $700 billion in value.

What was clear was that President Trump was getting back at Bezos for the way he was running the *Washington Post,* or rather the way he allowed the *Post* to run itself under his ownership.

Trump has every reason to be worried about the *Post.* In the 1970s, the *Post* had brought down President Nixon by exposing the Watergate scandal and publishing Bob Woodward's interviews with an FBI official turned informant code-named "Deep Throat" (Mark Felt). The *Post's* then owner Katharine Graham was put under enormous pressure to back off on coverage of the Nixon administration (she refused), but she confronted nothing like the vitriol hurled at Bezos by Donald Trump. The *Post,* Trump knew, could end a presidency, and he wanted to launch a preemptive strike that would put an end to its coverage of him. His attack on Amazon and Bezos was aimed at the *Post.*

Furthermore, Trump's suggestion that the *Post* should register with the federal government as a lobbyist, presumably under the Lobbying Disclosure Act of 1995, was ridiculous. The founders who drafted the First Amendment would have been aghast at the idea of requiring newspapers to register with the government, and the comparison of the *Post* with a paid lobbyist is absurd. The mere fact that a newspaper reports what happens in government, and sometimes expresses the opinions of its editors, does not make the paper a lobbying organization.

Trump moreover had his facts all wrong. There is absolutely no evidence that Bezos directs any of the reporting or editorial content of the *Post,* and the newspaper has never done any public relations or other work for Amazon.

Trump also repeated a story reported by right-wing conspiracy theorists who charged that the *Post* was in cahoots with the CIA, because the CIA contracts with Amazon to provide cloud-based data storage. InfoWars, one of the sites run by right-wing conspiracy theorists, wrote (in capital letters, no less): "BEZOS & DEEP STATE UNITE: LAUNCHES CLOUD SERVICE FOR CIA."

Like many of Trump's charges, this one was unfounded as well.

Once again Trump's allies helped him out with personal vendettas. In January 2019 David Pecker, owner of the *National Enquirer*, published on the cover of the magazine stolen photos of Jeff Bezos with his mistress, Lauren Sanchez. Inside, the magazine devoted eleven pages to his extramarital affair. The story apparently led to Bezos's divorce. Michael Sanchez, Lauren's brother, was accused of stealing the photos. When it was revealed that Sanchez was close friends with Trump dirty tricksters Roger Stone and Carter Page, naturally there arose the whiff that this was another Donald Trump smear job.

David Pecker has been close to Donald Trump for many years. The *National Enquirer* devoted its pages to electing Trump and disparaging Hillary Clinton whenever it could. Pecker paid for exclusive rights to stories about Trump's mistresses Stormy Daniels and Karen McDougal and then killed the stories to keep them from hurting Trump's election chances.

Over the years President Trump has been particularly brutal when it comes to CNN, which he is almost daily accusing of airing "fake news." But he has tried to harm CNN in other ways as well.

When AT&T and Time Warner, which owns CNN, sought to merge, the Justice Department sued to block the merger. Many antitrust experts described the DOJ's case as very weak, and others were shocked to see it brought by a Republican administration usually friendly to big business. But consistency and principle do not matter to Trump; personal loyalty and revenge matter a great deal. He was out for revenge. The DOJ suit against the AT&T and Time Warner merger was a disaster in court and was dismissed.

Even more troubling, Trump may have some allies on the Supreme Court in his attack on the media, and in particular a landmark 1964 Supreme Court holding, *New York Times Co. v. Sullivan,* that made it more difficult for public officials to sue newspapers for defamation. The *Sullivan* court held that a public official cannot win a suit for defamation unless the public official shows malice and an intentional disregard for the truth or falsity of reporting.

This standard has been applied also to defamation suits brought by political candidates and other public figures.

Trump, needless to say, hates the *Sullivan* standard and would like to sue newspapers under the ordinary negligence standard that applies to suits brought by private citizens who are not public figures. This is how he wants to "fix" our libel laws.

On February 18, 2019, Supreme Court Justice Clarence Thomas recommended taking another look at *New York Times v. Sullivan*.

Justice Thomas said the decision had no basis in the Constitution as it was understood by those who drafted and ratified it (he did not offer any evidence to support this assertion). Thomas's comments came after Trump's many complaints about his inability to sue media companies.

Thomas's criticism of the *Sullivan* holding produced shock waves through the media for about a week, but since then has been long forgotten.

Freedom of the press was so important that our founders incorporated it in the First Amendment to the Constitution. But we take it for granted. It is safe to say that millions more Americans know about *Roe v. Wade* than know about *New York Times v. Sullivan*.

We take freedom of the press for granted because we have had it since the founding. And we still have it.

For now.

CHAPTER 23

Trump the Campaigner

*The bosses of the Democratic party and the bosses of the Republican
party alike have a closer grip than ever before on the party machines in
the States and in the Nation. This crooked control of both the old parties
by the beneficiaries of political and business privilege renders it hopeless
to expect any far-reaching and fundamental service from either.*
—TEDDY ROOSEVELT

WITHOUT MONEY, POLITICIANS DON'T WIN ELECTIONS.
That has been true for a long time. That makes ordinary Americans
very angry.

Congress occasionally has responded to public outcry with reform legislation. Under the Theodore Roosevelt administration, direct contributions
from corporations to national elections were banned under the Tillman Act
of 1907. Limits on campaign donations and campaign spending were enacted
in the post-Watergate years. During the George W. Bush administration, lim-
itations on spending by outside groups were imposed in the McCain-Feingold
Act of 2001.

For much of our history, political corruption has not been a partisan issue.
Proponents of campaign finance reform included Barry Goldwater, the 1964

Republican presidential nominee who decried both corporate and union support for political campaigns in his book *The Conscience of a Conservative*, and John McCain, another senator from Arizona who was the Republican presidential nominee in 2008. Polling data consistently shows that Americans of all political convictions—right, left, and center—are sick of big money in politics.

That said, over the past several decades a legal and political war against limiting campaign expenditures has been waged by politicians who benefit from political contributions, and by organizations supported by wealthy campaign contributors such as the Koch brothers and Sheldon Adelson.

These groups scored a victory as early as 1976 when the Supreme Court in *Buckley v. Valeo* struck down limits on spending by political campaigns, although the court left intact statutory limits on contributions to political campaigns. Another huge victory came in 2010 with the Supreme Court ruling in *Citizens United*, giving corporations the go-ahead to plow billions of dollars into political campaigns via outside organizations organized under section 501(c)(4) of the Internal Revenue Code. Soon thereafter, the District of Columbia Court of Appeals, in a case called *Speech Now*, extended these "free speech" rights to super PACs funded with massive amounts of corporate and sometimes union money. Corporate electioneering expenditures—which the Tillman Act of 1907 had sought to prevent by banning direct corporate campaign contributions—were now permitted, and they became a constitutional right when delivered through the back door via a 501(c)(4) organization or super PAC.

No longer could ordinary people run for office. Without the backing of a 501(c)(4), a super PAC, or another big money organization, candidates didn't stand a chance.

Clearly the public was angry. The Supreme Court's decision allowing massive corruption of our campaign finance system came right on the heels of the 2008 financial collapse that was fueled by reckless conduct on Wall Street. Then there was the continuing disappearance of high-paying jobs as corporations moved factories to countries including Mexico and China. Americans knew the system was broken and looked for someone to blame.

Two easy targets were Bill and Hillary Clinton. President Clinton had been a prolific Democratic fundraiser and a champion of bipartisan free-trade agreements that were believed to have cost many Americans their jobs. The Clintons had many close friends on Wall Street and in Hollywood. Bill and Hillary Clinton left the White House with very little money, but by 2016 they had tens of millions of dollars. Hillary got $100,000 per appearance from corporations to make speeches after she left the State Department and Bill got even more. (He even raised his speaking fee after she became secretary of state in 2009.)

During the 2016 Democratic primary, Senator Bernie Sanders pointed out many of these problems with a Clinton candidacy, but in the end she won the Democratic nomination. Her experience, and the exciting prospect of electing our first woman president, put her over the top. There was considerable controversy about the nomination as well, as Sanders supporters with some justification believed that Democratic National Committee heavyweights had taken sides and sought to influence the primary to Clinton's advantage.

Enter our protagonist, Donald Trump.

Trump, who boasted of his billionaire status, wasn't going to do anything to get money out of politics, but at least he was smart enough to stand before disaffected Americans, ridicule the system, and tap into the anger of people left behind. His demeaning taunts toward government agencies struck a chord with those people. His rants against the Ivy League elites did too, even though he had gone to the University of Pennsylvania. He was also the first Republican presidential candidate in 2016 to go against the powerful Koch brothers faction in the GOP and attack the Supreme Court's decision in *Citizens United*—right before he accused all of his primary opponents of being bought by special interests.

Ironically, Trump was doing exactly what one of the authors of this book (Painter) had urged Republican candidates to do in his January 2016 book *Taxation Only with Representation: The Conservative Conscience and Campaign Finance Reform*. Political conservatives with a conscience should side with Barry Goldwater and John McCain, not Mitch McConnell, on campaign finance reform. Trump was right to criticize *Citizens United*. But he did so with no intent of actually fixing the system. (Mitch McConnell has screened and shepherded through Trump's judicial nominees, including two justices of the Supreme Court.) Trump also knew full well that he himself depended upon wealthy backers, both in the United States and abroad. He again relies on wealthy backers (and perhaps also the Russians) in his bid for reelection in 2020.

Americans who believed nothing was going to change, however, could identify with and revel in Trump's name-calling. Never mind that he'd spent a lifetime using his own money to influence politics, particularly in his home state of New York, where he was constantly greasing the skids for new real estate projects. Never mind that he had spent so much time and money schmoozing politicians—including even the Clintons—that for years nobody could tell if he was a Republican or a Democrat. People frustrated with the system wanted to believe in someone who would fix it, and many trusted Donald Trump.

That Trump had spent years spewing racist taunts didn't hurt with his populist base, either. His eight-year drumbeat aimed at President Obama and his birth certificate gave Trump an audience ready to vote for someone who promised to Make America Great Again. It was a brilliant slogan, a dog whistle to his followers. Above all Trump could be a man of the people—or at least white people. His vile rhetoric and juvenile, but effective, name-calling was enough to defeat such right-wing demagogues as Ted Cruz and fourteen other Republican candidates.

Trump was the rogue provocateur in the 2016 presidential election. Sarah Palin had promised a rogue agenda as the vice-presidential candidate with John McCain in 2008, but Palin was unprepared and seemed not very smart.

Trump didn't know much about much, but unlike Palin, he clearly knew how to win a verbal street fight. A mafia-like wordsmith, Trump ripped through his Republican opponents with rapier-sharp barbs.

In 2007 he signaled that he had little regard for his party when he said that George W. Bush was "probably the worst president in the history of the United States." In January 2015 he dismissed Mitt Romney as a viable 2016 presidential candidate.

"It can't be Mitt," he said. "Mitt ran and failed." Later he accused Romney of being "a frozen jellyfish" in the debates.

The first time Trump went after John McCain, he tweeted, "Sen. John McCain should be defeated in the primaries. Graduated last in his class at Annapolis—dummy."

Later Trump would famously say, "He's not a war hero. He's a war hero because he was captured. I like people who weren't captured."

McCain, a naval aviator, had been shot down during the Vietnam War and held prisoner for more than five years in Hanoi. He was repeatedly beaten, and when offered early release, he declined, saying he would not go until all his men could go with him.

This was perhaps Trump's most despicable attack in a most despicable campaign.

The stronger his opponent, the more effective the attack. Trump called Florida senator Marco Rubio "Little Marco," a derisive term that seemed to derail Rubio's candidacy. And so it was with "Low-Energy Jeb," former Florida governor Jeb Bush.

One of Trump's worst insinuations came against Texas senator Ted Cruz, whom he called "Lyin' Ted." As we mentioned earlier, he also accused Cruz's father of being seen with Lee Harvey Oswald shortly before the JFK assassination, a story that he got from the *National Enquirer*.

Rafael Cruz, an evangelical minister, had gone on Fox News to plead with evangelicals to vote for his son.

"I implore, I exhort every member of the body of Christ to vote according to the word of God and vote for the candidate that stands on the word of God and on the Constitution of the United States of America," said Rafael Cruz. "And I am convinced that man is my son, Ted Cruz. The alternative could be the destruction of America."

This was too much for Donald Trump, and during a phone interview with Fox News, Trump said, "His father was with Lee Harvey Oswald prior to Oswald's being—you know, shot. I mean, the whole thing is ridiculous. What is this, right prior to his being shot, and nobody even brings it up. They don't even talk about that. That was reported, and nobody talks about it.

"I mean, what was he doing—what was he doing with Lee Harvey Oswald shortly before the death? Before the shooting?

"It's horrible."

That the charge was absurd and unfounded didn't matter at all to Trump. The "truth" was what Trump said it was. Words were used as weapons, and Trump was a deadly shot. Trump then bragged that he, not Ted Cruz, was the candidate worthy of the evangelical vote.

Said Trump, "You look at so many of the ministers that are backing me, and they're backing me more so than they're backing Cruz, and I'm winning the evangelical vote.

"It's disgraceful that his father can go out and do that. And just—and so many people are angry about it. And the evangelicals are angry about it, the way he does that.

"But I think it's horrible. I think it's absolutely horrible that a man can go and do that, what he's saying there."

Cruz was the last of Trump's Republican opponents. After Cruz, Trump's path to the Republican nomination was clear.

Throughout his campaign Trump ran with the notion that he represented the little guy. Meanwhile, he lived in splendor. He bragged about being a billionaire, how successful he was, and what a great dealmaker he was, even though his companies had gone bankrupt at least three times.

That he was a little guy fighting against the rich and powerful was one of his more blatant and ridiculous assertions. Trump advertised himself as self-made, but as we know, Fred Trump had handed his son a small fortune to start his empire. Fred and son Donald would get huge tax breaks from city officials. Trump kept saying over and over that the system was rigged, that the fix was in against him, but the truth was that the fix was in *for* the Trumps.

When Trump shocked everyone by winning the Republican nomination, he turned his venom on his Democratic opponent, Hillary Clinton. A typical evening spew of lies came during the September 26, 2016, debate. Clinton told the national audience, "You know, Donald was very fortunate in his life and that's all to his benefit. He started his business with $14 million, borrowed from his father."

When it was Trump's turn, he started, "My father gave me a very small loan in 1975, and I built it into a company that's worth many, many billions of dollars."

The *Wall Street Journal* tracked down a casino license disclosure form from 1985 that showed that his father had lent him . . . $14 million.

A very small loan indeed.

In the debate, Mrs. Clinton accused Trump of saying that global warming was a hoax perpetrated by the Chinese.

"I did not say that," said Trump.

But in 2012 he said exactly that in a tweet.

Trump in 2016 accused the Fed of keeping interest rates low in order to protect Obama while he was president.

That was a baseless accusation; interest rates were low in part because the first half of the Obama presidency coincided with the deepest and longest recession since the 1930s. (In August 2019, after five years of steady economic growth during which interest rates ordinarily rise, Trump called for the Fed to drive interest rates down near zero to assure his own reelection in 2020, and in a tweet, he called the Fed chairman, a Trump appointee, an enemy of the United States for not lowering rates fast enough.)

Trump in the 2016 campaign said the Ford Motor Company was leaving for Mexico and that 78,300 jobs in Michigan and 75,800 in Ohio would be lost.

A Ford spokesman said that wasn't true.

Perhaps the most outrageous of Trump's claims during the debate was that Hillary Clinton had started the birther movement to beat Obama in the 2008 Democratic primary. Wrong—Clinton had nothing to do with "birtherism" and it was Trump who promoted this conspiracy theory; even after President Obama displayed his birth certificate, Trump continued to make the charge, hoping that white supremacists, neo-Nazis, the alt-right, and other racists would flock to his campaign.

Trump added two figures to his inner circle who were able and willing to spread his lies to their right-wing base.

Trump's wingman, Steve Bannon, CEO of Breitbart News, Harvard Business School grad, and an alumnus of Goldman Sachs, helped Trump with his false narratives in the campaign and in the White House as his chief strategist.

Breitbart News had little regard for the truth and had an unapologetic and loyal ultra-right-wing following. Breitbart's mission was to distort the truth to make liberals, Democrats, and the Obama administration look bad.

Breitbart in September 2009 sponsored two right-wing activists who visited ten ACORN (Association of Community Organizations for Reform Now—a community organizing group) offices with a hidden video camera. One claimed to be a prostitute and the other her friend, and they tried to trap the ACORN staff into advising them on how to buy a home to use for a prostitution ring. The video was doctored in a way to make ACORN look bad, but when their deceit was exposed, Breitbart said they should win the Pulitzer Prize for journalism. The phony video on Breitbart's website created tremendous controversy.

ACORN was exonerated of wrongdoing, but too late. ACORN closed offices in over a hundred cities.

Andrew Breitbart, like Trump, was a con artist who had mastered the new rules of political combat made possible by the internet and cable TV. In March 2012, Breitbart was walking to his home in Westwood, California, when he collapsed on the sidewalk and died of a heart attack at age forty-three.

After Breitbart's death, Steve Bannon took over and moved the organization even further to the right, albeit with a curious revolutionary twist borrowed from Marxist-Leninism and the fringe "deconstructionist" movement in academia.

"I'm a Leninist," said Bannon. "Lenin wanted to destroy the state, and that's my goal too. I want to bring everything crashing down, and destroy all of today's establishment."

Later Bannon denied making the statement. However, as Trump's campaign strategist and subsequently chief White House strategist, he clearly was the bull in the china shop. Bannon believed in nativism, America first, white nationalism, and blowing up the establishment. He predicted that under Trump, the Republican Party as a functional conservative party would be dead.

"It's going to be an insurgent, center-right populist movement that is virulently anti-establishment, and it's going to continue to hammer this city, both the progressive left and the institutional Republican Party," Bannon said.

Talking about women, Bannon said, "The women that would lead this country would be pro-family, they would have husbands, they would love their children. They wouldn't be a bunch of dykes that came from the Seven Sisters schools up in New England. That drives the left insane, and that's why they hate these women."

Bannon reserved his praise for Ann Coulter, Michele Bachmann, and Sarah Palin, three of the most extreme Republican female standard-bearers.

In Trump's campaign, Bannon's partner was campaign manager and chief spokesperson Kellyanne Conway, who switched loyalties from Ted Cruz to Trump as soon as Trump sealed the Republican nomination. Never worried about being truthful, she often made mincemeat of those who interviewed her, happily chattering away, spewing justifications for Trump's actions. Conway speaks in a rapid-fire patter and overwhelms interviewers with speed, outright falsehoods, and misdirection.

For Bannon and Conway, as with Trump, winning was everything.

Trump's embrace of Steve Bannon, Breitbart, and the alt-right blatantly indicated to African Americans and Hispanics he didn't care about them. Trump focused his attention on the workers (mostly white men) who lost their jobs to globalization, promising to return jobs to the coal and steel industries.

Trump liked to talk up his proposed tax overhaul to out-of-work Rust Belt voters, but his plan did not turn out to be the tax break he promised his followers. Rather, his tax plan—when it was enacted in 2017—was a boon for multimillionaires and billionaires, including himself, while raising working Americans' take-home pay $1.50 a week.

At the same time, Trump vowed to end the Affordable Care Act, promising a replacement for so-called Obamacare. In fact, he intended no such thing. His goal was to dismantle the Affordable Care Act, but he had nothing specific to suggest in its place.

His constant stream of lies would have disqualified him, but voters were sick of DC politicians, and they wanted change. Many didn't care that their agent of change was a serial liar, an abuser of women, a racist, and as it turned out, someone who didn't care a whit about them.

Days before the presidential election, Donald Trump was caught on video telling the country about what a sexual predator he was.

It was part of a tape shot in 2005 when Trump was on the set for a cameo role on *Days of Our Lives*, and it was kept in the archives of a TV show called

Access Hollywood. Trump was bragging about his sexual abilities to Billy Bush, a cousin of George W. Bush and one of the hosts of the show, while on the *Access Hollywood* bus. Trump talked about trying to have sex with an unidentified, beautiful married woman.

> **Trump:** I moved on her, actually. You know, she was down on Palm Beach. I moved on her, and I failed. I'll admit it. I did try and fuck her. She was married. I moved on her very heavily. In fact, I took her out furniture shopping. She wanted to get some furniture. I said, "I'll show you where they have some nice furniture." I took her out furniture shopping—I moved on her like a bitch. But I couldn't get there. And she was married. Then all of a sudden I see her, she's now got the big phony tits and everything. She's totally changed her look.

[They looked out the window of the bus and saw actress Arianne Zucker waiting for them as the bus came to a stop.]

> **Billy Bush:** Sheesh, your girl's hot as shit. In the purple.
>
> **Trump:** Whoa! Whoa!
>
> **Bush:** Yes! The Donald has scored. Whoa, my man!
>
> **Trump:** Look at you; you are a pussy.
>
> **Trump:** All right, you and I will walk out.
>
> **Trump:** Maybe it's a different one.
>
> **Bush:** It better not be the publicist. No, it's, it's her, it's—
>
> **Trump:** Yeah, that's her. With the gold. I better use some Tic Tacs just in case I start kissing her. You know, I'm automatically attracted to beautiful—I just start kissing them. It's like a magnet. Just kiss. I don't even wait. And when you're a star, they let you do it. You can do anything.
>
> **Bush:** Whatever you want.
>
> **Trump:** Grab 'em by the pussy. You can do anything.
>
> **Bush:** Uh, yeah, those legs, all I can see is the legs.
>
> **Trump:** Oh, it looks good.
>
> **Bush:** Come on, shorty.
>
> **Trump:** Ooh, nice legs, huh?

> **Bush:** Oof, get out of the way, honey. Oh, that's good legs. Go ahead.
> **Trump:** It's always good if you don't fall out of the bus. Like Ford,
>   Gerald Ford, remember?
> **Bush:** Down below, pull the handle.

The conversation, which landed on national television right before the presidential election, made it clear that the thrice-married Donald Trump had little regard for women. It was even worse than that. It made him out to be a sexual predator. How could anyone vote for him after hearing his now famous quote about grabbing women by the pussy?

How could Trump survive these vulgar, disgusting admissions? the public wondered.

After the *Access Hollywood* tape was released, Trump did what he often did when cornered: he denied he was that person talking on the bus. Then he changed course and said it was just "locker-room talk." When that failed, he attacked the Clintons. He said his "foolish" words were much different from the words and actions of Bill Clinton, whom he labeled an abuser of women, and he accused Hillary Clinton of having "bullied, shamed, and intimidated [Bill's] victims."

Trump went even further and appeared on television with women who had accused Bill Clinton of sexual misconduct, inviting Paula Jones to the presidential debate. His objective: to humiliate Hillary Clinton, to make the entire sexual assault story about her instead of about him.

"I've never said I'm a perfect person," said Trump, "nor pretended to be someone that I'm not. I've said and done things I regret, and the words released today on this more-than-a-decade-old video are one of them. Anyone who knows me knows these words don't reflect who I am."

In fact, they reflected *exactly* who he was. The tape should have wrecked his presidential bid, but the outrage and criticism didn't last.

One reason why Trump's defense was effective is that he is even more aggressive playing offense. His response to any criticism is to attack. Trump put Hillary Clinton in the crosshairs and took aim.

One cannot think of a more dangerous threat to the rule of law than a president ordering the Department of Justice to prosecute his political opponents, including his opponent in the preceding election. Such acts are not consistent with any representative democracy in the world.

The chant "Lock her up," aimed at Democratic presidential candidate Hillary Clinton, first arose in July 2016 during a speech given at a Trump rally by New Jersey governor Chris Christie, a conservative Republican who cited Clinton's "illegal" actions as secretary of state.

"Is she guilty or not guilty?" Christie asked after each accusation.

"Guilty," came back the lively response.

As Trump supporters became more and more animated, they waved their red, white, and blue Trump signs, shook their fists, and screamed and hollered, until the cry rang out, "Lock her up. Lock her up."

The next evening, when Trump spoke, every time he mentioned Clinton, whether her emails, Benghazi, or the Clinton Foundation, his supporters again shouted, "Lock her up. Lock her up."

It became the battle cry of Trump's campaign against Hillary Clinton.

In the debate on October 6, 2016, he said to her, "I'll tell you what. I didn't think I'd say this, but I'm going to say it, and I hate to say it. But if I win, I am going to instruct my attorney general to get a special prosecutor to look into your situation, because there has never been so many lies, so much deception. There has never been anything like it, and we're going to have a special prosecutor."

Three days later in a rally in Florida, Trump, talking about Clinton, told the crowd that "this corruption and collusion is just one more reason why I will ask my attorney general to appoint a special prosecutor."

When cornered, Trump said, "I don't want to hurt the Clintons. I really don't," but the chant continued to ring out at Trump rallies.

Trump was threatening to lock up a private citizen for a crime she had not and never would be charged with. In fact, Clinton had been investigated fully by the FBI for her use of a private email server to do government business, and she was cleared of any crime.

With his "Lock her up" threat, Trump sounded like an aspiring dictator. He was threatening our very system of government, and his fervent followers were happy to go along.

Then, in October 2016, one month before the presidential election, Donald Trump accused the Democrats of trying to *steal* the election. He predicted widespread voter fraud, and "a rigged outcome."

Never mind that—as discussed in the first part of Robert Mueller's 2019 report—Trump's campaign knew at the time that the Russians were meddling in the election on his behalf.

At a rally in Colorado Springs, he told supporters, "Voter fraud is all too common, and then they criticize us for saying that. But take a look at Philadelphia, what's been going on, take a look at Chicago, take a look at St. Louis. Take a look at some of these cities, where you see things happening that are horrendous."

At a rally in Pennsylvania, Trump said, "I hear these horror stories, and we have to make sure that this election is not stolen from us and is not taken away from us. And everybody knows what I'm talking about."

In fact, *no one* knew what he was talking about. He had made the whole thing up. As we wrote earlier, voter fraud of the sort Trump was talking about is exceedingly rare.

There was of course no mention by Trump of the Russians.

On his website Trump wrote, "Help me stop Crooked Hillary from rigging this election."

It was posited that Trump trotted out his voter fraud charge because he was certain he was going to lose the election. When it was revealed that Hillary Clinton garnered three million more votes than he did, he claimed that more than three million people voted illegally and demanded an investigation by the Justice Department.

Commented former Justice Department spokesman Matthew Miller, "Voter fraud is a crime, and DOJ usually begins investigations when they find evidence a crime was committed, not because the president has endorsed a conspiracy theory for which there is no evidence. Now, we're in a position where DOJ has to launch an investigation into a supposed crime just because the president is making up facts?"

No investigation was launched, but Trump has still not stopped talking about the fraudulent votes.

CHAPTER 24

Blowing Up Bridges, Building Walls

"I will build a great, great wall on our southern border"
and "have Mexico pay for that wall."
—DONALD TRUMP

The president has zero psychological ability to
recognize empathy or pity in any way.
—REINCE PRIEBUS

D ONALD TRUMP HAS A LONG HISTORY OF RACISM.
Donald and Fred Trump first appeared on the pages of the *New York Times* in the 1970s when the Trump Management Corporation, run by Fred Trump, was sued by the US Department of Justice for racial discrimination against African American renters in Brooklyn, Queens, and Staten Island. Black people who applied to rent one of his apartments were inevitably quoted prices higher than they could afford or were told that the apartment had already been rented and wasn't available.

Then in 1989, five African American and Hispanic teenagers were accused of raping a young white woman who was jogging in Central Park. Donald Trump ran a full-page ad in New York papers demanding the accused be given the death penalty. The teens would serve prison sentences of between seven and thirteen years before a court vacated the sentences. DNA evidence cleared them. They had been wrongly convicted, and in June 2014 they won a settlement of $41 million.

In October 2016 Trump nevertheless continued to insist they were guilty.

In 1991 Trump was quoted in a book by the former president of Trump Plaza Hotel and Casino saying, "Black guys counting my money! I hate it! The only kind of people I want counting my money are short guys that wear yarmulkes every day."

The next year the Trump Plaza Hotel and Casino paid a $200,000 fine for removing an African American dealer from poker tables when big-time gamblers demanded that only whites deal to them.

When Donald Trump ran for president, he clearly believed that race-baiting and Muslim baiting would be his meal ticket to the presidency. By displaying his disdain for minorities—and of President Barack Obama most of all—he planned to win over every man and woman who resented or hated that a black man was in the White House. On top of that hostility to Muslims, immigrants, federal judges, government, and the establishment (the "Deep State"), a growing online media market eager to compete with mainstream media by condemning it as unpatriotic, and a good dose of sexism (some voters of both sexes did not want any woman to be president), there was a lot for Trump to play with. He may have been playing with fire, but he didn't care, so long as he won.

The birther movement was one of many examples of the race game Trump played to win.

Other conspiracy theorists had started the lie about Obama being an illegitimate president because he was born outside the United States. (The Constitution requires that the president be a "natural born citizen.") Even after the Hawaii Department of Health released Obama's birth certificate, Jerome Corsi, author of the book *Obama Nation: Leftist Politics and the Cult of Personality*, told Fox News that the released birth certificate was a fake document.

Donald Trump, picking up the cudgel, launched his political career with a speech at the Conservative Political Action Conference in February 2011. He claimed that Obama "came out of nowhere. In fact, I'll take it even further: The people who went to school with him, they never saw him. They don't know who he is. It's crazy."

Trump repeated the claim that the released Obama birth certificate was a fraud.

In May 2011, a Gallup poll found that 13 percent of Americans believed the lie.

Donald Trump for five years remained at the forefront in the attack on Obama's legitimacy, even sending private detectives to Hawaii in 2011. Obama called Trump a "carnival barker." Trump claimed Obama wasn't a good enough student to get into Columbia or Harvard Law School, and called for the release of his student transcripts.

"I heard he was a terrible student," Trump said. "Terrible. How does a bad student go to Columbia and then to Harvard?"

Trump was making this up from the malevolent noises in his head. Obama had been elected president of the *Harvard Law Review*.

During campaign appearances across the country, Trump never let up on Obama. He soon saw that many of his constituents, his "base," were as racist as he was. Supporters in marches for Trump would carry signs with drawings of Obama looking like a monkey or with bones in his nose.

When Trump was endorsed by white supremacists and neo-Nazis, he retweeted their messages of support.

Not since George Wallace in 1968 had a presidential candidate been so open about his disdain for African Americans. As we showed earlier, racial inequality and race relations have been an Achilles' heel for American democracy for the entirety of this country's existence. Rather than help solve the problem, Trump took advantage of it throughout his campaign.

His presidency has been even worse.

A low point during Trump's presidency took place in Charlottesville, Virginia, on August 12, 2017, when a rowdy, organized group of white supremacists and neo-Nazis held a "Unite the Right" rally to protest the removal of a statute of Confederate general Robert E. Lee. The swastika-toting protesters swarmed the streets carrying torches and yelling racist and anti-Semitic slogans like "White lives matter" and "Blood and soil," a trademark Nazi mantra.

A large group of people gathered to protest white supremacy and Trump's racism, and fights broke out. In the midst of the melee, one of the white supremacists deliberately plowed his car into a crowd of civil rights defenders, killing a young woman, thirty-two-year-old Heather Heyer. Her murderer has since been sentenced to life in prison.

When asked about the conflict, Trump commented that there were "very fine people on both sides."

Richard Spencer, a highly visible white supremacist, praised Trump for "defending the truth."

The criticism from members of his cabinet was fierce, and the next day his advisors twisted his arm to read a statement in which he said, "We must love each other, show affection for each other, and unite together in a condemnation of hatred, bigotry, and violence."

Trump, whose philosophy was to never admit any wrongdoing no matter how wrong the doing, was furious about his capitulation.

"You never apologize," he told Rob Porter, his staff secretary. "I can't believe I was forced to do that. That's the worst speech I have ever given. I'm never going to do anything like that again."

Two days later during a press conference in the lobby of Trump Tower, while discussing Charlottesville, Trump attacked what he called the alt-left, "which also [is] very violent," and reverted to his earlier statement.

"There is blame on both sides. You also had people that were very fine people on both sides. You had a lot of bad people in the other group too . . . there are two sides to a story."

Trump bemoaned the loss of several monuments to Confederate heroes. Former Klan leader David Duke praised him, saying, "We are determined to take our country back."

That December Trump pardoned Arizona sheriff Joe Arpaio, whose brutal tactics against immigrants led to an investigation, an arrest for obstructing the investigation, conviction, and sentencing. Trump heaped praise on "Sheriff Joe" while pardoning him. Trump also verbally attacked black athletes, including NFL quarterback Colin Kaepernick, who knelt during the national anthem to protest the treatment of African Americans by the police, and basketball star Stephen Curry, who refused to visit the White House after the Golden State Warriors won the NBA championship.

And we will never forget his comment—before several high-ranking officials—that he would prefer immigrants from countries like Norway to those from "shithole countries" like Haiti and countries in Africa.

In this chapter we discuss how Trump exploited two serious issues—terrorism and immigration—to advance his brand of racism and appeal to the lowest common denominator in the American electorate. Instead of trying to solve problems and build bridges to Muslim and Hispanic communities, Trump has tried to build walls, literally and figuratively, to shut people out.

A WAR ON TERROR TURNED INTO A WAR ON ISLAM

In the days after the attacks of 9/11, President George W. Bush made it clear that we were at war with terrorism, not at war with Islam. Whatever one thinks of President Bush's wartime policies, he did not exploit this horrific attack on the United States to demonize the Muslim world. Bush—and Obama after him—understood that combatting terrorist groups required alliance with as many of the world's Muslims as possible. Indeed, the fact that Muslims are very often victims of terrorist attacks, particularly those that occur outside the United States, should make most of the Muslim world a natural ally in the war on terror.

Donald Trump took a different tack. President Trump has sent fewer American soldiers into war in Muslim countries than either of his two predecessors, Bush and Obama, but his war of words against Islam is virtually guaranteed to turn many of the world's over one billion Muslims against us. Winning the war on terror will be virtually impossible without strong allies in the Muslim world, but Trump does not care. Winning elections by hating Muslims is his priority.

In 2016 he got into a verbal dispute with the Muslim American father of a fallen US soldier after the father called out his racism. Attacking a gold-star family was acceptable for Trump—if they were Muslim.

Trump took on as advisors Steve Bannon, the face of the alt-right, and Sebastian Gorka, both of whom were forced to resign from the White House in August 2017 after the Charlottesville riot. Stephen Miller, who proposed separating immigrant parents from their children as punishment, remained at the White House and was put in charge of immigration policy. All of these men have made known their hatred of Muslims.

Trump repeatedly attacked Muslims during his campaign. On December 2, 2015, a US citizen, Syed Farook, and his wife, Tashfeen Malik, shot up a county department of public health center during a Christmas party, killing fourteen and injuring seventeen others. Farook, who was sympathetic to ISIS, was shot and killed. Six days later Trump, who was the presidential front-runner for the Republican Party, called for a ban on all Muslims entering the United States—immigrants and visitors alike.

During a debate in 2016, Trump was asked whether all 1.6 billion Muslims in the world hate the United States.

"I mean a lot of them," he said. "I mean a lot of them."

His proposed Muslim ban was unconstitutional under the First Amendment guarantee of free exercise of religion. Any first-year law student could have told him that. He didn't care—and didn't bother to change it into a "country-specific ban" (which was de facto still a Muslim ban) until he became president and his lawyers forced that change. On the campaign trail he called it a Muslim ban, and that is exactly what it was.

Upon becoming president, Trump signed the executive order that called for a ban on people from six predominantly Muslim countries from traveling to this country: Iraq, Iran, Libya, Somalia, Syria, and Yemen. Excluded from the travel ban, ironically, were most of the countries that historically have had the strongest ties to terrorism, including the attacks of 9/11, most notably Saudi Arabia. These countries not subject to the travel ban, the rich oil exporters, coincidently do business with the Trump Organization.

Just a coincidence? Right.

Twice courts said his ban was unconstitutional, but in a third attempt Trump managed to bolster his legal case just enough to skirt by. He dropped Iraq (which is presumably our ally after a war that since 2003 cost thousands of American lives and up to one trillion dollars) and added two non-Muslim

countries: Venezuela and North Korea. (North Korea was a ridiculous addition because almost nobody is allowed to leave North Korea.)

The United States Supreme Court, in a preliminary five to four ruling
split along the predictable partisan lines, accepted Trump's argument that the
travel ban is within his constitutional powers.

But everyone—including Donald Trump—knows that it is still a Muslim
ban. And everyone—including the entire world and many of the one billion
Muslims in it—knows that Donald Trump and the people working for him in
the White House hate Muslims.

What a pathetic way for the United States to lose a war on terrorism.

BUILDING THE WALL

Immigration is a second issue that has been difficult for the United States for
decades if not centuries. How many immigrants can we admit? What legal
and economic rights await them when they arrive? These are challenging
questions, particularly in times of economic stagnation and high unemployment, and also when we are considering bolstering basic social services in
healthcare and education to standards already obtained in much of the industrialized world.

Of course we cannot admit everyone, and of course we should take measures to prevent violations of our immigration laws. Every other president
has recognized the need to limit immigration, as well as the need to respect
immigrants for their valued contributions to our culture and economy. Every
other president has sought to work with Congress to achieve a compromise
on immigration policy, allowing some undocumented immigrants to remain
while requiring others to go home.

Once in a while somebody suggests a viable solution to the illegal immigration problem—for example, fining employers that hire undocumented
workers to avoid paying American citizens a living wage. Among those
employers has been the Trump Organization. But never mind—hypocrisy is
part of Trump's game.

What makes no sense is to approach the immigration problem using
racist and xenophobic rhetoric reminiscent of 1919. Immigration can be

an economic problem (and also an economic asset), but no thinking person sees immigration as a threat to our "culture" when our culture in the United States is not made up of a single ethnic group. The days when educated people thought that way in America are long gone.

Except for Donald Trump. He and his political advisors seek to appeal to voters who still see immigration in cultural terms. Enough so that framing the debate in cultural terms can win elections.

Trump committed himself to the "wall" early in his campaign.

"I will build a great wall—and nobody builds walls better than me, believe me—and I'll build them very inexpensively. I will build a great, great wall on our southern border, and I will make Mexico pay for that wall. Mark my words."

What's most remarkable about the entire Saga of the Wall is that it wasn't even Trump's idea. Trump's political advisors Roger Stone and Sam Nunberg thought his signature topic on the campaign trail should be immigration. So Stone and Nunberg came up with the idea of building a wall, a story line that allowed Trump to brag about his talents as a builder.

On June 23, 2015, Trump showed his utter contempt for Mexicans and Hispanic people emigrating from South and Central America. During a speech at the Maryland Republican Party's Twenty-Fifth Annual Red, White, and Blue Dinner, Trump for the first time vowed if he were elected president he would force Mexico to pay for a border wall to keep immigrants out of the United States.

"I'd build it," Trump said. "I'd build it very nicely. I'm very good at building things."

Trump commented that Mexican immigrants "aren't just bad."

"They are really bad," he said. "You have people coming in, and I'm not just saying Mexicans, I'm talking about people that are from all over that are killers and rapists and they're coming into the country.

"You have people coming through the border that are from all over. And they're bad. They're really bad."

Trump during the campaign repeatedly referred to the relatively rare instances of serious crimes committed by Latin American immigrants; he said that *Mexico* sent its "worst people" to the United States; he promised to build a wall on the US-Mexico border and make Mexico pay for it; he ranted about "bad hombres" crossing the border in speeches and debates; and he strongly implied that Mexican immigrants were not only a threat to American jobs but to our national identity. In the summer of 2016 he even verbally attacked a federal judge in the Trump University case, saying that the judge was biased because he was "Mexican."

Trump made it very clear not only that he had these attitudes, but that legal constraints on his use of presidential power might be ignored.

Through his entire presidency, he has spoken out against Latino immigrants. His fantasy has been that gangs sneak into this country from Mexico. In one speech he spoke of Latino gangs targeting "young, beautiful" girls, "slicing them and dicing them with a knife." (It was all a lie. Very few migrants are members of street gangs.)

Trump falsely accused all immigrants from Haiti of having AIDS.

Once he became president, Trump put his words into action. In May 2018 he ordered immigration officials to separate immigrant children from their parents upon arrival in the United States. The policy was pushed most strongly by his senior policy advisor, Stephen Miller. Thousands of children were detained in makeshift metal cages, and many more were transferred to detention centers far from the border and from their parents. They weren't marked with identification, and some of these children, too young to identify themselves, may never see their parents again.

"Ripping children out of their parents' arms to inflict harm on the child to influence the parents is unacceptable," said Senator Jeff Merkley of Oregon.

The backlash was fierce, and Trump mostly ended the practice, but not before great harm was inflicted on thousands of children and their parents.

Stephen Miller justified what he had wrought.

"No nation can have the policy that whole classes of people are immune from immigration law or enforcement," he said. "It was a simple decision by the administration to have a zero-tolerance policy for illegal entry, period."

Responded Merkley, "This is not a zero-tolerance policy; this is a zero-humanity policy, and we can't let it go on."

The asylum system, which is supposed to operate in accordance with statutes enacted by Congress, is in shambles. Early in 2019, Trump's Homeland

Security Secretary Kirstjen Nielsen, who had implemented most of his border policies, "resigned" because Trump simply wouldn't listen when she told him that his proposed policies for handling asylum seekers were illegal. He insisted that she violate the law anyway; when she refused, she was fired.

Amid all of this turmoil, Trump still had to have his wall. He was willing to do just about anything to get it.

During the two years the Republicans controlled both houses of Congress, there was no appropriation to build his wall, and the White House didn't really ask for it. No money was spent on the wall. Once the Democrats gained forty seats in the House in the 2018 midterm elections, it became clear that Trump no longer had the votes to get the money to build it.

On December 22, 2018, Trump shut down the government when Congress refused to spend $5.7 billion to build his proposed concrete wall along our southern border.

During the thirty-five-day government shutdown, nine federal departments were forced to close. Hundreds of other government operations were scaled back or shut down. The cost was upwards of six billion dollars. More than 800,000 federal workers would be laid off or have their pay withheld until the shutdown was over. Federal contractors were never paid the wages they lost during the shutdown.

Trump didn't care. He had told his base that he was going to build a wall, and he was taking a stand. No one was going to stop him.

Trump, under enormous pressure from House and Senate Republicans, finally relented and signed a bill reopening the government without an appropriation for the wall. But he said that if Congress didn't give him the money for the wall in three weeks, he'd shut down the government again. He also threatened to declare an emergency to pay for the wall.

In response to Trump's caving and signing the bill reopening the government, Ann Coulter tweeted, "Good news for George Herbert Walker Bush: As of today, he is no longer the biggest wimp ever to serve as President of the United States."

The three weeks went by, as a team of eight legislators, four from each party, crafted a bill that they felt the president should sign. The Republicans were compliant because of the backlash. A second shutdown, they knew, could be fatal to their chances in the 2020 election.

On February 15, waiting right to the deadline, President Trump caved and signed the bill that allowed $1.4 billion to build fifty-five miles of wall, averting another shutdown.

Trump next tried issuing an executive order to take money from various federal budgets, including the defense budget, to build his wall. To do this he declared an "emergency" under the National Emergencies Act and heightened his rhetoric about a "caravan" and "invasion" on our southern border. But this too was a stream of untruths. His caravan was comprised mostly of women and children seeking asylum from South and Central American countries where their lives were in danger either from oppressive governments or rapacious gangs.

This really was about Trump's inability to persuade Congress—even a Republican Congress—to appropriate money for a campaign promise. Now, in violation of the constitutional power of Congress to appropriate funds to federal departments through legislation, Trump was going to declare a fake "emergency" and spend the money as an autocrat would, at his own discretion with no consent from the legislature.

Congress has taken Trump to court, and the final outcome remains uncertain (there are several cases with different legal issues because Trump is raiding different pots of government money in different agencies in order to build his wall). But the precedent—the undermining of a fundamental constitutional power of Congress to control the purse strings—has worried even the most conservative Republicans. Many of these people, including Senate Majority Leader Mitch McConnell, won't stand up to Trump and have only themselves to blame. If a more liberal president someday chooses to declare another "emergency" to justify spending not approved by Congress (a "healthcare emergency," "transportation emergency," "environmental emergency," or "education emergency"), fiscal conservatives will rue the day they allowed Trump to get away with this.

A few Republicans in Congress were independent enough to publicly object.

"He is usurping congressional authority," said Republican senator Susan Collins of Maine. "This is a fundamental constitutional responsibility of Congress. We should be opposing this strongly."

But most Republicans were silent.

Democrats accused the president of needing to build his wall so badly that he was willing to shred the Constitution. They insisted this was no emergency, citing a statement Trump had made in a February 15 speech:

"I didn't need to do this," he said, "but I'd rather do it much faster."

On February 18, 2019, sixteen states, including New York and California, sued Trump over his phony emergency. Trump was unabashed. In a press conference he addressed the question. In a mocking singsong voice, he said, "We will have a national emergency. And we will then be sued, and they will sue us in the Ninth Circuit, even though it shouldn't be there. And we will possibly get a bad ruling, and then we'll get another bad ruling. And then we'll end up in the Supreme Court, and hopefully, we'll get a fair shake, and we'll win in the Supreme Court, just like the ban."

So, now that we are in in the midst of a "border crisis" and a "wall" emergency, what will be the next emergency?

In August 2019 Trump went so far as to tell administration officials that he would pardon them if they committed any crimes in the course of building his wall. He was telling people to commit crimes if they needed to in order to accomplish his political objective and promising them a pardon if they did.

What if Trump is impeached or he loses the 2020 election? Will he simply declare another national "emergency"?

Perhaps the most chilling outburst from Trump came in September 2018, when at campaign rally for Senator Josh Hawley of Missouri, Trump told the crowd, "They're so lucky that we're peaceful. Law enforcement, military, construction workers, Bikers for Trump—how about Bikers for Trump? They travel all over the country. They got Trump all over the place, and you're great. But these are tough people. But they're peaceful people, and Antifa and all—they'd better hope they stay that way. I hope they stay that way. I hope they stay that way."

Trump's definition of an "emergency" is about a lot more than his wall. It's about his narcissism, and that he sees an "emergency" whenever his conduct or ego comes into conflict with the rule of law.

CHAPTER 25

Two Tragic Figures

It is the first responsibility of every citizen to question authority.
—BENJAMIN FRANKLIN

HISTORIANS OF TOTALITARIAN REGIMES OFTEN WRITE about the people who supported and contributed to evil (collaborators) and those who opposed it (resisters). In addition, there are two other categories of actors. A great many people do nothing and remain silent in the face of evil. A fourth even more interesting category includes people who actively contributed to bringing about evil but then turned around and stood up to evil, paying for this decision with their careers and sometimes with their lives.

These people—those who actively do both evil and good—are in some ways the most tragic figures in tragic historical situations.

In the Nazi regime, for example, the first category included Hitler's confidants and a great many Nazi Party members who were loyal to the end, as well as much of the German military. Then there were resisters, many of whom were executed or perished in concentration camps. Third, there were millions of German citizens who may not have been enthusiastic about Hitler, but they kept quiet and often benefited from the evil as well as facilitated it. Fourth, there was a small group of people who started out helping Hitler and then turned against him, even if late in the game. Most notably, Claus von Stauffenberg and other conspirators had supported Nazism for years but on July 20, 1944, attempted to assassinate Hitler with a bomb. If successful, they probably would have saved hundreds of thousands if not millions of lives. The plot failed and these men paid with their own lives.

The United States is not a totalitarian state. We use the Constitution, not coups and assassination plots, to stand up to and remove totalitarian leaders. We are a nation of laws.

But here also, when we face the threat of authoritarian rule and constitutional crisis, there are people who fall into each of these four categories. There are those who collaborate with authoritarianism; people who resist and stand up for the rule of law regardless of personal and political loyalties; those who remain silent in the face of authoritarianism because it is politically convenient, even if the personal cost of speaking truth to power would be far less than in a true dictatorship; and then there are those who both contributed to the evil and opposed it.

These are the people, often quite powerful, who on the moral spectrum between right and wrong fall in between.

This chapter discusses two such men.

JAMES COMEY

In many respects, former FBI director James Comey is a tragic figure. A veteran prosecutor—and a Republican—he had been appointed to lead the FBI by President Obama because, among other things, during the Bush years he had been willing to stand up against illegal domestic surveillance tactics advocated by many in the White House and the CIA. Comey had an independent mind.

But then, as director of the FBI, he quickly was dragged into the investigation of Hillary Clinton's use of a private email server when she was secretary of state. Because the private email server *could* have contained classified information, it was important to involve the FBI at least to find out how much classified information there was (in fact very little) and whether it had been compromised. The idea that Clinton, apart from her negligence, had committed a crime was near laughable.

Negligent handling of classified information can technically be a crime, but there is virtually no record of anyone ever having been prosecuted for it.

The Republican-controlled House of Representatives, and most of all its Oversight and Government Affairs Committee, said this was different. Clinton had committed a serious crime, charged the Republicans, not because what she had done with her email was stupid (it was), but because she was Hillary Clinton. Republicans since 1992 had been accusing the Clintons of crimes ranging from rape to murder and even treason. Because Clinton was running for president in 2016, *whatever she did* was a crime in the eyes of a Republican-controlled House.

This was a situation that James Comey and the FBI should have avoided. He could not prevent politicized congressional investigations, which after 2012 focused more on Clinton than any other actors in the Obama administration. But Comey should have kept FBI involvement to a minimum and kept the FBI where it belongs—out of partisan politics.

At that he failed.

The story ends, as we know, in October 2016 when, just a week before the presidential election, for no good reason whatsoever, Comey sent a letter to the US House Oversight Committee suggesting that the FBI was continuing to look into Hillary Clinton's emails.

That single letter may very well have cost her the election.

This tragedy—for Comey and the FBI—began over a year earlier. The FBI spent months investigating whether Clinton's use of a private server was a criminal offense, and in July 2016, Comey said he would not seek to indict her. In a letter he explained the reasoning behind his decision. He went far beyond the comments that a prosecutor usually makes when deciding *not* to indict someone.

"Clinton had mishandled the classified information," he wrote, but then he gave his opinion that she was too inept to know the risks she was running; ergo, he couldn't prove she did it intentionally.

Although there is evidence of potential violations of the statutes regarding the handling of classified information, our judgment is that no reasonable prosecutor would bring such a case. Prosecutors necessarily weigh a number of factors before bringing charges. There are obvious considerations, like the strength of the evidence, especially regarding intent. Responsible decisions also consider the context of a person's actions, and how similar situations have been handled in the past.

In looking back at our investigations into mishandling or removal of classified information, we cannot find a case that would support bringing criminal charges on these facts. All the cases prosecuted involved some combination of: clearly intentional and willful mishandling of classified information; or vast quantities of materials exposed in such a way as to support an inference of intentional misconduct; or indications of disloyalty to the United States; or efforts to obstruct justice. We do not see those things here.

To be clear, this is not to suggest that in similar circumstances, a person who engaged in this activity would face no consequences. To the contrary, those individuals are often subject to security or administrative sanctions. But that is not what we are deciding now.

Director Comey thus said that he found Clinton's behavior to be unacceptable, if not criminal, and that he believed people who did what she did should suffer "consequences." This statement was almost an invitation to voters to impose "consequences" on Hillary Clinton in November.

Meanwhile, the FBI remained silent up through the election concerning what it knew about the far more dangerous situation of the Russians seeking to sabotage the election and possible ties between the Russians and Trump's associates. Trump may refer to this pre-election investigation of Russian activities as the FBI "spying" on his campaign, but it was a critically important counterespionage operation. American voters heard nothing about it until after the election, but they heard a lot about Hillary's email.

In this statement about Clinton, the FBI ventured where it never should—into a one-sided evaluation of the moral character of a presidential candidate, all while remaining silent about the enormous national security risk posed by her opponent, Donald Trump.

Democrats were scratching their heads over Comey's need to opine on the propriety of Clinton's actions, especially in light of the upcoming election four months hence.

Though Hillary Clinton was cleared of criminal behavior, Republicans insisted on accusing her anyway. The "Lock her up" chant went viral over the summer and at the Republican National Convention.

Comey then topped it all off with an October surprise. A week before the election he threw gasoline on the fire in such a way that Donald Trump and his supporters in Congress could make maximum hay over essentially nothing.

In a letter of October 28, 2016—sent just four days after WikiLeaks released John Podesta's stolen emails and eleven days before Election Day—Comey informed the House Oversight Committee that his agents had learned of new emails "pertinent" to their probe while working on an unrelated case. Comey told Congress that FBI agents needed to review those messages for classified information and any relevance to the now closed investigation of the Clinton email server. The letter in its entirety states:

> In previous congressional testimony, I referred to the fact that the Federal Bureau of Investigation (FBI) had completed its investigation of former Secretary Clinton's personal email server. Due to recent developments, I am writing to supplement my previous testimony.
>
> In connection with an unrelated case, the FBI has learned of the existence of emails that appear to be pertinent to the investigation. I am writing to inform you that the investigative team briefed me on this yesterday, and I agreed that the FBI should take appropriate investigative steps designed to allow investigators to review these emails to determine whether they contain classified information, as well as to assess their importance to our investigation.
>
> Although the FBI cannot yet assess whether or not this material may be significant, and I cannot predict how long it will take us to complete this additional work, I believe it is important to update your Committees about our efforts in light of my previous testimony.

A day later it was reported that the new emails didn't come from Hillary Clinton. They came from a computer obtained in the investigation of Anthony Weiner, the former congressman from New York who had been found guilty of sexting with a fifteen-year-old girl. Weiner was married to Huma Abedin, a top personal aide to Hillary Clinton. The emails, as Comey would learn—too late—were from the Weiner investigation, and any Clinton-related emails were almost certainly duplicates of emails that already were on the server that had already been examined by the FBI.

Nevertheless, when Comey was briefed on the existence of the "new" emails, he felt a need to tell the House Oversight Committee.

The letter was gleefully leaked to the press by Representative Jason Chaffetz, a Republican from Utah, and the letter went viral.

Trump was campaigning in Manchester, New Hampshire, when he heard the news.

"Perhaps, finally, justice will be done," he said, as his followers roared.

The FBI findings were "a damning and unprecedented indictment of her judgment, and the new statement doesn't change anything," said Republican National Committee Chairman Reince Priebus. He added, "None of this changes the fact that the FBI continues to investigate the Clinton Foundation for corruption involving her tenure as secretary of state."

Hillary Clinton, on her part, pleaded in vain with voters to "focus on the issues."

On October 30, two days after Comey's letter became public, one of our authors wrote an editorial in the *New York Times* contending that the actions of Comey and the FBI so close to the election were both highly improper and an abuse of power.

Said Painter, "The FBI's job is to investigate, not to influence the outcome of an election." He added that what Comey did was also a violation of the Hatch Act, which bars the use of an official position to influence an election.

"It is not clear whether Mr. Comey personally wanted to influence the outcome of the election, although his letter—which cast suspicion on Mrs. Clinton without revealing specifics—was concerning. Also concerning is the fact that Mr. Comey already made unusual public statements expressing his opinion about Mrs. Clinton's actions, calling her handling of classified information 'extremely careless,' when he announced this summer that the FBI was concluding its investigation of her email without filing any charges."

The piece concluded, "This is no trivial matter. We cannot allow the FBI or Justice Department officials to unnecessarily publicize pending investigations concerning candidates of either party while an election is underway.

That is an abuse of power. Allowing such a precedent to stand will invite more, and even worse, abuses of power in the future."

On November 6, 2016, just two days before the election, Comey wrote a second letter to the lawmakers informing them that his July conclusion hadn't changed. There were *no grounds* for prosecuting Hillary Clinton for her emails.

But the damage had been done.

The public reaction to the second letter was like a pebble in the ocean. The damage to Hillary Clinton's presidential campaign was irreparable. Comey's October 28 letter was used by the Republican majority in the House—and by Donald Trump—to help throw the election to Trump's favor.

According to analyst Nate Silver, Hillary Clinton would probably be president if FBI Director James Comey had not sent that letter. Said Silver, it "upended the news cycle and soon halved Clinton's lead in the polls, imperiling her position in the Electoral College."

Silver said Comey's letter wasn't the only reason she lost, but it played a big part.

"Because Clinton lost Michigan, Pennsylvania, and Wisconsin by less than one point," he said, "the letter was probably enough to change the outcome of the Electoral College."

One would think that Donald Trump would feel a deep gratitude to James Comey for helping him win the election. But Trump does not feel indebted to anyone. From his perspective, others are supposed to be in debt to him. Trump also had a problem. Comey was well aware he had been instrumental in installing Trump into the White House, and he had an obligation to complete the FBI's investigation of Russia's interference in the election.

Comey, like Trump, had sworn an oath of office to "support and defend the Constitution of the United States against all enemies foreign and domestic." Unlike Trump, Comey believed in the oath with all of his being. His loyalty came first to the United States and only secondarily to the president, and that created a serious problem for both of them.

Comey had used extraordinarily bad judgment in the Clinton email investigation, but he was a loyal American. If there was credible evidence that the Russians had interfered in an election, and that Americans may have helped them do it, he was going to investigate it.

During Trump's transition period, Comey presented him with evidence that Russia had collected compromising information about him. This information came from the Steele dossier and showed that Trump had ties to Russia long before the election.

On January 27, 2017, just seven days after assuming office, President Trump invited Comey to the White House for a tête-à-tête dinner meeting. Comey suspected that Trump was seeking to create a relationship, but Comey was taken aback when, as they ate, Trump said to him, "I need loyalty. I expect loyalty."

In response, Comey declared he would always be honest with the president, but told him, "I am not reliable in the conventional political sense."

Comey then attempted to explain to Trump how he saw his role as FBI director as it was proscribed by the Constitution. Comey told Trump the country would be best served if the FBI were independent of the president.

Trump, unhappy with Comey's answer, again told Comey he needed his loyalty.

Comey again said he would pledge his honesty and not his loyalty.

"Will it be honest loyalty?" Trump wanted to know.

"You will have that," Comey said.

Observers tried to explain away Trump's behavior by saying he didn't know that members of the FBI were not supposed to be politically loyal. Congress had given FBI directors a ten-year term to make them independent of the president. Trump either had no knowledge of the role of the FBI or most likely he didn't care. To Trump, loyalty *to him* is more important than competence, experience, or loyalty to the United States and to the rule of law.

Trump made this clear after Michael Flynn, who had been on his transition team, was caught talking to Russian ambassador Sergey Kislyak. When the FBI asked him about the phone calls, Flynn lied. Sally Yates, the acting attorney general, feared that Flynn would be subject to blackmail by the Russians because they knew he had lied. Presidential candidate Trump earlier had been informed by the FBI that Flynn was a paid lobbyist for the Turkish government during the campaign. He was committing a crime by not registering.

Despite these warnings, Trump promoted Flynn to national security advisor.

When Flynn's illicit activities became public a few weeks into his term, Trump had no choice but to fire Flynn. Shortly afterwards, FBI Director Comey launched an investigation into Flynn's activities.

Trump then met with Comey in a clumsy attempt to stop the investigation. In a meeting, he asked Comey to drop the probe.

"I hope you can see your way clear to letting this go, to letting Flynn go," said Trump. "He's a good guy. I hope you can let this go. Flynn hasn't done anything wrong."

Comey was horrified that Trump was putting him in such a compromising position.

"I agree he's a good guy," was Comey's response.

Comey would go on to keep notes on all his conversations with Trump. He did it for self-protection, considering Trump's reputation for lying.

"I was honestly concerned that he might lie about the nature of our meeting, so I thought it really important to document," he said during a later Senate hearing. "I knew there might come a day when I might need a record of what happened not only to defend myself but to protect the FBI."

As Comey predicted, Trump denied he ever said what Comey reported.

"The president has never asked Mr. Comey or anyone else to end any investigation, including any investigation involving General Flynn," said a White House statement. "The president has the utmost respect for our law enforcement agencies, and all investigations. This is not a truthful or accurate portrayal of the conversation between the president and Mr. Comey."

More important than the issue of who was lying was Trump's insistence on loyalty. In his private life, an employee's vow of loyalty to Trump was a precursor to getting hired.

In a truly stunning development, on Tuesday, May 8, 2017, Trump fired Comey, at the same time as Comey and the FBI were investigating Flynn and also whether anyone in the Trump campaign had conspired with Russia to influence the 2016 presidential election.

Trump clearly had fired Comey to remove him from the Russia investigation.

Trump must have had the sense that admitting his reason for firing Comey would expose him to criminal prosecution for obstructing justice, and so as his excuse, Trump said he was firing Comey for mishandling the FBI's investigation of Hillary Clinton.

The excuse was perplexing, because it had been Comey's letter about Clinton's email that helped to swing the election to Trump.

In his dismissal letter, Trump wrote to Comey, "I nevertheless concur with the judgment of the Department of Justice that you are not able to effectively lead the bureau."

Trump pushed the story line that Attorney General Jeff Sessions and Deputy Attorney General Rod Rosenstein were the ones pressing for Comey's dismissal. Rosenstein had written a letter saying, "I cannot defend the director's handling of the conclusion of the investigation of Secretary Clinton's emails, and I do not understand his refusal to accept the nearly universal judgment that he was mistaken."

Everyone was sure Rosenstein wrote the letter under Trump's orders. The last sentence sounded like it was written by Trump himself, who during the campaign and even after the election was full of fury that Hillary Clinton had been found innocent of any wrongdoing.

When Comey saw the announcement of his firing on television, he laughed, because it seemed so absurd. Not long afterwards he received Trump's letter of dismissal.

For many, the firing of James Comey reeked of obstruction of justice.

A few days later, Trump met with Russian foreign minister Sergey Lavrov.

The meeting added to the collusive smell.

In a hearing before the Senate a month later, in June 2017, Comey accused the Trump administration of spreading "lies, plain and simple," about him and the FBI.

During the hearing Senator Dianne Feinstein of California asked about the meeting in which Trump asked him to kill the Flynn investigation.

"Why didn't you stop and say, 'Mr. President, this is wrong'?" she asked Comey.

"That's a great question," said Comey. "Maybe if I were stronger I would have. I was so stunned by the conversation, I just took it in."

Comey was also asked whether Russia did, indeed, meddle in the 2016 election. Trump all along had been calling the investigation "fake news."

"There should be no fuzz on this," Comey said. "The Russians interfered. That happened. It's about as unfake as you can possibly get."

JEFF SESSIONS

Jeff Sessions is our second tragic figure.

Sessions—an extremely conservative senator from Alabama—was one of the first US senators to back Trump's presidential bid, and he was a very active leader in the Trump campaign.

In February 2017, during Sessions's confirmation hearing for attorney general, Senator Al Franken of Minnesota asked Sessions what he would do if he learned of evidence that anyone affiliated with the Trump campaign communicated with the Russian government in the course of the 2016 campaign. Sessions denied even knowing about such contacts, much less making them himself.

On his written Senate confirmation questionnaire, Sessions denied having any communication with the Russians. He also denied talking to the Russians about the 2016 presidential campaign.

Not true. Sessions had two conversations with Russian ambassador Kislyak in July and September 2016 when Sessions was an advisor to the Trump campaign.

A spokesperson tried to defend Sessions by saying his contacts with the Russian ambassador were made in his capacity as a member of the Senate Armed Forces Committee, not as a Trump campaign worker.

If that had been true, Sessions should have revealed that fact at the confirmation hearing. Instead, he had kept his conversations with Kislyak secret.

What Sessions had done was reminicient of the case of Richard Kleindienst, who in 1972 was confirmed as attorney general after John Mitchell resigned to run Nixon's reelection campaign. Kleindienst was asked several times during his Senate confirmation hearing whether he had interfered in the antitrust suit against ITT, a big-pockets contributor to the Nixon campaign. Kleindienst said no, but then special prosecutor Leon Jaworski uncovered a

White House tape of a phone call in which President Nixon told Kleindienst to drop the case against ITT. Kleindienst later pleaded guilty to misleading Congress, a misdemeanor. Most important, he had been forced to resign as attorney general.

When the Sessions news broke, many—including one of your authors (Painter) in an editorial in the *New York Times*—called for Sessions to be fired or to resign.

Concluded Painter in this editorial, "President Trump has already fired his national security advisor, Michael Flynn, for misleading Vice-President Pence about his conversations with the Russians. Misleading the United States Senate in testimony under oath is at least as serious. We do not yet know all the facts, but we know enough to see that Attorney General Sessions has to go as well."

One hundred members of the House of Representatives (all Democrats) signed a statement urging Sessions to step down. Said House Minority Leader Nancy Pelosi, "Attorney General Sessions must resign immediately. Our security and our democracy have been undermined by Russia's meddling, and this administration clearly cannot be trusted to investigate itself. There must be an independent, bipartisan, outside commission to investigate the full extent of the Trump political, personal, and financial connections to the Russians."

Sessions refused to resign, but on March 1, 2017, he recused himself from heading the Russian probe. Sessions had done wrong—he had helped Trump get elected and knew a lot more about the Russians than he had told his colleagues in the Senate, even under oath. But by recusing, he would do right.

Sessions had no choice, not just because of the embarrassment from having been caught stating an untruth under oath, whether inadvertently or intentionally, but also because federal ethics rules and lawyers' ethics rules prohibited him as the chief law enforcement officer in the United States from supervising an ongoing investigation of the Trump campaign when he had been a senior leader of the campaign during the entirety of the relevant time period when the Russians interfered with the election and had significant contacts with the campaign. Sessions could not investigate himself. He *had* to recuse.

By recusing himself, however, Sessions became a primary target for President Trump's wrath. Trump had expected Sessions to kill the investigation into Russian meddling in the election, but with Sessions's recusal, his ability to stop or hinder the investigation now had vanished.

When asked whether Sessions should have recused himself, President Trump said, "I don't think so."

Behind the scenes Trump ordered White House counsel Don McGahn to try to stop Sessions from recusing himself. When McGahn didn't succeed, Trump reacted angrily, saying he "needed his attorney general to protect him."

Two months later, on May 17, 2017, Trump was holding a meeting with Sessions, Vice President Mike Pence, and White House attorney Don McGahn to discuss who should replace FBI head Comey. During the meeting McGahn received a phone call. It was Assistant Attorney General Rod Rosenstein saying he had decided to appoint former FBI head Robert Mueller to head the Russian probe.

McGahn hung up and gave President Trump the news. His response was a string of insults. To Sessions's face, he said he blamed him for the tough spot he was in, and he said, "Choosing you to be attorney general was one of the worst decisions I ever made."

Trump said, "You're an idiot. You should resign."

Sessions told Trump he would resign and stormed out of the meeting.

Sessions would tell associates that it had been the most humiliating experience of his public life.

Sessions, shaken, immediately sent Trump a letter of resignation, but senior members of Trump's administration pleaded with Trump not to follow through. After all, Trump had already fired James Comey, his FBI director, and Michael Flynn, his national security advisor.

Two months later, in July 2017, Trump again considered firing Sessions, but again was talked out of it. Sessions told reporters he didn't want to quit because he wanted to bolster the country's strict immigration policies. On July 19 in an interview with the *New York Times,* Trump again commented that Sessions never should have recused himself.

"Jeff Sessions takes the job, gets into the job, recuses himself, which frankly I think is very unfair to the president," said Trump. "How do you take a job and then recuse yourself? If he would have recused himself before he took the job, I would have said, 'Thanks, Jeff, but I'm not going to take you.' It's extremely unfair—and that's a mild word—to the president."

He later told the *Wall Street Journal*, "I'm very disappointed in Jeff Sessions." Trump said Sessions would serve as attorney general "as long as it's appropriate."

Sessions remained in office, taking Trump's constant abuse. In his book *Fear*, Bob Woodward reported that Trump had called Sessions "mentally retarded" and a "dumb Southerner." (Trump then accused Woodward of telling lies and having lousy sources.)

Unable to abide Sessions any longer, on November 7, 2018, Trump demanded that he resign.

Upon leaving office, Sessions defended himself.

"In my time as attorney general we have restored and upheld the rule of law—a glorious tradition that each of us has a responsibility to safeguard. We have operated with integrity and have lawfully and aggressively advanced the policy agenda of this administration."

But like so many who toiled under President Trump, Sessions, who was hired in large part for his conservative views on social issues, his commitment to law enforcement, and his anti-immigrant stances, left as yet another victim of Trump's loyalty to no person other than himself.

CHAPTER 26

Robert Mueller: Trump's Worst Nightmare

When once a Republic is corrupted, there is no possibility of remedying
any of the growing evils but by removing the corruption and restoring
its lost principles; every other correction is either useless or a new evil.
—THOMAS JEFFERSON

O N MAY 19, 2017, DEPUTY ATTORNEY GENERAL ROD
Rosenstein, without consulting with White House lawyers or President
Donald Trump, named former FBI director Robert Mueller as the special
counsel to take over the investigation into Russian meddling in the 2016
election.

Mueller's appointment changed everything. The former FBI head was a
no-nonsense prosecutor with a stellar reputation for going after the bad guys
regardless of politics or favor. As House Democrats would later find out in
July of 2019, Mueller was not a telegenic personality for nationally televised
hearings, but for the special counsel's job that shouldn't matter. Mueller was
a thorough and impartial prosecutor.

Rosenstein needed to salvage his reputation. When James Comey was fired as FBI director, Rosenstein wrote a letter in which he covered for Trump by saying that Comey should be fired over his poor handling of Hillary Clinton's emails, even though Rosenstein knew that the Russia investigation was the real reason Trump was firing Comey. That was wrong, but Rosenstein did the right thing by appointing Robert Mueller. Rosenstein continued to do the right thing by refusing to fire, or to curtail, Robert Mueller throughout the investigation. If we were to add a third "tragic figure" to our discussion in the previous chapter, Rod Rosenstein would be it.

According to Rosenstein's order naming Mueller to the job, Mueller was authorized to investigate "any links and/or coordination between the Russian government and individuals associated with the campaign of Donald J. Trump" as well as other matters that "may arise directly from the investigation." Those matters included Trump's finances, associates, and family members, insofar as they were connected with the Russians.

Said Pat Buchanan, a former Republican presidential candidate, "A debilitating and potentially dangerous time for President Trump has now begun, courtesy of his deputy attorney general."

Trump, in an interview with Fox News, suggested that the investigation now headed by Mueller was political, that the Democrats were behind it. That Mueller had been a lifelong Republican didn't seem to enter into Trump's thinking. Trump said he was upset about the appointment because "well, he's very, very good friends with Comey, which is very bothersome. I can say that the people that have been hired are all Hillary Clinton supporters, some of them working for Hillary Clinton.

"I mean, the whole thing is ridiculous if you want to know the truth."

Trump later warned that if Mueller's investigation looked into the personal finances of the Trump family, "it will cross a line."

He added, "I think that's a violation. Look, this is about Russia."

Trump also got in a few licks against Rosenstein, who had been a federal prosecutor in Baltimore.

"There are very few Republicans in Baltimore, if any," said Trump, who then went after Comey, accusing him of lying about him in front of Congress. Trump was alluding to the meeting he and Comey had during which Comey showed him the Steele dossier. Comey said he had showed it to Trump before the press saw it, as a way of preventing embarrassment to Trump. Trump, paranoid and defensive, accused Comey of using the document as leverage against him.

"When he brought it to me," said Trump, "I said this is really made-up junk. I didn't think about any of it. I just thought about, man, this is such a phony deal."

It was only the second time the Justice Department named a special prosecutor using the rule Rosenstein invoked in his order. A law, the Special Counsel Act of 1999, had amended the federal code to replace provisions of the post-Watergate independent counsel statute (which had been allowed to expire) with provisions authorizing the attorney general to appoint a special counsel. That year Attorney General Janet Reno appointed John Danforth, a former Republican senator from Missouri, to investigate the federal raid on the compound in Waco, Texas, that killed seventy-six members of the Branch Davidian cult. Robert Mueller in 2017 was the next special counsel appointment.

Sadly, the Special Counsel Act of 1999 was much inferior to the post-Watergate independent counsel law that had preceded it because that earlier law prevented the president, or the attorney general, from firing the special prosecutor. Congress had not wanted this to happen again after President Nixon had fired Archibald Cox in the Saturday Night Massacre of 1973, so Congress created the office of special counsel and put the special prosecutor under the direction of a three-judge panel of the US Court of Appeals.

But, as we related earlier, special prosecutor and former federal judge Ken Starr, "supervised" by his former judicial colleagues on the US Court of Appeals for the District of Columbia Circuit, was widely believed to have abused his authority in investigating President Clinton, ultimately investigating White House sex instead of the Whitewater land deal. Congress in 1999 ditched the post-Watergate law and put the special counsel back under the authority of the attorney general. This meant Robert Mueller in 2017 would be in exactly the same place that his predecessor Archibald Cox had been forty-four years earlier. What happened to Archibald Cox in October 1973 could at any moment happen to Robert Mueller.

Government ethics commentators, including—ironically—former Nixon White House counsel John Dean, made weekly, and sometimes daily, appearances on cable news every time there was a threat—of which there were many—by Donald Trump to fire Robert Mueller.

It's worth noting that Robert Mueller and Donald Trump, born two years apart, had somewhat similar upbringings. Mueller was born in Manhattan in 1944, but his family moved to Princeton, New Jersey, where his father, Robert Mueller II, worked for DuPont after serving as a navy officer captaining a submarine chaser during World War II. Mueller's father insisted that Robert and his five younger sisters live by a strict moral code.

"A lie was the worst sin," said Mueller. "The one thing you didn't do was to give anything less than the truth to my mother and father." Mueller was enrolled in the Princeton Country Day School, until his family moved to Philadelphia. He then attended St. Paul's School in Concord, New Hampshire (former Watergate special prosecutor Archibald Cox had also attended St. Paul's in the 1930s), during much of the same time that Trump attended the decidedly less academic New York Military Academy. Mueller was the captain of St. Paul's soccer, lacrosse, and hockey teams, and in hockey he played on the same team with future secretary of state John Kerry.

One of Mueller's St. Paul's classmates, Maxwell King, who would go on to become an editor at the *Philadelphia Enquirer*, spoke about the respect the other boys had for Mueller. One day Mueller was at the Tuck, a snack shop at the school, and another student made a snide comment about a boy who wasn't there to defend himself.

"I don't want to hear that," Mueller told him.

"I mean," said King, "we all said disparaging things about each other face-to-face. But saying something about someone who wasn't there was something that Bob was uncomfortable with, and he let it be known and just walked out."

Trump went to the University of Pennsylvania, while Mueller followed in his father's footsteps and attended Princeton University, graduating in 1966. At Princeton, Mueller became close friends with David Hackett, who was a year ahead of him. Hackett had joined the Marines version of ROTC, training during the summertime. Mueller and Hackett played together on the lacrosse team, and Hackett became a role model to Mueller. When Hackett graduated in 1965, he joined the Marines, excelled at officer candidates' school, and went to Vietnam. Mueller vowed to join him when he graduated the coming year, but in April 1967, Hackett was killed by a sniper after an ambush by North Vietnamese troops.

Hackett's death steeled Mueller's resolve to join the Marines after graduation, but a knee injury from his years playing lacrosse and hockey at St. Paul's made him ineligible. He was told he would have to heal before he could enlist. *Robert Mueller went to a doctor to get healed so he could serve his country, not to get diagnosed with an ailment so he could avoid the draft.* Waiting to be healed, he married Ann Standish and enrolled at New York University to earn a master's degree in international relations.

When his knee finally healed, and military doctors gave him a clean bill of health, Mueller signed up for Officer Candidate School in Quantico, Virginia. This was about the same time Donald Trump was seeing his foot doctor (also a tenant of Fred Trump), who would diagnose his infamous "bone spurs" and help him avoid the draft.

Mueller shone at Officer Candidate School. When Mueller graduated OCS and went on to US Army Ranger School, Trump graduated from Penn and began working for his father's real estate company.

While Mueller was at Ranger School, he went on maneuvers for two days, with only two hours sleep and one meal a day. He then went to Airborne School, known as Jump School, where he learned to parachute out of a plane.

After landing in Okinawa in the fall of 1968, Mueller flew to the Dong Ha Combat Base near the DMZ. Mueller was assigned to H Company, referred to as Hotel Company, a famed Second Battalion infantry unit that had been fighting nonstop since the start of the war. Mueller was twenty-four years old when as a lieutenant he took over as one of ten new officers assigned to the forty-man unit.

His men, mostly from rural America with little education past high school, were wary of a platoon leader who had gone to an elite boarding school and Ivy League college. Quickly the men saw that Mueller was no snot-nosed elite. He was relentlessly curious about his job, asking questions of the veterans under him about soldiering on patrol in Vietnam's dense jungle.

It didn't take long for Mueller to earn his men's trust and respect.

In early December 1968, he and his company were ordered to retake a hill called Mutter's Ridge. When Fox Company was attacked by machine-gun fire, Mueller and his Hotel Company were on a neighboring hill. Mueller called for his men to go to Fox Company's rescue. It took them hours to go down a hill and up a ridge as they advanced through vegetation so thick the men needed machetes to cut through it. Once the company reached the top of the ridge, Mueller ordered everyone into battle.

The North Vietnamese sprayed them with machine-gun fire. Mueller stayed calm, positioning his fighters and calling in air cover. The battle went on for hours. Deaths mounted. At one point, Mueller dropped back to try to stem the bleeding of one of his men who had been shot. Eventually the North Vietnamese withdrew.

Mueller would be awarded a Bronze Star. His commendation read: "Second Lieutenant Mueller's courage, aggressive initiative and unwavering devotion to duty at great personal risk were instrumental in the defeat of the enemy force and were in keeping with the highest traditions of the Marine Corps and the United States Naval Service."

All told, thirteen of his men died and thirty-one were wounded in the battle of Mutter's Ridge. Mueller said his experience at Mutter's Ridge made everything that came afterward seem less stressful and dangerous.

Mueller always kept his composure.

Men continued to die. On April 10, 1969, soldiers from the Third Platoon were attacked while on patrol. There was an intense firefight, and when Mueller was hit, he was so focused that he didn't realize a bullet from an AK-47 had passed through his thigh.

He received a Navy Commendation medal as a result. His combat days ended when he was airlifted to a field hospital near Dong Ha. After three weeks of recovery, Mueller was sent to serve at command headquarters. He was appointed aide-de-camp to Major General William K. Jones, the head of the Third Marine Division.

From there, he worked at the Marine barracks near the Pentagon. He was admitted to the University of Virginia Law School.

Said Mueller years later, "I consider myself exceptionally lucky to have made it out of Vietnam. There were many—many—who did not. And perhaps because I did survive Vietnam, I have always felt compelled to contribute."

Mueller earned his JD in 1973. His first job was as a litigator at the law firm of Pillsbury, Madison & Sutro in San Francisco. He then became an assistant US attorney for the District of Northern California. He was promoted to chief of the criminal division in 1981. The next year he moved to Boston to work as an assistant US attorney for the District of Massachusetts. He worked on cases concerned with international money laundering, corruption, financial fraud, narcotics, and terrorism. In 1986 he was the district's acting US attorney, and after a year he joined the private law firm of Hill & Barlow.

In 1989 he returned to government work, joining the US Department of Justice as assistant to Attorney General Dick Thornburgh in the George H. W. Bush administration. He was also the acting deputy attorney general. He led the prosecution of Panamanian dictator Manuel Noriega; was the lead in the criminal case against the man accused of blowing up an airplane over Lockerbie, Scotland; and in his role as acting deputy attorney general, he formed a unit dedicated to cybersecurity.

Mueller returned to private practice in 1993, joining Hale and Dorr (later WilmerHale), a firm specializing in white-collar crime. In 1995 he went back to the public sector and joined the US attorney's office for the District of Columbia, where he soon rose to the post of senior litigator of the homicide division. From 1998 to 2001 he was the US attorney for the Northern District of California.

On July 5, 2001, President George W. Bush nominated Mueller to be the director of the FBI, replacing outgoing director Louis Freeh.

Mueller became the sixth director of the FBI on September 4, 2001, just a week before the terrorist attacks that would shape his FBI tenure.

Mueller was critical of the work done by the FBI prior to the attacks. Tips to field offices had not been communicated to the top brass, and Mueller made it his mission to reorganize the bureau, changing it into a high-tech global organization designed to head off terror threats, including cyberattacks. Some FBI veterans chafed at the change, but Mueller persisted in his view that cybersecurity would become the most important area of protection for this country.

For the next five years, Mueller's FBI was relatively incident free, but then in 2004, the Bush administration tried to make an end run around acting attorney general James Comey to extend a program that allowed for domestic spying without warrants. This Patriot Act program had been determined to be illegal by Justice Department lawyers.

White House Counsel Alberto Gonzales and President Bush's chief of staff, Andrew Card Jr., drove to the hospital where John Ashcroft, the attorney general, was lying in a bed, weak and unable to carry out his duties, with the intent of getting Ashcroft to sign an order approving the program.

With Comey looking on, Ashcroft refused to sign. Gonzales and Card left in a huff.

"I was angry," said Comey. "I thought I had just witnessed an effort to take advantage of a very sick man, who did not have the powers of the attorney general because they had been transferred to me."

The Bush administration decided to continue the warrantless wiretapping program anyway, which led to Comey, Mueller, and a half dozen other Justice Department officials threatening to resign unless the program was stopped. President Bush agreed to make changes.

Gonzales was called in front of the House Judiciary Committee, and he told the committee that Ashcroft "talked about the legal issues in a lucid form, as I've heard him talk about legal issues in the White House."

Mueller, who had taken notes about the Ashcroft incident from his conversations with Comey, told the committee otherwise. Mueller said that according to Comey, Ashcroft was recovering from gallbladder surgery and was disoriented and "pretty bad off," though he did speak with Gonzales and Card.

When the House Judiciary Committee asked to see Mueller's notes about the visit to Ashcroft, Mueller left portions of his unredacted notes about the events before and after the hospital visit.

What Mueller made clear was that Vice President Dick Cheney was very much involved in the warrantless wiretapping program. Mueller's notes showed Cheney's presence at the various meetings discussing the program with Gonzales and Card. The final meeting on March 23, 2004, was also attended by Vice President Cheney.

Where others wanted to play cover-up, Mueller went back to what he had learned as a child—no matter what, don't tell a lie. Mueller isn't a dramatic witness in a congressional hearing (he certainly was a very undramatic—in some ways even boring—witness years later in his July 2019 testimony before the House Judiciary Committee). But Mueller sees his role, whether as a witness or as a prosecutor, to be sticking to the facts and telling the truth. He is not there to play politics.

When President Barack Obama took office in 2009, he praised Mueller for the fine job reorganizing the FBI and offered to extend his ten-year term by another two years. Mueller accepted. With only four months to go before leaving office, he was awakened at one thirty in the morning of April 15, 2013, with the news that one of the suspects in the Boston Marathon bombing was dying and the other was on the run. The bombers had killed five people and injured more than 260 along the route of the marathon.

The bombers were the Tsarnaev brothers, natives of Chechnya, and Mueller was told that two years earlier, the FBI had interviewed the older brother, wrongly determined he wasn't a terrorist threat, and released him. Mueller made the information public even though he knew it would unleash a hail of criticism. Mueller could not tell a lie.

After serving longer as FBI director than anyone other than J. Edgar Hoover, Mueller rejoined his former firm of Hale and Dorr, now Wilmer-Hale. He handled some of the firm's most important cases, including a review of the NFL's punishment of Baltimore Ravens running back Ray Rice, who was caught on camera in a casino dragging his fiancée out of the elevator by her hair.

Roger Goodell, the commissioner of the NFL, had initially suspended Rice for two games, unleashing an outcry from women's groups. When a second video appeared on *TMZ* showing Rice punching his fiancée, the Ravens immediately released Rice. Goodell then suspended Rice permanently.

Rice sued the NFL, and on appeal he was reinstated.

Mueller spent four months investigating the case, and in his report backed Goodell, saying the commissioner hadn't seen the video before the public saw it. But Mueller did conclude that the NFL did not sufficiently address the problem of domestic abuse.

Lawrence J. Leigh, who worked with Bob Mueller years earlier when he was a US attorney in San Francisco, was not surprised when in 2017 Rod Rosenstein selected Mueller to be the special counsel in charge of the Russian investigation.

Leigh said that at first they weren't close, that Mueller's bona fides were in question when he came to work in the San Francisco area, the most liberal district in the country, because he was a Republican. But quickly Leigh became impressed by how Mueller ran things. He was thorough. He had high expectations of those working under him. He demanded excellence. He wanted his assistants to be the best.

Leigh was constantly impressed by the way his boss would scrutinize entire investigative case files before approving grand jury indictments. Leigh had written a sloppy appellate brief, and Mueller, a perfectionist, sent him for a writing refresher course.

Before Mueller came in, the office had experienced leaks to the press. Mueller quickly stopped assistants from talking to reporters. He ordered all press contacts to go through his press chief. The leaks stopped. Most importantly, Mueller was nonpartisan about everything, including hiring, prosecutions, and culture.

"I knew my close friends' party affiliations, but I could not tell you which party most assistants favored—although we were all on a first-name basis," wrote Leigh. "Although a Republican, he'd hire a talented Democrat over a mediocre Republican every time."

When asked his opinion of Mueller, Leigh responded, "The best, simply the best."

On October 31, 2017, someone used a congressional computer to alter the Wikipedia page of Special Counsel Robert Mueller. The page had read, "Mueller is of German, English, and Scottish descent."

The anonymous gremlin changed it to "Mueller is Donald Trump's worst nightmare."

CHAPTER 27

The Battle to Stop Robert Mueller

*We the people are the rightful masters of both Congress
and the courts, not to overthrow the Constitution but to
overthrow the men who pervert the Constitution.*
—*ABRAHAM LINCOLN*

*Russia has never tried to use leverage over me. I HAVE NOTHING TO
DO WITH RUSSIA—NO DEALS, NO LOANS, NO NOTHING!*
—*DONALD TRUMP*

T RUMP'S BATTLE AGAINST ROBERT MUELLER WAS AT
first a battle against James Comey and the FBI.

Although Comey and the FBI had been instrumental in handing the
2016 election to Donald Trump by reviving the Clinton email controversy
a week before Election Day, Trump and his far-right media allies quickly
turned against Comey for insisting that the FBI thoroughly investigate Russian interference in the election.

There was a lot to investigate.

That Russian operatives engaged in criminal conduct, including computer hacking and fraudulent use of social media accounts, is obvious. That

Donald Trump and his campaign knew about and benefited from those actions is also obvious. He even shouted encouragement to Putin, urging the Russian president on TV to "hack Hillary Clinton's emails."

What was not obvious, and what an investigation could reveal, was:

1. Who collaborated with the Russians;
2. Whether that collaboration was criminal conspiracy or noncriminal;
3. The impact on our national security (including whether the Russians could blackmail anyone in our government and whether anyone who had collaborated with the Russians, even if not criminally, held a high position in the US government and/or had a security clearance); and
4. How we could prevent a foreign power from ever attacking our electoral process again.

There needed to be an investigation.

But Trump never wanted an investigation, and he has spent his entire presidency trying to prevent it.

We now know that the available evidence hasn't proved that Trump personally conspired with the Russians to commit a crime (although nobody knows what he said in those private meetings with Putin). There apparently wasn't sufficient evidence of criminal conspiracy to justify a prosecution of any Americans for conspiracy with the Russians (the extent of that evidence remains a mystery because large portions of the first part of Robert Mueller's 2019 report have been redacted).

But collaboration, if not criminal conspiracy, was obvious. It was clear that Trump and people working in his campaign *knew* about a lot of what the Russians were doing and that he would benefit from it. There was also evidence of Trump campaign workers sharing polling data with the Russians. Then there was the Trump Tower meeting with Russian operatives who offered to get the "dirt" on Hillary Clinton. Also, the Trump campaign "coffee boy" George Papadopoulos, who sat at the table with campaign top brass (there's a photo of that) and met with his Russian handler, the "professor," when traveling to the United Kingdom. And there were many people closely connected to Donald Trump who lied about their contacts with the Russians, some of whom have been criminally convicted.

There needed to be an investigation.

But Donald Trump did not want an investigation. This conflict between what needed to happen—what the rule of law and national security required—and the narcissistic will of a single man from the outset put Trump on a collision course first with James Comey, then with Robert Mueller, and ultimately with Congress and the Constitution.

As is typical for Trump, his propaganda campaign began with speeches and tweets to his supporters as soon as the election was over. Trump called any attempt by the press to discuss Russian interference in the election "fake news" and a "witch hunt."

As soon as he took office on January 20, 2017, Trump was in a position to do a lot more than complain about the Russia investigation in speeches and tweets. As president he could obstruct the investigation.

And—as outlined in great detail in the second half of Robert Mueller's 2019 report—that is exactly what Trump did. Whether or not Trump had the constitutional power to obstruct an investigation conducted by an executive branch under his complete control is a *legal* question that Mueller did not definitively answer (his 2019 report strongly suggested that the answer is "no," an issue we discuss in Chapter 30). But the *fact* that Trump obstructed the investigation is obvious.

He started by putting the screws to FBI Director James Comey, asking for his loyalty.

When asked how he took the request, Comey later said he "took it as a direction. I took it as, this is what he wants me to do." Comey said it was "a very disturbing thing, very concerning." Comey said he discussed with other FBI officials whether to open an obstruction of justice investigation right there and then.

In March 2017, Trump asked Daniel Coats, the director of national intelligence, and Mike Pompeo, the CIA director, to speak with Comey directly to persuade him to back off from investigating Flynn.

When Comey in March revealed that the FBI was investigating possible collusion between the Trump campaign and the Russians, Trump asked

Coats and national security director Admiral Michael Rogers to publicly state that there was no evidence of such collusion.

Both Coats and Rogers were taken aback by the request and refused. Both exchanged notes about Trump's request.

Jeff Sessions, whom Trump chose to be his first attorney general, was one of Trump's most loyal supporters. Trump fully expected Sessions to be the firewall between him and any fallout from his illegal activities, but on March 1, 2017, Sessions gave Trump a jolt of reality by recusing himself from the Russian investigation. With Sessions stepping away, Comey was in charge, and it was clear to Trump that Comey had no intention of letting it go.

On May 9, 2017, Trump fired Comey.

The next day Trump told Russian officials that the firing had "taken off the great pressure" of the Russian investigation. Two days later, he told Lester Holt on *NBC Nightly News* that he fired Comey because of "this Russia thing." (A year later Trump, finally understanding the meaning of his confession, accused Holt in a tweet of "fudging my tape on Russia." Trump's attorney made the same assertion. Neither had any evidence to back up their claims.)

Firing Comey was obstruction of justice on its face. Here was the president of the United States interfering with an FBI investigation into the guilt or innocence of people who worked on his own campaign, including family members and potentially himself. Obstruction of the FBI investigation might not have been sufficiently within Trump's constitutional powers as president so that he could not be prosecuted for it criminally (that is the legal question addressed in the 2019 Mueller Report, which strongly suggested that the president did not have such powers). But it was obstruction of justice, and something for which Trump could be, and should be, impeached (the Mueller Report came close to suggesting that, without expressly telling Congress exactly what to do).

Wrote Trump to Comey in his firing letter, "While I greatly appreciate you informing me, on three separate occasions, that I am not under investigation, I nevertheless concur with the judgment of the Department of Justice that you are not able to effectively lead the bureau."

When Andrew McCabe became acting director of the FBI in May 2017, Trump had a conversation with him similar to the one he had had with

Comey, asking for loyalty. McCabe replied by saying he had not voted in the election. McCabe also took copious notes of the meeting.

As expected, Democratic legislators cried foul. So did Representative Justin Amash, a Michigan Republican who said he supported an independent commission to investigate the Russian links to Trump. As for Trump saying that Comey had cleared him three times, Amash said his claim was "bizarre."

Even more bizarre was Russian Foreign Minister Sergey Lavrov and Ambassador Kislyak meeting the next day in the Oval Office with Trump and Secretary of State Rex Tillerson.

More bizarre than that was that the American press, barred from attending the meeting, didn't even know that either Trump or Kislyak were there. The American public found out only because photos of the four men were posted on the Russian government's Twitter account.

Later it was reported that Trump had divulged classified information to the two Russians (most likely this was information obtained from Mossad, the Israeli intelligence agency).

The next day Deputy Attorney General Rod Rosenstein appointed Robert Mueller as special counsel to investigate Russia's interference in the 2016 election and possible collusion with the Trump campaign.

A day later on Twitter, Trump reverted to his witch-hunt charge.

"This is the single greatest witch hunt of a politician in American history," he said. Then he tweeted a misdirection: "With all of the illegal acts that took place in the Clinton campaign & Obama Administration, there was never a special counsel appointed!"

That afternoon he took questions from reporters and said, yet again, "There was no collusion."

As May blended into June, Trump continued to deny any wrongdoing. Once again he tried to turn the country's attention to things Hillary Clinton might have done. On June 15, 2017, he tweeted, "They made up a phony collusion with the Russians story, found zero proof, so now they go for obstruction of justice on the phony story. Nice . . . You are witnessing the single greatest WITCH HUNT in American political history—led by some very bad and conflicted people! . . . Why is [it] that Hillary Clintons family and Dems dealings with Russia are not looked at, but my non-dealings are? . . .

Crooked H destroyed phones w/ hammer, 'bleached' emails & had husband meet w/AG days before she was cleared—& they talk about obstruction?"

On July 6, 2017, the day before Trump was to meet with Vladimir Putin in Warsaw, Trump told reporters that "nobody knows for sure" whether Russia meddled in the election.

"Well, I think it was Russia, and I think it could have been other people and other countries. It could have been a lot of people interfered."

The next day in Hamburg, Germany, Trump met with Putin during a meeting of twenty world leaders. At first Trump only admitted meeting Putin one time. According to Secretary of State Rex Tillerson, Trump asked Putin about meddling in the election, and Putin once again denied any such thing.

It took an investigation by the *New York Times* to discover that Trump had met with Putin a second time for an hour. Trump, breaking protocol, went alone. There was no secretary or assistant to record what was said at the meeting. He spoke to Putin through a Russian translator. There has never been a report as to what the two talked about. Trump made sure of that.

Trump in a statement downplayed the significance of the meeting.

"It is not merely perfectly normal, it is part of a president's duties, to interact with world leaders," the statement said.

Then why had he not disclosed the one-on-one discussion with Putin?

Trump blasted the media for reporting on his undisclosed meeting with the Russian president, saying the "fake news" was "sick" and "dishonest." Trump misrepresented what was said about the meeting. He said the media had reported a "secret dinner," when it was, in fact, an undisclosed dinner. Without basis, he stated that the reporters knew all about the meeting, when they hadn't.

What was the meeting about? There was no way to know.

Trump's denials about the campaign colluding with the Russians during the run-up to the election became harder to swallow when on July 8, 2017, the *New York Times* revealed that in June 2016, Donald Trump Jr., campaign manager Paul Manafort, and son-in-law Jared Kushner had met at Trump Tower with Russian lawyer Natalia Veselnitskaya after the Russians promised Trump Jr. damaging information about Hillary Clinton. Veselnitskaya was married to a Russian deputy minister of transportation.

Donald Trump Jr. admitted to the *New York Times* that the meeting had, in fact, taken place, and the next day Trump Jr. said in a statement that they had met to discuss "adoptions." Why adoptions? Because the Russians had barred Americans from adopting Russian orphans in retaliation for sanctions. And that—adoptions—was the issue that would lead the top brass of Trump's campaign to meet with a Russian agent?

Trump Jr. was lying, of course. The adoption issue was just a smoke screen. At that Trump Tower meeting, the topic of discussion was the "dirt" the Russians had on Hillary Clinton and how the Trump campaign could use it, as well as concerns that the Russians had about American sanctions on Russia (which were tangentially connected to the baby adoption issue). There was no provable quid pro quo (dirt on Hillary in exchange for relief from the sanctions), but that was the obvious drift of the meeting.

The *Washington Post* then revealed that President Trump himself had written the statement delivered by his son about the Trump Tower meeting. A few days later Trump's lawyer Jay Sekulow lied to CNN, saying that neither he nor Trump were involved in writing that statement and that the meeting had been about adoption.

Exposure of the Trump Tower meeting represented the first public disclosure that high-ranking members of the Trump campaign were meeting with Russian agents and willing to accept Russian help. Robert Mueller in his 2019 report apparently concluded that the meeting was not a provable criminal conspiracy (not all collaboration between political campaigns and outside persons is criminal). Nonetheless, the meeting was a clear example of collusion, and it had to do with a lot more than Russian baby adoptions.

Trump, upon hearing of revelations about the Trump Tower meeting, attempted to deflect any criticism from himself.

"I strongly pressed President Putin twice about Russian meddling in our election. He vehemently denied it. I've already given my opinion . . . We negotiated a ceasefire in parts of Syria which will save lives. Now it is time to move forward in working instructively with Russia! . . . Putin & I discussed forming an impenetrable Cyber Security unit so that election hacking & many other negative things, will be guarded . . . Sanctions were not discussed at my meeting with President Putin. Nothing will be done until the Ukrainian & Syrian problems are solved."

Trump was going to team up with the Russians to form a cybersecurity unit to prevent election hacking? Was he trying to be funny? Short of sharing our nuclear codes with the Kremlin, it is hard to imagine a crazier idea.

Donald Trump Jr., meanwhile, cast the Russian agent at the meeting, Natalia Veselnitskaya, as a woman who was "vague, ambiguous, and made no sense."

Said Trump Jr., "It quickly became clear that she had no meaningful information. Then she changed subjects and began talking about the adoption of Russian children and mentioned the Magnitsky Act." Trump Jr. concluded that this had been her primary purpose all along.

Veselnitskaya, backpedaling as fast as the Trump team, denied the discussion had anything to do with the presidential campaign, and she denied acting on behalf of the Russian government.

"I never discussed any of these matters with any representative of the Russian government," she said.

Trump Jr.'s problem was that the *New York Times* had copies of his emails. One of them was from Rob Goldstone, a British music publicist, who at the behest of a Russian client informed Trump Jr. that the information Veselnitskaya would give him at the meeting was from the Russia government's efforts to help his father win the presidency. Veselnitskaya worked for Yuri Chaika, Russia's prosecutor general.

When Trump Jr. learned that the *Times* had his emails, he hastily released them himself. In one of them, Goldstone promised him "information that would incriminate Hillary and her dealings with Russia and would be very useful to your father. The information is part of Russia and its government's support for Mr. Trump."

Replied Trump Jr., "If it is what you say, I love it, especially later in the summer."

Here was an operative of a foreign adversary giving the Trump campaign information on their opponent in an attempt to compromise the election. Most any other campaign operative would have called the FBI.

Instead Donald Trump Jr. replied, "I love it."

That night Trump Jr. was interviewed by Fox News sycophant Sean Hannity. Trump Jr. said that the meeting was "such a nothing." He also admitted he should have "done things a little differently."

On July 16, Jay Sekulow repeated the lie that President Trump wasn't involved in preparing the statement about the meeting with Natalia Veselnitskaya.

To this day, President Trump stands by his assertion that, if a foreign agent offers an American political candidate dirt on his opponent, the candidate should "listen" to what the agent has to say. As Trump said in a June 2019 interview with ABC's George Stephanopoulos, he could, of course, listen to the foreign agent and not call the FBI ("Who calls the FBI?"). When FBI Director Chris Wray countered with the view that a person presented with potentially stolen information should call the FBI, Trump said, "The FBI director is wrong."

The news of the various Russian connections to Trump and his team must have been weighing on him heavily, when on July 19, 2017, Trump in an interview with the *New York Times* complained bitterly about having appointed Jeff Sessions to be his attorney general. Sessions's recusal, Trump said, was "very unfair to the president." Trump wanted Sessions to un-recuse from the Russia investigation and rein in—or fire—Robert Mueller.

A day after that admission, Trump's legal team spokesperson, Mark Corallo, quit after only two months on the job. Trump that day reportedly asked his lawyers whether he could pardon his campaign team, his family members, and even himself should he be found guilty of collusion with the Russians. Incredibly, he even asked about his power to issue pardons in a Twitter rant.

"While all agree the U.S. President has the complete power to pardon, why think of that when only crime so far is LEAKS against us. FAKE NEWS . . . My son Donald openly gave his emails to the media & authorities whereas Crooked Hillary Clinton deleted (& acid washed) her 33,000 emails!"

In another display of anger, Trump again went after Sessions as well as Adam Schiff, the leading Democrat on the House Intelligence Committee.

"So why aren't the Committees and investigators, and of course our beleaguered A.G., looking into Crooked Hillarys crimes & Russia relations? . . . Attorney General Jeff Sessions has taken a VERY weak position on Hillary Clinton crimes (where are E-mails & DNC server) & Intel leakers! . . . Problem is that the acting head of the FBI & the person in charge of the Hillary investigation, Andrew McCabe, got $700,000 from H for wife!"

That day, July 25, 2017, the House passed sanctions on Russia. The vote was 419 to 3. The days of Putin thinking that Trump could make a deal and do away with American sanctions on Russia were over.

That same day FBI agents raided the home of Paul Manafort, collecting documents and computer files. In response, Trump again went after Sessions.

"Why didn't A.G. Sessions replace Acting FBI Director Andrew McCabe, a Comey friend who was in charge of Clinton investigation but got . . . big dollars ($700,000) for his wife's political run from Hillary Clinton and her representatives? Drain the Swamp!"

The next day George Papadopoulos was arrested at Dulles International Airport. (He later pleaded guilty to one count of making false statements to investigators.) Back in the Senate, despite opposition from Trump, the bill to *add* sanctions to Russia passed by a 98 to 2 vote.

On September 5, Putin commented, " [Trump is] not my bride, and I am not his groom."

In September 2017, Facebook agreed to provide congressional committees investigating Russian meddling with details about Russian bots that influenced the election. Trump tweeted, "What about the totally biased and dishonest Media coverage in favor of Hillary Clinton?"

When in late October 2017 it was revealed that Christopher Steele, the author of the dossier, had been hired by Marc Elias, a lawyer for the Clinton campaign after the initial funding by Republican opponents of Trump, Trump countered that the collusion with the Russians wasn't by his campaign, but rather Hillary Clinton's.

The noose tightened in late October when Paul Manafort and his aide Rick Gates turned themselves in to the FBI after being indicted for money laundering and making false statements. Trump fell back to the position that Manafort did what he was accused of, long before he joined the Trump campaign, and that the campaign had nothing to do with it. George Papadopoulos, meanwhile, made a plea deal with Robert Mueller to cooperate with prosecutors.

Since Robert Mueller took over the investigation in May 2017, it is clear that Trump had done all he could to obstruct the investigation. That is the focus of the entire second half of Mueller's 2019 report, which outlines a dozen separate incidents in which Trump obstructed justice in the investigation.

Mueller sought to question Trump about the firings of both Michael Flynn and James Comey, but to no avail. Trump made it clear that he would resist a one-on-one interview with Mueller. Mueller eventually decided to forgo this interview rather than delay the investigation for months, if not years. Waiting to interview Trump under court order (assuming Mueller was able to get a court order and defend it all the way to the Supreme Court) would have delayed considerably the release of the Mueller Report, which the House believed it needed to proceed with further investigations and possible impeachment. Not to mention the fact that, in any such interview, Trump likely would do what he does best—lie.

Mueller interviewed Andrew McCabe and Jeff Sessions. He interviewed Mark Corallo, the former spokesperson for Trump's legal team, and Hope Hicks, a longtime aide, about whether Trump obstructed justice. Corallo had resigned over his concern that Trump had done just that. Mueller interviewed White House counsel Don McGahn, who disclosed that Trump had ordered him to contact the Department of Justice to get Mueller fired. (Trump of course denies this ever happened.)

As Mueller was building cases against Paul Manafort and Michael Flynn, Trump's attorney John Dowd talked to Manafort and Flynn's personal attorneys about the possibility of both of them getting pardoned by Trump. There was a report in March 2018 that Manafort was considering just that option. Dangling pardons to witnesses was yet another instance where Trump sought to obstruct justice in the Mueller investigation.

In January 2018, Trump's attorneys wrote a letter to Mueller arguing that Trump as the president cannot obstruct justice, because the Constitution grants him full authority over all federal investigations.

"If he wished, [he could] terminate the inquiry, or even exercise his power to pardon."

In sum, Trump not only fired FBI Director Comey to stop the Russia investigation, but he was going to do everything possible to obstruct Mueller as well. The full details of his obstruction of the investigation were not made public until publication of Mueller's (heavily redacted) report in May 2019. It is very clear that Trump did a lot of obstructing.

When Comey went before the Senate Intelligence Committee in June 2017, he testified he was certain he had been fired because of Trump's concern about the Russia investigation, not because of the FBI investigation of Hillary Clinton's emails.

"I was fired, in some way, to change—or the endeavor was to change the way the Russia investigation was being conducted," Comey testified.

Comey also testified that three times he had told Trump he was not under investigation.

In response Trump tweeted that he felt "total and complete vindication."

On June 15, 2017, Trump went on what is now known as a tweet storm.

At 5:55 AM he tweeted, "They made up a phony collusion with the Russians story, found zero proof, so now they go to obstruction of justice on the phone story. Nice."

At 6:57 he tweeted, "You are witnessing the single greatest WITCH HUNT in American political history—led by some very bad and conflicted people! #MAGA."

At 2:34 PM Trump tweeted, "Why is that Hillary Clintons family and Dems dealing with Russia are not looked at, but my non-dealings are?"

Thirteen minutes later he added, "Crooked H destroyed phones w/ hammer, 'bleached' emails, & had husband meet w/AG days before she was cleared—& they talk about obstruction?"

Never mind that Hillary Clinton never personally destroyed her phone with a hammer. One of Clinton's aides told the FBI that, on two occasions, he disposed of her unwanted mobile devices by breaking or hammering them. Cell phone owners commonly destroy old phones to keep others from using them. Furthermore, it was true that Bill Clinton met with Attorney General Loretta Lynch days before Hillary Clinton was cleared of any wrongdoing with respect to her emails, but that had nothing to do with the Russia investigation. As usual, months after the 2016 presidential election, Trump deflected by playing the Hillary card.

A month later, in mid-July 2017, Trump threatened Mueller and his investigation, again calling it a "witch hunt" and warning Mueller that if he looked into his personal finances, that would be a "violation." Trump stated that any member of Mueller's team who had ever contributed to the Democratic Party was ethically compromised.

Trump and his team were reportedly stockpiling information to use against Mueller in order to discredit the investigation.

His spokesperson, Sarah Sanders, said that Trump reserved the right to remove Mueller.

By December 2017, experts were saying that Trump was trying to undermine the special counsel in order to sow doubt and shape public perception in the event Trump decided to pardon some of his officials who were being investigated or indicted by Mueller. If Americans believed Mueller was politically motivated, Trump thought, the political blowback from pardons would be less severe. Experts also said it was a better strategy than terminating Mueller, because of the storm of criticism that yet another firing would unleash after the Comey dismissal.

Mueller, meanwhile, continued his investigation, silent and resilient, his visage looming large over the Trump presidency. In April 2018 Mueller's team raided the home of Trump's fixer and personal lawyer Michael Cohen. Around that time, Trump pardoned Scooter Libby (former vice president Cheney's chief of staff, convicted of perjury a decade earlier) and the far-right commentator Dinesh D'Souza (convicted of felony campaign finance violations). Trump was accused of advertising his pardon power to say to those who Mueller indicted, including Cohen and former campaign manager Paul Manafort, that if they refused to cooperate with the special counsel, Trump would pardon them as well.

When in June 2018 Trump ramped up his attacks on Mueller, former CIA director John Brennan said of Trump, "Your fear of exposure is palpable. Your desperation even more so."

Brennan then asked, "When will those of conscience among your cabinet, inner circle, and Republican leadership realize that your unprincipled and unethical behavior, as well as your incompetence, are seriously damaging our nation?"

In July 2018 Trump returned to his rant against the Steele dossier, tweeting a series of false claims, including his charge that the 2016 FISA (a Foreign Intelligence Surveillance Act court) warrant application against Carter Page was responsible for starting Mueller's investigation. The final line of his tweet was that "Fake Dirty Dossier, that was paid for by Crooked Hillary Clinton and the DNC, that was knowingly and falsely submitted to FISA and which was responsible for starting the totally conflicted and discredited Mueller

Witch Hunt!" Here Trump picked up on another conspiracy theory—that the entire Russia investigation was a hoax the FBI had started under President Obama to gather incriminating information and falsely link the Trump campaign to the Russians. The FISA submissions had been made by the FBI to a FISA judge for purposes of obtaining search warrants because the FBI had suspected certain Trump associates of collaborating with the Russians. Trump now claimed these FISA warrants—approved by judges—were somehow part of a domestic spying conspiracy against him.

Trump also tweeted, "Carter Page wasn't a spy, wasn't an agent of the Russians—he would have cooperated with the FBI. It was a fraud and a hoax designed to target Trump."

In mid-August 2018, Trump tweeted that Mueller was "disgraced and discredited" all the while calling his team of prosecutors a "National Disgrace."

It soon became apparent that Trump's verbal barrage against Mueller was having little effect. A Fox News poll showed that 59 percent of registered voters approved of Mueller's investigation.

Initially, Trump's former campaign manager Paul Manafort, knowing himself to be in deep trouble for money laundering and other crimes, cooperated with the special counsel. But on November 27, 2018, Mueller accused Manafort of lying and breaking his cooperation agreement.

In response Trump went on another Twitter tirade:

"The Fake News Media builds Bob Mueller up as a Saint, when in actuality he is the exact opposite. He is doing TREMENDOUS damage to our Criminal Justice System, where he is only looking at one side and not the other. Heroes will come to this, and it won't be Mueller and his terrible gang of Angry Democrats. Look at their past, and look where they come from. The now $30,000,000 Witch Hunt continues and they've got nothing but ruined lives. Where is the Server? Let these terrible people go back to the Clinton Foundation and 'Justice' Department."

On December 7, 2018, Trump vowed to release a counter report to Mueller's findings and said eighty-seven pages were already written.

Plenty of right-wing political commentators were allies in Trump's all-out attack on the Justice Department, the FBI, and Mueller. When Mueller announced his first indictments in the Russia investigation in late October

2017, Sebastian Gorka, a former White House official, and Trump's long-time friend and advisor Roger Stone tweeted attacks on Mueller.

Tweeted Gorka, "I guess that both ex-G-Men have forgotten the 'I' in the @FBI motto stands for INTEGRITY."

He also tweeted, "If this man's team executes warrants this weekend he should [be] stripped of his authority by @realDonald Trump."

Stone was more sarcastic. He tweeted, "Breaking: Mueller indicts @ PaulManafort's maid for tearing labels of sofa cushions." And "Yeah, I hear Deep State stooge is indicting Manafort's driver for double parking, u little shithead."

Not to be outdone, Fox News's Sean Hannity tweeted, "This has been a HORRIBLE week for Mueller, Special Counsel's office. THIS IS ALL A DISTRACTION. Monday I'll have the details. TICK TOCK….!"

Some Republicans in Congress also came to Trump's defense. Representative Trent Franks called for Mueller to resign, saying Mueller was compromised because of his relationship with James Comey. Frank cited Trump's argument that Democratic donors funded the Steele dossier, which Republicans say was a phony document that set the Russia investigation in motion, and he cited a discredited report that Hillary Clinton was involved in the sale of uranium to a Russian company.

The attacks on Mueller seemed to have little traction.

But in December 2018 the attacks intensified. The more Mueller imperiled Trump, the more McCarthy-like Trump and his allies became in making unfounded accusations against career government officials, including Mueller. Their objective was to derail the investigation and bury the facts in falsehoods.

Former House Speaker Newt Gingrich said on Fox News, "Mueller is corrupt. The senior FBI is corrupt. The system is corrupt." House Speaker Paul Ryan, who had been sharply critical of Trump during the 2016 election, did nothing to defend Mueller or the investigation. Many in his GOP caucus were even worse in jumping on the anti-Mueller bandwagon.

And even the underlying accusation itself—collaboration with Russia—could be turned on its head. Fox legal analyst Gregg Jarrett exclaimed that Mueller was using the FBI "just like the old KGB."

Fox host Jeanine Pirro piled on, saying, "There is a cleansing needed at the FBI and Department of Justice. It needs to be cleansed of individuals who should not just be fired but need to be taken out in handcuffs."

Pirro was focusing on a relationship between two FBI agents, Peter Strzok and Lisa Page, who were having an affair and wrote text messages critical of Trump to each other. Strzok was reassigned from the Mueller team almost immediately, but the Republicans cited the texts as proof of bias. Pirro—laughably—would go on to call the FBI "a crime family" under the leadership of James Comey.

No longer were Trump and his Fox News allies and other right-wing commentators just arguing that the Russia probe was fake news and a witch hunt. Now they argued that the FBI probe was prejudiced against Trump because six of the fifteen FBI investigators had given money to Democratic candidates. (Never mind that the people at the top of the probe—Mueller, Rosenstein, FBI Director Christopher Wray, and former FBI director Comey—were all Republicans.) Undermining Mueller's investigation, they knew, was the key to saving Trump's presidency.

Three Republicans in the House of Representatives, Jim Jordan of Ohio, Matt Gaetz of Florida, and Devin Nunes of California, chairman of the House Intelligence Committee, all screamed for Mueller's dismissal and even prosecution. Representative Ron DeSantis of Florida, a House Judiciary member, called for the scope and funding of Mueller's investigation to be severely limited. DeSantis was richly rewarded with Trump's support during his campaign to become Florida's next governor.

Nunes, Jordan, and Gaetz had been secretly meeting with a group from the House Intelligence Committee to make the case that heads of the Justice Department and the FBI had mishandled the contents of the Steele dossier. In April 2018 it was revealed that Nunes, head of the House Intelligence Committee, was bringing classified information about the investigation to President Trump in the White House without telling the other members of the committee. Nunes was doing all he could to sabotage or even close down the House investigation. He even went so far as to threaten to issue a report exposing corruption at the FBI.

Other Republicans, however, worried that the attacks on the FBI and Justice Department would foster a distrust of our most important legal institutions.

Said Representative Charlie Dent of Pennsylvania, a moderate Republican, "Most of my Republican colleagues feel as I do that we have confidence in law enforcement. I don't know why that should change now that we have a Republican administration." Dent added that law enforcement officials should only be punished for their political opinions if they act on them.

Added Representative Thomas Rooney of Florida, "Those are political cheap shots that sound good on Fox News but in the real world are completely unfair to a guy who has given his life to serving this country."

Senator Marco Rubio of Florida, also a Republican, said, "From his reputation and everything I know about him, I remain convinced that when this is all said and done, Mueller is going to only pursue things that are true, and he will do it in a fair and balanced way." Rubio advised the president to allow Mueller to complete his investigation.

Hearing some Republicans uphold the rule of law was heartening, but it didn't slow the criticisms from Trump and his most loyal supporters. In March 2018 Devin Nunes, head of the House Intelligence Committee, announced that the Republicans on the committee had ended the investigation into Russian interference in the election and found no evidence of wrongdoing.

Meanwhile, Nunes continued to attack the Mueller investigation.

"A dangerous new era of alternative reality is advancing," said a March 14, 2018, op-ed in the *New York Times*, co-authored by former Republican representative Claudine Schneider of Rhode Island, "and House Republicans are signaling that, like their president, they intend to ignore, bend or assail truth to fight the Mueller investigation (and presumably that of the Senate Intelligence Committee as well, should it reach inconvenient conclusions)."

Trump, like all who spurn democracy in favor of oligarchy, had another extremely powerful ally in his attempts to thwart Robert Mueller and his investigation: Fox News commentator Sean Hannity, with whom President Trump had nightly conversations from his White House bedroom. According to *New York Magazine*, Trump and Hannity at night would discuss the Mueller "witch hunt." They also gabbed about media ratings, sports, and Kanye West.

Hannity, even from outside the White House, replaced Steve Bannon as Trump's most trusted advisor after Bannon left the White House team. The two would discuss next moves whenever Trump was criticized in the newspapers and on CNN and MSNBC. On his Fox News program, Hannity would blast away at the critics and heap congratulatory praise at Trump. More than anything, Hannity repeated Trump's false claims about Mueller and reverted to the notion that Hillary Clinton should have been indicted for her use of private emails.

Sean Hannity started his career as a shock jock on a college radio station, KCSB in Santa Barbara, California, but was fired after calling gays "disgusting people" who were "brainwashing" the public. Then he moved to Alabama to work at WVNN, and then to Georgia to work for WGST talk radio in Atlanta.

Roger Ailes hired him for Fox News in 1996. In 2011 he gave Trump a platform for his birtherism myth, and they became friends in 2016, when Hannity helped Trump get elected and Trump helped Hannity become a popular face of cable news.

Hannity on December 5, 2017, went on a ten-minute diatribe against Mueller. He said, "Let's start off with the head of the snake. Mueller's credibility is in the gutter tonight with these new discoveries; his conflicts of interests, his clear bias, the corruption are on full display. Mueller is frankly a disgrace to the American justice system and has put the country now on the brink of becoming a banana republic."

He blasted some of the investigators for being Democrats, called out "Mueller's band of Clinton lovers," and mentioned "$50,000 in donations to Democrats" from members of Mueller's team.

For months after Robert Mueller's appointment in May 2017, little was heard from the special counsel while Trump was filling the airways and newspapers with his tweets deriding Mueller and his investigation. As bad as the leaks had been in the White House, the opposite was true from Mueller's vaunted team of attorneys. The public—and the White House—had no idea what Mueller and his staff were up to.

Then on July 27, 2017, George Papadopoulos, Trump's former campaign foreign policy adviser, walked off a Lufthansa flight from Munich at Dulles International Airport where FBI agents met him and placed him under arrest. He was booked into the city detention center in Alexandria, Virginia, the next day.

Papadopoulos was charged with lying to the FBI about his contacts with pro-Russian advocates and with obstruction of justice.

When Papadoupolos, shaken, agreed to plead guilty and cooperate about Russian interference in the 2016 election, Mueller dropped the obstruction charge.

Reports trickled in about who Mueller was calling in to testify before a grand jury: first came Russian American lobbyist Rinat Akhmetshin, who had ties to Russian military counterintelligence and who was in the room when Donald Trump Jr., Paul Manafort, and Jared Kushner met with Natalia Veselnitskaya at the all-important June 9, 2016, Trump Tower meeting.

Other Trump appointees appeared before a grand jury. Paul Manafort's spokesman Jason Maloni presumably was asked about what Manafort told him about the Trump Tower meeting, and then came Keith Kellogg, who served as acting national security adviser to President Trump following the resignation of Michael Flynn. Kellogg was also an advisor to Trump during the campaign.

Mueller then interviewed former White House chief of staff Reince Priebus, former press secretary Sean Spicer, and Trump campaign foreign policy advisory member Sam Clovis. Clovis was asked what he knew about George Papadopoulos talking to the Russians.

None of this made much of an impression on the public, but then on October 30, 2017, Mueller's team brought a twelve-count indictment against Paul Manafort and his associate Rick Gates. Both were charged with being unregistered agents of the government of Ukraine. They were accused of generating tens of millions of dollars in income and hiding the money from US authorities.

According to the indictment, Manafort and Gates "laundered the money through scores of United States and foreign corporations, partnerships, and bank accounts." They did all of this to avoid detection of their violations of, among other laws, the Foreign Agents Registration Act of 1938 (FARA). Congress enacted FARA to require anyone working as an agent of a foreign government to register with the Department of Justice (in 1938, Germany, Japan, Italy, and the USSR topped the list of countries trying to influence the United States government, and the USSR and the former Soviet republics have been trying to infiltrate the US government in just about all of the eighty years since FARA was enacted).

In furtherance of the scheme, said the indictment, Manafort and Gates funneled millions of dollars in payments to foreign companies and bank accounts in foreign countries, all the while hiding the existence of these foreign companies and banks. They reported none of this money on their income tax forms.

As lobbyists on behalf of a foreign government, they were required to report their work and fees under FARA. Instead, they hid that information. When the Department of Justice asked them about it, they lied.

Said the indictment, "Manafort also used these offshore accounts to purchase multimillion-dollar properties in the United States. Manafort then borrowed millions of dollars in loans using these properties as collateral, thereby obtaining cash in the United States without reporting and paying taxes on the income. In order to increase the amount of money he could access in the United States, Manafort defrauded the institutions that loaned money on these properties so that they would lend him more money at more favorable rates than he would otherwise be able to obtain."

More than $75 million flowed through the offshore accounts. Manafort laundered more than $18 million, which he used to buy property, goods, and services in the United States, income that he concealed from the United States Treasury, the Department of Justice, and others. Gates transferred more than $3 million from the offshore accounts to other accounts he controlled.

Anyone who read the indictment would have been overwhelmed by Manafort and Gates's incredible lawlessness. The question, of course, was why Trump chose Manafort to be his campaign chairman and Gates to be Manafort's right-hand man. The man who would soon become president of the United States could not keep an unregistered foreign agent out of the top job in his own political campaign—or perhaps Trump knew and didn't care.

On the day Papadopoulos's name surfaced again, it was reported that he had signed a statement admitting he had lied to the FBI.

More interviews followed. In early November 2017, Jared Kushner was asked about the role of Michael Flynn. Stephen Miller, a Trump advisor, was interviewed, as was Don McGahn. Then on December 1, Michael Flynn,

Trump's former national security advisor (who only lasted in that job for a few weeks in early 2017 before he was forced to resign), pleaded guilty to lying to the FBI about conversations with Russian ambassador Sergey Kislyak, part of a coordinated effort by Trump and his appointees to form foreign policy even before taking office and while Obama was still president.

Flynn agreed to cooperate with the investigation in exchange for leniency for his son, who had some exposure to charges on related matters, and a lighter sentence for himself. Flynn agreed to testify about Trump's efforts to get the FBI to shut down the Flynn investigation.

If Trump had promised to lift the Obama administration's US sanctions against Russia in exchange for Russian help in winning the 2016 election, Flynn would very likely have been involved. He was certainly a key witness. An express quid pro quo agreement between Trump and the Russians on such a deal probably would have been bribery even if Trump did not hold public office at the time the deal was made.

But there also could have been a "wink-wink, nod-nod" that fell short of proverbial criminal bribery. Mueller would have to find out. Discovering what had happened—whether or not Trump associates' actions with the Russians were *criminal*—was an important point of Mueller's investigation. It should be kept in mind that the suspected quid pro quo in this instance was highly unusual in that it did not involve a deal between a US political candidate and US nationals—for example a domestic bank, healthcare company, or fossil fuel company contributing PAC money to a politician—but a foreign government that since the 1917 Russian Revolution had been committed to undermining, and even overthrowing, the US government.

Any express or implied quid pro quo with the Russians, or any dependency between the Russians and a US candidate, much less a US president, was a cause for enormous concern for US national security. Allowing the Mueller investigation to proceed—and witnesses such as Flynn to testify fully and truthfully—should have been an utmost priority for any loyal American.

If Trump had been innocent, and at all rational, completing the Mueller investigation without interference on his part would have been his priority as well.

Hope Hicks, the White House communications director, was interviewed in December 2017 about Trump's conversations with Russians and the doings of Paul Manafort, with whom she also worked. Mueller in mid-January 2018 then interviewed Attorney General Jeff Sessions as Mueller began to focus on Trump's behavior in office, whether the president was attempting to obstruct justice by firing FBI Director James Comey, as well as possible ties to the Russians. As head of the Trump campaign's foreign policy team, Sessions had met with Russians. That was why Sessions had recused himself from the investigation.

Silence once again fell on the investigation until February 16, 2018, when Mueller indicted thirteen Russian nationals and three organizations linked to the Internet Research Agency, known in Russia as the Kremlin's troll factory. These were the Russians who conducted the information warfare on Hillary Clinton for the benefit of Donald Trump. According to Mueller, the disinformation campaign began in 2014 and continued through the election. The goal was "to sow discord in the United States political system." The Russians posted derogatory information about a number of candidates and bought ads and communicated with "unwitting" people tied to the Trump campaign and others.

The indictment included a February 2016 memo to the staff of the Internet Research Agency telling them to post political content on US social media sites and "use any opportunity to criticize Hillary and the rest (except [Bernie] Sanders and Trump—we support them)." Twelve of those indicted worked for the Internet Research Agency. One of those charged was Yevgeny Prigozhin, an oligarch who controlled Concord Catering, a group that funded the Internet Research Agency. The indictment said the company spent more than $1.25 million a month during the election year. Some defendants traveled to the United States to gather intelligence.

On that day Richard Pinedo, an unknown figure, pleaded guilty to identity fraud for selling stolen bank account numbers to Russians involved in election interference. He transferred, possessed, and used strangers' identities so that the Russians could have PayPal accounts under fake names. He faces up to fifteen years in prison and a $250,000 fine. He agreed to cooperate with Mueller's investigation.

On February 20, 2018, Alex van der Zwaan, a Dutch lawyer, pleaded guilty to lying to the FBI about working with Rick Gates and an individual identified as "Person A." On February 22, Mueller filed thirty-two additional charges against Manafort and Gates, accusing them of money laundering and bank fraud. A day later, Gates cut a deal with Mueller.

The next day a federal grand jury indicted Manafort, alleging he had "secretly retained a group of former senior European politicians to take positions favorable to the Ukraine, including lobbying in the United States."

Everyone wondered, *What was that all about?*

On April 3, 2018, the mysterious Alex van der Zwaan was sentenced to thirty days in jail and $20,000 in fines for lying to FBI investigators. Van der Zwaan was the first person indicted by Mueller to go to jail.

Then, on April 9, 2018, Mueller made headlines when the FBI raided the hotel room and office of Trump's personal advisor and "fixer," Michael Cohen. A month later Mueller brought new charges against Manafort and also charged Konstantin Kilimnik, a former aide to Manafort with suspected ties to Russian intelligence. Manafort and Kilimnik were both charged with conspiracy and obstruction of justice for attempting to get others to lie in their testimony. Mueller also charged Manafort with conspiracy to launder money, acting as an unregistered foreign agent, and lying to authorities.

The next broadside of indictments was filed on July 13, 2018, when Mueller indicted twelve Russian military intelligence officers for hacking and releasing the Democratic emails during the 2016 presidential campaign.

A month later, on August 21, Manafort was found guilty in a Virginia courtroom of eight counts of fraud. That same day Michael Cohen—in a separate case brought by the United States Attorney for the Southern District of New York—pleaded guilty in a Manhattan courtroom to eight counts of tax fraud and campaign finance violations. Some of these charges arose out of Cohen's payment on behalf of an unindicted co-conspirator, "Individual 1," of $130,000 in hush money to Stormy Daniels in exchange for her silence about her affair with Donald Trump. Individual 1 is no doubt Donald Trump himself.

On September 7, Papadopoulos was sentenced to fourteen days in prison for lying to the FBI. On November 29, Michael Cohen pleaded guilty to lying to Congress about what he knew about the proposal for a Trump Tower deal in Moscow.

On December 12, 2018, Michael Cohen was sentenced to three years in prison on charges relating to campaign finance violations, tax evasion, and lying to Congress.

To the public this didn't sound like much, but Mueller was slowly putting the large jigsaw puzzle together, and when combined with Trump's actions to strengthen Russia and to weaken America, it was becoming clearer and clearer that if Trump wasn't in Putin's pocket, either voluntarily or because of blackmail, then Trump certainly had enough of a bromance with Putin to do his bidding. Why did Trump change the Republican Party's platform on Ukraine to benefit Putin? How was it that Trump derided NATO and treated the English and German leaders terribly while praising Putin for his leadership?

Why and how indeed.

Whether or not an express quid pro quo with the Russians could be proven, there was strong *circumstantial* evidence of a close relationship between Trump and Russia—a *dependency* at minimum. For years we have grown accustomed to hearing that so and so is "the oil companies' man in the Senate," or "the bankers' man in the House," even if bribery indictments are almost never handed down. Now we confront the extremely dangerous situation that the Russians could have their man in the White House.

Trump could see that Mueller slowly but surely was closing in. Trump knew that conclusions from the investigation would be rich fodder for his impeachment and possible removal from office. With the aid of his White House legal team, Trump rolled out a couple more tricks to hinder the investigation and prevent the issuance of Mueller's final report.

CHAPTER 28

The Supreme Court

He [George Washington] may have had a bad past. Who knows?
—DONALD TRUMP

TRUMP KNEW HE NEEDED THE COURTS ON HIS SIDE TO blunt, if not stop, the Mueller investigation and any future congressional investigations should the Democrats win control of the House (which they did in 2018). If he could pack the courts, and in particular the United States Supreme Court, with judges who believed philosophically in virtually unlimited presidential power ("unitary executive theory") and who believed in presidential immunity from investigations, he could avoid investigations, avoid complying with subpoenas, and ultimately get himself off the hook for wrongdoing.

The ghost of Richard Nixon has always loomed large over Trump. The *United States v. Nixon* case was a turning point in the Watergate scandal, and if the Supreme Court had not ordered Nixon to turn over the White House tapes to the special prosecutor, Nixon almost certainly would have survived the scandal and served the rest of his term. Trump did not want to go down the road that Nixon did; this explains much of his obsession with trying to silence the *Washington Post*, which had blown the lid off Watergate. Nixon lost in the Supreme Court and as a result lost his presidency. But for President Ford's pardon, he might have gone to jail. Trump was determined not to lose the Supreme Court.

Trump was already blessed with a Supreme Court much more conservative than the Supreme Court of the 1970s, and furthermore, Trump hoped to appoint "loyal" justices of his own. Squarely on his side in confirming new judges and justices were Republicans in the Senate, and an army of conservative media pundits, provided the judges Trump appointed weren't just strong believers in executive power (unitary executive theory) but also conservative on social issues such as abortion, sympathetic to business, and committed to states' rights.

When Justice Antonin Scalia died in early 2016, Mitch McConnell, the Senate majority leader, set it up for the winner of the 2016 presidential election to choose the next Supreme Court justice by vowing not to allow the Senate to vote on President Barack Obama's nomination of Judge Merrick Garland.

When the Republicans kept control of the Senate and Trump was elected, the Republicans had clear sailing to swing the court. Trump on January 31, 2017, named Neil Gorsuch, a federal appeals court judge based in Denver. Democrats, still fuming over the failure of the Republicans to take up the nomination of Merrick Garland, were enraged at Trump's more conservative choice. But Republicans had the votes and Gorsuch was confirmed. Thus far, Justice Gorsuch has sided with the Trump administration in most executive power cases, although it's not certain how he would rule if a case related to a congressional subpoena or an impeachment investigation were to come before the court.

Then in June 2018, Justice Anthony Kennedy announced he was retiring. Kennedy was the critical swing vote on the court.

On July 8, 2018, Trump nominated Brett Kavanaugh, a judge of the United States Court of Appeals for the District of Columbia Circuit.

He is "one of the finest and sharpest legal minds in our time," said Trump, who with a straight face said that Kavanaugh, if appointed, would put aside his political views and apply the Constitution "as written."

Kavanaugh's views on executive power were in line with Trump's. Even though he had been a top lawyer for Ken Starr in his investigation of President Bill Clinton, Kavanaugh's years as a White House lawyer and then staff secretary for President Bush had convinced Kavanaugh that in fact the president should almost never be investigated for anything while in office. Kavanaugh not only changed his mind on presidential immunity but wrote it down in a detailed 2009 article in the *Minnesota Law Review*. Although Kavanaugh never expressly called for *United States v. Nixon* to be overruled, there were strong hints that he might severely narrow its scope if a similar case were to come before the court involving President Trump.

Kavanaugh's publication record made him the perfect court pick. Whether Mueller were to seek White House communications (a repeat of the *United States v. Nixon* showdown over the White House tapes in 1974), or Congress were to issue subpoenas to administration officials (in 2019 dozens of such subpoenas were issued, most of them ignored), or the New York attorney general were to try to indict Trump while he was in office, Trump needed all the help he could get on the court. Large chunks of a future court opinion—or at least the opinion that Trump wanted—were already published, with Kavanaugh's name on them in the *Minnesota Law Review*. Or so Trump surely thought when he nominated Kavanaugh.

Then the plan almost fell apart. In September 2018, before his confirmation hearing, several women said that they had been sexually assaulted by Kavanaugh decades earlier when he was in high school and during his first year of college at Yale. One, Christine Blasey Ford, told the *Washington Post* that when she was fifteen and he was seventeen, Kavanaugh had assaulted her at a party. She said Kavanaugh pinned her on the bed, tried to take off her clothes, and covered her mouth to keep her from screaming.

"I thought he might inadvertently kill me," she said.

At the time of the assault, Blasey Ford was a student at the Holton-Arms School, a private girls' prep school in Bethesda, Maryland. Kavanaugh was a student at Georgetown Prep, an all-boys Catholic prep school where traditional Jesuit values apparently were not always observed—Kavanaugh's classmate and best friend Mark Judge later wrote a book about their high school years titled *Wasted.*

Blasey Ford testified for several hours before the Senate Judiciary Committee, and many observers believed her to be credible. She told the panel, "I am here today not because I want to be. I am terrified. I am here because I believe it is my civic duty to tell you what happened to me while Brett Kavanaugh and I were in high school."

Further allegations against Kavanaugh were brought by two other women, Deborah Ramirez (a Yale classmate) and Julie Swetnick (whose allegations also involved parties during Kavanaugh's years at Georgetown Prep when she was in high school).

At this point the appropriate course of action for the White House was to do what the George H. W. Bush White House had done when allegations were made against Judge Clarence Thomas during his confirmation hearing in 1991. That was to have the FBI thoroughly investigate the allegations so a report could be made to the Senate before a vote on the nomination. Although the Trump White House eventually relented and asked the FBI to conduct the investigation, it took weeks to begin because the White House, its allies in the media, and several senators, most notably Lindsey Graham, decried the need for an investigation claiming that this was yet another "witch hunt."

Whether it was Trump's hatred of FBI investigations or his desire to ram through the Kavanaugh nomination at any cost, this stubborn refusal even to investigate made the situation even worse. In the end the FBI investigation took less than a week, a fraction of the time spent arguing about whether there should be an investigation.

Kavanaugh's response to Blasey Ford's story was angry and defiant. He blamed the Democrats.

"You sowed the wind for decades to come," he said. "I fear that the whole country will reap the whirlwind."

His face showing his rage, he told the committee, "This whole two-week effort has been a calculated and orchestrated political hit, fueled with apparent pent-up anger about President Trump and the 2016 election. Fear that has been unfairly stoked about my judicial record. Revenge on behalf of the Clintons, and millions of dollars of money from outside left-wing opposition groups."

If Trump had ever considered pulling the nomination, this testimony no doubt made Kavanaugh an even more attractive Supreme Court justice in Trump's eyes. Having been on the receiving end of an investigation—or "witch hunt"—Kavanaugh would be virtually certain to sympathize with Trump in his own predicament. And Kavanaugh had even mentioned in his testimony Trump's favorite targets of denunciation—the Clintons! He was the perfect Trump Supreme Court justice.

This was fantasy straight out of the Salem witch trials. When accused of something, simply turn the tables and accuse your accuser, someone who supports your accuser, or someone else.

Kavanaugh's speech got rave reviews in the right-wing media. One conservative pundit with no hint of irony even called it a "Churchillian" moment.

Senator Lindsey Graham bolstered Kavanaugh's absurd claim of a left-wing conspiracy when he said that the Democratic handling of Blasey Ford's claims was an "unethical sham" and "the most despicable thing I have seen in my time in politics."

Whether or not one believed Blasey Ford's recollection of events thirty-five years earlier, or of the identity of her attacker at that party, it is absurd to attack a witness in this manner. Even a vote to confirm Kavanaugh in the face of this factual uncertainty did not require such a denunciation of Blasey Ford or of the Democrats who wanted to give her testimony a fair hearing. But for Trump and Lindsey Graham, the battle was to be won at all costs, even if that required denunciation of the confirmation process itself and of anyone who participated in it.

After the confirmation of Justice Kavanaugh, Trump continued to do everything possible to obstruct the Mueller investigation and now is doing everything possible to obstruct subsequent investigations by Congress, including the House Judiciary Committee investigation that by 2019 had clearly become an impeachment investigation.

The Trump administration thus far has ignored many of the House of Representatives' subpoenas, refusing to turn over the president's tax returns, the redacted portions of the Mueller Report, and other critical information. If any cases related to those investigations ever reach the Supreme Court, Trump hopes that he has two new justices on his side.

One thing America learned from the Mueller investigation—and the Kavanaugh hearing—was not only how much Trump and his allies hated thorough investigations of credible evidence of wrongdoing, but the lengths that they were willing to go to stop an investigation—and to personally attack anyone who dared say that allegations of any sort should be taken seriously.

CHAPTER 29

Barr's Inside Job

In William Barr, Donald Trump Has Finally Found His Roy Cohn.
—THE NATION

HAVING SECURED THE APPOINTMENT OF TWO SUPREME Court justices, Trump went about cleaning up his own Department of Justice—or rather cleaning out people who weren't Trump loyalists.

That was his idea of "draining the swamp."

Trump's lawyers, particularly his private lawyers, told him that he could do anything he wanted to do at the Department of Justice.

Private lawyer William Barr, who had previously served as attorney general under President George H. W. Bush, wrote a memorandum for defense lawyers in the Mueller investigation arguing much the same: the president could not be criminally charged for obstructing his own executive branch investigation by firing people in the Justice Department. The president's executive power over the Justice Department was near absolute.

Barr—touting this extreme version of unitary executive theory—had interviewed with Donald Trump to be his personal attorney in the investigation. Barr was never paid for any of this work, but he was clearly looking for an appointment of some sort. Trump obviously liked Barr's views on executive power and eventually found a job for him.

But first, on November 8, 2018, Trump, desperate to find a way to submarine the Mueller investigation, after firing Jeff Sessions, appointed Matthew Whitaker to be acting attorney general.

Whitaker, who in 2004 had been appointed United States attorney for the Southern District of Iowa by George W. Bush, had helped run Texas governor Rick Perry's presidential campaign in 2012. Whitaker ran for the US Senate in 2014 and lost. That same year, he was a paid advisor for World Patent Marketing, a company shut down by federal regulators for cheating customers out of $26 million. Before the 2016 election he had been paid over $900,000 to head a nonprofit organization, FACT, that focused almost exclusively on the "unethical" conduct of Hillary Clinton. Where FACT got its dollars (assuming they raised dollars rather than rubles) is not known. Nonprofit organizations, even very political ones, do not need to disclose their donors.

Whitaker had been Jeff Sessions's chief of staff. He had publicly auditioned for the appointment to replace Sessions by criticizing the Mueller investigation on CNN, calling it a lynch mob "going too far." He suggested the investigation could be closed down by "starving it of resources." He also said that if Mueller investigated the president's finances, it "would raise serious concerns that the special counsel's investigation was a mere witch hunt."

Whitaker in July 2017 appeared as a legal commentator on CNN and mused about whether Trump might fire Sessions and appoint a temporary replacement.

"That temporary replacement," Whitaker said in one of his commentaries, "could move to choke off Mueller's funding. So I could see a scenario where Jeff Sessions is replaced with a recess appointment, and that attorney general doesn't fire Bob Mueller, but he just reduces his budget to so low that his investigation grinds to almost a halt."

Whitaker also wrote an op-ed piece for CNN entitled "Mueller investigation of Trump is going too far," in which he urged Rod Rosenstein to "limit the scope of the investigation."

Whitaker scoffed at the idea that Trump had done anything wrong during his Trump Tower meeting with the Russians.

"You would always take the meeting," Whitaker said. He apparently saw no difference between a meeting with an American industry group or union, and a meeting with Russian agents promising to deliver dirt on an opponent.

Whitaker was fishing for a new job.

Apparently, Trump felt Whitaker's history was perfect for his personal attorney general.

Under most circumstances Rod Rosenstein, the deputy attorney general, should have been appointed. But Rosenstein was honest and he wasn't loyal, and Trump didn't want that. Whitaker got the appointment instead, even though he had never been confirmed by the Senate for *any* position in the Trump administration (under the Vacancies Act, an acting cabinet-level appointment is supposed to be granted to someone who has been confirmed by the Senate for whatever position they currently hold, but this legal "technicality" was simply ignored).

On November 14, 2018, in an interview on the Daily Caller, Trump was asked who he might nominate to be the new permanent attorney general.

Naming Whitaker, Trump said, "As far as I'm concerned this is an investigation that never should have been brought. It's an illegal investigation."

Democrats saw his appointment as part of Trump's "pattern of obstruction."

When asked, Trump denied he had ever read or heard about Whitaker's criticism of the Mueller investigation.

"There is no collusion," said Trump. "He happened to have been right. I think he's astute politically. He's going to do what's right."

The reaction was swift and harsh.

"In appointing Matthew Whitaker as acting attorney-general," commented Steve Denning in *Forbes* magazine, "President Trump again risks appearing to obstruct justice in plain sight."

Commented Denning, "If President Trump had taken these steps in secret, they would have constituted elements for a complaint of obstructing justice. The fact that they were done in plain view of the public doesn't make them any less questionable."

A top Justice Department official who refused to identify himself said he and a group of four Justice Department officials met with Whitaker three times to advise him on the ethics and transition to the job. The advice was to recuse himself out of an "abundance of caution."

Whitaker refused.

Conservative lawyer George Conway and former acting solicitor general of the United States Neal Katyal wrote an editorial in the *New York Times* saying that Trump's appointment of Whitaker was unconstitutional under the appointment clause of the Constitution, which provides:

> [The President] shall nominate, and by and with the Advice and Consent of the Senate, shall appoint Ambassadors, other public Ministers and Consuls, Judges of the supreme Court, and all other Officers of the United States, whose Appointments are not herein otherwise provided for, and which shall be established by Law: but the Congress may by Law vest the Appointment of such inferior Officers, as they think proper, in the President alone, in the Courts of Law, or in the Heads of Departments.

Whitaker was not a "principal officer," who reports directly to the president because he had never been confirmed by the Senate to any position. Because he was not a principal officer, his appointment to be acting attorney general would have to be ratified by the Senate.

As a result, said Conway and Katyal, anything Whitaker did as acting attorney general would be invalid. The two lawyers concluded, "We cannot tolerate such an evasion of the Constitution's very explicit, textually precise design. Senate confirmation exists for a simple, and good, reason. Constitutionally, Matthew Whitaker is a nobody. His job as Mr. Session's chief of staff did not require Senate confirmation. (Yes, he was confirmed as a federal prosecutor in Iowa, in 2004, but Mr. Trump can't cut and paste that old, lapsed confirmation [from the Bush administration] to today.) For the president to install Mr. Whitaker as our chief law enforcement officer is to betray the entire structure of our charter document."

Commentators also wondered what Whitaker would do with the Mueller Report once Mueller submitted it to the Department of Justice. Would Trump's handpicked errand boy give the report over to Congress, or to Trump's television lawyer, Rudy Giuliani? Would Whitaker edit the report with "redactions" before allowing Congress to see it? Would he ignore a subpoena from the House of Representatives seeking the full unredacted report?

In Trump's war with the FBI and the Justice Department to avoid being impeached, his opponents realized he would take any steps necessary to protect himself from the Mueller investigation. But with Conway and other lawyers checkmating him with unassailable arguments under the Vacancies Act and the Constitution, the Whitaker appointment was a bridge too far.

Trump's plan to hire Whitaker for his "inside job"—undermining the Mueller investigation from inside the Justice Department—was not going to work.

After three weeks of listening to the harsh conclusions of Whitaker's critics, Trump decided to pick someone else, and on December 8, 2018, he named William Barr to the post.

Barr had already been the attorney general under George H. W. Bush from 1991 to 1993. He was widely respected in Washington, at least among Republicans, and his confirmation by a Republican Senate was just about a sure thing. Mueller had served as an assistant attorney general in charge of the criminal division when Barr was attorney general. Barr was the perfect person to try to rein in Mueller.

And Barr appeared more than willing to do just that. Barr had written an op-ed in the *Washington Post* defending Trump's right to fire Jim Comey. Barr argued that since Comey, the FBI director, wasn't really in charge of the investigation, which was the responsibility of the Justice Department, "Comey's removal simply has no relevance to the integrity of the Russian investigation as it moves ahead."

Barr had offered other negative comments about the investigation. He noted that a number of Mueller's prosecutors had made contributions to the Democratic Party. In 2017, in a conversation with the *Washington Post,* Barr said that "prosecutors who make political contributions are identifying fairly strongly with a political party. I would have liked Mueller to have more balance in this group." No mention of the fact that Mueller himself was a Republican who had worked with Barr in a Republican administration.

Barr also said that the Clintons should have been investigated for their ties to a uranium mining firm that had benefited from a decision Hillary Clinton made while she was secretary of state. The Justice Department was wrong, he said, for not investigating her. Red meat for Donald Trump and Fox News.

In fact, Barr was already working on the Mueller investigation—for the defense. After Trump fired James Comey, Barr wrote a twenty-page memo, circulated to the defense lawyers representing targets of the Mueller investigation, saying that Trump could not be found to have obstructed justice when he fired the FBI director. Barr wrote that it was "quite understandable that the administration would not want an FBI director who did not recognize established limits on his power. . . Mueller should not be permitted to demand that the president submit to interrogation about alleged obstruction. Apart from whether Mueller has a strong enough factual basis for doing so, Mueller's obstruction theory is fatally misconceived."

Barr had actually interviewed with Trump to join his private defense team, and very likely would have been offered that position if Trump had not preferred to hire Barr to help him handle the investigation from the inside. And that could most effectively be done from inside the Department of Justice itself.

Observers noted that when President George H. W. Bush in 1993 pardoned six men convicted of offenses as part of the Iran-Contra investigation, Barr approved. He clearly knew how to handle pardons—including the preemptive pardons that Trump might need to reduce the likelihood of cooperating witnesses in the Mueller investigation.

Barr, because he had already been attorney general, could easily be confirmed by the Senate, and in his public statements and his actual work for the defense team in the Mueller investigation, could be counted upon to execute Trump's plan for an "inside job."

With Barr firmly in place as attorney general—in effect Mueller's boss for the length of the investigation—Trump's plan to obstruct the investigation would be complete.

At his Senate confirmation hearing on January 12, 2019, Barr said forcefully that he intended to leave Mueller alone to finish his investigation and that he would bring it to the public after it was written. "It is in the best interest of everyone—the president, Congress, and, most importantly, the American people—that this matter be resolved by allowing the special counsel to complete his work."

He added: "I will follow the special counsel regulations scrupulously and in good faith, and on my watch, Bob will be allowed to finish."

He then backtracked by repeatedly telling the Senate Judiciary Committee that he was committed to making as much information public *as he can* about Special Counsel Mueller's investigation. Barr suggested that what would eventually be released might not be Mueller's report or even a redacted version of it, but instead a report from the attorney general on what the special counsel had concluded.

"Under the current regulations, the special counsel report is confidential, and the report that goes public would be a report by the attorney general," Barr told lawmakers.

Those caring about the rule of law were horrified, but it was music to President Trump's ears.

But it was wrong.

As attorney general, Barr *should not have had anything to do with the Mueller investigation.* He had already participated as a lawyer on the side of the defense; he had written a detailed memo for the defense lawyers, and had even interviewed with Donald Trump himself to join that team. It was *unconscionable* that Barr would now be allowed to supervise the prosecution and decide what to do with Mueller's report. That would be the ultimate inside job. Both federal ethics rules (5 CFR Section 2635.502) and American Bar Association ethics rules for lawyers (Model Rule 1.11(d)) specifically address this issue by requiring recusal of a government lawyer in these circumstances.

The government lawyer must recuse from an investigation or other party matter in which he has already participated in the private sector unless the conflict is waived by a supervisor or someone else with authority to waive the conflict.

And of course there's the rub. Barr's supervisor was none other than Donald Trump. And Trump was more than happy to waive the conflict. Ethics experts cried foul, saying that Donald Trump, as a target of the Mueller investigation, could not give Barr this consent, and that agency ethics lawyers instead should be heeded. But the Senate did not care and confirmed Barr anyway without any promise from him to recuse from the Mueller investigation.

In sum, not only could Trump fire FBI directors and attorneys general in order to stop the Mueller investigation, but he also could order his new attorney general to switch sides from working for the defense to supervising the prosecution.

Why? Because Trump is president. Many of Trump's supporters embrace the view that a president—under an extremely broad interpretation of the unitary executive theory championed by conservative constitutional law scholars whenever a Republican is president—can do just about *anything* he wants.

If he wants, he can be an American Nero.

CHAPTER 30

The Mueller Report

MUELLER FINISHED THE INVESTIGATION A FEW WEEKS after Barr's confirmation. Mueller submitted his four-hundred-page report to the attorney general. He had already indicted Trump associate Roger Stone and over a dozen Russian agents (who remained in Russia and refused to show up for trial). Mueller had obtained criminal convictions against Trump's campaign manager Paul Manafort, his deputy campaign manager Rick Gates, Trump campaign operative George Papadopoulos, and Trump's former top national security advisor in the White House, Michael Flynn.

Mueller did not indict President Trump, any members of his family, or anyone in the Trump campaign for criminal conspiracy with the Russians. Mueller's report, divided into two parts, explained the facts that the investigation had uncovered in two key areas: First, collaboration between the Trump campaign and the Russians and whether or not such collaboration was criminal, and, second, Trump's efforts to stop the investigation and whether Trump had criminally obstructed justice.

Upon receiving Mueller's report, Attorney General Barr could have released the full text or at least the summary portions of the report that had already been prepared by Mueller's team. The report did not need another summary.

Instead Barr prepared his own four-page summary letter to Congress. This letter was inaccurate at best. Barr concluded that Mueller could not prove collusion with the Russians. (Wrong—Mueller had not said there was no collusion; rather, Mueller said that whatever happened there was not sufficient evidence to prove a *criminal conspiracy* between the Trump campaign and the Russians.) As for the charge of obstruction of justice, Barr said that "while the report does not conclude that the President committed a crime, it also doesn't exonerate him." An understatement to say the least.

Barr said he would make the Mueller Report public after "determining what can be released in light of applicable law, regulations, and departmental polices."

Trump gloated.

Before getting on Air Force One on March 24, 2019, Trump reacted to Barr's finding.

"It was just announced," he said. "There was no collusion with Russia, the most ridiculous thing I've ever heard. There was no collusion with Russia. There was no obstruction and none whatsoever. And it was a complete and total exoneration.

"It's a shame our country had to go through this. To be honest, it's a shame your president had to go through this. Before I ever got elected it began. And it began illegally. And hopefully someone is going to look at the other side. This was an illegal takedown that failed. And hopefully someone is going to be looking at the other side. It's complete exoneration. No collusion. No obstruction.

"Thank you very much."

Two days later in the Oval Office, Trump said about the Mueller investigation, "A lot of people out there that have done some very, very evil things, very bad things. I would say treasonous things about our country."

Lindsey Graham, who had spent the afternoon playing golf with Trump at Mar-a-Largo, held a news conference to announce that the Senate Judiciary Committee, which he chaired, would launch an investigation into what he called "all of the abuse by the Department of Justice and the FBI" during the 2016 election.

"Time to investigate the Obama officials who concocted and spread the Russian conspiracy hoax," wrote Kentucky senator Rand Paul, another who golfed with Trump.

Commented Sean Hannity on Fox News, "We will hold every deep-state official who abused power accountable. We will hold every fake news media liar accountable. We will hold every liar in Congress accountable."

White House counselor Kellyanne Conway called on House Intelligence Committee chairman Adam Schiff to resign. House minority leader Kevin McCarthy also called for Schiff to resign.

Barr's wildly inaccurate summary of the Mueller Report allowed the Trump media machine inside and outside the White House to swing into action and call the entire investigation a hoax.

Barr's title was attorney general of the United States, but he had actually joined the Department of Alternative Facts.

Barr stalled for four more weeks before releasing a redacted portion of the Mueller Report. All the public got was his four-page "summary." These four weeks gave the Trump spin machine more than enough time to tilt the story—and gave the public a chance to forget about the Mueller investigation.

Finally, in late April 2019, the Mueller Report was released to Congress and the public. Actually, it wasn't. A heavily redacted version of the Mueller Report was released.

Several excuses were given for these redactions. Some information was classified. This information could be shared with members of Congress who have security clearances, but that hasn't happened. Some of the redacted information relates to pending grand jury investigations, suggesting that there are more criminal cases related to the Mueller Report. This information, however, can be shared confidentially with members of Congress, with permission from the federal judge overseeing the grand jury. This hasn't happened because Barr's Justice Department hasn't bothered to ask the judge. Yet other information is redacted because of "privacy" concerns for unindicted persons. A lot of Trump family and perhaps Kushner family financial information, as well as information about personal connections in Russia, may very well fall into this category. We don't know—it's all redacted.

Most of the redactions are in the first half of the Mueller Report concerning collusion with the Russians. All we know is that Mueller found that the collusion did not amount to a provable criminal conspiracy under federal law.

Because much of the report is redacted, we cannot discern:

1. The extent of the collusion;
2. The extent of Russia ties; or
3. Whether President Trump, high-ranking members of his administration, or his family are vulnerable to blackmail by the Russians, or could even be working for the Russians.

Congress—which has not been allowed to see the redacted portions of the report—can't discern these facts either.

What do we know from the unredacted portions of the Mueller Report?

We will not provide a comprehensive summary of the report. The report is easily available online, and Americans should read the entire report—all of it. Americans should also demand that the redacted portions be revealed.

But a few highlights follow.

The first part of the report addresses collusion with the Russians. It is obvious that there was plenty of collusion, much of which we knew about before the report was released. This includes the Trump Tower meeting with a Russian agent about "dirt" on Hillary Clinton, as well as a Trump campaign "coffee boy" meeting with his Russian handler in the UK.

Discussed also are the various Trump campaign contacts with WikiLeaks, which, about the same time, was being contacted by Russian spies with information hacked from Democratic National Committee email and other email accounts associated with Clinton.

There was plenty of collusion—and that's only what we know about from the unredacted portion of the Mueller Report. Contacts with the Russians that the public did not already know about most certainly were redacted by Attorney General Barr.

Lots of collusion.

But legally not all collusion is a criminal conspiracy.

Putting the Russians aside for a moment, political campaigns often collude with organizations and persons without engaging in a criminal conspiracy. These include labor unions, corporations, civic groups, and grassroots-issue-oriented organizations. Political campaigns collude with law-abiding Americans—and some lawbreaking Americans—to help candidates get elected.

But they collude with Americans—not Russians. There is scant evidence of any prior American presidential campaign colluding with any foreign government—much less the Russians—to win an election. The closest we have come to improper contacts with foreign governments is when Nixon let the South Vietnamese government know that they would get a better peace deal from him than from LBJ if they stalled on negotiations until Nixon won the election. That was wrong—indeed a violation of the Logan Act—but was nothing like what clearly happened between the Trump campaign and the Russians.

Collusion by presidential campaigns also does not ordinarily include collusion with known criminals. Yes, there were rumors that the mob helped deliver Illinois electoral votes to John F. Kennedy in 1960, but there was no evidence of Kennedy campaign workers being in contact with the mob, and in fact, as attorney general, Bobby Kennedy ruthlessly prosecuted the mob.

The 1972 Nixon reelection campaign did collude with known criminals including the Watergate burglars, and we know exactly where that endeavor led. If campaign officials know that someone else is hacking people's email, breaking into buildings, or engaging in other criminal activity, those campaign officials should stay away and report what they know about it to the FBI. If they don't, the entire campaign is very likely to be embroiled in an investigation just like the investigation conducted by Robert Mueller.

Collusion with known criminals is not always criminal conspiracy. But collusion with known criminals is a great way to get investigated for criminal conspiracy. And it's an obvious way to never be allowed a security clearance by the United States government.

Yes, there are people who benefit from known criminal activity without reporting it to law enforcement. Landlords look the other way and rent rooms to drug dealers and prostitution rings, and some merchants earn huge markups by dealing in stolen merchandise (the separate crime of receipt of stolen merchandise was created in some jurisdictions to close this loophole in criminal conspiracy law). Prosecution of such people for criminal conspiracy in these cases is often unworkable. But these types of people should not be running our government or getting security clearances from our government.

Criminal conspiracy is a much narrower set of circumstances than collusion, even collusion with known criminals. A criminal conviction for conspiracy requires first an agreement (in this case between the Trump campaign and the Russians) to commit a certain underlying crime (such as computer hacking) and second an overt act by the defendant (in this case someone in the Trump campaign) in furtherance of the conspiracy.

These are the elements that Robert Mueller apparently believed could not be proven beyond a reasonable doubt against anyone in the Trump campaign. The Russians did not need someone in the Trump campaign to help them hack DNC email or any other email. Russians, particularly Russian security operatives, are perfectly good at computer hacking on their own. The Russians had probably already hacked the emails by the time they contacted the Trump campaign. They did not need Trump campaign workers to help them contact WikiLeaks. The Russians knew how to do that on their own. The Russians gave the Trump campaign a heads-up about what they were doing (the precise details of this are very likely buried in the redacted portions of the Mueller Report). But getting a heads-up about a crime, and even benefiting from the crime, without calling the FBI, and having private meetings with the people who commit the crime, is not itself criminal conspiracy unless all of the elements of the crime of conspiracy can be proven beyond a reasonable doubt.

Needless to say, when the criminals are not ordinary criminals, but Russian spies, and the persons collaborating with them work for the president of the United States, a lot more is at stake than whether a prosecutor can prove a criminal conspiracy case beyond a reasonable doubt. The fact that nobody in the Trump campaign reported to the FBI the multiple contacts made by the Russians is a concern. The fact that some people, including Michael Flynn, chose to lie about contacts with the Russians is also a concern. Whether the Russians are in a position to blackmail the president or anyone who works for him is also a concern.

As of the printing of this book, the public does not have the information in the redacted portions of the Mueller Report. Neither does Congress. Attorney General Barr has ignored the subpoena from the House of Representatives for the unredacted report. He is in contempt of Congress, but he considers that a joke. When he saw Speaker Nancy Pelosi in the halls of the Capitol,

Barr joked, "Did you bring your handcuffs?" Unless the House impeaches Trump, it could be difficult to get courts to enforce this or any other House subpoena in a timely manner (House subpoenas of the Justice Department from the Obama administration took years to resolve in the federal courts).

The second part of the Mueller Report addresses the question of whether Donald Trump himself committed the crime of obstruction of justice in his repeated efforts to derail the Russia investigation, including his firing of James Comey and his attempt to get the Department of Justice to fire Robert Mueller, as well as dangling pardons before witnesses, influencing witnesses, and more.

Mueller's job was principally to investigate the *facts*, and then to bring criminal charges if the facts showed that there was a crime that could be proven beyond a reasonable doubt under the *law*. If there were different interpretations of the law, particularly constitutional law, it was not Mueller's job definitively to resolve those questions. That would be the job of the federal courts if and when the Justice Department chose to prosecute.

Moreover, that prosecution decision was not Robert Mueller's to make. Each indictment had to be approved by top Justice Department officials. Before William Barr became attorney general, the approval was from Rod Rosenstein, but now that approval had to be from Barr.

Two constitutional law questions stood between President Trump and a criminal indictment for obstruction of justice. Barr could use these questions to stop a prosecution of Trump dead in its tracks, even if Barr's interpretation of constitutional law was incorrect.

The first was the question of whether a sitting president can ever be criminally charged for anything while in office, or whether the Constitution requires that the president first be impeached or have his term expire. One would think that the founders, if they had wanted to make the president immune from prosecution while in office, would have explicitly said so. They didn't. The Constitution is silent on this point.

What the founders did say—and very often—is that no man should be above the law. They did not want another King George III or an American version of the Roman emperor Nero who only faced justice for his crimes when he was finally tried by the Roman senators. The founders wanted an elected president with limited powers.

Nonetheless, arguments have been made that prosecuting a president during his term would be so disruptive that it should be postponed until after he leaves office. Even though the Supreme Court has already decided in the *Clinton v. Jones* sexual harassment case that a president can be *civilly* sued while in office, the court has never expressly said that a president can be *criminally* charged. A few legal scholars, including now Supreme Court justice Brett Kavanaugh in his 2009 article in the *Minnesota Law Review*, suggest that would likely be unconstitutional. We do not know how the Supreme Court would decide this question, but we aren't going to find out.

The reason has nothing to do with Mueller, but rather the fact that the Justice Department under William Barr sticks to the position (admittedly a position that the Justice Department has adhered to in the past) that criminal prosecution of a sitting president is unconstitutional. Because of this, the Justice Department will refuse to bring charges.

Yes, the president could shoot someone dead in the middle of Fifth Avenue in New York City (Trump once boasted he could do just that with impunity), or commit any other crime, and the president wouldn't be prosecuted. The position of the Department of Justice is that the president cannot be criminally charged until he is impeached by the House and removed by two-thirds of the Senate. If the president shoots another person in the middle of Fifth Avenue, same answer. Unless a majority of the House and two-thirds of the Senate are willing to remove him from office, he can just keep on going until his term expires. Only then can he be prosecuted.

That's the Constitution according to William Barr.

In his May 2019 news conference, Robert Mueller made it very clear that an important reason—if not *the* reason—why he did not indict President Trump was that it is the position of the Department of Justice that a sitting president cannot be indicted for *anything*. It does not matter what the president did. It is up to the House to impeach him and the Senate to remove him. That is the only remedy. Mueller is not the attorney general and there is nothing he could do to change it. A recommendation to prosecute Trump sent to the attorney general's desk would have been dead on arrival.

Mueller thus could not criminally prosecute Trump for anything. He was told that by Attorney General Barr; Barr was his superior, and he had no choice but to adhere to that order—or to resign.

The second constitutional question is whether a president can ever, even after leaving office, be criminally charged for obstructing a criminal investigation by his own Justice Department when the president, as head of the executive branch, has power to direct the policy of the Justice Department and to hire and fire presidential appointees in the Justice Department. Does a president have the power to use Donald Trump's two favorite words—"You're fired!"—to kill a Department of Justice investigation of himself, his family members, and his campaign?

In a country committed to the rule of law, the answer to this question should be an unequivocal "no." A president can control Justice Department policy, and he can hire and fire senior officials, but he cannot use these powers to obstruct a criminal investigation, particularly an investigation of himself. A president has broad powers as head of the executive branch, but there are limits. He cannot take bribes (for example, he could not have taken $100,000 in return for firing James Comey as head of the FBI). He also cannot obstruct justice.

The reason: no man, even the president, is above the law.

But there is another alternative theory—the unitary executive theory. The idea is that the president as head of the Justice Department, or any other part of the executive branch, can decide what gets investigated and what doesn't. If investigating his political opponents—for example, Hillary Clinton—is a priority, and investigating Russian interference with the election is "bad policy," the president can decide that. Anyone who doesn't go along with the president's "policy" decisions—whether Sally Yates, James Comey, or Robert Mueller—can simply be told "You're fired."

In sum, under this unitary executive theory, the president is not exactly the same as a king because he does not have a lifetime appointment and does not pass the office to his heirs, but the president has much the same power as a king for four years. Not only may the president grant pardons (a prerogative expressly bestowed by the Constitution), but he can decide who doesn't get prosecuted or even investigated (a prerogative not expressly bestowed by the Constitution but implied under the unitary executive theory). And he can do so for any reason he wants.

According to this constitutional theory, things didn't change that much after the American Revolution against King George III except that our king-president is elected and serves for four years. Then we decide whether to keep him or elect a new one. If he cheats in the election, or even colludes with a foreign power, that is a matter that doesn't even get investigated by the Justice Department unless he, as head of the unitary executive branch, decides it should be investigated. Anyone in the executive branch who disobeys his orders gets fired.

Sounds ridiculous. Yes. But this unitary executive theory is popular among some conservative legal scholars, with strong traces of it appearing, among other places, in the writings of Justice Kavanaugh. This theory was also much talked about in the early 2000s when then White House associate counsel Brett Kavanaugh served under President Bush.

This theory has not been tested in the courts in a criminal case against a president or a former president for obstruction of justice during his presidency. We probably would have had a criminal obstruction of justice trial against former president Nixon in the 1970s but for his pardon by President Ford. One cost of the Nixon pardon—one underappreciated at the time—was that federal courts never ruled on whether a president has not only the constitutional power, but also the legal right, to obstruct a federal investigation while in office. President Ford genuinely wanted to put an end to the "long national nightmare" of Watergate, but the Nixon pardon made it more likely that we would have another nightmare in the future.

Was Nixon's obstruction of justice, including his Saturday Night Massacre firing of special prosecutor Archibald Cox in 1973, actually obstruction of justice or within his powers as president under the unitary executive theory? We never got a definitive answer to that question. Forty-five years later, we still don't have a definitive answer.

We have no definitive answer from the courts to this part of the bigger question of whether the president for practical purposes is above the law.

All we have is William Barr's answer.

And Barr knows what the answer is. That's why he is attorney general. He buys the unitary executive theory 100 percent, particularly as it applies to Donald Trump.

Barr was very quick to decide this constitutional law question. Never mind that Mueller's report discussed extensively reasons why such constitutional theories could not be used to justify Trump's actions, and reasons why Donald Trump's actions did amount to criminal obstruction of justice. Never mind that the Mueller Report specifically noted both the impeachment remedy and the possibility that a president could be criminally charged after leaving office. And that the report specifically said that President Trump, in the view of Mueller and his staff, was not exonerated.

Barr decided otherwise. In his March 24, 2019, four-page summary of Mueller's report, Barr concluded that "the evidence developed during the Special Counsel's investigation is not sufficient to establish that the President committed an obstruction-of-justice offense." That's not what the Mueller Report said, but it's what Barr said, and he was the attorney general, appointed by the president, so that was that. Or so it seemed.

This was the same conclusion that Barr had already reached in memos he circulated in 2018 to defense lawyers representing targets in the Mueller investigation including Trump, and the same conclusion that Barr had reached as a private lawyer in his own lengthy memorandum of June 8, 2018, to Deputy Attorney General Rod Rosenstein and Assistant Attorney General Steven Engel with the heading "Mueller's 'Obstruction' Theory." Before he became Trump's attorney general, Barr had denigrated Mueller's investigation of Trump for obstruction of justice, and now Barr was doing exactly what Trump had hired him to do—shoot down the "obstruction theory" from his perch atop the Department of Justice.

The fact that Barr was now doing this not as a defense lawyer but in his new capacity as Mueller's boss, purporting to "summarize" the conclusions that Mueller had reached, was ludicrous if not absurd. Mueller was disturbed by this "summary" of his conclusions, and wrote Barr a March 27, 2019, letter citing "public confusion about critical aspects of the results of our investigation." Mueller continued, "This threatens to undermine a central purpose for which the Department appointed the Special Counsel: to assure full public confidence in the outcome of the investigations."

But that letter apparently was ignored. Barr also "forgot" about it when he testified at an April 9, 2019, House hearing when Representative Charlie Crist (D-FL) asked him if he knew why members of Mueller's team were frustrated with his March 24 letter.

"No. I don't," Barr said.

In sum, Barr had relied upon two legal theories not supported by controlling case law—the theory that a sitting president could not be charged for any crime while in office, and an extreme version of the unitary executive theory under which it was virtually impossible for a president to obstruct justice—to sink an otherwise very strong obstruction of justice case against President Trump. Barr did what he was hired to do.

But what about the facts?

Those were bad—very bad.

For a defendant who is not president—a mere mortal who is not somehow constitutionally above the law because William Barr says so—an obstruction of justice charge requires three things: 1) that the person commit an obstructive act, 2) a nexus of that act with an official proceeding, and 3) a corrupt intent of that person in committing the act. The person must do something to obstruct; there must be a connection between that act of obstruction and an official proceeding such as the Russia investigation; and the person must have a corrupt intent in committing the act of obstruction.

The facts already discussed at length show that Donald Trump's conduct satisfies all three elements of the crime of obstruction of justice in multiple instances:

- Trump's conduct to obstruct the investigation into Michael Flynn
- Trump's firing of Comey
- Trump's efforts to fire Mueller and to curtail Mueller's investigation
- Trump's efforts to have Sessions "un-recuse" and take control of the investigation
- Trump's order to White House counsel Don McGahn to lie about Trump's earlier attempt to fire Mueller and Trump's order to McGahn to create a false record "for our files"

Trump's conduct in other instances also may have satisfied the elements of a criminal case for obstruction of justice.

In sum, we have a president whose campaign collaborated with Russian agents, and even though that collaboration did not amount to a provable criminal conspiracy, several of his highest associates lied about their contacts with the Russians and have been criminally convicted for lying. Furthermore, the president has clearly engaged in conduct that would be obstruction of justice for any ordinary citizen.

President Trump has not been criminally charged because his own attorney general believes the president is above the law. Attorney General Barr's constitutional law theories—both of them—would apply only in a criminal case and would not be binding on the House and Senate in an impeachment trial where representatives and senators can define for themselves the meaning of "high crimes and misdemeanors."

The Mueller Report is a clear road map for impeachment.

CHAPTER 31

Ukraine, China, Syria, and More

Against the insidious wiles of foreign influence . . . the
jealousy of a free people ought to be constantly awake.
—*GEORGE WASHINGTON, FAREWELL ADDRESS*

You can't impeach a president for doing a great job.
—*DONALD TRUMP*

MANY OF OUR FOUNDERS, INCLUDING GEORGE WASH-ington and James Madison, feared a president who might "betray his trust to foreign powers."

In *The Federalist Papers* No. 68, Alexander Hamilton wrote in 1788 that the election of the president was a particular worry for the framers of the Constitution.

> Nothing was more to be desired than that every practicable obstacle should
> be opposed to cabal, intrigue, and corruption. These most deadly adversaries
> of republican government might naturally have been expected to make their
> approaches from more than one quarter, but chiefly from the desire in foreign
> powers to gain an improper ascendant in our councils.

As explained in Volume I of the 2019 Mueller Report (the publicly available version is heavily redacted), and as we have already discussed in detail in this book, improper foreign influence on the election of the president is exactly what happened in 2016. There was abundant "cabal, intrigue, and corruption." We now face the very real prospect that it will happen again in 2020.

A "hoax" was how Trump described the Mueller Report, which concluded that the Kremlin not only sought to help elect Trump, but that Trump *welcomed* Russia's help.

Said Trump during the 2016 campaign, "Russia, if you are listening, I hope you're able to find the thirty thousand [Hillary Clinton] emails that are missing. I think you will probably be rewarded mightily by our press."

Despite the findings of the Mueller Report, Nancy Pelosi, the Speaker of the House, did not deem Trump's dangerous behavior sufficient to launch an impeachment inquiry, even though federal law expressly states that it is illegal for "a person to solicit, accept, or receive" anything of value from a foreign national in connection with a federal election.

President Trump, unpunished and unrepentant for inviting a foreign power to interfere in a US election, figured he could get away with it again. This time he sought to get foreign governments to go after his likely opponents in 2020, including Joe Biden, who was for much of 2019 the top-polling Democratic candidate for president.

Trump's actions were so alarming that in late September of 2019, a whistle-blower from an intelligence agency came forward to reveal that, during the summer, Trump had made a phone call to the new Ukrainian president, Volodymyr Zelensky, asking him to investigate whether Ukraine, and *not Russia*, had been responsible for meddling in the 2016 election. He also wanted Zelensky to investigate the "corruption" of Democratic presidential candidate Joe Biden and his son Hunter. If Zelensky would do him that favor, *if and only then* would Ukraine get the $391 million in aid that Congress had voted for Ukraine's missile defense against threats from Russia.

The whistle-blower also charged that Trump, aware of the illegality of arm-twisting a foreign power in order to interfere in an American election, hid all records of the phone call, especially the word-for-word transcript of the conversation produced by the White House situation room, by locking them down in a secret server. Lawyers from the White House counsel's office apparently participated in this cover-up.

There was more. Rudy Giuliani, Trump's personal attorney, and William Barr, the attorney general, were actively pushing Trump's false narrative, acting as shadow diplomats, approaching Ukrainian officials and demanding they look into Ukrainian interference in the 2016 election and investigate Biden and his son. Top US intelligence officials and diplomats were circumvented—and shocked when they learned about it.

What was made clear to Zelensky was that Trump would not give him the $391 million voted by Congress until Trump saw that the Ukrainian president had done what he had asked. Quid pro quo.

For Zelensky, the requests had to have been bizarre and troubling, because there was no evidence of Ukrainian interference in the 2016 US election or of corruption in Ukraine on the part of Joe Biden and his son. Both were figments of Donald Trump's conspiracy-fed imagination.

Hunter Biden had been on the board of Burisma Holdings, the largest Ukrainian natural gas company, while Joe Biden was vice president, but investigations determined that, though Hunter may have benefited professionally from the prestige of his father's position, neither he nor his father had done anything illegal. His father had not violated any federal ethics rules. The notion that there was something illegal to be investigated by the Ukrainian government was all in Donald Trump's mind, as the president attempted to influence the 2020 election by smearing the reputation of his leading Democratic opponent.

Trump, lashing out at the whistle-blower, called him a "treasonous spy" and suggested he be executed by hinting that the whistle-blower suffer the same punishment the US "used to do in the old days when we were smart with spies and treason, right?"

Trump, who often accused others of doing what he himself was doing, also claimed that Joe Biden had made the same extortion threats to a foreign power. Trump accused Biden, when he was vice president, of withholding a billion dollars in foreign aid unless then Ukrainian president Petro Poroshenko fired a Ukrainian prosecutor to keep him from investigating Biden's son.

Trump's story, not surprisingly, wasn't true. In fact, it was the opposite of true.

Said Daria Kaleniuk, Ukraine's leading anti-corruption activist, the story is "absolute nonsense."

The real story was that Viktor Shokin, the Ukrainian prosecutor, was fired from office after attacking the reformers within the attorney general's office. Shokin was refusing to investigate corruption, embezzlement, and misconduct of public officials following the 2014 popular uprising that deposed President Viktor Yanukovych. The Obama administration threatened to withhold a billion dollars of American aid until Shokin was removed, and it was Vice President Biden who conveyed that message, but there is no evidence this had anything to do with Hunter Biden.

Biden, our vice president, was acting as the point man for a coordinated international effort to dump Shokin. Corruption was killing Ukraine financially, and the reformers wanted him removed. As for Biden's son Hunter, Shokin was actually *protecting* the head of Burisma, Hunter Biden's boss, and Shokin's removal made it more likely that Burisma would be investigated. Biden's threat of withholding the billion dollars in aid was the only way to get Shokin removed, and he acted despite how it might have adversely affected a company that his son worked for.

Of course, the falsity of the allegation about Biden's role in all of this didn't stop Trump and his minions from trashing the former vice president and his son.

When news of Trump's telephone call with President Zelensky came to light, the outcry demanding Trump's impeachment this time was loud and long. Seven Democratic House members representing right-leaning districts wrote an op-ed in the *Washington Post* demanding that Trump be impeached for inviting a foreign power to meddle in the 2020 election.

House Democrats demanded that a transcript of the conversation be made public. It was locked safely away along with a trove of other documents and transcripts of phone calls. Trump refused to release it, but instead made public what he described as a "full, rough transcript of the conversation based on voice-activated software."

The transcript, which was a partial recitation of the conversation between Trump and Zelensky, proved that Trump had done exactly what he was accused of doing. The number of House members supporting an impeachment investigation continued to grow up to and above the 218-vote threshold required for impeachment. On September 24, 2019, Speaker Pelosi announced that there would be a formal impeachment inquiry.

"We are at a different level of lawlessness," said Pelosi.

The phone conversation that launched this groundswell of support for an impeachment inquiry began with Trump, speaking of the Ukrainian presidential election, congratulating Zelensky "on a great victory." Zelensky then stroked Trump's fragile ego. He really piled it on.

"We worked a lot but I would like to confess to you that I had an opportunity to learn from you. We used quite a few of your skills and knowledge and were able to use it as an example to our elections, and yes it is true that these were unique elections." He went on to say, "I think I should run more often so you can call me more often and we can talk over the phone more often."

Zelensky told Trump, "To tell you the truth, we are trying to work hard because we wanted to drain the swamp here in our country . . . You are a great teacher for us and in that."

Trump then patted himself on the back saying, "I will say that we do a lot for Ukraine . . . Much more than the European countries are doing, and they should be helping you more than they are."

Zelensky agreed with him, and said, "I'm very grateful to you for that because the United States is doing quite a lot for Ukraine. Much more than the European Union especially when we are talking about sanctions against the Russian Federation. I would also like to thank you for your great support in the area of defense. We are ready to continue to cooperate for the next steps specifically we are almost ready to buy more Javelins from the United States for defense purposes."

Responded Trump, "I would like you to do us a favor *though* [italics ours]."

The word "though" caught everyone's attention, because Zelensky and Trump had been talking about military aid, and Trump then mentioned the conspiracy theory that Ukraine helped Hillary Clinton during the 2016 election, and then he told Zelensky he wanted him to talk with Attorney General Bill Barr about that "to get to the bottom of it."

Said Trump, "As you saw yesterday, that whole nonsense [the investigation into Russian interference in the 2016 election] ended with a very poor performance by a man named Robert Mueller, an incompetent performance, but they say a lot of it started with Ukraine. Whatever you can do, it's very important that you do it if that's possible."

Zelensky talked about how important it was for him to cooperate with Trump. He added, "I will personally tell you that one of my assistants spoke with Mr. Giuliani just recently, and we are hoping very much that Mr. Giuliani will be able to travel to Ukraine, and we will meet once he comes to Ukraine." He then told Trump that "we are friends. We are great friends."

"Good," said Trump, "because I heard you had a prosecutor who was very good, and he was shut down, and that's really unfair." Trump talked about Giuliani, that he was mayor of New York, "a great mayor, and I would like him to call you. I will ask him to call you along with the attorney general.

"The other thing, there's a lot of talk about Biden's son, that Biden stopped the prosecution, and a lot of people want to find out about that so whatever you can do with the attorney general would be great. Biden went around bragging that he stopped the prosecution so if you can look into it. It sounds horrible to me."

Zelensky didn't respond directly on that subject, but they did talk about Trump's firing in May of Marie Yovanovitch, the American ambassador to Ukraine, whom Trump called "bad news."

She was apparently "bad news" because Trump and his henchmen needed to get rid of her if their plot to smear Biden and his son was to get any traction.

And there was more. Two associates of Rudy Giuliani, Lev Parnas and Igor Fruman, sent illegal contributions to the 2018 reelection campaign of Peter Sessions, a congressman who was head of the House Rules Committee, whom they used to get rid of Ambassador Yovanovitch. In a letter to Secretary of State Mike Pompeo, Sessions accused Yovanovitch of being disloyal to President Trump. Parnas and Fruman both were arrested by police at Dulles Airport in Virginia, outside of Washington, DC, in October 2019 as they attempted to leave the country. They were charged with conspiring to violate the ban on foreign donations and contributions in connection with federal and state elections. In addition, they were charged with conspiring to make contributions in connection with federal elections in the names of others, and with making false statements and falsifying records to obstruct the administration of a matter within the jurisdiction of the Federal Election Commission.

Yovanovitch had been a thirty-three-year State Department veteran who had also been vilified in the right-wing media. Appointed as ambassador to Ukraine by President Obama, she was a critic of the rife corruption. Without any evidence, she was accused of being disloyal to the president by former federal prosecutor Joseph diGenova on Fox News. Two days later, Trump tweeted he had been trying to fire her for a year. Secretary of State Mike Pompeo refused to answer questions about why she had been recalled.

In the July 25 phone call, Zelensky, continuing to kowtow, told Trump, "You were the first one who told me that she was a bad ambassador. I agree with you one hundred percent."

Trump then reiterated that Barr and Giuliani would call him, "and we will get to the bottom of it. I'm sure you will figure it out. I heard the prosecutor was treated very badly, and he was a very fair prosecutor, so good luck with everything."

Zelensky informed Trump that, the last time he'd visited the United States, he had stayed at Trump Tower. He agreed to talk to Giuliani and Barr, and he finished, "We are great friends, and you Mr. President have friends in our country so we can continue our strategic partnership. I also plan to surround myself with great people and in addition to that investigation, I guarantee as the president of Ukraine that all the investigations will be done openly and candidly. That I can assure you."

Trump and a number of his Republican allies refused to categorize the conversation as a quid pro quo—"It was a perfect conversation," said Trump—but at least one career diplomat working in Ukraine was horrified by the exchange that he heard.

In text messages, Ambassador William Taylor, the chargé d'affaires at the US embassy in Kiev, repeatedly questioned the decision to withhold millions of dollars of aid to Ukraine unless the Ukrainian president conducted the investigations that Trump was demanding.

On October 3, 2019, the House impeachment inquiry released twenty-two pages of text messages between a group of top diplomats involved with Ukraine. The texts, released by Kurt Volker, the special US envoy to

Ukraine, showed conclusively that Trump committed the impeachable offense described by the whistle-blower.

"Are we now saying that security assistance and WH meeting are conditioned on investigations?" texted William Taylor to US ambassador to the European Union, Gordon Sondland, on September 1, 2019, after Trump skipped a trip to Poland, during which he was supposed to meet with Zelensky. They then talked on the telephone.

A week later Taylor texted to Sondland, "As I said on the phone, I think it's crazy to withhold security assistance for help with a political campaign." Taylor complained that Trump's decision to hold back congressionally approved aid to Ukraine had created a "nightmare scenario."

Sondland, realizing how this text message looked, quickly went into cover-your-ass mode.

"The president has been crystal clear no quid pro quo's [sic] of any kind," he texted. He then texted, "I suggest we stop the back and forth by text."

The cover-up had begun. Trump forbade anyone involved in the impeachment investigation from testifying before Congress.

He then went on television to admit what he had done. He defended his phone call to Zelensky as being "entirely appropriate," and admitted they had talked about Joe Biden and Biden's son's corruption as part of the conversation.

"The conversation we had was largely congratulatory, with largely corruption, all of the corruption taking place and largely the fact that we don't want our people like Vice President Biden and his son creating the corruption already in the Ukraine."

Trump then doubled down. On October 3, he stood before reporters prior to boarding Marine One, and without any evidence whatsoever, he accused China of paying Hunter Biden $1.5 billion to influence his father to win trade deals for some of China's biggest financial companies.

"And that's probably why China, for so many years, has had a sweetheart deal where China rips off the USA—because they deal like people with Biden, where they give their son a billion and a half dollars. And that's probably why China has such a sweetheart deal that, for so many years, they've been ripping off our country."

The attack on the Bidens by Trump came after it was revealed that members of Trump's extended family, including daughter Ivanka and son-in-law Jared Kushner, were awarded dozens of potentially valuable patents by the Chinese government, and Kushner's sister Nicole Meyer used her connections with the president to lure Chinese investors into buying into a development in New Jersey.

Standing on the South Lawn of the White House, Trump spoke to reporters about opening trade talks with China. He said, "If they don't do what we want, we have tremendous power." Then he said, "China should start an investigation into the Bidens, because what happened in China is just about as bad as what happened in the Ukraine."

Facing intense criticism for soliciting assistance from foreign powers to discredit political opponents, Trump argued there was nothing wrong with seeking foreign help to fight corruption.

"As president of the United States," he wrote on Twitter, "I have an absolute right, perhaps even a duty, to investigate, or have investigated CORRUPTION, and that would include asking, or suggesting, other Countries to help us out!"

It was as though Trump was daring the House of Representatives to impeach him. At the same time, Trump and his right-wing echo chamber were claiming that the impeachment hearing against him was part of a coup.

"As I learn more and more each day," Trump tweeted, "I am coming to the conclusion that what is taking place is not an impeachment, it is a COUP, intended to take away the Power of the People, their VOTE, their Freedoms, their Second Amendment, Religion, Military Border Wall, and their God-given rights as a Citizen of the United States of America."

Trump had tweeted earlier, "Why isn't Congressman Adam Schiff being brought up on charges for fraudulently making up a statement and reading it to Congress as if this statement, which was very dishonest and bad for me, was directly made by the President of the United States. This should never be allowed."

As the president raged, the House, including its Judiciary Committee and Intelligence Committee, continued its work on impeachment.

With the Ukraine scandal, House investigators finally had that which everyone suspected, but which Robert Mueller could not prove definitively in the Russia investigation: a quid pro quo in which Trump offered official action of the United States government in exchange for foreign government assistance for his political campaign. There had been abundant evidence that Russia released the hacked Clinton emails and interfered in the 2016 election in order to get the economic sanctions against Russia lifted (both subjects were brought up repeatedly, including at the infamous June 2016 Trump Tower meeting with a Russian agent). Still, Mueller did not find a smoking gun email, telephone call, or other communication in which Trump or anyone working for him presented such a quid pro quo to the Russians. The circumstantial evidence (much of it redacted from Volume I of the Mueller Report) was substantial, but not sufficient for criminal charges.

Now, in 2019, Trump had been caught red-handed—this time in his capacity as president, not just as a candidate. He was on tape (wherever that tape might be hidden in a White House vault) in a phone call offering a remarkably similar proposition to the president of Ukraine: give me dirt on Joe Biden that I can use against him in 2020, give me an investigation that undermines the US investigation of what Russia did in the 2016 election, and I will give you vital US military aid for Ukraine.

A quid pro quo. Solicitation of a bribe. Extortion. Illegal. Impeachable.

Then, while the world was focusing on Trump and his dealings with Ukraine, on October 6, 2019, Trump hung up on a call with Turkish president Recep Tayyip Erdoğan and ordered American troops to leave Syria and get out of the way so that Erdoğan could mount an invasion to attack the Kurds and wipe them out. Even though the Kurds were our allies, Trump removed the American troops protecting them despite opposition from the State Department and the military.

It wasn't the first time Trump signaled a willingness to bow to Erdoğan's wishes. In December of 2018, Erdoğan had asked Trump to remove the American troops so he could attack the Kurds. American officials warned Trump that some troops had to remain in order to contain ISIS, which was (and is) a guerilla army. Erdoğan then offered to take over from the American troops, and Trump agreed, sending the generals into a state of shock and bewilderment.

Defense Secretary James Mattis, furious about a number of things, including that Trump would betray the Kurds, submitted his resignation.

Brett McGurk, the American envoy to the coalition against ISIS, did as well. On December 23, 2018, Trump announced he was accelerating Mattis's departure.

With Mattis gone, Trump gave Erdoğan the okay to attack the Kurds. Republicans, who kept strangely silent after the Ukraine fiasco, howled in protest. Senate Majority Leader Mitch McConnell warned that Trump's withdrawal would benefit Russia, Iran, Syria, and the Islamic State.

"Exercise American leadership," McConnell intoned.

Another strong Trump supporter, Senator Lindsey Graham, said he wanted to block what the president did and keep our troops in place.

"This impulsive decision by the president has undone all the gains we've made, thrown the region into further chaos; Iran is licking its chops, and if I'm an ISIS fighter, I've got a second lease on life," he said on *Fox & Friends*.

"To those who think ISIS has been defeated, you will soon see; and to Turkey, you have destroyed the relationship, what little you had, with the US Congress, and I will do everything I can to sanction Turkey's military and their economy if they step one foot into Syria," Graham added.

Meanwhile, a Fox News poll showed that more and more registered voters favored Trump's impeachment. Of those surveyed, 51 percent said they want Trump impeached and removed from office. Forty percent opposed impeachment.

Fox News also found that 66 percent of voters found that asking a foreign leader to investigate a political opponent was "generally inappropriate."

Trump tweeted that "I have NEVER had a good @FoxNews poll. Whoever the pollster is, they suck." He complained, "FoxNews doesn't deliver for US anymore. It is so different than it used to be."

"Oh well, I'm President!" he added.

It remained to be seen for how much longer.

Why was Trump so deferential to Erdoğan and his Turkish government? Why was he abandoning the Kurds, who had helped us fight Saddam Hussein in Iraq and then had helped us fight ISIS, to be slaughtered?

As Trump professed his wish to scale back on American troop presence in the Middle East, that very same week he ordered a deployment of 2,800 additional US troops to Saudi Arabia, an oil-rich nation very capable of defending itself. Trump's Middle East policy has been confusing to say the least. Could the motivating factor be that the Trump Organization has business dealings with Saudi Arabia and none in Syria? Could it be that we are experiencing the very fears that the founders had when they drafted the emoluments clause of the Constitution?

As for Turkey and Erdoğan, Trump's policy is also a mystery.

Or perhaps not. Recall this infamous April 20, 2012, tweet from Ivanka Trump that we mentioned in an earlier chapter: "Thank you Prime Minister Erdogan for joining us yesterday to celebrate the launch of #TrumpTowers Istanbul!"

CONCLUSION

Looking Ahead

No man has a good enough memory to be a successful liar.
—ABRAHAM LINCOLN

A S THIS BOOK GOES TO PRINT, THE FUTURE OF THE
Trump presidency remains uncertain.

Trump himself remains delusional. He is the same person we describe
in the Introduction to this book—a narcissist on a scale not seen since King
George III and the Roman emperor Nero. Trump *is* the American Nero.

Trump not only thinks he can finish his term but that he can win a second
term. He has not been indicted for obstruction of justice because his handpicked attorney general believes in two constitutional law theories that put the
president above the law. Robert Mueller, in his report, laid out a clear path
for impeachment and conviction. The Ukraine scandal makes the case for
impeachment that much more compelling.

And thus Trump goes about what he has done since the beginning of his
term—he shows no respect for the rule of law.

Nobody high up in the executive branch itself is willing to stand up to
Trump. Trump's cabinet and senior White House staff are mostly egging him

on rather than pointing out to him the perilous situation that he has created for himself and the country. Those who dared to stand up to him—including a secretary of state, an attorney general, a defense secretary, two chiefs of staff, a White House counsel—all were forced to leave within the first two years. Trump started in 2017 with a team of yes-men and yes-women. Through frequent purges and "resignations," he has been able to make his team even more loyal to him—if not loyal to the United States.

Hopes of invoking the Twenty-Fifth Amendment and removing the president for mental incapacity have dimmed as the cabinet—the body responsible for initiating such proceedings—becomes ever more personally loyal to Trump. Anyone who questions Trump's mental capacities—as Secretary of State Tillerson was once reported to have done—is gone.

The rule of law set forth in our Constitution provides for checks and balances that *are supposed to* prevent a man like King George III, or Nero, or Trump from using the presidency to exercise the powers of an autocrat.

The founders believed the checks and balances in the Constitution to be sufficient to prevent this eventuality because they thought that if they gave other branches of government the power to keep the presidency in check, those other branches of government would do their job.

The most powerful branch is Congress. Congress not only has the power of the purse strings, but also the power to investigate, impeach, and remove the president for treason or for high crimes or misdemeanors.

The 2018 election brought a sea change in the House of Representatives.

The Democrats gained forty seats in the House and took over control of that body. As a result, Nancy Pelosi once again is the Speaker of the House, and the House Intelligence Committee, having tossed out Trump devotee Devin Nunes, suddenly had California's Adam Schiff, a Democrat, in charge. Representative Jerry Nadler of New York took over the House Judiciary Committee.

Schiff commenced hearings on Trump and Russia, and he has tried to use his subpoena power to make sure the evidence from Robert Mueller's investigation would see the light of day through his committee. But so far not even members of Congress with security clearances have seen the unredacted Mueller Report. Subpoenas are simply ignored. The attorney general is in contempt of Congress but doesn't care.

Would the Democrats prioritize picking up where Mueller left off, taking up Mueller's clear signal that the House should impeach Trump? Or would Democrats complain about Trump's corruption, and try to investigate it, but focus mostly on policy issues that appeal to the Democratic base such as immigration, healthcare, abortion and other social issues, and climate change?

The Democrats control the House. They have the power to impeach Trump. After the Ukraine scandal, they finally did so.

On December 18, 2019 the House of Representative by a vote of 230 to 197 voted to impeach President Trump. Not a single Republican voted for impeachment. Justin Amash (I-MI), who had been a Republican but became an Independent earlier in 2019, voted for impeachment. Every single Democrat except two voted in favor of impeachment. Jeff Van Drew (D-NJ) voted against impeachment and quickly switched parties to become a Republican. Collin Peterson (D-MN) a reactionary Democrat from northwestern Minnesota voted against impeachment, claiming to represent the views of his district. One Democrat, Jared Golden (D-ME) voted for the first article of impeachment but not the second.

In order to achieve near unanimity in the Democratic caucus, the House leaders did not include charges against Trump for obstruction of justice in the Mueller investigation, violations of the emoluments clause of the Constitution, or other high crimes and misdemeanors that would have been supported by the evidence had the House chosen to impeach him for them.

The Articles of Impeachment in their entirety read as follows:

Resolved, That Donald J. Trump, President of the United States, is impeached for high crimes and misdemeanors and that the following articles of impeachment be exhibited to the United States Senate:

Articles of impeachment exhibited by the House of Representatives of the United States of America in the name of itself and of the people of the United States of America, against Donald J. Trump, President of the United States of America, in maintenance and support of its impeachment against him for high crimes and misdemeanors.

Article I: Abuse of power

The Constitution provides that the House of Representatives "shall have the sole Power of Impeachment and that the President shall be removed from Office on Impeachment for, and Conviction of, Treason, Bribery, or other high Crimes and Misdemeanors". In his conduct of the office of President of the United States—and in violation of his constitutional oath faithfully to execute the office of President of the United States and, to the best of his ability, preserve, protect, and defend the Constitution of the United States, and in violation of his constitutional duty to take care that the laws be faithfully executed—Donald J. Trump has abused the powers of the Presidency, in that:

Using the powers of his high office, President Trump solicited the interference of a foreign government, Ukraine, in the 2020 United States Presidential election. He did so through a scheme or course of conduct that included soliciting the Government of Ukraine to publicly announce investigations that would benefit his reelection, harm the election prospects of a political opponent, and influence the 2020 United States Presidential election to his advantage. President Trump also sought to pressure the Government of Ukraine to take these steps by conditioning official United States Government acts of significant value to Ukraine on its public announcement of the investigations. President Trump engaged in this scheme or course of conduct for corrupt purposes in pursuit of personal political benefit. In so doing, President Trump used the powers of the Presidency in a manner that compromised the national security of the United States and undermined the integrity of the United States democratic process. He thus ignored and injured the interests of the Nation.

President Trump engaged in this scheme or course of conduct through the following means:

(1) President Trump—acting both directly and through his agents Within and Outside the United States Government—corruptly solicited the Government of Ukraine to publicly announce investigations into—

(A) a political opponent, former Vice President Joseph R. Biden, Jr.; and

(B) a discredited theory promoted by Russia alleging that Ukraine—rather than Russia—interfered in the 2016 United States Presidential election.

(2) With the same corrupt motives, President Trump—acting both directly and through his agents within and outside the United States Government–conditioned two official acts on the public announcements that he had requested—

(A) the release of $391 million of United 5 States taxpayer funds that Congress had appropriated on a bipartisan basis for the purpose of providing vital military and security assistance to Ukraine to oppose Russian aggression and which President Trump had ordered suspended; and

(B) a head of state meeting at the White House, which the President of Ukraine sought to demonstrate continued United States support for the Government of Ukraine in the face of Russian aggression.

(3) Faced with the public revelation of his actions, President Trump ultimately released the military and security assistance to the Government of Ukraine, but has persisted in openly and corruptly urging and soliciting Ukraine to undertake investigations for his personal political benefit.

These actions were consistent with President Trump's previous invitations of foreign interference in United States elections.

In all this, President Trump abused the powers of the Presidency by ignoring and injuring national security and other vital national interests to obtain an improper personal political benefit. He has also betrayed the Nation by abusing his high office to enlist a foreign power in corrupting democratic elections.

Wherefore President Trump, by such conduct, has demonstrated that he will remain a threat to national security and the Constitution if allowed to remain in office, and has acted in a manner grossly incompatible with self-governance and the rule of law. President Trump thus warrants impeachment and trial, removal from office, and disqualification to hold and enjoy any Office of honor, trust, or profit under the United States.

Article II: Obstruction of Congress

The Constitution provides that the House of Representatives "shall have the sole Power of Impeachment" and that the President "shall be removed from Office on Impeachment for, and Conviction of, Treason, Bribery, or other high Crimes and Misdemeanors". In his conduct of the office of President of the United States—and in violation of his constitutional oath faithfully to execute the office of President of the United States and, to the best of his ability, preserve, protect, and defend the Constitution of the United States, and in violation of his constitutional duty to take care that the laws be faithfully executed—

Donald J. Trump has directed the unprecedented, categorical, and indiscriminate defiance of subpoenas issued by the House of Representatives pursuant to its sole Power of Impeachment. President Trump has abused the powers of the Presidency in a manner offensive to, and subversive of, the Constitution, in that:

The House of Representatives has engaged in an impeachment inquiry focused on President Trump's corrupt solicitation of the Government of Ukraine to interfere in the 2020 United States Presidential election. As part of this impeachment inquiry, the Committees undertaking the investigation served subpoenas seeking documents and testimony deemed vital to the inquiry from various Executive Branch agencies and offices, and current and former officials.

In response, without lawful cause or excuse, President Trump directed Executive Branch agencies, offices, and officials not to comply with those subpoenas. President Trump thus interposed the powers of the Presidency against the lawful subpoenas of the House of Representatives, and assumed to himself functions and judgments necessary to the exercise of the "sole Power of Impeachment" vested by the Constitution in the House of Representatives. President Trump abused the powers of his high office through the following means:

(1) Directing the White House to defy a lawful subpoena by withholding the production of documents sought therein by the Committees.

(2) Directing other Executive Branch agencies and offices to defy lawful subpoenas and withhold the production of documents and records from the Committees—in response to which the Department of State, Office of Management and Budget, Department of Energy, and Department of Defense refused to produce a single document or record.

(3) Directing current and former Executive Branch officials not to cooperate with the Committees—in response to which nine Administration officials defied subpoenas for testimony, namely John Michael "Mick" Mulvaney, Robert B. Blair, John A. Eisenberg, Michael Ellis, Preston Wells Griffith, Russell T. Vought, Michael Duffey, Brian McCormack, and T. Ulrich Brechbuhl.

These actions were consistent with President Trump's previous efforts to undermine United States Government investigations into foreign interference in United States elections.

Through these actions, President Trump sought to arrogate to himself the right to determine the propriety, scope, and nature of an impeachment inquiry into his own conduct, as well as the unilateral prerogative to deny any and all information to the House of Representatives in the exercise of its "sole Power of Impeachment". In the history of the Republic, no President has ever ordered the complete defiance of an impeachment inquiry or sought to obstruct and impede so comprehensively the ability of the House of Representatives to investigate "high Crimes and Misdemeanors". This abuse of office served to cover up the President's own repeated misconduct and to seize and control the power of impeachment and thus to nullify a vital constitutional safeguard vested solely in the House of Representatives.

In all of this, President Trump has acted in a manner contrary to his trust as President and subversive of constitutional government, to the great prejudice of the cause of law and justice, and to the manifest injury of the people of the United States.

Wherefore, President Trump, by such conduct, has demonstrated that he will remain a threat to the Constitution if allowed to remain in office, and has acted in a manner grossly incompatible with self-governance and the rule of law. President Trump thus warrants impeachment and trial, removal from office, and disqualification to hold and enjoy any office of honor, trust, or profit under the United States.

Speaker Nancy Pelosi, as of January 2020, had not yet delivered these articles of impeachment to the Senate and implied that she would not do so until the Senate agreed to procedures for a fair impeachment trial. Senate Majority Leader Mitch McConnell has made clear his intention to hold an abbreviated trial with few if any witnesses, or simply have a vote to dismiss the articles of impeachment. It will take a handful of Republican senators to join Senate Democrats to achieve the fifty-one votes needed to approve procedures required for a fair impeachment trial, and, as this book goes to press, it is not certain that will happen. Sixty-seven votes will be needed to convict Trump.

Not impeaching Trump would have been a moral disaster for House Democrats and could have been a political disaster. The sandbagged 2020 Democratic nominee for president would have had to defend the indefensible House decision not to impeach Trump or repudiate it.

By impeaching Trump, the House did the right thing.

What about the Republicans?

Secretly many of them despise Trump.

One Republican congressman, who insisted on anonymity, in April 2018 gave this appraisal of the president during a meeting at a Safeway store in Washington, DC, with conservative blogger and TV host Erick Erickson. As they walked past the cereal and the dairy aisle, the congressman, who on Fox News often praised the president, told Erickson exactly what he thought of Trump in a profanity-laced diatribe.

"He may be an idiot," said the congressman, "but he's still the president and leader of my party and he is capable of doing some things right. But dammit, he's taking us all down with him. We are well and truly fucked in November." (He was right. In November 2018 the Republicans lost forty seats in the House and lost control of the chamber.) "I say a lot of shit on TV defending him, even over this. But honestly, I wish the motherfucker would just go away. We're going to lose the House, lose the Senate, and lose a bunch of states because of him. All his supporters will blame us for what we have or have not done, but he hasn't led. He wakes up in the morning, shits all over

Twitter, shits all over us, shits all over his staff, then hits golf balls. Fuck him. Of course, I can't say that in public or I'd get run out of town."

So why won't any of these Republicans do anything about Trump? Why not send the message that if the House impeaches Trump, powerful GOP senators will go over to the White House and tell Trump to resign? That's what happened with Nixon. Why not do the same with Trump?

The bottom line is that the Republicans are scared of Trump.

Trump will wreak maximum havoc if the Republicans try to remove him from office or take the 2020 nomination away from him. If he didn't get the nomination, he could run as a third-party candidate and peel off a portion of the Republican base, assuring Republican defeat in the general election. Trump, if he goes down in a Senate impeachment trial, would take the entire GOP ship down with him. If he survived the "coup" (as he calls it), he would purge from the GOP anybody who participated.

The second problem for Republicans is how to deal with Trump's political base were he to leave office, particularly if his departure were to be ugly. Mike Pence could likely motivate Catholic and evangelical conservatives. But the more secular white working-class base that was so critical in Ohio, Pennsylvania, Michigan, and Wisconsin—true swing voters who have supported Democrats in the past—owe their allegiance to Trump because of his harsh stance on immigration, his vocal advocacy for older industries (steel and coal), and to some extent his hostility to minority ethnic groups. Trump brought these people into the Republican fold, and another Republican, even Pence, might not be able to keep them in.

And then there are the Russians. Do they have damaging information on Republican leaders in Congress? If so, the Russians could shut down any movement in the GOP to remove and replace Trump through blackmail or providing damaging information about key Republican leaders.

We have no idea what dirt the Russians have on top Republicans. What we do know is that the Russians have been hacking computers for a long time, and that many Americans, including members of Congress, do many stupid things on their computers.

Several key Republican leaders are acting so irrationally that it isn't hard to conclude that Russia might have something on them, as detailed in an article written by one of your authors (Painter) and clinical psychologist Leanne Watt:

Although former Republican National Conference (RNC) chairman, Reince Priebus, repeatedly denied that the RNC emails were violated, it has been established by the FBI that the Russians successfully hacked the RNC's emails, possibly exposing weaknesses within the Republican leadership. In fact, it appears that the Russians now possess approximately ten years' worth of GOP emails, through 2015, when SMARTech, an email- and web-hosting firm, stopped hosting the Republican Party's email accounts. (Tom Del Beccaro, the ex-chairman of the California Republican Party, reported to The Smoking Gun that SMARTech has "admitted being hacked.") . . .

It would be naïve to ignore that Vladimir Putin likes to leverage "secrets." If the Russians discovered any hidden scandals within the Republican hacked emails, then this is exactly what Putin would attempt to do. It is well-known within the intelligence community that Russian intelligence officers are highly skilled at exploiting people's weaknesses with the goal of securing their cooperation. Putin, a former KGB operative and former FSB head, is Russia's most masterful "behaviorist," especially adept at identifying vulnerabilities in targets, skillfully manipulating and cultivating cooperation from his victims.
. . .

We begin our exploration by looking at the irrational behavior exhibited by House Intelligence Committee (HIC) Chairman Devin Nunes, in relationship to the president and the HIC probe into Russian election interference . . . There is no logical reason for Nunes to go so far in trying to obstruct the Russian investigation unless he has something personal at stake. Why else would Nunes use up his own political capital to attack the Mueller investigation and interfere with the House's investigation of Russian interference in the election?

[Senator] Lindsey Graham (R-SC) is also on our roster of Congress members behaving in an unreasonable fashion. Most striking is the senator's dramatic reversal in tone and words regarding the president, coupled with his unprecedented shift of character. Graham's remarkable pivot is especially noteworthy, because the senator has been long known for his predictable, principled, and independent character style; these traits were all on display in his May 2016 remarks, when he stated that he would not be voting for Trump in the general election, asserting that the Republican Party had been "conned." For many years, Graham was one of Donald Trump's harshest critics. In 2015, he described Donald Trump as a "race-baiting xenophobic bigot." In 2016, Graham said of Trump: "I think he's a kook. I think he's crazy. I think he's unfit for office." During the first eight months of Trump's presidency, Graham continued to criticize Trump . . .

Graham's striking U-turn took place later in 2017, when he suddenly, almost overnight, became one of the president's staunchest allies. In October of 2017, Graham played golf with Trump for the first time—and twice in the same week. During their week of golf dates, the *LA Times* reports that ". . . other senators have said Trump and Graham now talk so frequently it's as if they are on speed-dial with one another." Based upon the timing of his dramatic shift and their golf games, we assume that the conversations Senator Graham had with Trump on the golf course played a role in his sharp reversal.

Following their October 2017 tête-à-tête, Graham began to contradict himself in a way that was totally out of character for him. In November of 2017, the senator repudiated his earlier remarks on Trump's character, stating: "What concerns me about the American press is this endless, endless attempt to label [Trump] as some kind of kook, not fit to be president." And Graham now claims that he has "never heard him (Trump) make a single racist statement." And in August of 2018, Senator Graham defended Trump's desire to fire Jeff Sessions, insisting that the president is "entitled to an attorney general he has faith in."

. . .

We know that Senator Graham's emails were stolen by the Russians, based upon his own admission in a December of 2016 interview. Most of Graham's hacked emails have not been released, so it is reasonable to consider the possibility that many of his emails are still in play . . .

And alarmingly, [these men] continue to be willing to protect Trump, even though their association with him will undermine their future political careers, and in spite of the fact that he is a danger to our nation.

As this book is going to press, it appears that, for various reasons, almost all of the Republicans in Congress will not undertake their constitutional duty to remove Trump's "cancer on the presidency." Nonetheless, developments in 2019, including the Ukraine scandal, Trump allowing Turkey to invade

Syria and slaughter our Kurdish allies, all while enjoying profits and benefits (emoluments) from Trump Tower Istanbul, and Trump's incredibly brazen attempt to solicit yet more foreign emoluments by offering to host the 2020 G7 meeting at his Doral golf resort, may lead some Republicans to finally say that they are fed up. At some point, the calculus shifts in favor of doing what the Republican leaders did in 1974 when they asked the president to resign. This would mean installing Pence in the presidency with the benefits and difficulties of running with him in 2020 instead of Trump. As of the printing of this book we are apparently not at this point yet, but we could be close. If it happens, it will likely happen quite suddenly as twenty or more Republican senators together come out and say "ENOUGH. DONALD TRUMP, YOU'RE FIRED!"

But what if the opposite happens and Trump is not convicted by the Senate?

If Trump is reelected, we may have to deal with the very real possibility that he will not want to leave office when his second term expires. The Constitution only allows a president two terms, but the Constitution also says a president may not receive emoluments from foreign governments and that the freedom of the press is protected. The Constitution has been ignored thus far in the Trump presidency and may be ignored again.

What about prosecution of Trump, and perhaps others, for crimes committed during his presidency? Will justice ever be done?

A federal prosecution of the president while he is in office is, we believe, constitutional, but Trump's attorney general, William Barr, has foreclosed that. Mueller had no choice but not to indict and instead to send his report to Congress to consider for impeachment. The state of New York could try to indict Trump, and test his immunity from prosecution in the courts, but thus far that has not happened.

It could be a different story after Trump leaves office. He would no longer be a sitting president, removing the first constitutional argument against his indictment. A new attorney general could also repudiate the second constitutional argument—the extreme version of the unitary executive theory that purports to allow a president to obstruct a Justice Department investigation while he is in office.

Such a prosecution of Trump, as a former president, should of course be handled by an independent prosecutor, not by political appointees of a new president.

Democratic candidates for president, and a future Democratic president, should never revert to the "lock him up" mentality that helped create this constitutional debacle. A prosecution of Trump for his crimes in office should be carried out in accordance with the rule of law—and should not be a rallying cry for Democratic presidential candidates or at the Democratic National Convention—but it should take place.

The rule of law requires it.

But do Americans care? We should, but do we?

Too many Americans are numb to Trump's behavior and rhetoric. They don't seem to be aware of how Trump's actions and words threaten the rule of law and our democracy.

Moreover, besides the rule of law, there are political issues that Americans care about. For the vast majority of voters, particularly swing voters in the middle of the political spectrum, those issues are economic. Democrats may not have learned their lesson from the 2016 election—particularly the need to focus on economic issues and the declining middle class.

Democrats also need a realistic platform on immigration, the issue that may have won Trump the 2016 election.

Trump's "wall" is a narcissistic ego trip, not a solution, but denying that illegal immigration is a problem is also foolhardy. It remains to be seen whether Democrats will articulate workable solutions such as cracking down on employers of undocumented workers (like the Trump Organization) with strict enforcement and heavy fines.

Democrats also could run too far to the left on social issues—or more likely talk too much about social issues that appeal to partisan voters who have already made up their minds, and not talk enough about economic issues that appeal to swing voters. This would allow Trump once again to paint a picture of Democrats abandoning the middle class.

Russian trolls—pretending to be "Democrats"—are all too happy to help with stirring the identity-politics pot. The Russians, we can be certain, will still be up to their game in 2020.

Dan Coats, the director of national intelligence, in February 2019 told reporters at a White House briefing that Russia was behind "a pervasive messaging campaign" to undermine the November 2018 congressional elections as well as the 2020 presidential election.

Said Coats, "We also know the Russians tried to hack into and steal information from candidates and government officials alike."

Coats said that the Russians' intention was to suppress voting, provide illegal campaign financing, and make cyberattacks against our voting mechanism along with computer hacks that target elected officials and others.

By late July 2019, Coats resigned his position after a tenure marked by tension with the White House.

FBI Director Christopher Wray has reached similar conclusions about Russia, and thus far remains in his job.

It remains to be seen whether our intelligence agencies can play defense effectively or whether future elections will be compromised by Russian hacking.

We know whose side Trump is on. He would be happy to have the Russians compromise the coming elections and keep him in office.

On January 3, 2020 Trump found another way to distract from his impending impeachment trial in the Senate. He authorized a military strike that killed Iran's top security and intelligence commander Major General Qassem Soleimani in a drone strike at Baghdad International Airport in Iraq. The reasons Soleimani had been in Iraq were unclear, but it may have been to help coordinate Iranian and Iraqi efforts to combat ISIS. Trump claimed that Soleimani had also been responsible for Iran's sponsorship of terrorist attacks on Americans and that killing him saved countless lives. The immediate response to the killing was outrage in Iran, and almost as much outrage in Iraq, where the Parliament days later voted to expel all foreign soldiers—including Americans—from Iraqi territory. Trump responded with threats to impose sanctions on Iraq and also exchanged belligerent military threats with top officials in Iran. Trump even threatened—on Twitter of course—to destroy major cultural sites in Iran, which would be a clear violation of international treaty obligations and a war crime under the War Crimes Act. Trump doesn't care.

America's relationship with Iraq, which was hosting Soleimani when he was attacked, is now in shambles, despite the United States having invested trillions of dollars—and losing thousands of soldiers' lives—stabilizing Iraq over the past seventeen years. Trump doesn't care.

As this book goes to print, Iran is threatening retaliatory military action against the United States and Trump is very much hoping that Iran will do just that. Getting into a war with Iran on the eve of his Senate impeachment trial is for him a dream come true, even if it could mean the deaths of thousands of Americans and Iranians, and perhaps millions killed if nuclear weapons are used.

Going back to President Lincoln's suspension of habeas corpus during the Civil War and eighty years later the internment of Japanese Americans during World War II, war has inevitably brought an expansion of presidential power. War is a "hall pass" for presidents. Trump, on the eve of impeachment badly needs a hall pass. And Iran, by retaliating against the United States, may very well give it to him.

Today, we have to ask ourselves: How much do we care about preserving the Union and the rule of law set forth in the Constitution that governs it? Do we care at least as much about the country as a whole as its separate parts? Will we learn to love our fellow Americans enough that we are not more afraid of neighbors of a different race, religion, or political ideology than we are afraid of a foreign adversary that wants to destabilize our government and undermine the rule of law in the United States?

The founders gave us a Constitution that, as we have amended it over the years, continues to guide the United States on the path of being a large and prosperous representative democracy. We will never stop arguing with each other (that is part of democracy), but we also need to recognize our common goals. We need to recognize the fact that our adversaries in the world—Russia among them—are not always wishing us success and, if they have a chance, will take advantage of our divisions to undermine us. To assure the future of the rule of law in our country, we have to recognize that what we share as Americans is far more important than anything that can divide us.

Abraham Lincoln urged the country to unite after the horrific Civil War. We could have lost everything the founders envisioned. At Gettysburg, Lincoln said to the nation:

It is rather for us to be here dedicated to the great task remaining before us—that from these honored dead we take increased devotion to that cause for which they gave the last full measure of devotion—that we here highly resolve that these dead shall not have died in vain—that this nation, under God, shall have a new birth of freedom—and that government of the people, by the people, for the people, shall not perish from the earth.

Today our country and the rule of law are under attack from both homegrown nativism and from powerful Russian forces that appear determined to keep Donald Trump in office. Our Senate has thus far abandoned its constitutional duty to remove a narcissistic, criminal, and authoritarian president—an American Nero—from office.

It is now up to us, the people, to make sure that our government, in Lincoln's words, does not perish from the earth.

NOTES

INTRODUCTION

Page 1 See *Annals of Tacitus*, Books XIII through XVI (covering the reign of Nero up through 66 CE). Suetonius and Cassius Dio also wrote histories of Nero several decades after his death. All three of these authors were severely critical of Nero, but they also give conflicting accounts. Modern historians have questioned their accounts. See Edward Champlin, *Nero* (Cambridge, MA: Harvard University Press, 2005). One criticism of Tacitus, Suetonius, and Cassius Dio is that all three were members of the elite senatorial class impacted by Nero's populist appeal and perceived assault on the rule of law. This is not a book on Roman history. Our prototype is the Nero described by Tacitus and we leave aside further inquiry into what the actual Nero was like. We note, however, that the allegation that Tacitus, Suetonius, and Cassius Dio because of their elite status were biased against Nero and Nero's populism is itself a recurring phenomenon in history. Donald Trump has repeatedly said that the Republican and Democratic Party "elites" are against him and that he is on the side of the people.

Page 2 Thrasea was forced to commit suicide. Mary Beard, *SPQR: A History of Ancient Rome* (New York: Liveright, 2016).

Page 4 . . . had to sit on him to keep him safe on the floor. Lucy Worsley, "What was the truth about the madness of King George?" *Magazine: BBC News*, April 15, 2013. www.bbc.com/news/magazine 22122407.

Page 4 . . . and the pension of the royal laundress. Willard Sterne Randolph, "America's last king: The unsettling parallels between King George III and Donald Trump," *Salon*, June 25, 2017.

Page 4 For a more favorable biography of George III, see Christopher Hibbert, *George III: A Personal History* (New York: Basic Books, 2000). See also John Brooke, *King George III* (New York: McGraw-Hill, 1972). Recent scholars have sought to conduct psychological analysis of King George III's correspondence. See Vassiliki Rentoumi, Timothy Peters, Jonathan Conlin, and Peter Garrard, "The acute mania of King George III: A computational linguistic analysis," *PLOS One*, March 22, 2017, which explains, "We used a computational linguistic approach, exploiting machine learning techniques, to examine the letters written by King George III during mentally healthy and apparently mentally ill periods of his life. The aims of the study were: first, to establish the existence of alterations in the King's written language at the onset of his first manic episode; and secondly to identify salient sources of variation contributing to the changes."

Page 5 In a separate article written with clinical psychologist Dr. Leanne Watt, Richard Painter observed that Trump has the personality disorder of narcissism so acute that he is incapable of leading. Richard Painter and Leanne Watt, "The 25th Amendment proves why Trump's mental health matters," *NBC News*, October 18, 2017.

Page 5 At best Trump is a real threat to our democracy and the rule of law. Several books and articles have already been written about this threat, including two to which Richard Painter, one of these authors, contributed a chapter: *Rocket Man: Nuclear Madness and the Mind of Donald Trump*, eds. John Gartner and Steven Buser (Asheville, NC: Chiron Publications, 2019), and *The Dangerous Case of Donald Trump*, ed. Bandy Lee (New York: Thomas Dunne Books, 2017).

CHAPTER 1: THE RULE OF LAW IN AMERICA

Page 10 "The natural liberty of man is to be free from any superior power on earth." John Locke, *Second Treatise of Civil Government*, ch. IV, sec 22 (1690).

CHAPTER 2: ASSAULTS ON THE RULE OF LAW IN EARLY AMERICA

Page 14 The deer antlers, a symbol of leadership, would be removed from his headgear, and he'd return to private life (Ultrakulture.com, December 14, 2014). See William Fenton, *The Great Law and the Longhouse: A Political History of the Iroquois Confederacy* (Norman, OK: University of Oklahoma Press, 1998); Kayanesenh Paul Williams, *Kayanerenkó:wa: The Great Law of Peace* (Winnipeg, MB, Canada: University of Manitoba Press, 2018); Bruce Elliott Johansen, *The Native Peoples of North America: A History*, vol. 1 (New Brunswick, NJ: Rutgers University Press, 2005), page 161: "The Traditional headdress of the Iroquois leader (an emblem of office) includes deer antlers which are said to have been 'knocked off' if the sachem has been impeached"; "Chiefs of the Iroquois League are instructed to take criticism honestly and that their skins should be seven spans thick to absorb the criticism of the people they represent in public councils"; "The Great Law also provides for the removal from office of sachems who can no longer adequately function in office, a measure remarkably similar to a constitutional amendment [the 25th Amendment] adopted in the late 20th century providing for the removal of an incapacitated president"; "In some ways the Grand Council acts like the United States House of Representatives and Senate, with their conference committees."

Page 14 For more information on how our Constitution was modeled in part upon the Great Law of Peace, we recommend Gregory Schaaf, *The U.S. Constitution and the Great Law of Peace* (Center for Indigenous Arts and Culture, 2004). See U.S. S. Con. Res. 76, December 2, 1987.

Page 18 "We maintain therefore that in matters of religion, no man's right is abridged by the institution of Civil Society, and that Religion is wholly exempt from its cognizance." James Madison, "A Memorial and Remonstrance Against Religious Assessments," https://billofrightsinstitute.org/founding-documents/primary-source-documents/memorial-and-remonstrance.

Page 24 "If Attorney General Bradley can prove the words were not true," said Hamilton, "I will agree they were libelous." *A Brief Narrative of the Case and Tryal of John Peter Zenger, Printer of the New-York Weekly Journal*, was first published in 1736.

Page 24 "We maintain therefore that in matters of religion, no man's right is abridged by the institution of Civil Society, and that Religion is wholly exempt from its cognizance." Madison, "Memorial and Remonstrance." Jon Meacham, *American Gospel: God, the Founding Fathers, and the Making of a Nation* (New York: Random House, 2006), analyzes these writings and reproduces some of them in appendices. Vincent Phillip Muñoz, *God and the Fathers: Madison, Washington and Jefferson* (Cambridge, UK: Cambridge University Press, 2009), analyzes the different perspective on church and state of three of the Founders and applies their perspective to contemporary questions, such as the balance between secular law and religious freedom. Some "separation of church and state" arguments can be taken to an extreme and depart from the intent of the framers. Philip Hamburger, *Separation of Church and State* (Cambridge, MA: Harvard University Press, 2002), challenges more far-reaching views on separation of church and state in modern scholarship and commentary as having no basis in the First Amendment.

CHAPTER 3: FROM THE CIVIL WAR TO THE OHIO GANG

Page 32 The policy was first implemented by Secretary of State William Seward and then by Secretary of War Edwin Stanton. As many as 38,000 people were imprisoned and held without a hearing during the war. See Mark E. Neely, "The Lincoln Administration and Arbitrary Arrests: A Reconsideration Journal of the Abraham Lincoln Association," *Journal of the Abraham Lincoln Association* 5 (1983): 6–24 ("the lowest estimate is 13,535 arrests from February 15, 1862, to the end of the war"); Mark E. Neely, *The Fate of Liberty: Abraham Lincoln and Civil Liberties* (Oxford, UK: Oxford University Press, 1992).

Page 32 Taney wrote an opinion that Lincoln's action was unconstitutional. He said that only Congress could suspend habeas corpus. *Ex parte Merryman*, 17 F. Cas. 144 (C.C.D. Md. 1861) (No. 9487). Chief Justice of the United States Roger Taney's opinion in this case was not an opinion of the Supreme Court but his own opinion filed with the federal district court in Maryland holding that Lincoln's action was unconstitutional. He said that only Congress could suspend habeas corpus. Chief Justice Taney before the Civil War had been the author of one on the Supreme Court's most notorious pro-slavery opinions. *Dred Scott v. Sandford*, 60 U.S. (19 How.) 393 (1857), holding that the Constitution did not extend citizenship to African Americans whether they were enslaved or free and that therefore they were not entitled to the protections extended to citizens under the Constitution.

Page 33 Following the battle of Antietam on September 24, 1862, Lincoln broadened his expansion of the writ of habeas corpus. Dennis Keating, "Lincoln's Suspension of Habeas Corpus," *Cleveland Civil War Roundtable*, June 29, 2018.

Page 33 Once again, Lincoln ignored Congress's mandate. Mark Neely, *Fate of Liberty: Abraham Lincoln and Civil Liberties* (Oxford, UK: Oxford University Press, 1991). Lincoln thus acted outside the rule of law, although Congress later authorized the suspension of habeas corpus in the Habeas Corpus Suspension Act, 12 Stat. 755 (1863).

Page 34 The act allowed the president to call upon the army to quell a disturbance and to send federal marshals to polling places if violations of the act were detected, https://www.revolvy.com/page/Enforcement-Act-of-1870. See generally Stephen Cresswell, "Enforcing the Enforcement Acts: The Department of Justice in Northern Mississippi, 1870–1890," *Journal of Southern History* 53 (1987): 421–40. The Enforcement Act of 1870, "An Act to enforce the Right of Citizens of the United States to vote in the several States of this Union, and for other Purposes," 41st Congress, Sess. 2, 16 Stat. 140, May 31, 1870.

Page 34 Riding in large groups, the Klan terrorized the former slaves and those who supported them with intimidation, assaults, destruction of property, and murder. Elaine Frantz Parsons, *Ku-Klux: The Birth of the Klan during Reconstruction* (Chapel Hill, NC: University of North Carolina Press, 2015).

Page 36 Protégé of Andrew Jackson. David Herbert Donald, "Why they impeached Andrew Johnson," *American Heritage* 8 (December 1956).

Page 37 The South Carolina, Alabama, and Mississippi laws. Ibid.

Page 37 Annette Gordon-Reed, "The fight over Andrew Johnson's impeachment was a fight for the Future of the United States," *Smithsonian Magazine*, January 2018.

Page 38 The firing of Stanton was the last straw. Ibid.

Page 38 Wade was one reason why the impeachment failed. Robert Black, "Politics, prejudice and procedure: The impeachment trial of Andrew Johnson," *Institute for Historical Review* 7 (Summer 1986): 175–92.

Page 39 He refused to attend Grant's inauguration. David Crary, "Andrew Johnson back in the spotlight for 1868 impeachment brush," *Miami Herald*, October 12, 2019.

Page 39 Among those indicted were Babcock and Grant's other private secretary, Horace Porter. Mary Louise Hinsdale, *A History of the President's Cabinet* (Ann Arbor, MI: University of Michigan Press, 1911).

Page 39 According to Marsh, William Belknap received a total of approximately $20,000. Edward S. Cooper, *William Worth Belknap: An American Disgrace* (Vancouver, BC, Canada: Fairleigh Dickinson University Press, 2003).

Page 39 Belknap resigned to avoid impeachment but was impeached anyway. Ibid. Cooper discusses House deliberations over whether to impeach Belknap after he had left office to prevent him from taking future office. A majority of the Senate voted to impeach but not the required two-thirds majority, so Belknap was acquitted.

Page 40 The committee believed Robeson had embezzled it. See *Responses of the Presidents to Charges of Misconduct*, C. Vann Woodward, ed. (New York: Delacorte Press, 1974): 133–162.

Page 40 George Robeson was suspected of embezzling large sums of money from the Navy. Robert P.

Broadwater, *Ulysses S. Grant: A Biography* (Westport, CT: Greenwood Press, 2012). Report, Investigation of the Navy Department, 45th Congress, 3rd Session, House of Representatives, Report 112 (February 21, 1879) page 28: "Resolved [that Robeson's and others'] sale and disposition of public property, in their making of public contracts and in involving the government in indebtedness over and beyond the appropriations made by Congress for the support of the Navy, deserve and should receive the severest censure and condemnation." This is one of the earliest documented congressional investigations of military spending getting out of control.

Page 40 All the committee could do was admonish him. Ibid.

Page 41 The corrupt agents then substituted fake evidence that was designed to show that prosecutor Alexander was involved in the theft of the papers in the safe. Andrew L. Slap, *The Doom of Reconstruction: The Liberal Republicans in the Civil Rights Era* (New York: Fordham University Press, 2006).

Page 41 Babcock was acquitted. Later it was revealed that the jury had been tampered with. Ibid.

Page 41 Gould gave assistant Secretary of the Treasury Daniel Butterfield a $10,000 bribe. Kenneth D. Ackerman, *The Gold Ring: Jim Fisk, Jay Gould, and Black Friday, 1869* (Washington, DC: Viral History Press, 1988).

Page 41 Boutwell had been selling $1 million worth of gold a week. Ibid.

Page 42 This stopped Gould and Fisk from cornering the market, and at the same time financially ruined many other investors. Ibid.

Page 42 Benjamin Freed, "D.C. police once gave the president a speeding ticket," *DCist*, October 4, 2012.

Page 42 Michael Rosenwald, "The police officer who arrested a US president—could it happen again?" *Sydney Morning Herald*, December 17, 2018.

Page 42 J. LeCount Chestnut, "Ulysses Grant arrested for speeding," *Washington Post*, November 7, 1925.

Page 47 "The bullet is in me now, so that I cannot make a very long speech, but I will do my best." "Mr. Wilson has done precisely and exactly nothing about the trusts." "Mr. Wilson has distinctly committed itself to the old flintlock, muzzle-loaded doctrine of States' rights, and I have said distinctly that we are for the people's rights." "I only want to say this: Mr. Wilson has said that the States are the proper authorities to deal with the trusts. Well, about eighty percent of the trusts are organized in New Jersey. The Standard Oil, the tobacco, the sugar, the beef, all those trusts are organized in New Jersey." "I will say that, friends, because the Republican Party is beaten. Nobody needs to have any idea that anything can be done with the Republican Party." Theodore Roosevelt speech of October 14, 1912.

Page 49 The group had staked 33 claims, although Alaska land laws were designed to benefit small farmers and prevent monopoly and thus required each claimant to prove that he or she was acting on his or her own behalf, as well as limited each claimant to 160 acres. Henry Pringle, *The Life and Times of William Howard Taft* (New York: Farrar & Rinehart, 1939).

Page 49 A scandal in the press followed, and the progressive wing of the Republican Party split and joined the Democrats by the 1912 election. Ibid.

Page 49 The Ohio Gang, members of Harding's administration had taken bribes in exchange for leasing oil reserves at Teapot Dome in Wyoming to private companies. Robert K. Murray, *The Harding Era: Warren G. Harding and His Administration* (Newtown, CT: American Political Biography Press, 2000).

Page 49 Blacks were excluded from federal employment, and more so than during the preceding Teddy Roosevelt and William Taft administrations, and the president was allied with powerful Southern governors. Nicholas Patler, *Jim Crow and the Wilson Administration: Protesting Federal Segregation in the Early Twentieth Century* (Boulder, CO: University Press of Colorado, 2004), discusses how federal civil service laws were supposed to protect African Americans in federal employment but were often avoided; Eric S. Yellin, *Racism in the Nation's Service: Government Workers and the Color Line in Woodrow Wilson's America* (Chapel Hill, NC: University of North Carolina Press, 2013), describes a relative freedom for black federal workers during the Republican era from 1867 to 1913, followed by the Wilson Administration's use of progressive politics and civil service reform to purge the federal government of black workers; Yellin, page 3, discusses how much of the discrimination and purging of African American federal workers was done by men whom Wilson appointed to key government posts, including Assistant Treasury Secretary John Skelton Williams; see also Yellin, page 4 (before Wilson became president in 1913, "government employment and Republican politics safeguarded Washington as a place of relative opportunity for black Americans"). For a discussion of Wilson's complex morality on a range of issues, including race, see Patricia O'Toole, *The Moralist: Woodrow Wilson and the World That He Made* (New York: Simon & Schuster, 2018), which discusses how Wilson pursed both a progressive economic agenda and a segregationist social agenda: "He knew that segregation was morally indefensible, but ending it would have cost him the votes of every Southerner in Congress." See also two other recent Wilson biographies: John M. Cooper, *Woodrow Wilson: A Biography* (New York: Knopf, 2009), and A. Scott Berg, *Wilson* (New York: G. P. Putnam's Sons, 2013).

Page 49 Harry Sinclair, founder of Sinclair Oil, went to jail for contempt of court and for bribing the jurors. Ibid. See "Sinclair's last night in jail," *Milwaukee Sentinel* (A), November 19, 1929, which describes Sinclair's six-month sentence for contempt of court and shadowing jurors.

CHAPTER 4: THE IMMIGRATION ISSUE: THE RED SCARE TO JAPANESE INTERNMENT

Page 53 Wilson called them "creatures of passion, disloyalty, and anarchy," and declared that they "must be crushed out." Mario DiNunzio, *Woodrow Wilson: Essential Writings and Speeches of the Scholar President* (New York: New York University Press, 2006). See also John Higham, *Strangers in the Land: Patterns of American Nativism, 1860–1925* (New Brunswick, NJ: Rutgers University Press, 1955, 2002 edition) page 200, quoting President Wilson's speech.

Page 55 Hoover's job was to name members of radical groups and investigate their activities. See Curt Gentry, *J. Edgar Hoover, The Man and the Secrets* (New York: W.W. Norton & Co., 1991). For an account of Hoover's personal as well as professional life, see Anthony Summers, *Official and Confidential: The Secret Life of J. Edgar Hoover* (New York: Open Road, 1993): "A homosexual F.B.I. Director, in charge of the nation's internal security, was a classic target for any hostile intelligence service—especially that of the Soviet Union."

Page 55 In New York City alone, 650 people were swept up and arrested. Louis F. Post, *The Deportations Delirium of Nineteen-Twenty: A Personal Narrative of an Historic Official Experience* (Chicago: Charles H. Kerr & Co., 1923).

Page 56 Sometimes every person there was arrested, whether or not that person belonged to the group. Some were American citizens. Ibid. See generally Louis F. Post, *Attorney General A. Mitchell Palmer on Charges Made Against Department of Justice*, vols. 1–2 (Hearings before the Committee on Rules, House of Representatives, Sixty-sixth Congress, 2nd sess., 1920). Palmer's feud with Post arose because Post, as Assistant Secretary of Labor and Acting Secretary of Labor, was administering the Bureau of Immigration, then under the Labor Department. Post had freed from detention immigrants whom Palmer had ordered be detained. Palmer, who was running for the Democratic nomination for president in 1920, failed to get President Wilson to fire Post, and tried to start a House investigation and impeachment proceeding against Post but this effort backfired; Post kept his job and the House report was largely unfavorable to Palmer.

Page 57 ". . . any disgrace should be forever removed from their names." Report to the Governor in the matter of Sacco and Vanzetti (Boston: Commonwealth of Massachusetts, 1977).

Page 58 Richard Reeves, *Infamy: The Shocking Story of the Japanese American Internment in World War II* (New York: Henry Holt and Company, 2015); Greg Robinson, *A Tragedy of Democracy: Japanese Confinement in North America* (New York: Columbia University Press, 2009); Greg Robinson, *By Order of the President: F.D.R. and the Internment of Japanese Americans* (Cambridge, MA: Harvard University Press, 2009), explains FDR's role; Jerry Stanley, *I Am an American: A True Story of Japanese Internment* (New York: Crown Publishing, 1996).

Page 59 "Racial antagonisms never can." *Korematsu v. United States*, 323 U.S. 214 (Washington, DC: Supreme Court of the United States, 1944). Justice Robert Jackson challenged the inherent racism of the Japanese exclusion area in his dissent: "A citizen's presence in the locality, however, was made a crime only if his parents were of Japanese birth. Had Korematsu been one of four—the others being, say, a German alien enemy, an Italian alien enemy, and a citizen of American-born ancestors, convicted of treason but out on parole—only Korematsu's presence would have violated the order. The difference between their innocence and his crime would result, not from anything he did, said, or thought, different than they, but only in that he was born of different racial stock."

Page 59 The U.S. Supreme Court held there was no legitimate, legally sanctioned reason for holding loyal, law-abiding Japanese-American citizens in internment camps once the government determined they weren't threats to the nation's security. *Ex parte Mitsuye Endo*, 323 U.S. 283 (1944).

Pages 59–69 "A million Italian-Americans served in the war, and more than half that number had to worry about owning a flashlight and carrying an Enemy Alien card. It makes me angry to this day." Rock Positano and John Positano, *Dinner with DiMaggio* (New York: Simon & Schuster, 2017).

CHAPTER 5: RUSSIAN ASSAULTS ON THE RULE OF LAW

Page 62 . . . and so the Russians came up with a plan to stir up trouble between the two countries. Will Englund, "When Russian meddling in the US got so bad the ambassador got the boot," *Washington Post*, November 12, 2017.

Page 66 Sadly for Stalin and Russia, Hitler would come to power and bring death and destruction on the Soviet Union. Countrystudies.us/russia/10.htm. See Timothy Snyder, *Bloodlands: Europe Between Hitler and Stalin* (New York: Basic Books, 2012), a history of the mass murders committed by the Nazi and Stalinist regimes in the 1930s and 1940s in the vast geographic area between Germany and Russia; Roger Moorhouse, *The Devils' Alliance: Hitler's Pact with Stalin, 1939–1941* (New York: Basic Books, 2014); John Lukacs, *June 1941, Hitler and Stalin* (New Haven, CT: Yale University Press, 2006), chronicles the relationship between the two dictators and Hitler's decision to invade Russia in June 1941, at page 3 ("In 1941 and exactly on 22 June 1941 everything depended upon two men, Hitler and Stalin. This in itself refutes the social-scientific and current opinion according to which history, especially as we advance into the mass age, is ruled by vast economic and material forces and not by individual persons.")

Page 68 Over the years, more than a hundred such devices were found in American embassies throughout the Communist Bloc. James Lint, "Russia's long history of election meddling and espionage," *In Homeland Security*, March 5, 2018.

Page 69 Harvard later settled the suit with USAID in 2005 for $26.5 million. Zachary M. Seward, "Harvard to pay $26.5 million in HIID settlement," *Harvard Crimson*, July 29, 2005.

CHAPTER 6: THE NAZIS' ASSAULT ON THE RULE OF LAW

Page 72 As a boy living in Vienna, Austria, Hitler adopted a nationalist stance. An extreme narcissist lacking in empathy, Hitler in 1921 began preaching a virulent, violent anti-Semitism, speaking of putting Jews in concentration camps and even exterminating them. Alex Ross, "The Hitler vortex," *The New Yorker*, April 30, 2018.

Page 74 He reduced law to power relationships, and in the end Schmidt and other university professors ended up becoming members of the Nazi party. Claudia Koonz, *The Nazi Conscience* (Cambridge, MA: Belknap Press, 2005).

Page 75 Hitler was not interested in the state, did not understand the state, and actually did not think much of it. Sebastian Haffner, *The Meaning of Hitler* (Cambridge, MA: Harvard University Press, 1983), p. 86.

Page 75 The press in Germany was no longer free. The news was what Hitler said it was. Ibid.

Page 77 He was party to the burning of books by Jewish authors and even ordered the burning of books by authors who might have been influenced by Jewish authors. Ibid.

Page 78 The Communist Party was dismantled and its real estate holdings taken from them. The History Place, "Genocide in the 20th century: The Nazi Holocaust, 1938–1945, 6,000,000 deaths," http://www. historyplace.com/worldhistory/genocide/holocaust.htm.

Page 78 The decree, called "For the Protection of the People and State," remained in effect until the end of World War II. Ibid.

Page 78 Stormtroopers raided homes, rounded up citizens, especially Jews, and took them to a barracks, where they were beaten and tortured. Ibid.

Page 78 All political opposition was destroyed, and Hitler was free to do as he wished. Unions were dissolved. Many clergy were arrested. Ibid.

Page 79 Dachau, the first, was built to hold political prisoners, especially Jews and gays. Ibid.

Page 79 In 1934, the S. D. hired Adolph Eichmann to be its Nazi expert on the Jews. He spied on Jewish organizations in Germany. Ibid.

Page 79 In *Der Stermer*, it was written, "Now judgment has begun and it will reach its conclusion only when knowledge of the Jews has been erased from the earth." Ibid.

Page 81 Bernhard Rieger, *The People's Car: A Global History of the Volkswagen Beetle* (Cambridge, MA: Harvard University Press, 2013). Ferdinand Porsche said of the car: "Its purpose is to answer their transportation needs, and it is intended to give them joy." https://www.history.com/this-day-in-history/volkswagen-is-founded.

CHAPTER 7: MCCARTHYISM

Page 86 Eight hundred public school teachers were targeted. See Peter Golenbock, *In the Country of Brooklyn* (New York: William Morrow, 2008).

Page 91 Said Richard Gid Powers, a historian who has written extensively on Hoover and the FBI, "All the institutions young Hoover joined—Sunday school, church, Central High—regarded themselves as defenses against the immigrant threat to the nation, hegemony, its character as all-but-officially Christian nation, and to the national leadership of the old-stock American." Richard Gid Powers, *Secrecy and Power: The Life of J. Edgar Hoover* (New York: The Free Press, 1987).

Page 92 *The Crucible*, by Arthur Miller, first produced in 1953, was set in Salem, Massachusetts, during the witch trials, but also incorporates themes from McCarthyism.

Page 92 David Oshinsky, *A Conspiracy So Immense: The World of Joe McCarthy* (Oxford, UK: Oxford University Press, 2005).

Page 94 Nicholas Von Hoffman, *Citizen Cohn* (New York: Doubleday, 1988). This is a biography of McCarthy's chief counsel who later returned to New York City to represent clients including Fred and Donald Trump.

CHAPTER 8: RACE AND THE RULE OF LAW

Page 98 In Virginia, Senator Harry Byrd organized a movement that closed schools rather than integrate them. William Yardley, "Harry F. Byrd, Virginia senator, dies at 98," *New York Times*, July 30, 2103. The opposition in Congress and from elected state officials, almost all Democrats, was fierce. See J. Harvie Wilkinson, *Harry Byrd and the Changing Face of Virginia Politics, 1945–1966* (Charlottesville, VA: University of Virginia Press, 1968), for an interesting account of Byrd by a lawyer who would later become a prominent conservative jurist on the Fourth Circuit Court of Appeals.

Page 98 In Florida, the state legislature passed a resolution denouncing the *Brown v. Board* decision and declared it null and void. (House Concurrent Resolution No. 174.)

Page 98 He argued that the overturning of Brown should only be done legally. https://www.floridamemory.com/exhibits/floridahighlights/Collins.

Page 98 In Arkansas, Eisenhower answered Faubus's challenge by sending members of the 101st Airborne Division from Fort Campbell, Kentucky, to Arkansas. He also federalized the Arkansas National Guard. https://archive.nytimes.com/www.nytimes.com/learning/general/onthisday/big/0925.html. David A. Nichols, *A Matter of Justice: Eisenhower and the Beginning of the Civil Rights Revolution* (New York: Simon & Schuster, 2007), examines Eisenhower's actions during the civil rights movement and concludes that, despite his cautious words, he was more willing than his predecessor Harry Truman to take action to advance civil rights.

Page 99 Thirty-one years after the murder, De La Beckwith was finally convicted. https://www.history.com/this-day-in-history/beckwith-convicted-of-killing-medgar-evers.

Page 99 He capitulated only when President John F. Kennedy intervened, and Wallace was ordered by General Henry Graham of the Alabama National Guard to step aside. Tribune News Services, "General who faced down George Wallace in 1963," *Chicago Tribune*, March 26, 1999. http://www.chicagotribune.com/news/ct-xpm-1999-03-26-9903260281-story.html.

Page 100 Kennedy had said to a Justice Department official, "Can't you get your goddamned friends off those buses? Stop them." www.pbs.org/wgbh/americanexperience/features/kennedys-and-civil-rights.

Page 102 President Johnson commented to his chief of staff, Bill Moyers, "I think we just gave the South to the Republicans for your lifetime and mine." https://answers.yahoo.com/question/index?qid=1006030502842.

Page 103 Whites-only primaries continued. https://www.courtlistener.com/opinion/101911/Nixon-v-condon.

Page 105 Said Kevin Phillips in his book, *The Emerging Republican Majority* (New Rochelle, NY: Arlington House, 1969), "The more negroes who register as Democrats in the South, the sooner the negrophobe whites will quit the Democrats and become Republicans." Eugene Robinson, "Needed: Competition for black votes," *Real Clear Politics*, October 8, 2010. https://www.realclearpolitics.com/articles/2010/10/08/needed_competition_for_black_votes_107484.html.

Page 107 Carter named more blacks, Latinos, and women to the federal judiciary than all previous administrations combined. Ari Berman, "Op-Ed: How Jimmy Carter championed civil rights—and Ronald Reagan didn't," *Los Angeles Times*, September 3, 2015.

Page 109 In 1980, almost a quarter of all Democratic voters switched and voted for Reagan. In 1984, Reagan got 90 percent of the white vote. Ninety percent of blacks voted against him. https://ropercenter.cornell.edu/polls/us-elections/how-groups-voted/how-groups-voted-1984.

Page 110 When George H. W. Bush ran for president, he told the country to "leave that tired old baggage of bigotry behind." https://potus-geeks.livejournal.com/172919.html.

Page 111 Said Jennifer Clark of the Brennan Center for Justice, "[Voter fraud] is not a significant concern." Sami Edge, "No, voter fraud actually isn't a persistent problem," *Washington Post*, September 1, 2016.

Page 111 Obama achieved most of these goals, though no significant civil rights legislation for African Americans was brought forth. The focus was on enforcing the existing laws. David Cole, "Obama's civil rights legacy—and ours," *The Nation*, December 8, 2016.

Page 115 Alana Abramson, "How Donald Trump perpetrated the 'birther' movement for years," *ABC News*, September 16, 2016.

CHAPTER 9: THE PHONY WAR: SCIENCE V. RELIGION

Page 118 See Ernan McMullin, *The Church and Galileo* (Notre Dame, IN: University of Notre Dame Press, 2005), a collection of essays by scholars examining the confrontation between Galileo and the Church); Dom Paschal Scotti, *Galileo Revisited: The Galileo Affair in Context* (San Francisco: Ignatius Press, 2017).

Page 119 Argued Clarence Darrow for the defense, "We find today as brazen and as bold an attempt to destroy learning as was even made in the Middle Ages." http://teva.contentdm.oclc.org/cdm/landingpage/collection/scopes.

Page 119 Darrow concluded his examination by saying, "I am examining you on your fool ideas that no intelligent Christian on earth believes." Ibid.

Page 119 In 1973, Tennessee passed a bill saying that the Genesis account in the Bible had to be given equal weight when evolution was taught. https://www.nytimes.com/1973/05/09/archives/tennessee-law-equalizes-all-teachings-on-creation.html.

Page 119 Two years later, the law was declared unconstitutional by a federal appeals court. Glenn Branch and Ann Reid, "50 years ago: Repeal of Tennessee's 'Monkey Law,'" *Scientific American*, May 10, 2017.

Page 120 "We are taking the creator, the one that created everything, we're just trying to kick Him out and He's not happy with that." Heather Clark, *Christian News*, September 15, 2014.

Page 122 ". . . and since the reproductive function is so vital to the upkeep of the race, and since any exception to this law would be multiplied indefinitely, every act of contraception frustration is a gravely immoral act, or, in Catholic terminology, a mortal sin." Father Francis J. Connell, "Birth control: The case for the Catholic," *The Atlantic*, October 1939.

Page 123 They were fined $100 each. https://www.thirteen.org/wnet/supremecourt/rights/landmark_griswold.html.

Page 123 In 1972, in the case of *Eisenstadt v. Baird*, the court extended the right of privacy in the use of contraceptives to all women, married or not. https://embryo.asu.edu/pages/eisenstadt-v-baird-1972.

Page 123 When the U.S. Court of Appeals for the First Circuit found his conviction to be unconstitutional, he was released. Ibid.

Page 125 The rationale behind all ten reasons was either religious (abortion is "evil") or the premise that human life begins at conception ("abortion is murder"). https://www.tfpstudentaction.org/resources/fliers/10-reasons-why-abortion-is-evil. More sophisticated commentary on *Roe v. Wade* from both sides of the debate is extensive. For insight into how the debate was viewed at the time, see David J. Garrow, *Liberty and Sexuality: The Right to Privacy and the Making of Roe v. Wade* (Berkeley, CA: University of California Press 1994, 1998), which discusses how the right to privacy in *Roe* emerged out of the *Griswold v. Connecticut* holding on birth control; *The Morality of Abortion*, John T. Noonan, ed. (Cambridge, MA: Harvard University Press, 1970), discusses the moral and legal issues of the abortion controversy by authors who generally conclude that unrestricted abortion is wrong; Rosemary Nossiff, *Before Roe: Abortion Policy in the States* (Philadelphia: Temple University Press, 2001), describes abortion restrictions in the various states and the impact on women; Leslie J. Reagan, *When Abortion Was a Crime: Women, Medicine, and Law in the United States* (Berkeley, CA: University of California Press, 1998).

Page 126 "The commandment gave life to what otherwise would have been only rational calculation." Dave Andrusko, "50 years ago today Colorado passed an historic abortion law which unleashed the abortion machinery," *National Right to Life News Today*, April 25, 2017.

Page 127 To avoid the glare of the cops, many gays who lived in Greenwich Village went to the Stonewall Inn, a safe haven for gay, lesbian, and transgender people. https://www.history.com/topics/gay-rights/the-stonewall-riots.

Pages 127–128 This was thought to be a scientific fact as early as 1990, but only in 2014 in a report released by the Academy of Science South Africa was the theory substantiated. Michael Sean Pepper and Beverly Kramer, "Here's what we know about the science of sexual orientation," *Slate*, June 11, 2015.

Page 128 Scientific studies also showed the harmful effects of trying to deny one's orientation. Studies showed that keeping one's sexual orientation hidden (in the closet) and dealing with the social stigma of homosexuality can add to the stress of being gay or bisexual. https://www.cdc.gov/msmhealth/mental-health.htm.

Page 128 Among those strongly opposed to gay and lesbian rights in at least some of these areas have been the Catholic Church, Orthodox Jews, Southern Baptists, and other evangelical Protestant denominations. David Masci and Michael Lipka, "Where Christian churches, other religions stand on gay marriage,"

Pew Research Center, December 21, 2015.

Page 128   Among those who do so are Reform and Conservative Jews, Unitarians, Episcopalians, many Presbyterians and Lutherans, and the Congregationalists in the United Church of Christ. Ibid.

Page 129   In *Bowers v. Hardwick*, 478 U.S. 186 (1986), the Supreme Court had upheld a Georgia anti-sodomy law. The Court reversed its position and struck down a similar Texas law in *Lawrence v. Texas*, 539 U.S. 558 (2003). See Dale Carpenter, *Flagrant Conduct: The Story of Lawrence v. Texas* (New York: W. W. Norton, 2012). The next major Supreme Court victories for gay and lesbian rights were *United States v. Windsor*, 570 U.S. 744 (2013), striking down the federal "Defense of Marriage Act," which had refused federal recognition to same-sex marriages under state law, and *Obergefell v. Hodges*, 135 S. Ct. 2584 (2015), requiring states to grant marriage licenses to same-sex couples.

CHAPTER 10: THE STAIN OF VIETNAM

Page 136   The generals promised them safe conduct, but after they were captured, they were brutally murdered. https://www.history.com/this-day-in-history/diem-murdered-during-coup.

Page 136   He pulled 1,000 American troops out, and he then signed an order to withdraw the rest of them by 1965. James K. Galbraith, "JFK's Vietnam withdrawal plan is a fact, not speculation," *The Nation*, November 22, 2013. Scores of books have been written about how the Johnson Administration became embroiled in Vietnam and couldn't find a way out. Books on this topic include George C. Herring, *LBJ and Vietnam: A Different Kind of War* (Austin, TX: University of Texas Press, 1994); Brian VanDeMark, *Into the Quagmire: Lyndon Johnson and the Escalation of the Vietnam War* (Oxford, UK: Oxford University Press, 1995); Michael H. Hunt, *Lyndon Johnson's War: America's Cold War Crusade in Vietnam, 1945–1968* (New York: Farrar, Straus and Giroux, 2011); and a fascinating book written by an army officer who would later become President Trump's National Security advisor, H. R. McMaster, *Dereliction of Duty: Johnson, McNamara, the Joint Chiefs of Staff and the Lies That Led to Vietnam* (New York: Harper Collins, 1998).

Page 137   Only years later did we learn that on that day Secretary of Defense Robert S. McNamara apparently misled LBJ by withholding from him the information that the U.S. commander in the Gulf had serious doubts there had been an attack. Gareth Porter, "Robert S. McNamara and the real Tonkin Gulf deception," *CounterPunch*, August 5, 2014.

Page 140   "I feel like a great and very brave soldier." https://www.usmagazine.com/celebrity-news/news/donald-trump-calls-sleeping-around-as-his-personal-vietnam-w432176/.

CHAPTER 11: TRICKY DICK AND DIRTY TRICKS

Page 141   Nixon won by 15,000 votes. Jerry Voorhis and Paul Bullock, *The Idealist as Politician* (New York: Vantage Press, 1978). Michael A. Cohen, *American Maelstrom: The 1968 Election and the Politics of Division* (Oxford, UK: Oxford University Press, 2016), discusses the political strategies and manipulation implemented in the 1968 election and the impact on American democracy. An analysis of the 1968 election that focuses on what went wrong on the Democratic side and the papers of Hubert Humphrey, appears in Michael Schumacher, *The Contest: The 1968 Election and the War for America's Soul* (Minneapolis, MN: University of Minnesota Press, 2018).

Page 142   Nixon's response: "I'll castrate her." Irwin Gellman, *The Contender* (New York: The Free Press, 1999). See also Greg Mitchell, *Tricky Dick and the Pink Lady: Richard Nixon vs. Helen Gahagan Douglas—Sexual Politics and the Red Scare, 1950* (New York: Random House, 1998).

Page 142   In subsequent rallies, Nixon kept repeating that Douglas was "pink right down to her underwear." Colleen M. O'Connor, "'Pink right down to her underwear,'" *Los Angeles Times*, April 9, 1990. Sally Denton, *The Pink Lady: The Many Lives of Helen Gahagan Douglas* (London: Bloomsbury Press, 2009), discusses how Nixon's sexist attack was received at the time and newspaper cartoons depicting Helen Douglas's underwear.

Page 143 He told the American public he had a "secret plan to win the war," and then through a Nixon fund-raiser by the name of Anna Chennault, he sent a message to South Vietnam president Nguyen Van Thieu to say that if Thieu waited until *after* the election, that he, Nixon, could get Thieu a better deal for South Vietnam. John A. Farrell, "Nixon's Vietnam treachery," *New York Times*, December 31, 2016.

Page 143 Rostow, Johnson's national security aide, was ordered to hide the dossier. Meteor Blades, "What's new in BBC report on Nixon's treason on Vietnam? Not much," *Daily Kos*, March 17, 2013.

Page 144 Nixon had made himself an enemies' list, and on that list was MIT professor Daniel Ellsberg. See Daniel G. Axtell, "The complete annotated Nixon's Enemies List," EnemiesList.info, 2019.

Page 144 Hunt teamed up with former FBI agent G. Gordon Liddy and a group of right-wing Cuban émigrés to burglarize the office of Ellsberg's psychiatrist Lewis Fielding to gain information about the man who leaked the Pentagon Papers in order to discredit him. Egil Krough, "The break-in that history forgot," *New York Times*, June 30, 2007.

Page 144 To make sure no one found out about Nixon's treachery, they planned to firebomb the Brookings Institution. John Dean, the White House counsel, said he heard Nixon "literally pounding on his desk, saying, 'I want that break-in at the Brookings-[Institution].'" Allen McDuffee, "Charles Colson, Watergate figure who proposed firebombing Brookings, said near death," *Washington Post*, April 19, 2012.

Page 145 Later Ken Clawson, deputy director of White House communications, admitted writing the letter. Then he denied writing the letter. David A. Andelman, "L.I. Muskie camp cries 'sabotage,'" *New York Times*, May 22, 1972.

Page 145 They also sent out a mass mailing to Democratic voters in Florida saying that Muskie was for busing, was against FBI director J. Edgar Hoover, and was against the space shuttle. Theodore White, *The Making of the President 1972* (New York: HarperCollins, 1972).

Page 145 Nixon and Chief of Staff H. R. Haldeman even discussed sending campaign contributions to Jesse Jackson in an attempt to get him to run for president as an Independent. Ibid.

Page 146 On September 15, 1972, the five burglars were indicted by a Grand Jury along with G. Gordon Liddy, a former FBI agent, treasury official, and counsel to the Finance Committee to Reelect the President, and E. Howard Hunt, a former White House consultant and CIA employee. https://www.nytimes.com/1974/03/02/archives/federal-grand-jury-indicts-7-nixon-aides-on-charges-of-conspiracy.html.

Page 147 Butterfield was relieved he wasn't going to be called. Alicia Shepard, "The man who revealed the Nixon tapes," *Washington Post*, June 14, 2012.

Page 148 The next day, October 20, 1973, Richardson was called to a meeting at the Justice Department. Nixon had ordered him to fire Cox. He refused. He said he would resign as attorney general. https://www.nytimes.com/1973/10/21/archives/richardson-quits-over-order-on-cox-attorney-general-says-he-couldnt.html.

Page 148 Ruckelshaus wrote a letter saying his conscience would not allow him to fire Cox. Ibid.

Page 148 That night the fired Cox issued a statement: "Whether ours shall continue to be a government of laws and not of men is now for Congress and ultimately the American people." Carroll Kilpatrick, "Nixon forces firing of Cox; Richardson, Ruckelshaus quit," *Washington Post*, October 21, 1973.

Page 149 Levi saw that Richard Nixon, like other presidents, had power, and with that power sought to use the Justice Department as a weapon against his enemies. There were 207 names on Nixon's enemies list. Among them were senators including Edward Kennedy, George McGovern, and Walter Mondale; members of the House, including Bella Abzug; and 12 black Congressmen, including John Conyers, Ronald Dellums, and Charles Rangel. On the list were organizations like the Brookings Institute, SANE, and the Southern Christian Leadership Conference; labor leaders; members of the media, including Jack Anderson, Pete Hamill, and Thomas Braden; 11 celebrities, including Carol

Channing, Paul Newman, Dick Gregory, and Barbra Streisand; a raft of businessmen; and Daniel Ellsberg, Arthur Schlesinger, and J. Kenneth Galbraith. EnemiesList.info, 2019.

Page 149 Hoover had bugged King's phone conversations, and he used them to try to destroy King's marriage. David Leonhardt, "The sense of justice that we're losing," *New York Times*, April 29, 2018.

CHAPTER 12: IRAN CONTRA

Page 155 Secordgetsmystery$500,000.https://www.sun-sentinel.com/news/fl-xpm-1987-06-24-8702240130-story.html.

CHAPTER 13: THE IMPEACHMENT OF BILL CLINTON

Page 160 CBSNEWS.com staff, "Hillary Clinton in clear on Travelgate," *CBS News*, June 22, 2000.

Page 161 On the Whitewater scandal, see Dylan Matthews, "Whitewater, explained for people who don't remember the Clinton presidency," *Vox*, April 13, 2015.

Page 164 On the role of Linda Tripp, see Jane Mayer, "Portrait of a whistleblower," *The New Yorker*, March 23, 1998.

Page 167 Alison Mitchell, "Impeachment: The overview," *New York Times*, December 20, 1998. See generally Jeffrey Toobin, *A Vast Conspiracy: The Real Story of the Sex Scandal That Nearly Brought Down a President* (New York: Random House, 2012); Richard A. Posner, *An Affair of State: The Investigation, Impeachment, and Trial of President Clinton* (Cambridge, MA: Harvard University Press, 2009).

Page 167 On the Clinton impeachment, see Charles Pierce, "1998: Bill Clinton and the year America changed," *Esquire*, September 23, 2013; Olivia Waxman and Merrill Fahy, "From an anonymous tip to an impeachment, *TIME*, May 4, 2018.

CHAPTER 14: W

Page 170 Dexter Filkins and Dana Canedy, "The Brooks Brothers Riot," *New York Times*, November 23, 2000.

Page 170 Edward Foley, "George W. Bush vs. Al Gore, 15 years later: We really did inaugurate the wrong guy," *Salon*, December 19, 2015. See also Jeffrey Toobin, *Too Close to Call: The Thirty-Six Day Battle to Decide the 2000 Election* (New York: Random House, 2002).

Page 172 The lies leading to the Iraqi war. Christopher Scheer, "Ten appalling lies we were told about Iraq," *Alternet*, June 26, 2003.

Page 172 *How the Bush Administration Sold the Iraq War*, MSNBC documentary, aired October 14, 2013.

Page 172 Robert Jervis, *Why Intelligence Fails: Lessons from the Iranian Revolution and Iraq War* (Ithaca, NY: Cornell University Press, 2010); Paul R. Pillar, *Intelligence and U.S. Foreign Policy: Iraq, 9/11, and Misguided Reform* (New York: Columbia University Press, 2011); *Understanding the U.S. Wars in Iraq and Afghanistan*, Beth Bailey and Richard H. Immerman, eds. (New York: New York University Press, 2015) includes essays by national security experts. Multiple official reports on the origins and conduct of the Iraq war have been prepared in the U.S. and U.K. See, e.g., "Review of Intelligence on Weapons of Mass Destruction" (London, UK: Stationary Office of the House of Commons, 2004), a report of the inquiry by the five-member committee, chaired by Lord Butler. The United States Army study of the entire war was completed in 2019. See *The U.S. Army in the Iraq War*, vol. 1, Joel D. Rayburn, ed. (Carlisle, PA: Army War College Press, 2019).

Page 174 James Risen, "A warning on Blackwater," *New York Times*, June 29, 2014. Peter Singer, "The dark truth about Blackwater," *Brookings*, October 2, 2007.

Page 175 Detainee ##### reported that an Iraqi policeman (1) held a knife to his throat and (2) placed a pistol to his head and pulled the trigger. He further alleged that American forces (1) punched him and hit him with weapons, (2) threw urine on him, and (3) applied electric shocks to his body. Kris Jepson, *Channel 4 News*, October 22, 2005. See U.S. Senate Select Committee on Intelligence, "Report on Torture: Committee Study of the Central Intelligence Agency's Detention and Interrogation Program" (Washington, DC: U.S. Senate, 2014); David Cole, *Torture Memos: Rationalizing the Unthinkable* (New York: The New Press, 2009) contains key documents, including the infamous "torture memos" from the Department of Justice Office of Legal Counsel, compiled with introductory and explanatory material.

Page 176 Julian Bolger, "Senate report on the CIA's torture," *Guardian*, December 9, 2014; Charles Pierce, "CIA torture," *Esquire*, September 9, 2016.

Page 177 Peter Dizikes, "Bush Administration scandals," *Salon*, January 18, 2005.

Page 177 Nina Burleigh, "The Bush White House lost 22 million emails," *Newsweek*, September 12, 2016.

CHAPTER 15: BUT HER EMAILS . . .

Page 181 "Rep. Joe Wilson yells out 'You lie!' during Obama's health care speech," *CNN*, November 9, 2009.

Page 182 Mary Elizabeth Williams, "Dinesh D'Souza, adulterous felon and disgraced academic," *Salon*, October 21, 2016.

Page 184 By 2012 the Republicans hoped to use some of this anger to oust Obama. Said House Speaker John Boehner, "We're going to do everything—and I mean everything we can do—to kill it, stop it, slow it down, whatever we can." Andy Barr, "John Boehner: 'We will not compromise,'" *Politico*, October 28, 2010. Carl Hulse and Adam Nagourney, "Senate GOP leader finds weapon in unity," *New York Times*, May 16, 2010.

Page 184 Clyde Wayne Crews Jr., "Obama's legacy: Here's a raft of executive actions Trump may target," *Forbes*, January 16, 2017.

Page 186 "Debra Maggart, former GOP lawmaker targeted by NRA: 'They turned on me,'" *Huffington Post*, December 18, 2012. Also see Richard Painter, "The NRA protection racket," *New York Times*, December 19, 2012.

Page 189 Kristen Lee, "Rush Limbaugh claims Obama hates America," *New York Daily News*, July 17, 2012.

CHAPTER 16: WHO IS DONALD TRUMP?

Pages 193–194 When it came time for young Donald to go to prep school. Paul Schwartzman and Michael Miller, "Confident. Incorrigible. Bully: Little Donny was a lot like candidate Donald Trump," *Washington Post*, June 22, 2016.

Page 194 "I was promoted," he said. "The word is promoted. Mark it down." Lawrence Swaim, "Surviving Trump: What happens when you wake up in an alternative universe run by a narcissistic sociopath," *Medium*, March 22, 2017.

Page 197 "I don't want to be a loser," he told them. "I've never been a loser before … and I'm not going to be a failure." Jeff Pearlman, *Football for a Buck: The Crazy Rise and Crazier Demise of the USFL* (Boston: Houghton Mifflin Harcourt, 2018).

Page 197 Trump became known as a "charlatan, dead set on getting his way." Ibid.

Page 198 At the end of the meeting, Roselle told him, "Mr. Trump, as long as I or my heirs are involved in the NFL, you will never be a franchise owner in the league." Ibid.

Page 198 "He was the personification of slime." Ibid.

Page 200 Before the lawsuits were settled, Trump in 2016 launched an attack on the judge, Gonzalo Curiel, saying that because the judge was "Mexican," he couldn't be impartial. Matt Ford, "Trump attacks a 'Mexican' U.S. federal judge," *The Atlantic*, May 28, 2016.

Page 201 Burnett needed to determine which city and to find a host. He was looking for someone "bigger than life and very colorful, someone who would be likable, tough, and fascinating enough to interest an audience for a full season." Michael Kranish and Marc Fisher, "The inside story of how 'The Apprentice' rescued Donald Trump," *FORTUNE*, September 8, 2016.

Page 201 He would be judge, jury, and executioner in a weekly contest to see which desperate go-getter would get the work in one of Trump's businesses for a salary of $250,000 a year. Ibid.

Page 202 "And as the master, I want to pass along some of my knowledge to somebody else." Ibid.

Page 202 "*The Apprentice* offered a promise not only of enrichment," wrote David Frum, "but of justice, at a time when Americans craved that fantasy even more than usual." David Frum, "The great illusion of *The Apprentice,*" *The Atlantic,* January 6, 2018. Also see ibid.

Page 203 "It would be a hymn to the glory of Russia," he said. Patrick Radden Keefe, "Winning: The TV producer who rehabilitated Trump's image," *The New Yorker,* January 7, 2019.

CHAPTER 17: CON ARTIST AND HUSTLER

Page 211 His interests range from management deals with golf courses in the UAE, branding agreements with real estate projects that bear Trump's name in India as well as companies that have been involved with beverage sales in Israel. https://www.cnn.com/2016/11/21/politics/trump-overseas-business-interests/index.html.

Page 212 His "Make America Great Again" hats were made in Southern California. Michelle Yee, "How many Trump products were made overseas? Here's the complete list," *Washington Post*, August 26, 2016.

Page 212 The autocrats in his circle include Anar Mammadov, a millionaire playboy who lives in Azerbaijan, a country known as the "world's most corrupt regime." In 2015 Anar and his father, who are called "the Corleones of the Caspian," helped finance the Trump Istanbul Hotel and Tower. *Rolling Stone Magazine,* July 29, 2015.

Page 222 Every time there was a financial transaction between a foreign government—or a company controlled by a foreign government—and any Trump entity, there would be a potential for favorable treatment that could violate this limitation, as well as the anti-bribery laws. Norman Eisen, Richard Painter, and Laurence Tribe, "Report: The Emoluments Clause: Its text, meaning, and application to Donald J. Trump," *Brookings*, December 16, 2016.

Page 224 Mr. Trump's businesses owe hundreds of millions to Deutsche Bank, which is currently negotiating a multibillion-dollar settlement with the U.S. Department of Justice, a settlement that will now be overseen by an attorney general and many other appointees selected by and serving at the pleasure of Mr. Trump. Ibid.

Page 226 Even more important, in its decision the Court interpreted the Emoluments Clause essentially the same way as the plaintiffs did, as did CREW in the earlier suit in New York. *District of Columbia and Maryland v. Trump* (D. MD 2018), citing ibid. Unfortunately, this same case in July 2019 was dismissed by the U.S. Court of Appeals for the Fourth Circuit, which held that the State of Maryland and the District of Columbia did not have standing to sue Trump over the Emoluments Clause in federal court, regardless of how the substantive prohibition in that clause is interpreted.

CHAPTER 18: DRAINING THE SWAMP

Page 228 The third plank of Trump's platform to "Make America Great Again" was his statement that he would "drain the swamp" of lobbyists and career government employees whom he associated with President Obama and the Clintons. Theodoric Meyer, "Lobbyists say business is better than ever," *Politico*, October 19, 2017.

Page 228 Lachlan Markay, "How Trump let the swamp drain him," *Daily Beast*, April 27, 2017.

Page 232 Peter Baker, Glenn Thrush, and Maggie Haberman, "Health Secretary Tom Price resigns after drawing ire for chartered flights," *New York Times*, September 29, 2017.

Page 233 Pruitt rented his living quarters in Washington, D.C., for $50 a night from a "friend" who is an energy lobbyist. Eric Lipton, "Pruitt had a $50-a-day condo linked to lobbyists. Their client's project got approved," *New York Times*, April 2, 2018.

Page 233 Davenport et al., "EPA chief Scott Pruitt Resigns."

Page 233 His unethical behavior became so pronounced that Laura Ingraham, the conservative talk show host on Fox, tweeted, "Pruitt is the swamp. Drain it." Carol Davenport, Lisa Friedman, and Maggie Haberman, "EPA chief Scott Pruitt resigns under a cloud of ethics scandals," *New York Times*, July 5, 2018.

Page 233 Alexander Kaufman, "At least 23 ethical issues are dogging EPA administrator Scott Pruitt," *Huffington Post*, April 5, 2018.

Page 235 Jessica Estepa, "Steve Bannon steps down from Breitbart after break with Trump," *USA Today*, January 9, 2018.

Page 235 They were fine with a president who sided with Vladimir Putin in a traitorous exchange in Helsinki. See David Remnick, "The unwinding of Donald Trump," *The New Yorker*, July 17, 2018.

Page 236 For Trump's new fixers, Cohen gave them an answer: "I did the same thing you're doing now." Timothy Egan, "After Cohen, Republicans are now Trump's fixers," *New York Times*, March 2, 2019.

CHAPTER 19: THE STEELE DOSSIER

Page 237 On January 10, 2017, President Obama and President-elect Trump were told that the Russians had compromising information on Trump. Trump called it fake news. Feliks Garcia, "Intelligence chiefs allege Russians have compromising personal information on Donald Trump," *Independent*, January 11, 2017.

Page 238 Who is Christopher Steele? See Jane Mayer, "Christopher Steele, the man behind the Trump dossier," *The New Yorker*, March 5, 2018. Also see Kenneth Vogel, "The Trump dossier: What we know and who paid for it," *New York Times*, March 5, 2018.

Page 242 Putin's spokesman told the audience, "The Kremlin has no compromising dossier on Trump. Such information isn't consistent with reality and is nothing but an absolute fantasy." Kevin Hagen, "Trump received unsubstantiated report that Russia had damaging information about him," *New York Times*, January 10, 2017.

Page 243 Oleg Erovinkin, a key aide to Igor Sechin, who was named in the dossier, was murdered. Robert Mendick, "Mystery death of ex-KGB chief linked to M16 spy's dossier on Donald Trump," *Telegraph*, January 27, 2017.

Page 243 Mysterious disappearances of Mikhailov, Dokuchaev, and Stoyanov. See Steve LeVine, "Three Russian cyber arrests, one suspicious death, and a new twist in the US election hack," *Quartz*, January 31, 2017.

Page 244 Oronov, who was the father of Cohen's brother's wife, lived in one of Trump's buildings. He also was said to have died of a heart attack, an all too common occurrence for prominent Russian businessmen and government officials who get too close to sensitive situations. Martin Longman, "How did Alex Oronov die and why does it matter?" *Washington Monthly*, March 6, 2017. See also Rachel Roberts, "Ukrainian businessman with links to Donald Trump and Russia dies in unexplained circumstances," *Independent*, March 6, 2017.

Page 244 That's a lot of dead Russians. See Bill Palmer, *Palmer Report*, March 12, 2017.

Page 244 Peter Smith, one of the GOP operatives who was said to have told the Russians to turn over the stolen Clinton emails to WikiLeaks, committed suicide in a hotel room in Rochester, Minnesota. Tom Porter, "Trump Russia investigation: Does the case of GOP 'dirty tricks' operative Peter W. Smith hold the key to the election hacking allegations?" *Newsweek*, October 21, 2017.

Page 245 We should also ask ourselves, why didn't the FBI take action after receiving the Steele dossier in July of 2016? Kim Sengupta, "Former M16 agent Christopher Steele's frustration as FBI sat on Donald Trump's Russia file for months," *Independent,* January 13, 2017.

Page 246 Trump and the Blackstone Bayrock group. Jeff Nesbit, "Donald Trump's many, many, many, many ties to Russia," *TIME*, August 15, 2016.

Page 246 Trump's deals with Bayrock. Timothy O'Brien, "Trump, Russia and a shadowy business partnership," *Bloomberg Opinion,* June 21, 2017.

Page 247 Kriss said Bayrock executives skimmed cash, dodged taxes, and cheated him out of a million dollars. Ibid.

Page 247 "If he were sitting in the room right now, I really wouldn't know what he looked like." Ibid.

Page 248 Rozov signed a letter of intent that he sent to Cohen. Trump countersigned it. Emily Price, "Yep, Trump did sign a letter of intent for a Trump Tower in Moscow," *FORTUNE*, December 19, 2018.

Page 248 Trump at times denied knowing anything about these projects in Russia during the presidential campaign. Carol Leonnig, Tom Hamburger, and Rosalind Helderman, "Trump's business sought deal on Trump Tower in Moscow while he ran for president," *Washington Post*, August 27, 2017.

Page 249 Flynn secretly met with Kislyak to discuss the impact of Obama's sanctions. Mark Mazzetti and Michael Schmidt, "Flynn said Russian sanctions would be 'ripped up,' whistle-blower says," *New York Times*, December 6, 2017.

Page 249 In the end, Trump Tower Moscow was never built. Frank Vyan Walton, "Trump Tower Moscow was a much larger deal—and potential crime—than anyone has realized," *Daily Kos,* January 27, 2019. On September 15, 2015, Rozov wrote to Cohen, "The building design you sent over is very interesting and will be an architectural and luxury triumph. I believe the tallest building in Europe should be in Moscow, and I am prepared to build it." Ibid. Emily Goodin and David Martosko, "Trump Tower Moscow proposal included architect's drawing of what would have been Europe's tallest building despite Giuliani's claim 'no plans were ever made' and 'there were NO drafts,'" *Daily Mail,* January 22, 2019. See also Dan Alexander and Richard Behar, "The truth behind Trump Tower Moscow: How Trump risked everything for a (relatively) tiny deal," *Forbes*, May 23, 2019. ("Sater says he was cooking up a plan to raise huge sums from additional investors, including two of Vladimir Putin's closest cronies, Boris and Arkady Rotenberg. 'We would have gone to them and asked them for four or five hundred million dollars cash,' Sater says . . . It seems more likely that Trump would have walked away with roughly $35 million up front and $2.6 million or so in annual fees, if everything went according to plan. In the rosiest of scenarios, Sater says, Trump could have gotten about $50 million. A lot of money to most people but less than 2% of the president's net worth.")

Page 252 Trump very much seems to enjoy meeting secretly with Vladimir Putin. Peter Baker, "Trump and Putin: Five meetings infused with mystery," *New York Times,* January 16, 2019.

Page 252 On the flight back to Washington that night, Trump told reporters that at the June 2016 Trump Tower meeting of his top campaign officials with a Russian agent. Sonam Sheth, "Donald Trump Jr.'s 'staggering admissions' about meeting with a Russian lawyer are skirting a huge question," *Business Insider,* July 10, 2017.

Pages 253-254 *The Washington Post* reported that Jeff Sessions had spoken with Russian ambassador Kislyak during the campaign. See Richard Painter, "Jeff Sessions needs to go," *New York Times* op-ed page, March 2, 2017. For the definitive Trump-Russia timeline of events, see Matthew Nussbaum, "Today in Trumpworld—March 3," *Politico*, March 3, 2017.

CHAPTER 20: RUSSIA HACKS THE WORLD

Page 257 Putin rebuilds Soviet Russia. See Oliver Bullough, "Vladimir Putin: The rebuilding of 'Soviet' Russia," *BBC Magazine*, March 28, 2014.

Page 259 On Russian meddling in France, see Leigh Ann Caldwell and Emmanuelle Saliba, "U.S. eyes Russian meddling in French presidential campaign," *NBC*, April 21, 2017. Also see Laura Daniels, "How Russia hacked the French election," *Politico*, April 23, 2017.

Page 261 On Russia's interference in Germany, see Constanze Stelzenmüller, "The impact of Russian interference on Germany's 2017 elections," *Brookings*, June 28, 2017.

Page 262 On Russian oligarch Arron Banks's connection to Brexit, see David Kirkpatrick and Matthew Rosenberg, "Russians offered business deals to Brexit's biggest backer," *New York Times*, June 30, 2018.

Page 262 For information on Russia's interference on Brexit, see Jonathan Chait, "Britain has a Russian collusion scandal now. It looks exactly like Trump's," *New York Magazine*, June 22, 2018; Jonathan Chait, "The other Russia collusion scandal is breaking wide open," *New York Magazine*, June 30, 2018.

Page 263 Corbyn apparently was the preferred candidate for the Russians. Heather Stewart and Larry Elliott, "Jeremy Corbyn defies critics and calls for calm over Russia," *Guardian*, March 15, 2018; Jake Ryan, "How Russia backed Jeremy Corbyn and the Kremlin trolls targeting the UK," *The Sun*, March 10, 2018.

Page 263 On the disarray in Great Britain, see Griff Witte, Karla Adam, and William Booth, "May vows to stay course on Brexit, but resignation pressure build after stunning loss," *Washington Post*, June 9, 2017.

Page 264 For information on Russia's election interference around the world, see Sam Becker, "These countries have been the target of Russian election interference," *Cheat Sheet*, March 25, 2018.

CHAPTER 21: PUTIN CROWNS OUR PRESIDENT

Page 265 Jeff Nesbit, "Donald Trump's many, many, many, many ties to Russia," *TIME*, August 15, 2016.

Page 267 Elise Viebeck, "What Podesta's emails reveal about Clinton's ties to the progressive left," *Washington Post*, October 28, 2016.

Page 270 After the election was over, the report said, the Russians posted on Facebook and Instagram 70 times mocking claims that the Russians had interfered in the election. Scott Shane and Sheera Frenkel, "Russia 2016 influence operation targeted African-Americans on social media," *New York Times*, December 18, 2018.

Page 270 Natasha Bertrand, "It looks like Russia hired internet trolls to pose as pro-Trump Americans," *Business Insider*, July 27, 2016.

Page 270 Scott Shane, "The fake Americans Russia created to influence the election," *New York Times*, September 7, 2017.

Page 271 Three days later, Assange released to the public thousands of John Podesta's emails. Charlie Savage, "Assange, avowed foe of Clinton, times email release for Democratic Convention," *New York Times*, July 26, 2016.

Also see:

Page 273 Russia: "There were contacts" with Donald Trump's campaign before election. David Filipov and Andrew Roth, "Moscow had contacts with Trump team during campaign Russian diplomat says," *Washington Post*, November 10, 2016.

Page 273 Sharon LaFraniere and Adam Goldman, "US outlines web of sex, lies and ties to Russian operatives," *New York Times*, July 19, 2018.

Page 273 Jonathan Chait, "What if Trump has been a Russian asset since 1987?" *New York Magazine*, July 8, 2018.

Page 273 Christina Maza, "Russia picked Donald Trump and ran him for president, former Israeli intelligence officer says," *Newsweek*, December 27, 2018.

CHAPTER 22: FAKE NEWS
AND OTHER PRESIDENTIAL LIES

Page 279   The *Washington Post* kept track of Trump's lies during the first year in office and came up with more than two thousand. Meg Kelly, "President Trump has made 2,436 false or misleading claims so far," *Washington Post*, March 1, 2018.

Page 280   "But I would never kill them. I hate them. Some of them are such lying, disgusting people. It's true." Colin Campbell, "Donald Trump on reporters: 'I would never kill them. But I do hate them,'" *Business Insider*, December 21, 2015.

Page 281   "... So when *The New York Times* writes a hit piece which is a total disgrace or when *The Washington Post*, which is there for other reasons, writes a hit piece, we can sue them and win money instead of having no chance of winning, because they're totally protected." James Joyner, *Outside the Beltway*, February 27, 2016.

Page 281   Ben Jacobs, "Donald Trump threatens to sue *New York Times* over 'irresponsible intent,'" *Guardian*, September 17, 2016.

Page 281   David Graham, "Trump wants to censor the media," *The Atlantic*, October 5, 2017.

Page 281   Trump again said the media was the enemy of the people, complaining that the *New York Times* "is so evil and so bad, because they write lies." Michael Grynbaum, "Trump calls the news media the 'enemy of the American people,'" *New York Times*, February 17, 2017.

Page 281   Trevor Timm, "Trump's many, many threats to sue the press since launching his campaign," *Columbia Journalism Review*, October 3, 2016.

Page 285   Another favorite of Trump is Sinclair Broadcasting Group, which is controlled by the family of its founder, Julian Sinclair Smith. Eli Rosenberg, "Trump said Sinclair is 'far superior to CNN.' What we know about the conservative media giant," *Washington Post*, April 3, 2018.

Page 285   Margaret Harding McGill and John Hendel, "Trump tweet seen as boost for Sinclair deal," *Politico*, April 2, 2018.

Page 285   In early April of 2018, the executives of the Sinclair Broadcast Group issued an ultimatum to its TV anchors across the country to read a script that echoed Trump's calling out of "fake news." Jacey Fortin and Jonah Engel Bromwich, "Sinclair made dozens of local news anchors recite the same script," *New York Times*, April 2, 2018.

Page 286   On March 29, 2017, President Trump threatened to raise postal rates on Amazon, owned by Jeff Bezos, who also owns the *Washington Post*. Cristiano Lima, "Trump draws blood in feud with Amazon, Washington Post," *Politico*, April 2, 2018.

Page 289   On February 18, 2019, Supreme Court Justice Clarence Thomas raised the issue of taking another look at *New York Times v. Sullivan*. Adam Liptak, "Justice Clarence Thomas calls for reconsideration of landmark libel ruling," *New York Times*, February 19, 2019.

Page 289   "Our fact checks of the first debate," *New York Times*, September 26, 2016.

Page 289   Dylan Dyers, "Donald Trump's 'sleaze' attack on reporters hits new level of media animosity," *CNN*, May 31, 2016.

Page 289   "The Trump Administration's war on the press," *Media Matters*, February 1, 2017.

Page 289   Jeremy Diamond, "Trump launches all-out attack on the press," *CNN*, June 1, 2016.

CHAPTER 23: TRUMP THE CAMPAIGNER

Page 301   The chant, "Lock Her Up," aimed at Democratic presidential candidate Hillary Clinton, first arose in July of 2016 during a speech given at a Trump rally by New Jersey governor Chris Christie. Peter Stevenson, "A brief history of the 'Lock Her Up!' chant by Trump supporters against Clinton," *Washington Post*, November 22, 2016.

CHAPTER 24: BLOWING UP BRIDGES, BUILDING WALLS

Page 303 German Lopez, "Donald Trump's long history of racism, from the 1970s to 2019," *Vox*, January 14, 2018. See Tim Alberta, *American Carnage: Behind the Scenes of the Republican Civil War and the Rise of Trump* (New York: HarperCollins, 2019), in which the chief political correspondent of *Politico* looks inside the Republican Party and how a decade of cultural upheaval, populist outrage, and ideological warfare made the GOP vulnerable to a hostile takeover from Donald Trump. The book is full of good quotes, including ones from John Boehner, House Speaker up until 2015, who says Congress is filled with "some of the nicest people" and "some that are Nazis," and from Mitt Romney, "Sometimes you have to light a prairie fire to win . . . But sometimes it comes back and burns your house down."

Page 305 A low point during Trump's presidency took place in Charlottesville, Virginia. Jamie Kizzire, Brad Bennett, Will Tucker, and Booth Gunter, "America the Trumped: 10 ways the administration attacked civil rights in year one," Southern Poverty Law Center, January 19, 2018.

Page 310 The wall wasn't even Trump's idea. Cody Fenwick, "Here are 5 of Trump's lies from his Oval Office speech about his ridiculous border wall demands," *AlterNet*, January 9, 2019.

Page 311 Matthew Rozsa, "Trump advisor Stephen Miller threatens to do 'whatever is necessary to build the border wall,'" *Salon*, December 16, 2018.

Page 311 Responded Merkley, "This is not a zero tolerance policy, this is a zero humanity policy, and we can't let it go on." Julie Hirschfeld Davis and Michael D. Shear, "How Trump came to enforce a practice of separating migrant families," *New York Times*, June 16, 2018.

Page 313 "He is usurping congressional authority," said Republican senator Susan Collins of Maine. "This is a fundamental constitutional responsibility of Congress. We should be opposing this strongly." Carl Hulse and Glenn Thrush, "Trump's attempt to circumvent Congress leaves uneasy Senate Republicans with hard choice," *New York Times*, February 17, 2019.

Page 313 S.V. Date, "Trump on track to sign another spending bill that fails to pay for his wall," *Huffington Post*, September 25, 2018.

Page 313 Felicia Sonmez, "Trump threatens to shut down southern border as government funding stalemate drags on," *Washington Post*, December 28, 2018.

Page 314 Julie Hirschfield Davis and Peter Baker, "How the border wall is boxing Trump in," *New York Times*, January 5, 2019.

CHAPTER 25: TWO TRAGIC FIGURES

Page 317 Stephen Dinan, "FBI reopens Clinton email investigation," *Washington Times*, October 28, 2016.

Page 317 Nate Silver, "The Comey letter probably cost Clinton the election," *FiveThirtyEight.com*, May 3, 2017. "Because Clinton lost Michigan, Pennsylvania, and Wisconsin by less than 1 point," he said, "the letter was probably enough to change the outcome of the Electoral College."

Page 317 Sari Horwitz, "Read the letter Comey sent to FBI employees explaining his controversial decision on the Clinton email investigation," *Washington Post*, October 28, 2016.

Page 317 Richard W. Painter, "On Clinton emails, did the F.B.I. director abuse his power?" *New York Times*, October 30, 2016, argues that F.B.I. director James Comey in sending this letter a week before the election violated the Hatch Act prohibition on using an official position to influence a partisan election.

Page 317 Amber Phillips, "'It's a firing offense': Why James Comey may have broken the law with Clinton emails," *Washington Post*, October 30, 2016.

Page 322 Michael Shear and Matt Apuzzo, "FBI director James Comey is fired by Trump," *New York Times*, May 8, 2017.

Page 322 Devlin Barrett, "'I expect loyalty,' Trump told Comey, according to written testimony," *Pittsburgh Post-Gazette*, June 7, 2017.

Page 323 Rick Noack, "Comey said working with Trump reminded him of the Mob—let's break that comment down," *Washington Post*, April 13, 2018.

Page 324 Michael Schmidt, "Comey memo says Trump asked him to end Flynn investigation," *New York Times*, May 16, 2017.

Page 327 For a timeline on Jeff Sessions's rocky relationship with President Trump, see Tessa Berenson and Katie Reilly, "Jeff Sessions just resigned as attorney general. Here's a timeline of his rocky relationship with President Trump," *TIME*, November 7, 2018.

Page 327 Abby Phillip and Sari Horwitz, "Trump blasts AG Sessions for recusing himself from the Russia probe," *Washington Post*, July 19, 2017.

Page 327 Michael Schmidt and Maggie Haberman, "Trump humiliated Jeff Sessions after Mueller appointment," *New York Times*, September 14, 2017.

Page 327 Sessions would tell associates that it had been the most humiliating experience of his public life. Schmidt and Haberman, "Trump humiliated Jeff Sessions."

CHAPTER 26: ROBERT MUELLER: TRUMP'S WORST NIGHTMARE

Page 329 On May 19, 2017, Deputy Attorney General Rod Rosenstein, without consulting with White House lawyers or President Donald Trump, named former FBI director Robert Mueller as the special counsel. Patrick Buchanan, *Newsmax TV*, May 19, 2017; Rebecca Ruiz and Mark Landler, "Robert Mueller, former F.B.I. director, is named special counsel for Russia investigation," *New York Times*, May 17, 2017.

Page 332 "I mean," said King, "we all said disparaging things about each other face to face. But saying something about someone who wasn't there was something that Bob was uncomfortable with, and he let it be known and just walked out." Marc Fisher and Sari Horwitz, "Mueller and Trump: Born to wealth, raised to lead. Then, sharply different choices," *Washington Post*, February 23, 2018.

Page 332 "A lie was the worst sin," said Mueller. "The one thing you didn't do was to give anything less than the truth to my mother and father." Graff, "The untold story."

Page 333 On his military career, see Garrett Graff, "The untold story of Robert Mueller's time in combat," *WIRED*, May 15, 2018.

Page 336 Gonzalez, who strongly defended the controversial program, and Card shoved the papers in front of Ashcroft, but with Comey looking on, Ashcroft refused to sign them. Dan Eggen, *Washington Post*, August 17, 2007.

Page 336 "I was angry," said Comey. "I thought I had just witnessed an effort to take advantage of a very sick man, who did not have the powers of the attorney general because they had been transferred to me." https://www.nytimes.com/2013/05/30/us/politics/obama-to-pick-james-b-comey-to-lead-fbi.html.

Page 336 Dan Eggen and Paul Kane, "Gonzalez hospital episode detailed," *Washington Post*, May 16, 2007.

Page 337 Douglas Frantz, "Mueller defends FBI in Boston bombing," *Washington Post*, May 16, 2013.

Page 337 Martha Schick, "Lewandowski (falsely) claims Comey was partly responsible for Boston Marathon bombing," *Boston Globe*, April 18, 2018.

Page 337 Sheryl Gay Stolberg and Michael Schmidt, "Bombings make a bitter bookend for FBI director," *New York Times*, May 9, 2013.

Page 337 Cindy Boren, "Mueller report: Five takeaways from the Ray Rice investigation," *Washington Post*, January 8, 2015.

Page 338 Lawrence Leigh, who worked with Bob Mueller when he was a U.S. attorney in San Francisco, was not surprised when Rod Rosenstein selected Mueller to be the special counsel in charge of the Russian investigation. Lawrence Leigh, "Commentary: The Robert Mueller I know," *Salt Lake Tribune,* November 10, 2018.

CHAPTER 27: THE BATTLE TO STOP ROBERT MUELLER

Page 346 Veselnitskaya worked for Yuri Chaika, Russia's prosecutor general. See Andrew Kramer and Sharon LaFraniere, "Lawyer who offered dirt on Clinton is tied to a Kremlin official," *New York Times*, April 28, 2018.

Page 350 "I was fired, in some way, to change—or the endeavor was to change the way the Russia investigation was being conducted," Comey testified. Devlin Barrett, "Special counsel is investigating Trump for possible obstruction," *Washington Post,* June 14, 2017.

Page 352 Devlin Barrett, Spencer Hsu, and Rosalind Helderman, "Special counsel Mueller indicts Paul Manafort," *Washington Post,* June 8, 2018.

Page 354 Fox host Jeanine Pirro piled on. David Graham, "The partisan, nihilist case against Robert Mueller," *The Atlantic*, December 11, 2017.

Page 354 Three Republicans . . . all screamed for Mueller's dismissal and even prosecution. Natasha Bertrand, "A trio of House Republicans lobbing attacks on Mueller have been in touch with the White House," *Business Insider*, December 21, 2017.

Page 354 Karoun Demirjian, "Devin Nunes, targeting Mueller and the FBI, alarms Democrats and some Republicans with his tactics," *Washington Post*, December 31, 2017. Claudine Schneider, Eliot Cohen, and Norman Eisen, "Beware of Devin Nunes's next move," *New York Times*, March 14, 2018. Eric Boehlert, "Ryan endorses Nunes' attack on Mueller probe, Justice Department," *National Memo*, May 10, 2018.

Page 354 Other Republicans, however, expressed their worry that the attacks on the FBI and Justice Department would foster a distrust of our most important legal institutions. Nicholas Fandos, "Republican attacks on Mueller and FBI open new rift in GOP," *New York Times*, December 30, 2017.

Page 354 Noah Bookbinder, Norman Eisen, Caroline Fredrickson, and Kristin Amerling, "The smear campaign against Mueller: Debunking the Nunes memo and the other attacks on the Russia investigation," American Constitution Society, January 31, 2018.

Page 355 Rubio advised the president to allow Mueller to complete his investigation. Nicholas Fandos, "Republican attacks on Mueller and FBI open new rift in GOP," *New York Times*, December 30, 2018.

Page 355 "A dangerous new era of alternative reality is advancing," said a March 14, 2018, op-ed in the *New York Times,* co-authored by former Republican representative Claudine Schneider of Rhode Island, "and House Republicans are signaling that, like their president, they intend to ignore, bend or assail truth to fight the Mueller investigation (and presumably that of the Senate Intelligence Committee as well, should it reach inconvenient conclusions)." Claudine Schneider, Eliot Cohen, and Norman Elsen, "Beware of Devin Nunes's next move," *New York Times*, March 14, 2018.

Page 356 Andrew Blake, "Sean Hannity: Robert Mueller is 'a disgrace to the American justice system,'" *Washington Times*, December 6, 2017.

Page 361 Kara Scannell, David Shortell, and Veronica Stracqualursi, "Mueller indicts 13 Russian nationals," *CNN*, February 17, 2018.

Page 362 Whether or not an express *quid pro quo* with the Russians could be proven, there was strong *circumstantial* evidence of a close relationship between Trump and Russia. Adam Serwer, "There is only one Trump scandal," *The Atlantic*, April 21, 2018.

CHAPTER 28: THE SUPREME COURT

Page 365 "I thought he might inadvertently kill me," she said. Christine Hauser, *New York Times*, September 26, 2018. https://www.nytimes.com/2018/09/26/us/politics/brett-kavanaugh-accusers-women.html.

Page 366 Further allegations against Kavanaugh were brought by two other women. Christine Hauser, "The Women who have accused Brett Kavanaugh," *New York Times*, September 26, 2018.

Page 366 Kavanaugh's response to Blasey-Ford's story was an angry, defiant response. See David Brooks, "A complete national disgrace," *New York Times*, October 4, 2018.

Page 366 "He channeled both the widespread fear that the Me Too movement was becoming so careless that it could take down innocent men and the well-justified loathing of the shameless collusion in the elected Democrat-activist-media triangle." Kyle Smith, "Brett Kavanaugh's history-changing speech," *National Review*, September 28, 2018.

CHAPTER 29: BARR'S INSIDE JOB

Page 370 After he fired Jeff Sessions, [he] appointed Matthew Whitaker to be acting attorney general. Steve Denning, "Trump: Replacing Sessions with Whitaker appears to obstruct justice," *Forbes*, November 8, 2018.

Page 372 Conservative lawyer George Conway (husband of Trump advisor Kellyanne Conway) and former acting solicitor general of the United States Neal Katyal wrote an editorial in the *New York Times* saying that Trump's appointment of Whitaker was unconstitutional under the appointment clause of the Constitution. Neal Katyal and George Conway III, "Trump's appointment of the acting attorney general is unconstitutional," *New York Times*, November 8, 2018.

Page 372 Michael Balsamo, "Whitaker rejected advice to recuse from Russia probe," *Associated Press*, December 20, 2018.

Page 373 On December 8, 2018, he named William Barr to the post. Michael Isikoff and Daniel Klaidman, "Trump first wanted his attorney general pick William Barr for another job: Defense lawyer," *Yahoo News*, December 8, 2018.

Page 374 Aaron Blake, "The red flags on Trump's new attorney general pick, William Barr," *Washington Post*, December 7, 2018.

Page 375 William Barr had an insurmountable conflict of interest on account of his having worked extensively with the targets of the Mueller investigation and their lawyers before he became attorney general. See Richard W. Painter and Virginia Canter, "William Barr's view of Russia recusal could undermine all government ethics programs," *USA Today*, January 29, 2019.

Page 376 William Saletan, "Bill Barr's weasel words," *Slate*, March 24, 2019.

CHAPTER 30: THE MUELLER REPORT

Page 377 He had already indicted Trump associate Roger Stone and over a dozen Russian agents. Mark Mazzetti, Eileen Sullivan, and Maggie Haberman, "Indicting Roger Stone, Mueller shows link between Trump campaign and WikiLeaks," *New York Times*, January 25, 2019.

Page 377 Special Counsel Robert S. Mueller III, Report on the Investigation into Russian Interference in the 2016 Presidential Election, vols. I and II, U.S. Department of Justice, March 2019 (submitted pursuant to 28 C.F.R. Section 600.8(c)).

Page 379 See Ibid. Volume I is a heavily redacted discussion of Russian interference in the election and the conduct of Trump campaign officials and others. See also Seth Abramson, *Proof of Collusion: How Trump Betrayed America* (New York: Simon & Schuster, 2018). This book, published before release of the 2019 Mueller Report, along with volume I of the Mueller Report (to date heavily redacted), is probably the most thorough explanation of how the Trump campaign colluded with the Russians. The evidence of collusion—including the infamous Trump Tower meeting and more—is obvious even if campaign officials' conduct did not amount to a criminal conspiracy that could be prosecuted under existing federal laws.

Page 384 Ibid. Volume II at page 1 notes that the Department of Justice's Office of Legal Counsel (OLC) has taken the position that a sitting president cannot be indicted, that the Special Counsel is part of the Department of Justice, and thus the Special Counsel cannot prosecute the president. Ibid at page 2 states that the Special Counsel, not being able to indict the president, will not reach a traditional prosecutorial determination of whether he committed a crime, and at pages 1–2 notes that a president can be prosecuted after he leaves office for crimes committed while he was in office, and that "we conducted a thorough factual investigation in order to preserve the evidence when memories were fresh and documentary materials available."

Page 384 Ibid. Volume II at page 182: "Because we determined not to make a traditional prosecutorial judgment, we did not draw ultimate conclusions about the President's conduct."

Page 385 Ibid. Volume II at page 168 discusses "Constitutional Defenses to Applying Obstruction-of-Justice Statutes to Presidential Conduct." The report rejects a lot of the constitutional arguments made to defend Trump's conduct. See, e.g., ibid at page 178: "[W]e were not persuaded by the argument that the President has blanket constitutional immunity to engage in acts that would corruptly obstruct justice through the exercise of otherwise valid Article II powers."

Page 387 Ibid. Volume II at pages 2 and 8: "If at the same time we had confidence after a thorough investigation of the facts that the President clearly did not commit obstruction of justice, we would so state. Based on the facts and the applicable legal standards, we are unable to reach that judgment. Accordingly, while this report does not conclude that the President committed a crime, it does not exonerate him."

CHAPTER 31: THE UKRAINE, CHINA, AND THE KURDS

Page 390 "The desire in foreign powers to gain an improper ascendant in our councils." Peter Baker, "Impeachment battle to turn for first time on a president's ties to a foreign country," *New York Times*, September 29, 2019.

Page 391 . . . the Kremlin not only sought to help elect Trump . . . Ibid.

Page 392 . . . called him a "treasonous spy." Michael Shear, "White House tried to 'lock down' Ukraine call records, whistle-blower says," *New York Times*, September 27, 2019.

Page 392 Sheryl Gay Stolberg, Maggie Haberman, and Peter Becker, "Trump's bogus conspiracy theory," *New York Times*, September 30, 2019.

Page 394 "We are at a different level of lawlessness." Ibid.

Page 395 Two associates of Rudy Giuliani, Lev Parnea and Igor Fruman. Kenneth Vogel, "Giuliani is said to be under investigation for Ukraine work," *New York Times*, October 11, 2019.

Page 396 Sharon LaFraniere, Kenneth Vogel, and Peter Baker, "The firing of Marie Yovanovitch," *New York Times*, September 27, 2019.

Page 397 . . . admitted they talked about Joe Biden. Nicholas Fandos, Jonathan Martin, and Maggie Haberman, "As Trump confirms he discussed Biden with Ukraine, pressure to impeach builds," *New York Times*, October 8, 2019.

Page 397 "The conversation I had was largely congratulatory." Ibid.

Page 397 Sharon LaFraniere and Michael Forsythe, "Trump accused China of paying Hunter Biden $1.5 million," *New York Times*, October 3, 2019.

Page 398 "I have an absolute right, perhaps even a duty, to investigate." Peter Baker and Eileen Sullivan, "Trump publicly urges China to investigate the Bidens," *New York Times*, October 3, 2019.

Page 398 "What is taking place is not an impeachment, it is a coup…" Davey Alba and Nick Corasaniti, "False 'coup' claims by Trump echo as unifying theme against impeachment," *New York Times*, October 2, 2019.

Page 400 "I have never had a good @FoxNews poll . . ." Allan Smith, "Trump lashes out over Fox News poll that show majority support his impeachment," *NBC News*, October 10, 2019.

Page 408 But the modern GOP as a whole is overwhelmingly fanatical, corrupt, or both . . . Paul Krugman, *New York Times*, November 22, 2019.

CONCLUSION: LOOKING FORWARD

Page 409-410 "He wakes up in the morning, shits all over Twitter, shits all over us, shits all over his staff, then hits golf balls. Fuck him. Of course, I can't say that in public or I'd get run out of town." Erick Erickson, April 11, 2018, as reported by Conor Friedersdorf, "The GOP's problems are bigger than Trump," *The Atlantic*, April 19, 2018.

Page 411 "It is also rational to, at least, consider the possibility that Putin may have accessed some of these 'buried bodies' through the RNC emails and that he could be using this material to threaten certain members of Congress today." Richard W. Painter and Leanne Watt, "Hidden motives behind key GOP leaders' cooperation with Trump & Russia: An Evidence-based examination of irrational behaviors & the Republican Congress members who exhibit them," *Medium*, November 3, 2018.

Page 412 And alarmingly, they continue to be willing to protect Trump, even though their association with him will undermine their future political careers, and in spite of the fact that he is a danger to our nation. Ibid.

Page 415 It remains to be seen whether our intelligence agencies can play defense effectively or whether our future elections will be compromised by Russian hacking. Todd Beamon, "US intelligence officials: Russia still meddling in our elections," *Newsmax*, August 2, 2018. Editorial Board, "From the Czech Republic, a warning for our midterms: The Russians are still meddling, *Washington Post*, January 29, 2018.

INDEX

ACKNOWLEDGMENTS

Richard Painter is grateful for the support provided by the S. Walter Richey Professorship at the University of Minnesota Law School, and also for the support and encouragement from his wife Karen Painter and their three children Elizabeth, William, and Anne. Peter Golenbock wishes to single out Vivienne Sohn, who has been so wonderful to me and Wendy over the years. We miss you dearly.

The authors wish to thank Lee Oglesby, Alexa Stevenson, Alicia Kania, Scott Calamar, and Karen Levy of BenBella Books for all their assistance, and we want to thank our literary agent Michael Wright for his fine work.

ABOUT THE AUTHORS

Richard Painter, a former Republican who is now an Independent, worked in the George W. Bush administration as associate counsel to the President in the White House Counsel's office from February 2005 to July of 2007. His specialties are government ethics, business ethics, and lawyers' ethics. Since Donald Trump began his run for the presidency in 2016, Painter has been an outspoken critic of candidate Trump and President Trump, appearing frequently on such popular cable news stations as CNN and MSNBC. The author of two books, he has also appeared on NPR's *All Things Considered* and recently was a guest on *The Bill Maher Show*. Norman Eisen, President Barack Obama's ethics chief, described Painter as "the number one scholar in the country on government ethics." Painter, like the President, has a dedicated and faithful Twitter following.

Peter Golenbock is the author of 10 *New York Times* best sellers. Among these are *American Prince* with Tony Curtis and *Presumed Guilty* with Jose Baez, the lawyer for Casey Anthony. Golenbock lives in St. Petersburg, Florida, where he is an adjunct professor of history at the University of South Florida, St. Pete campus.